THE GREAT EJECTMENT OF 1662

The Great Ejectment of 1662

Its Antecedents, Aftermath, and
Ecumenical Significance

EDITED BY

ALAN P. F. SELL

PICKWICK *Publications* · Eugene, Oregon

THE GREAT EJECTMENT OF 1662
Its Antecedents, Aftermath, and Ecumenical Significance

Pickwick Publications
An Imprint of Wipf and Stock Publishers
199 W. 8th Ave., Suite 3
Eugene, OR 97401

www.wipfandstock.com

ISBN 13: 978-1-61097-388-5

Cataloging-in-Publication data:

The Great Ejectment of 1662 : its antecedents, aftermath, and ecumenical significance / edited by Alan P. F. Sell.

xii + 282 p. ; 23 cm. Includes bibliographical references and index.

ISBN 13: 978-1-61097-388-5

1. Puritans—Great Britain. 2. Dissenters, Religious—England—History—17th century. 3. Presbyterian Church—History—17th century. I. Sell, Alan P. F. II. Jones, J. Gwynfor. III. Appleby, David, 1960. IV. White, Eryn Mant. V. Title.

BX5085 S45 2012

Manufactured in the U.S.A.

"As dying men, once more we put you in mind of some things unquestionably great and weighty: our pilgrimage has been through various trials in very unsettled times, under which having obtained mercy to be found faithful in some measure, our great care is, that the work of God may outlive us, and prosper more in your hands."

—From the elderly ejected ministers to ministers raised up since the Ejectment

Contents

Contributors

John Gwynfor Jones is Emeritus Professor of Welsh History at the University of Cardiff. He has published extensively in English and Welsh, mainly on early modern Welsh religious, administrative, social, and cultural themes. Among his recent publications are *Aspects of Religious Life in Wales c. 1536–1660: Leadership, Opinion and the Local Community* (2004); an updated text, with commentary and notes, of George Owen's *The Dialogue of the Government of Wales (1594)* (2010); *Crefydd a Chymdeithas: Astudiaethau ar Hanes y Fydd Brotestannaidd yng Nghymru c.1559–1750* (2007); and, as editor and contributor, *Hanes Methodistiaeth Galfinaidd Cymru c. 1814–1914: Y Twf a'r Cadarnhau* (2011). He is currently preparing a monograph on the sixteenth-century Puritan John Penry.

David J. Appleby is Lecturer in Early Modern British History at the University of Nottingham, and a Fellow of the Royal Historical Society. He has published and lectured in Britain and the USA on several aspects of the post-conflict culture of Britain and the Atlantic World after 1660. In 2010 his monograph, *Black Bartholomew's Day: Preaching, Polemic and Restoration Nonconformity* (2007) was awarded the Richard L. Greaves Prize by the International John Bunyan Society. He is currently working on a monograph on the experiences of parliamentarian veterans after the Restoration, entitled *In Redcoat Rags*.

Eryn M. White is Senior Lecturer in Welsh History in the Department of History and Welsh History at Aberystwyth University. She is the author of *The Welsh Bible* (2007), and co-author of *Calendar of Trev-ecka Letters* (2003) and *The Elect Methodists: Calvinistic Methodism in England and Wales, 1735–1811* (2012).

Alan P. F. Sell is a philosopher-theologian and ecumenist, with strong interests in the history of Christian thought. He has held academic posts in England, Canada, and Wales, and ecclesiastical posts in England and Geneva. He publishes and lectures widely at home and abroad. His most recent books are *Hinterland Theology: A Stimulus to Theological Construction* (2008); *Four Philosophical Anglicans: W. G. De Burgh, W. R. Matthews, O. C. Quick and H. A. Hodges* (2010); *Convinced, Concise and Christian: The Thought of Huw Parri Owen* (2012); and *Christ and Controversy: The Person of Christ in Noncon-formist Thought and Ecclesial Experience* (2012).

Preface

It had long been my intention to publish a collection of papers to mark the 350th Anniversary of the Great Ejectment. The objective was a scholarly volume that would throw fresh light upon the antecedents and aftermath of the Ejectment in both England and Wales; that would provide an assessment of its doctrinal and ecumenical significance; and that would afford future scholars an insight into the way in which some of their forebears viewed the matter in the early decades of the twenty-first century. My first expression of thanks must be to the three historians, Professor J. Gwynfor Jones, Dr. David J. Appleby and Dr. Eryn M. White for their willing participation in the venture, and for the promptness with which they completed their most informative chapters.

The execution of this project has fallen during my period as Chairman of the Committee of the Friends of the Congregational Library. It seemed to me that to associate this book with that Library would be particularly appropriate, and the Committee was in cordial agreement. The Library was founded in 1831 and, with a view to commemorating the Bicentenary of the Great Ejectment, it was resolved to build the Memorial Hall in Farringdon Street, London. The new building opened in 1875, ironically on the site of the old Fleet Prison in which a number of Separatists had been incarcerated, and to it the Library was removed. Now housed at Dr. Williams's Library, London, the Congregational Library is an important repository of archives and printed material relating to Dissenting history in general and Congregationalism in particular. My second expression of thanks is to the Chairman and Council Members of the Congregational

Memorial Hall Trust for their generous grant towards the cost of publishing this book.

The authors of the following chapters will be presenting summaries of their work at a symposium to take place at Dr. Williams's Library on 9 June 2012, and on the same day this book will be launched. With this I come to another institution with Congregational roots, and to a third expression of thanks. The Congregational Insurance Company was founded in 1891 by the Reverend Samuel Robert Antliff (1851–1927), an alumnus of Lancashire Independent College, during his ministry at Ramsden Street Church, Huddersfield. In addition to providing insurance, the Company has, for more than a century, supported Congregational (and nowadays United Reformed) churches and individuals in countless ways. It has generously made itself responsible for the entire cost of forthcoming symposium—meals, travel costs, accommodation and publicity—and for this I and my Committee are most grateful to the Managing Director, Mr. Carlo Cavaliere, and his colleagues.

As on previous occasions I warmly thank Dr. K. C. Hanson, the editor-in-chief of Wipf and Stock, Dr. Robin Parry, the editor of this book, and all their colleagues, for their interest in the project and their never-failing courtesy and skill.

ALAN P. F. SELL
Milton Keynes, U.K.

Part One: **HISTORICAL**

1

The Growth of Puritanism
c.1559–1662[1]

John Gwynfor Jones

Historians have differed in their definition of 'Puritanism' in Elizabethan England and the impact it had in a period that saw far-reaching changes in politics, social life, and economy as well as religion. A. G. Dickens, Patrick Collinson, Peter Lake, Christopher Haigh, Paul Christianson, and Basil Hall among several others have attempted to evaluate what constituted the Puritan ethos and have come to varying conclusions.[2] It was the Puritan Richard Baxter who stated in 1680 that those who were called Puritans were 'the most serious, conscionable, practical, sober and charitable Christians that ever

---

1. The following abbreviations are used in this chapter: CSPD: *Calendar of State Papers, Domestic*; EHD: *English Historical Documents*; ODNB: *Oxford Dictionary of National Biography*.

2. Doran, *Elizabeth I and Religion*, 23–30; Elton, *England Under the Tudors*, 309–14, 423–26; Collinson, *English Puritanism*, 7–11.

he knew . . . the apple of God's eye.'[3] Such a definition was far too rash, vague, and contradictory when it is considered that he had already three years earlier stated that 'Puritan . . . is an ambiguous ill-made word used in many ways.'[4] There are many other more dispassionate concepts of Puritanism that are offered according to the manner in which historians and theologians interpret a movement and period which were to have a tremendous impact on the history of a wide spectrum of historical experience over the last five centuries. What is broadly acceptable to most historians, however, is that Puritans, unlike conformist Protestants, believed more intensely in the need for further reform in the Elizabethan settlement of 1559 while remaining within the Church. They were also known as precisionists because of their attention to duties of conduct, especially with regard to religious observance. That was reflected in their pietism and discipline and their firm adherence to Calvinist teachings. They comprised moderate as well as extreme minority groups who, created a 'religious sub-culture' separate from Protestant conformism attempting to amalgamate various interpretations of the Scriptures. 'The meaning of Puritanism,' Collinson maintains, 'is not only doctrine, applied and internalized, but a social situation . . . which contributed to a significant change in the pattern of cultural and social relations.'[5]

The origins of Puritanism go back before the days of Elizabeth I. Some historians in the past have associated it with the growth of Lollardy in the fifteenth century and the anabaptism movement on the continent. While it cannot be denied that there were traits that might be associated with earlier movements, the chief features of English Puritanism were its connections with Genevan Calvinism rather than with Barrowites and Brownists, the seed of future separatism.[6] The reformist exiles that returned to England on Elizabeth's accession were reluctant to conform fully with her new Church

3. Baxter, *History of the Governors of Bishops*, fig. a 3.

4. Baxter, *Naked Papacy*, 30.

5. Collinson, *Elizabethan Puritan Movement*, 12–13; Collinson, *Religion of Protestants*, 230.

6. Among major works to be consulted on English Puritanism and its impact in this period are Knappen, *Tudor Puritanism*; Collinson, *Elizabethan Puritanism*; Collinson, *Godly People*; Lake, *Moderate Puritans*; Watts, *Dissenters* I; McGrath, *Papists and Puritans*; Nuttall, *Puritan Spirit*; Jones, *Congregationalism*; Hill, *Society and Puritanism*; MacCulloch, *Later Reformation*.

Settlement in the following year and aimed to reform it from within.[7] In other words, they wished to see the Reformation progress to its natural conclusion, rejecting what they regarded as vestiges of popery in the new Church and the apostolic succession. Puritanism emphasized justification by faith and the literal acceptance of God's Word in the Scriptures. This lay at the basis of Presbyterianism, the reform movement within the Elizabethan church. To them episcopalianism lay not at the root of the early Christian church but rather was a system, as prescribed in the Book of Acts, based on ministers and elders within a parochial or presbyterial structure and regional synods. That implied that Presbyterianism co-operated with the state but remained independent of it.

On her accession in 1558 Elizabeth I, who had inherited much of her father's character and determination, regarded her primary task to be to establish her authority in ecclesiastical and secular affairs within her realm. From the outset she set about tackling the problems that threatened the unity of church and state. The Church of England had experienced many upheavals during the previous two decades because changes in religious policies and the long-term impact of her father's reign had forced Elizabeth, judiciously applying her authority, to face the challenge to defend the realm's interests at home and abroad. Much was expected of her and the pageants performed on her coronation underlined a strong feeling of a restored Tudor stability. Among the similies used to describe her, one of the most appropriate was that of Deborah, the judge and 'prophet of Israel,' who reigned firmly for forty years and became a symbol of power and unity.[8] The English realm needed a ruler who would adopt a strong policy at the outset to restore political stability after Mary's reign. Elizabeth was soon to be regarded as the powerful leader known for her strong will, self-confidence, and arrogance, and although lacking in experience she doubtless possessed remarkable political acumen which made her mindful of the problems that beset her realm on her accession to the throne and Church Settlement. As a younger daughter of Henry VIII, reared as a Protestant, she had to tread carefully. The shadow of Mary's reign still hung over her and in order to strengthen her realm she soon became aware of the need to establish her rule on

7. Loades, *Revolution in Religion*, 56–59.
8. A prophetess and Judge. *Judges*, chaps. 4–5.

firm foundations. She insisted on conformity and made that clear to Archbishop Matthew Parker in a letter on 25 January 1564, barely six years after her accession. She had become aware of 'diversities of opinion' and 'novelties of rites and manners' which had grown within her realm, and she reminded the primate that she had no intention 'to have . . . dissension or variety grow, by suffering of persons, which maintain the same, to remain in authority.' And she continued: 'yet in sundry places of our realm of late . . . with sufferance of sundry varieties and novelties, not only in opinions, but in external ceremonies and rites, there is crept and brought into the Church by some few persons, abounding more in their own senses then wisdom would, and delighting in singularies and changes, an open and manifest disorder, and offence to the godly, wise and obedient persons, by diversity of opinions, and specially in the external decent, and lawful rites and ceremonies to bee used in the churches.'[9]

Bishops in their dioceses, particularly the remoter ones, found it a frustrating task to enforce obedience to the new religious settlement. John Best, Bishop of Carlisle, for example, had to contend with the hostility of conservative Catholic families of aristocratic stock, such as the Dacres and Cliffords, and he despondently reported to Sir William Cecil, the Queen's Chief Secretary, in January 1562:

> The rulers and justices of peace wink at all things and look through their fingers. For my exhortation to have such punished I have had privy displeasure. Before the great men came into these parts I could do more in a day concerning Christ's gospel nor since that time in two months. I have no probable cause to allege but that for punishing and depriving certain evil men which neither would do their office according to the good laws of this realm, neither acknowledge the Queen's Majesty's supremacy, neither yet obey me as ordinary.[10]

On the death of her half-sister Mary in 1558 Elizabeth inherited a weak Church. The further away dioceses were situated from central control the more difficult for the bishops it was to command obedience. Shortage of clergy and the poor quality of their education left much to be desired. Marian priests still held office and the laity were slow to enforce royal policy. At the end of her reign the second

9. EHD, (1558–1603), 171.

10. Ibid., 153–54.

Reformation in England had not been a complete success. It took considerable time for illiterate parishioners to become aware of, and well versed in, the basic beliefs of the Protestant faith. It was one matter to abandon the 'Old Faith' but an entirely different one to embrace the new. The situation in Welsh dioceses, for example, explains the problem clearly, particularly regarding the situation in simple monoglot rural communities. In such remote regions the progress of the reform programme in Elizabeth's reign could be frustratingly very slow, and Nicholas Robinson, Bishop of Bangor made the point very clear in a letter to Sir William Cecil in October 1567:

> the people Liue in much obedience, fredome and quiet . . . But touching ye Welshe peoples receauing of ye ghospell I finde by my small experience among them here, yt ignorance contineweth many in ye dregges of superstition, which did grow chefely apon ye blyndnes of the clergie ioyned with greediness of getting in so bare a cuntrey, and also apon ye closing vp of gods worde from them in an vnknown tounge . . . for the most part of ye priestes are to olde . . . now to be put to schole . . . Apon this inhabilitie to teache gods worde . . . I have found . . . Images and aulters standing in churches undefaced, lewde and undecent vigils and watches observed, much pilgrimage going, many candels sett up to ye honour of sainctes, much reliquies yet carried about, and all ye Countries full of bedes and knottes . . .[11]

This section of his apologetic letter threw into high relief the dire condition of the Church in such backward areas as Snowdonia. He drew attention to poverty, conservatism, ignorance, superstition, and the poor quality of the clergy as well as the greed of gentry landowners constantly seeking the main chance through the acquisition of church properties. Above all else a monoglot society without the Scriptures in their own language at that time stifled the promotion of Protestantism in local communities. Similar circumstances whereby ignorance and apathy stalled the progress of religious change were evident in other parts of the realm, particularly in the remoter areas of the midlands and north of England where Roman Catholic recusancy was a constant threat to religious uniformity. There were sharp divisions between regions, but the government had to contend with the

11. CSPD, 1547–1580, 301 (no. 27) [SP 12 44 7476].

conservatism in most backward parts of the country, a factor that was clearly publicized in episcopal reports.

Despite the decline of Roman Catholicism traditional beliefs and practices still remained major drawbacks to uniformity. Church courts needed reforming and the standards of the episcopalian system were not of the quality required to stabilize a new Religious Settlement. Indeed, radical reforms were often ignored in the less well-endowed dioceses. It is true, however, that the latter part of Elizabeth's reign showed more encouraging tendencies in the show of greater resilience and improvement in the standards of the clergy and church courts. Because of severe persecution and the increase in Protestant literature the 'Old Faith' lost ground. Iconophobia and Protestant-worded wills became more common and the persistent policies to promote the New Faith meant that the transition from one generation to another gradually led to the acceptance of new religious values. Preaching and local lectureships increased and the quality of lay and clerical education improved by the close of the Tudor century. Regardless of Puritan opposition and the survival of Roman Catholicism the Reformation under Elizabeth's rule was achieved without any political unrest.[12]

From the Queen's early years on the throne it was evident that religion was but one of several problems that she had to resolve. Politics and the role of Parliament, growing opposition to royal prerogative powers, social and economic instability were pressing issues, and religious tensions increased with the return of Protestant exiles from the continent deeply influenced by the Reformed faith. The Queen's religious policy, therefore, aimed at forming a religious settlement that would combine the loyalties of both Protestants and Catholics to the throne. The returned Protestants were determined to reform the Church of England and liberate it from the 'Old Faith.' They were intent on reviving the preaching tradition and institution of 'godly preachers,' helping to consolidate Protestant teaching, and advancing the 'evangelism' normally associated with Puritanism, all of which would reinforce the new Church established by statutes in 1559. The Act of Supremacy proclaimed the Queen to be 'supreme governor' of the Church of England, thus placing her authority below that of Christ, but she continued to exercise her father's authority over

---

12. McGrath, *Papists and Puritans*, 48–49.

religious affairs.[13] Roman Catholicism was gradually placed under pressure following the Oath of Supremacy imposed on clergy and laity whereby they undertook to reinforce the Church established by law. Likewise, the Act of Uniformity made compulsory attendance at parish churches on Sundays and Holy Days and the use of the revised *Book of Common Prayer*, which differed little from that issued in 1552 by Thomas Cranmer, was sanctioned. The 'black rubric' of 1552, which denied corporeal presence, was omitted, transubstantiation and mass vestments were rejected and a wooden table installed to replace the stone altar. The Queen had no wish to suppress Catholic rites and images and proclamations were issued to safeguard ancient monuments and memorials. She made no declaration of faith because that was considered to be a matter for the Church and did not wish to embroil herself in religious disputes. Rather, she regarded her settlement as being essentially secular, and to say that she created a *via media* between Rome and Geneva is misleading. It was a political compromise formed owing to tensions between herself and the bishops. It was not an 'Anglican' church either, as it has so often been described. The English Church was not cut off from the continent as that title seems to suggest. Rather it was the Protestant Church of England with the Queen as its supreme governor. Matthew Parker, her first Archbishop of Canterbury, was an able administrator and leader, who had not had the experience of being among continental reformers but who served the Crown with 'firmness and moderation,' intent on establishing a new religious settlement without upheaval.

The Church's theology was a mixture of Lutheran, Zwinglian, and Calvinist doctrines; Cranmer's *Prayer Book*, issued in Edward VI's reign, was restored and in 1563 royal sanction was given the *Thirty-Nine Articles* which were based on the *Forty-Two Articles* of 1552. Its basis was Laodicean in that it was accommodating, and within it growing opposition emerged among reformers who rejected its secular spirit. Its leaders emphasized historical continuity and the belief that it was a Church restored to its ancient purity. In his *Address to the Welsh* People, the preamble to the translation of the New Testament into Welsh in 1567, Richard Davies, Bishop of St. David's, made the point clearly: 'I will recall one excellent virtue which is equivalent to all the above, which adorned thee of old, and gave thee a privilege

---

13. EHD, (1558–1603), 36.

and a pre-eminence, namely, undefiled religion, pure Christianity, and an effective fruitful faith.'[14] Davies's comment was Protestant propaganda, wholly assertive and embedded in mythology and spurious history. Reformers in the Church, many of who were returned exiles, sharply objected to this interpretation for they demanded further reform whereby the Church would be liberated from what they regarded as 'the dregs of Popery.' They demanded that the Church should be based on the Word of God and Christ's teaching to the Apostles. For them the Church should be freed from all superstitions, papal vestiges considered by them to be 'Antichrist.' The appearance of the Geneva (or Breeches) Bible in 1560, translated by Puritan exiles, principally William Whittingham, Anthony Gilbey, and Thomas Sampson, assisted the Puritan cause with its marginal Calvinist comments which disapproved of bishops. It is therefore understandable why the Bishops' Bible (1568)—fully approved by the Queen and the establishment—became less popular. The Geneva version was based on the Great Bible (1539) and appealed to the common man.[15]

The Vestiarian Controversy which arose from the disagreements had much wider implications than merely the use of vestments for it became an attack on ecclesiastical organisation and led to a conflict over the episcopalian system and the Queen's authority to appoint bishops and vest in them the power to act in their dioceses, the House of Lords, and in Convocation. The main opponent who strongly voiced his disapproval of episcopal authority was Dr. Thomas Cartwright, Lady Margaret Professor of Divinity at Cambridge, the chief Puritan leader who believed that the Scriptures were the basis of the Church's authority.[16] He argued that emphasis should be placed exclusively on preaching and teaching the Word, and it was he who gave John Field and Thomas Wilcox the incentive to publish *An Admonition to Parliament* (1572), a Presbyterian manifesto severely critical of episcopalianism. A second *Admonition* soon followed, attributed to Cartwright but possibly written by Christopher Goodman, a radical Protestant,[17] and Cartwright defended both works in 1573, which led to the bitter controversy between him and John Whitgift, vice-

14. Evans, *Legality*, 84–85; Williams, *Reformation Views*, ch. 5.

15. Daniell, *Bible in English*, 198–220, 291–319, 338–47.

16. For a study of Cartwright see Pearson, *Cartwright and Elizabethan Puritanism*.

17. ODNB, 22, 792–94.

chancellor of Cambridge and Dean of Lincoln following Whitgift's *The defense of the Aunswere to the Admonition* in 1574. Cartwright favoured ministers being elected by congregations and rejected the mythical 'Protestant Church theory.' His comments on the negligence of bishops and clergy in attending to the spiritual needs of parishioners at times of confession revealed his hatred of them. In a letter by him to 'a godly merchant' on 'the true way of confessing our sinnes,' he made his views clear about the need to abandon Popish practices and confess all sins:

> so deepelye are the Popishe traditions printed in their tender Consciences, esteeming the breache of them to be a greater offence, the[n] idolatrye, blasphemye, periurie, theft, slaunder, or any transgression of Gods holy commaundements. Whiche thinge oughte to make all the Babilonicall Bishoppes ashamed (but yt they are past all shame already) because they suffer Gods people to be so drowned in ignoraunce, that they can not discern the commaundements of God, fro[m] the dirtye dregs of Papisticall traditions.[18]

The term 'Puritan' requires definition for it is central to religious disputes and conflicts from early in Elizabeth's reign onwards.[19] There had been growing opposition to the Church since Henry VIII's latter years but it cannot be said that Puritans early in Elizabeth's reign violently opposed the new established Church. Puritanism became evident first of all on the continent in the 1550s where English and Welsh exiles, opposed to Marian policies, were free from persecution and receptive of reforming ideas in the strong Protestant centres of Geneva, Strasbourg, Basel, Zürich, and Frankfurt. As stated above, they were preachers and scholars who enthusiastically returned on Mary's death to reform religion based on their convictions. Similarly in Scotland John Knox, that fiery anti-Catholic reformer, returned to become the influential leader of the reforming party. It is evident that a 'Calvinistic consensus' had emerged in Parliament in 1559. 'Puritan' was often a term of abuse but was identified with the Presbyterians who disregarded episcopal power but accepted royal supremacy. According to Collinson, the term requires a broader interpretation for it involved

18. Peel and Carlson (eds.), *Cartwrightiana*, 110.

19. Collinson, *Elizabethan Puritanism*, 22–28; Collinson, *Godly People*, ch. 1; Hall, "Problem of Definition," 283–96.

the role of the laity as well as the clergy.[20] There were moderate clergy inclined towards Puritanism who complied with the requirements of the law because they feared losing a living or preaching licence. Moreover, there are several aspects to Puritanism which need broader treatment for the different interpretations given it associated it with political ideologies, social and economic tensions and conflicts as well as theological disputes. It can be said that Puritans became more vocal during the Vestiarian controversy of the early 1570s, when they were regarded as a minority that refused to conform to the *Prayer Book*.

Several Elizabethan bishops showed puritanical leanings—such as Edmund Grindal, John Jewel, Richard Cox, and James Pilkington—all of whom were returned exiles from the continent intent on pressing for reform. In 1574 Cartwright left a second time for Germany but not before translating Walter Travers's *Ecclesiasticae Disciplinae Explicatio*, called 'a textbook for English Presbyterians,' another outspoken exposition of Protestant nonconformity emphasizing the need for ecclesiastical self-government.[21] This Presbyterian sect campaigned for a Genevan system of government by ministers and synods governed by elected elders, prominence being given to the central control exercised by ministers, deacons, and ruling elders. The episcopal bench was rejected, for Presbyterians believed in individual responsibility towards God and rejection of the spiritual powers of bishops. This meant that they disregarded the 'apostolic succession' of episcopal ordination which led to their refusal to accept the Order of Service in the *Book of Common Prayer* and rules regarding vestments and ornaments in Archbishop Parker's *Book of Advertisements*(1566).[22] They linked episcopacy with the absolute authority of the Crown conferred by God, a claim that Presbyterians totally rejected. In the Commons in April 1571 the radical Puritan William Strickland, among other matters spoke further in favour of reforming the Common Prayer, and referred to abuses within the Church that should not be tolerated. His petition was rejected by the Lord Treasurer on the grounds that the 'matters of ceremony,' which Strickland wished Parliament to refer to the Queen as Supreme head of the Church, violated her prerogative

---

20. Collinson, *Elizabethan Puritanism*, 22–28; Hall, "Problems of Definition," 283–96.

21. McGrath, *Papists and Puritans*, 140.

22. Ibid., 89–90.

powers 'who hath authority as chief of the Church to deal therein. And for us to meddle with matters of her prerogative . . . it were not expedient.'[23] Issues involving divine privilege were beginning to loom large in the relations between the Queen and the Commons.

Another aspect of Puritan activity were the 'prophesyings,' set up at Northampton in 1573 and based on the study of the Scriptures with the intention of improving the quality of the clergy. They were often referred to as the 'exercise of prophesying,' chiefly to improve their preaching skills before an audience of fellow clergy, an activity regarded as 'in-training for the ministry.'[24] The word 'prophesying' was originally adopted from that used by St. Paul for preaching publicly in urban centres at regular intervals, usually on market days. It was an organization supported by Edmund Grindal who followed Matthew Parker as Archbishop of Canterbury in 1575. Grindal defended prophesyings to the Queen in December 1576: 'The reading of the godly homilies hath his commodity,' he stated, 'but is nothing comparable to the office of preaching. The godly preacher is termed in the Gospel "a faithful servant" . . . who can apply his speech according to the diversity of times, places, and hearers, which cannot be done in homilies.'[25] How much impact they had is difficult to assess, but the presence of laity, deeply affected by them, posed a threat to Elizabethan government that could not be ignored. Preaching of this kind was considered to have the desired effect for the most ardent Presbyterians eager to promote their faith. The efforts made to silence them were at best weak and ineffective and were mainly confined to the diocese of Norwich. The Queen feared that they would damage the royal prerogative and in May 1577, in response to Grindal's favourable view of these prophesyings, ordered him to suppress them:

> We hear . . . that in sundry parts of our realm there are no small numbers of persons presuming to be teachers and preachers of the Church . . . which, contrary to our laws established for the public divine service of Almighty God . . . do daily devise, imagine, propound, and put in execution sundry new rites and forms in the Church, as well by their preaching, reading and ministering the sacraments, as well by procuring unlawful assemblies of a great number of our people out of

23. EHD, (1558–1603), 178.

24. For 'prophesyings' see Collinson, *Elizabethan Puritan Movement*, 168–76.

25. EHD (1558–1603), 835.

their ordinary parishes and from place far distant . . . to be hearers of their disputations and new devised opinions upon points of divinity . . .[26]

Such was Grindal's support for these activities, however, that it led to his suspension in 1583[27] and he was followed at Canterbury by John Whitgift who, despite his Puritan leanings, as an active supporter of the Crown pursued a harsh policy of suppressing Puritanism. Subsequently, the *Six Articles* (1583) enforced the Crown's ecclesiastical policy together with the *Thirty-Nine Articles* and *Book of Common Prayer*, all of which led to 200 clergy being suspended for nonconformity. They believed that neither the 'infallibility' of the Church nor the authority of the Court of High Commission—first established in 1559 at Canterbury and York—could be defended at the time when Whitgift strove hard to destroy religious dissent. His policy dealt the Puritan movement a heavy blow. However, the 'classical movement'— local groups, which were synods of Puritan clergy—continued the campaign for ecclesiastical reform, and prophesyings in the Church became methods used to advance Presbyterianism within it, preparing candidates for the ministry and providing Puritan expositions of the Scriptures. Grindal's message was loud and clear: 'Public and continual preaching of God's word is the ordinary mean and instrument of the salvation of mankind . . . By preaching also due obedience to Christian princes and magistrates is planted in the hearts of subjects . . . So as generally where preaching wanteth, obedience faileth.'[28]

The 'classis,' the first of which appeared in Suffolk and soon spread to Essex, was used to 'confer and exercise' in prophesying, or in interpreting the Scriptures and enforcing discipline among its members. They were most popular in the South East, and many who attended pursued devotional matters and discussed the *Book of Common Prayer* rather than promoting Presbyterianism. The Puritan movement, then within the Church, utilized what methods it had at its command to advance its aims to reform the Church and undermine the ecclesiastical hierarchy.

26. Ibid., 841.

27. Collinson, "Downfall," 371–97. For Grindal's career see Collinson, *Archbishop Grindal.*

28. EHD (1558–1603), 834.

The Presbyterian 'classis' was designed to enable its members to discuss their affairs without Episcopal interference. Led by John Field, considered to be one of the 'godly young men' who refused to wear vestments in 1566, they were interested in campaigning to overthrow the 1559 settlement and to promote the use of a Genevan Prayer Book, an aim that was not fulfilled because of increasing pressures upon them.[29] Field, a follower of Cartwright, was an ardent Puritan who, with Thomas Wilcox, curate of All Hallows, Honey Lane, London, presented the *Admonition to the Parliament* in 1571. Thus the controversy arose concerning church government in which Cartwright and his enemy John Whitgift were involved; a controversy that extended into fields beyond scriptural authority such as relations between the Christian community and secular authority.[30] It was described as 'a brilliant piece of journalism' by Collinson, and 'the first popular manifesto of English Presbyterianism,'[31] a lively and strongly-worded rejection of the Elizabethan Church and its episcopal and other high ecclesiastical offices:

> In that the lord bishops . . . and such ravening rabblers, take upon them, which is most horrible, the rule of God's Church, spoiling the pastor of his lawful jurisdiction over his own flock given by the word, thrusting away most sacrilegiously that order which Christ hath left to His Church, and which the primitive Church hath used, they show they hold the doctrine with us, but in unrighteousness, with an outward show of godliness, but having denied the power thereof, entering not in by Christ, but by a popish and unlawful vocation.[32]

A much longer *Second Admonition* was presented to Parliament soon afterwards in 1572 which also contained severe attacks on the episcopacy and Puritan proposals for a reformed ministry, principally advocating the appointment of 'preaching pastors' in every parish. Both Admonitions, in fact, were Presbyterian manifestos that were strongly anti-papal.[33] Field and Wilcox held 'classical' conferences in which 'Calvinist ecclesiology' was the basic study. Field was one of the

29. Collinson, "John Field," 335–70.

30. Lake, *Anglicans and Puritans*, 13–70.

31. Ibid., 339; Lake, *Puritan Movement*, 118–21.

32. EHD (1558–1603), 181.

33. Ibid., 183–89.

most radical of Puritans whose career was untimely cut short in 1588. His patron, Robert Dudley, earl of Leicester, died in the same year, as did others who supported religious radicals, and subsequently the Presbyterian movement lost much of its impetus. Field, according to Collinson, was 'the linchpin of a precociously organised Presbyterian movement' who seriously threatened the Church, its hierarchy and its doctrine.[34]

Although articles of reform were introduced in Convocation in 1585 in an attempt to undermine Presbyterian activity opposition continued. In addition to Field's activity, Puritan members of Parliament, such as the brothers Peter and Paul Wentworth, increasingly attacked the Church and royal prerogative and campaigned for freedom of speech. On 28 February 1587 Sir Anthony Cope, member of Parliament for Banbury, eager to establish a Presbyterian system, presented the *Bill and Book* to Parliament advocating the abolition of the episcopal hierarchy and the establishment of a synodical government instead of the Church. It is possible that the Welsh layman John Penry of Brecknockshire, whose first treatise on the poor condition of the Church in his native country in that year, included bitter comments with a view to supporting Cope.[35] It is of interest to note that Penry's main supporters in presenting the *Aequity of an Humble Supplication* early in 1587 were two strong Puritans, Edward Dunn Lee, member of Parliament for Carmarthen boroughs, and Job Throckmorton, member for Warwickshire who was associated with the Marprelate Tracts. Penry was particularly concerned about the lack of competent preachers to serve his fellow Welshmen, and in his preface referred to their dire spiritual condition:

> Therefore in the name of God I require al of you, that you hinder not his honour, the saluation of perishing souls, and the good to the common wealth hereby inte[n]ded. If you do otherwise, I praie God, so many souls, as perish in miserable Wales for want of preaching, be not required at your hands in the daie of iudgement . . . My brethren for the most part know not what preaching meaneth, much lesse think the same nec-

34. "Field," 339–40; ODNB, 19, 476.

35. For detail on Penry and his career see Pierce, *John Penry*; McGinn, *John Penry and the Marprelate Controversy*; Williams, "Marprelate and Patriot," 361–72; Jones, "John Penry," 361–72.

essarie to saluation. Though they graunt it needeful, they think
it sufficient to heare one sermon once perhaps in al their life.[36]

By implication, Penry's plea drew attention to the widespread illiteracy and poor social conditions that hampered the progress of the Reformation in a backward part of the realm, a fact to which he and others constantly drew the attention of the authorities.

In the 1580s developments soon occurred whereby small but more extreme groups emerged and left the Church, thus establishing the 'separatist' movement. It emphasized the free congregation that rejected the alliance between Church and State to which Presbyterianism was attached. The main leaders were very resourceful, particularly Henry Barrow and the strong-willed Robert Browne, both of minor gentry stock, who advocated in their writings and sermons the role of the free congregation and rejected the episcopal system and ecclesiastical order. Barrow was a pioneer in this respect and John Greenwood, who was educated at Cambridge and deprived of his living in 1585, drove himself to a position in which he denied that the Church had a legitimate ministry, asserting that its assemblies were not based in Scripture but rather on papal canons. The irreverent anti-establishment Marprelate Tracts, whose authorship still remains a mystery, severely hampered the Church's counter-attacks and badly damaged its credibility. Heavy fines, imprisonment, and execution followed a total disregard for the ecclesiastical settlement, and some early separatists were not spared. Barrow, Greenwood and Penry—a Presbyterian turned separatist—were hanged in 1593 and Robert Browne, despite having defected from the separatists, published one of the most hostile and lengthy of anti-settlement tracts entitled *A Treatise of reformation without Tarying for anie* (1582). He is regarded as one of 'the most enigmatic figures' in the history of early dissent, and this treatise set out to declare that reform of 'wicked' ministers was urgently needed in a Church 'which will not reforme till the Magistrate commaunde or compell them.'[37] The magistrate, the civil officer of law, who awaited the Queen's command to act, he maintained, 'needs to be overridden and reform proceeding apace' and he continued: 'Woe to you therefore ye blinde Preachers and hypocrites: for ye spread a vaile of darkenes vpon the people, and bring vpon them a cursed couering, because

---

36. Williams, *Three Treatises*, 4, 7.

37. Peel and Carlson (eds.), *Harrison and Browne*, 15–17, 151.

by your policie you hide them vnder the power of Antichrist, and keepe from their eyes the kingdome of Christe.'[38] At Norwich Browne befriended Robert Harrison, both having studied at Cambridge where they were deeply influenced by Thomas Cartwright's teaching. Harrison became master of St. Giles's hospital at Norwich and both of them became Congregationalists—separatist groups that broke away from the Church. They did not at all times see eye to eye on matters of doctrine but in 1581 they fled with their followers to Middelburg in the Netherlands to avoid persecution.

John Penry, a Presbyterian turned separatist, was equally resentful of episcopal powers within the Church, and in his second treatise, *An exhortation vnto the gouernors, and people . . . of Wales* (1588), he sharply rebuked its unworthiness in his native country: 'Therefore wo be to the shepheards of Wales, saith Iehouah which feede themselues, shoul;d not the shepheards feed their flocks, you eat the fat and cloath you with the wooll, but you feede not the flocke . . . Take this from me also, that vnlesse you forsake your idleness, those personages and those chaires of pestilence wherein you sit, I mean your Bishops seas will spue you out.'[39] Harsh words indeed, written at a time of unrelenting internal and external pressures, soon after the outbreak of war with Spain in 1585. Puritan attacks on the Church, particularly by Congregationalists, were intended to damage its integrity, and the government adopted a severe policy of suppression against both Roman Catholic and Protestant dissidents. Their followers, however, regarded their leaders as martyrs who had sacrificed themselves in a campaign against what they considered to be a corrupt ecclesiastical order. Queen Elizabeth, besieged by increasing problems during the war with Spain, especially economic stringency and the Catholic threat, faced a more volatile Parliament eager to defend its privileges, especially freedom of speech, adopted a weak line of resistance against militant Puritans. They, at the time, were confronted by a dilemma, namely, either to satisfy their conscience or, as citizens of the realm, to defend it in its hour of need. As the century drew to a close the Crown allied itself more with the Church than Parliament because it safeguarded its prerogatives, a situation that angered Puritans further. John Whitgift, appointed Archbishop of Canterbury in 1583, follow-

38. Ibid., 167.

39. Williams, *Three Treatises*, 65.

ing his early moderate Puritan tendencies, hardened his opposition to them and used the Court of High Commission to repress them.[40] In that year a royal proclamation denounced 'seditious, schismatical and erroneous' printed books by Browne and Robert Harrison,[41] and a decade later an act was passed 'for retaining the Queen's subjects in their due obedience' which punished by exile or death all those who refused to attend church or persuaded others not to do so.[42]

For a number of reasons it cannot be said that the Presbyterian movement was a success. In fact, it had never been a strong force. Although secret methods were used to advance its campaign, based on Walter Travers's *Book of Discipline* (1584), it was unable to overcome the pro-establishment forces in church and state. Circumstances militated against it, such as the death of leaders, one of them being the stalwart John Field, the increase in influential offices given to some of them, the adverse impact upon them of the Marprelate Tracts which declared Presbyterianism to be subversive and, in 1588, the defeat of the Spanish Armada, which regenerated English national feeling and support for the Church. Moreover, the High Commission, fully supported by Whitgift and Richard Bancroft, Bishop of London, became more actively engaged in suppressing the 'classical movement' in 1591. Bancroft led a persistent campaign against Puritans, especially by investigating the press for seditious evidence. The Puritans themselves also felt a lack of unity among themselves in theological matters. Browne and Robert Harrison differed in their attitudes towards the Church, and varying opinions voiced by other leaders led to a failure to achieve collective agreement in their conferences, chiefly over subscriptions to the *Book of Discipline*. Some unease was felt by members of the 'classical movement' about it and, in a wider context, Puritans found themselves to be more isolated at Court, particularly after the death of the earl of Leicester in 1588. He had been a staunch supporter of Puritans, and in a letter to the preacher Thomas Wood in August 1576 he recalled some of his services in their aid:

> that there is no man I know in this realm of one calling or other that hath showed a better mind to the furthering of true religion than I have done . . . And when times of some trouble

40. Dawley, *John Whitgift*, 133–94.

41. Hughes and Larkin, *Tudor Royal Proclamations, II, 1553–1587*, 501–2.

42. *Statutes of the Realm*, IV(ii), 841–43.

hath been among the preachers and ministers of the church for matters of ceremonies and such like . . . who did move for them . . . Or who in England had more blame of both for the success that followed thereby than myself? I would fain know at the most devilish enemy's hand that I have what one act have I done to hinder or diminish the church of God . . . ? I defy their worst. For my conscience doth witness the contrary . . .[43]

Gradually the Puritan spirit lost much of its impetus, the Presbyterians, bent on reducing royal supremacy over the Church, being unable to combat the greater emphasis placed by Bancroft and Dr. John Bridges, Dean of Salisbury, on the divine right of episcopacy.[44] Bridges published a massive work entitled *A Defence of the Government established in the Church of England* (1587), denounced by John Penry as 'plaine popery' and a transgression of the Scriptures, which had not created episcopacy.[45] He ridiculed Bridges, almost in libellous fashion, thus placing him in a most vulnerable position, but his conscience dictated that he should defend his standpoint in a most forceful manner, and that appeared in his third major treatise *A Supplication vnto the High Court of Parliament* (1588):

I do therefore in this point also, for the discharge of my dutie and conscience towards the Lord, his Church, my countrie, and the whol estate of this kingdom . . . that our dumbe ministers, that the callings of our L[ord] B[ishops], archdea[cons], commiss[ioners], with al other remnants of the sacriledge brought into the Church by that Roman strumpet . . . are intolerable before the Lorde, and that it is not likely that euer you tolerating these things any longer, shall escape Gods fierie wrath . . . These thing I offer to proue against M[aster] D[octor] Bridges, who lately in a large volume, hath undertaken their defence. In which book of his, he hath offered her Maiestie & the Parliament most vndutifull injurie, by going about for the maintenance of his own belly, & the belies of the rest of his coat, to allienat the hearts of the loyallest subiects in the lande, from their most carefull prince and gouernors.[46]

43. Collinson (ed.), *Letters of Thomas Wood*, 13.

44. ODNB, 7, 583–85.

45. Williams, *Three Treatises*, 123.

46. Ibid., 123.

Preaching outside the Church continued to be a prominent feature of Puritan activity, and it gathered support among Puritan gentry, members of which held local offices and served as powerful members of the Court and Parliament and local agencies of the Crown. The role of the small number of separatists became more evident in the latter years of Elizabeth's reign. They had abandoned the Church since they did not regard it as the true servant of God, and organised their own scattered congregations, known as 'gathered churches', and some Presbyterians joined them. The seeds of sectarianism had been well sown under the leadership of Browne and Harrison, both of them having established a 'gathered church' at Norwich in 1580. Soon after the 'classical movement' ended the separatists, led by Henry Barrow and John Greenwood, maintained their stand against the Church, and despite their imprisonment their influence was still felt among minority groups. On his release in 1582, Barrow moved to the Netherlands where his works were published. He was eager to defend the position of separatists against the attacks by Church of England apologists, one of the most devious being George Gifford, a clergyman who vehemently dismissed them as Anabaptists, schismatics, heretics, and Donatists [members of an ancient Christian sect believing that they were the only true Christians], an accusation which Barrow totally refuted. The dispute led to Barrow's lengthy *Plaine Refutation of M. Giffardes . . . short treatise against the Donatists of England*, published in 1591. His onslaught on the Church was maintained throughout this diatribe and declared that the Church was not truly the Church of God:

> And for the Church of England we neither did or doe condemne
> it . . . but we condemned the publick worship of their Church
> of England presently injoyned, received and used, as devised by
> men, popish, superstitious, idolatrous, abhominable, not such
> as God commandeth, requireth, or accepteth, and therfore not
> such as anie faithfull Christian may offer unto God, compelled,
> or consent unto . . . wee condemne not the Church of England
> as separate from Christ . . . But rather as never rightly gathered
> to Christ, for that al the prophane and wicked are received and
> retayned as members of their churche.[47]

Barrow hit hard at the heart of the Church's teaching, dismissing entirely the accusation that separatists considered themselves, as did

47. Carlson (ed.), *Writings of Henry Barrow (1590–1591)*, 326.

Donatists, the only pure sect that believed that the baptisms and ordi-
nations of others were invalid. In his treatise he examined in detail four
fundamental weaknesses in the Church in the Tudor state. First, it was
guilty of false worship, created by man, imposed by the hierarchy and
based on Catholic tradition as revealed in the *Book of Common Prayer*.
His beliefs, that the Bible is the absolute authority, God's supremacy
above that of the Church, were those taught by Thomas Cartwright,
Theodore Beza and John Calvin. *The Book of Common Prayer*, he further stated, had its origins in papal liturgies, a human invention totally
idolatrous. Secondly, the Church received all, whether true believers
or 'the profane ungodlie multitude.'[48] Only those who had entered a
covenant with God and had kept His Commandments could be accepted as members of the true Church, those who professed faith and
took a vow of obedience to Him. The third accusation touched upon
the quality of the ministry, and Barrow contrasted the 'reigning order'
of the Church with the New Testament pattern which gave rise to the
structure of pastors, teachers, elders, deacons, and relievers, individuals ordained by congregations to care for the ill and impoverished.
Bishops, he maintained, were 'blasphemous and unwarranted . . .
arrogant and presumptuous.' In 1559, when the Church settlement
came about, no attempt was made to distinguish between them, and
among them, Barrow declared, there were papists or heretics. In his
view, this made the Church confused, sacrilegious and secularised,
major offices being grasped by those who usurped the dignities which
only Christ himself possessed. 'For if it be blasphemy for anie mortal
man to receive . . . those names, titles, dignities, or offices which are
peculiar and proper to Christe's sacred person alone, then are these
chief ministers of the Church of England . . . highlie guilty of blas-
phemie . . .'[49] Fourthly, the governmental structure of the Church was
not based on that laid down in the primitive church described in the
New Testament Thus, Barrow questioned the claim of the Church to
be 'the true spouse of Christ.'[50] 'No true established church of Christe,'
he declared, 'may willingie receive, or wittingly stand subject under
anie other ecclesiasticall government than Christ hath prescribed and
instituted.' Since the Church of England, according to Barrow, was not

48. Ibid., 3–18, 102.
49. Ibid., 192, 206.
50. Ibid., 285–86; Carlson (ed.), *Writings of Henry Barrow (1587-1590)*, 143.

created according to that prescribed by the New Testament then it was 'not the true established Church of Christ.'[51]

Barrow did not live long enough to continue his dispute with Gifford for, on his return from the continent, he was imprisoned and, like Greenwood, was hanged in 1593. Barrow's memory, however, was still revered by his followers, and his reputation lived after him in his slanderous anti-Church book headed A *Brief Discovery of the False Church*, written during his imprisonment in the Fleet in 1589. In it, his sharp wit, like that of other Puritans, stood out:

> All the lawes of God are heere broken and rejected . . . both of the ecclesiasticall and civille and of everie particular person in both, both in the worship of God, and in civile justice and conversation: all things being innovate in both, according to the lustes and pleasures of men, the law and word of God being quite rejected and cast aside, as may appeare, if the estate either of the church or common welth be examined or tried by the word of God . . . And what then are the enormities that ensue therof to everie estate, degree and person. This need no other demonstration, than the general excesse, pride, superfluitie, covetousness, rapine, crueltie, deceit, malice, debate, inordinate affections, unbridled lustes, dissolutnes, disobedience, etc which we found most rife, even in all estates and degrees amongst them. Neither hath all kind of sinne and wickednes more universally raigned in any nation at any time, than heere at this present in this land; where all are received into the church, all made members of Christ.[52]

Such a harsh condemnation of the state Church and its leaders clearly declared the position taken by this minority of separatists in the last decade of Elizabeth's reign. Whereas Presbyterianism had lost much of its impetus the resilient attacks by Congregationalists and Baptists continued undeterred, even extending to the continent, as did the London congregation which settled in Amsterdam, and it was there that they established a new religious tradition. Congregationalists became active in parts of the east midlands, Nottinghamshire, Lincolnshire and south Yorkshire, and it was among their 'gathered churches' that a new spirit arose determined to promote further reform.

51. Carlson (ed.), *Writings of Henry Barrow (1587–1590)*, 285.

52. Ibid., 282–83.

I

On the accession of James I to the English throne in 1603 the situation between the Church and separatists, while not being entirely satisfactory, had eased, since it was expected that the Scottish king, who had inherited a new kingdom, would wish to compromise on both sides. On the occasion of his journey from Edinburgh to London the Millenary Petition, presented to him, clearly indicated that moderate Puritans wished to impress him and present their grievances to him at the earliest opportunity. It was partly drawn up by Henry Jacob, a moderate separatist, and Stephen Merton, minister of St. Anne's, Blackfriars; its main demands being the abolition of Popish features such as vestments and ceremonies, which they regarded as being repulsive in the Church. They also objected to other practices like the sign of the cross in baptism and the use of the ring in marriage, and demanded improvements in the ministry. They were concerned about the educational standards of the clergy and the practice of pluralities, and called for a conference to be convened to discuss these matters, many of which were of minor concern. The Petition, however, came to nothing. It was a none-starter from its inception for, in the first instance, separatist ill-feeling had manifested itself in several parts of England in the same year and, more importantly, King James wished to avoid 'nourishing schism' in the kingdom and to suppress all 'turbulent humours' opposed to all that the Church stood for.[53] Conflicts also arose following the Canons of 1604 passed by Convocation, which revealed James's lack of sympathy for Puritanism. They were designed—insensitively perhaps—by Bancroft, not only to reform pluralities and non-residence but also to reinforce the Church's position, for example, in maintaining the *Articles*, the *Book of Common Prayer* and the episcopal office as well as all other rites and ceremonies.[54] These Canons caused much controversy, and although they were not passed by Parliament and were therefore not binding on the laity, the Canons led 300 ministers to secede from the Church. They declared that any person who believed that the *Prayer Book* and episcopal authority were contrary to the word of God was to be punished severely, a clause which led to an increase in small 'gathered' churches led by John Smyth, John Robinson, Richard Bernard, and William Brewster

53. Coward, *Stuart Age*, 110.

54. EHD (1603–1660), 269–72.

and others, some of whom left for the continent. Others, among the Congregationalists, being more moderate, showed less hostility towards the Church and were prepared to conciliate while maintaining their stand to campaign for religious freedom.

In this tense atmosphere, which could have erupted as a major confrontation between the Crown, with the Church as its ally, and the separatists with their 'tender consciences', the situation was partly relieved because James agreed to convene a conference between delegates from the Church and moderate Puritans at Hampton Court early in 1604 (14–16 January) to discuss religious issues which caused major grievances. In spite of his sceptical attitude it was James himself, in fact, who decided that such a conference should be held, over which he himself presided. Doubtless he was eager to avoid any further disruption, but at the same time he was determined to act as the 'grand arbitrator', fully aware of his ability to fill the role. Historians have generally considered the conference to have been a failure, chiefly because of James's stern, even stubborn, opposition to the matters raised by Presbyterians. He had sad even bitter memories of his harsh upbringing among Presbyterians in Scotland, and any attempt to amend any part of the religious settlement, by then well established, would certainly anger him. S. R. Gardiner and R. G. Usher, for example, believed that he and members of the episcopal deputation rejected almost completely the Puritan proposals. They were firm in their view that James was determined to 'make them conform to existing usage' or he would 'harry them out of the land'; or, in Gardiner's words, he would send 'the defenders of an apparently hopeless cause . . . back to their labours, to struggle on as best they might.'[55] The Puritan lobby, however, was not as easily cast aside as some historians have thought, and it is now generally accepted that the conference, in certain directions, encouraged the Puritan deputation to revive their aims and to carry them into the political arena, as revealed in James's first Parliament in 1604. Patrick Collinson has clarified the fact that these Presbyterians had not existed as a sect in the early years of Elizabeth's reign but rather a presence within the Church who believed much of what other Protestants held but more intensely. The increased tensions which occurred between them and the Church had galvanised them to such a degree that they were well prepared to confront a sovereign

55. Gardiner, *History of England*, 158–59.

who hold strong views on divine right of kings.[56] Among those who
were 'harried out of the land' were John Smyth and Thomas Helwys,
who sought freedom in the Netherlands in 1608. Both were General
Baptists and Helwys, who favoured religious toleration, returned to
England in 1611 and formed the first Baptist church on English soil in
the following year.

The Puritan deputation at Hampton Court sought changes in
the *Book of Common Prayer* and other ceremonial reforms, which
revealed that they were prepared to compromise on certain issues. In
Scotland James had learned that the Church was not his kingdom but
rather the kingdom of Christ and that he was a member of it like all
other Christians, but the Puritan deputation was not ready to probe
such deep-seated concepts. In his *Basilikon Doron* (1603) James stated,
when referring to Puritans: 'No, I am so farre from being contentious
in these things (which for my own part I euer esteemed as indifferent)
as I doe equally loue and honour the learned and graue men of either
of these opinions.'[57] Doubtless he welcomed rational discussion with
moderate Puritans for his experiences in Scotland had well-prepared
him to encounter them and the more extreme whom he regarded as
'seditious schismatics.'[58] At one stage he became annoyed when John
Rainolds, leader of the Puritan delegation, Provost of Corpus Christi,
Oxford, and a highly reputable theological scholar, suggested that
'Presbyteries' should be established. It led James later to totally oppose any suggestion that a Presbyterian system might be established
in the Church. Rainolds, the chief Puritan spokesman, was joined
in the deputation by John Knewstub, Church of England clergyman
turned Puritan, Laurence Chaderton,[59] Master of Emmanuel College,
Cambridge, and Thomas Sparke, a Church of England clergyman
who had puritan sympathies. Rainolds and his deputation were faced
by a group of Anglican bishops and scholars eager to maintain the
Church settlement and undermine the arguments put forward by
their Puritan counterparts.

---

56. Collinson, *Puritan Movement*, 29; Lake, "Calvinism and the English Church,"
114.

57. C. H. McIlwain, *Political Works of James I*. 8.

58. Ibid., 6–8, 23, 24.

59. Hunt, "Chaderton and Hampton Court," 207–28.

The king's well-known retort on hearing the word 'presbytery' threatened to bring the conference abruptly to an end. It 'as well agreeth with a monarchy as God and the Devil,' he stated, 'No bishop, no king.' Although James's mind was clear his disagreements with the Puritans did not lead him unceremoniously to dismiss Rainolds and his co-delegates from the conference and bring proceedings to an untimely end.[60]

The details of discussions at the conference were recorded in detail by the anti-Puritan William Barlow, Dean of Chester, who compiled his biased *The Summe and Substance of the Conference* (1604). The Anglican leader was Richard Bancroft, Bishop of London and another ardent opponent of Puritanism, soon to become Archbishop of Canterbury on Whitgift's death. John Rainolds proposed that the clergy should convene once every three weeks in rural deaneries to hear prophesyings and to refer any ecclesiastical matters to the archdeacons on their visitations and episcopal synod where bishops might settle disputes in a presbytery. Whether that proposal was misunderstood or not it was evident that Rainolds had no intention of proposing that the episcopal office be abolished. He wished rather to reform ecclesiastical organisation, to 'purify' the Church and establish a system whereby bishops might function within presbyteries, and not create a Presbyterian polity. On that occasion James's Scottish upbringing caused his misinterpretation since he failed to understand what the Puritan delegation had in mind. He sat on the throne 'to maintain the religion presently professed within their Countrie, according to lawes whereby it is established, and to punish all those that should preise to alter or disturbe the profession thereof.'[61] Such a statement was a saving device allying the king with the established order but also widening the breach between him and the most moderate group of Puritans eager to gain his favour.

In James's early days on the English throne the Church had experienced a resurgence through the leadership of Richard Hooker and Lancelot Andrewes, acclaimed Anglican scholars and preachers. Andrewes, later to become Bishop of Winchester, was a highly regarded churchman and one of the most pious and erudite ecclesiastical scholars of his day. Hooker had come to prominence following his

---

60. Bingham, *James I of England*, 35, 38–39.

61. Sommerville, "Trew Law," 64–65.

extensive eight-volume study in defence of the Elizabethan Church entitled *Of the Laws of Ecclesiastical Polity* (1594–1600), a masterpiece which lay the basis for several other theological works.[62] He sought unity in the Church and expounded the medieval belief that it and the state were one and the same. The Church, he declared, had powers to make laws and establish a polity for the good of the realm, and he appealed to Puritans to consider their position yielding to reason and tradition so that stability might be achieved. Although he conceded that there was need for reform and queried the apostolic succession, he upheld episcopal authority and rejected the Puritan emphasis on the Scriptures as the basis of the Church. Both Andrewes and Hooker defended the Church and adopted an Anglican theology that defied Puritan beliefs.

Despite the partial achievement in matters relating to external reforms the failure to achieve all that was proposed at Hampton Court created a further division between the Crown and Puritans. Of all modern historians Mark Curtis is one of those who have studied the conference more positively and has interpreted it as an attempt to draw both factions together.[63] He believes that James, like the Puritans, wished to safeguard purity within the Church, to place preaching ministers in each parish and ensure that the *Book of Common Prayer* promoted godliness. Bancroft, however, prejudiced against the Puritans, considered that the conference had achieved very little, and doubted that any important issues had in fact been resolved. In the proclamation he had prepared to publicise the changes made to the *Prayer Book* he revealed his dissatisfaction:

> We leave to the report of those who heard the same, contenting our Selfe with the sinceritie of Our own heart within. But we cannot conceal that the success of that conference was such as happeneth to many other things which moving great expectation before they be entered into, in their issue produce small effect. For we found mighty and vehement informations supported with so weak and tender proofs, as it appeared unto us and our council that there was no cause why any changes

---

62. Lake, "Richard Hooker," 146–64.

63. Curtis, "Hampton Court Conference," 1–16 (2–3); Shriver, "Hampton Court Revisited," 48–71, especially 62..

should have been at all in that which was most impugned, the
Book of Common Prayer . . .[64]

Bancroft's opinion was similar to that published by William Barlow
who considered the Puritan case to be weak and 'poorly grounded.'[65]
The bishops, influenced largely by him, failed to meet all the requirements of the conference. The reforms proposed to curtail pluralism
and non-residence, and the promotion of a preaching ministry, modi-
fications to the *Book of Common Prayer* and Catechism, education,
censure of schismatics and other outstanding abuses, were only partly
given attention, thus revealing how reluctant Bancroft and his fellow
bishops were to accede to the requirements of the Puritan deputation.[66]

The main Puritan achievement at Hampton Court, however,
was the decision to provide a new 'authenticall' version of the Bible, a
proposal put forward by Rainolds who believed that parts of the biblical text were corrupt or misleading, not a view eagerly accepted by
some of the Anglican deputation, including Bancroft, who stated that
'if every mans humor should be followed, there would be no end of
translating.'[67] Since he and his colleagues were aware that the Geneva
and Bishops' Bible were still available and popular they did not wish to
yield any advantage to the opposing side at the conference. The King
agreed that there should be a new version because he thought that the
Geneva Bible, which had marginal notes added to the text, contained
'untrue, seditious,' material, 'savouring too much of dangerous, and
traitorous conceits.'[68] James objected to that version because it condemned royal rule and the word 'tyrant' was too frequently used in
the text. The translation was to be reviewed by bishops and the best
scholars made available to accomplish the task. It was then to be presented to the Privy Council and ratified by the King 'to be read in the
whole church, and no other.'[69]

A number of highly-qualified scholars, divided into six groups—
two at Oxford, two at Cambridge, and two at Westminster—was appointed to undertake the arduous task of providing a new version,

64. Larkin and Hughes (eds.) I, *Stuart Royal Proclamations* I, 75.

65. Barlow, *Summe and Substance*, 46.

66. Curtis, "Hampton Court Conference," 14–15.

67. Barlow, *Summe and Substance*, 46.

68. Ibid., 14; Daniell, *Bible in English*, 434; Bruce, *History of the Bible*, 96–97.

69. Daniell, *Bible in English*, 433–34.

drawing upon the rich biblical heritage of the past, and based mainly on the translations of Tyndale and Coverdale.[70] It has misleadingly been described as King James's 'authorised' version because it was not officially sanctioned in Convocation or Parliament. What James did was simply to approve the translation at Hampton Court and to express his opinion of the Geneva Bible in derogatory words: 'I profess, I could never yet see a Bible well translated in English; but I think that, of all, that of Geneva is the worst. I wish some special pains were taken for an uniform translation, which should be done by the best-learned men in both Universities.'[71] James charged them to correct or amend errors in matters of faith and ensure that other vague words or phrases would have glosses attached.

The work was eventually completed and published, including the Apocrypha, in 1611. It was an immense achievement by forty-seven named scholars (some say fifty-four) who were required to observe fifteen rules, the first being that they were to follow the text of the 1568 Bishops' Bible 'and ensure that, as [be] altered, as the truth of the original will permit.' John Rainolds made up the team of seven scholars, including Miles Smith, Canon of Hereford (later Bishop of Gloucester), in the first Oxford company to undertake the task of translating the Old Testament books from Isaiah to Malachi, but he died before his work was completed in 1607.

The outcome of this vast project was the publication of what is considered to be one of the finest examples of English prose, which had a significant influence on noteworthy English litterateurs such as William Shakespeare (in his latter years), John Donne, George Herbert, John Milton, and John Bunyan. The principles upon which the translators based their work were clearly stipulated in the admirably detailed introduction—'The Translators to the Reader'—compiled by Miles Smith, assisted by Thomas Bilson, Bishop of Winchester:

> Truly, good Christian Reader, we never thought from the beginning that we should need to make a new translation, nor yet to make of a bad one a good one . . . but to make a good one better, or out of many good ones one principal good one, not justly to be excepted against; that hath been our endeavour, that our mark. To that purpose there were many chosen,

70. Ibid., 431–42.
71. Ibid., 433–34.

that were greater in other men's eyes than their own, and that sought the treuth rather than their own praise.[72]

It was on the second day of the conference that the Puritan deputation was given the opportunity to voice its grievances, but the proceedings were more constructive than is often believed. It was not a Convocation but rather a formal gathering to see whether or not some reconciliation might be achieved. Several such conferences had been held in the past, for example, at Lambeth in 1584. In 1604 doubtless the Puritan delegates were well aware of the divine right powers claimed by James, a concept which might easily have caused a serious hindrance to any progressive discussions. James was so eager to defend his prerogatives that he could be tedious and unreasonable, not only in religious matters but also more strikingly in his relations with a Parliament which had already demonstrated its growing strength in the latter decades of Elizabeth's reign.

At Hampton Court the Puritans were not seeking any radical changes that would undermine the Church's theology but rather reiterated largely what had been presented to the King in the Millenary Petition, especially the rejection of Catholic rites and other matters relating to ceremonial. Among them were the rejection of the cross in baptism, the appointment of better-educated church ministers, matters relating to church livings, the maintenance of the clergy, and church discipline. The petition ended partly on a hopeful and partly on a cautionary note: 'God, we trust, hath appointed your Highness our physician to heal these diseases . . . Thus your Majesty shall do that which . . . shall be acceptable to God; honourable to your Majesty . . . comfortable to your ministers . . . and prejudicial to none, but to those that seek their own quiet, credit and profit in the world.'[73]

Puritanism had declined in the latter years of the sixteenth century, especially after the failure of the Presbyterians in 1586–87 to abolish episcopacy and Catholic ritual, but Hampton Court gave its leaders a glimmer of hope that they might achieve a more positive outcome with the accession of a new king whom they considered would be prepared to compromise. Moderate Puritans, while they disapproved of James's policy in issuing the Declaration of Sports in 1618, became less prepared to oppose James's determination to maintain

72. Bible 1611 [ix]; Pollard (ed.), *Holy Bible*, [14].
73. EHD (1558–1603), 263.

the structure of the Elizabethan Church. Their more moderate radical standpoint was such that Church of England leaders considered that there were no 'issues around which it could organise a general assault on Puritan piety and its alleged subversive implications.'[74]

Richard Bancroft—by then Archbishop of Canterbury—had been more intent on seeing the 1604 Canons accepted in Convocation to maintain the king's supremacy—'the high majesty of monarchy'— over the Church, to reinforce the doctrine and liturgy of the Church and to detail the abuses subject to censure. It is not correct, however, to regard Bancroft as an anti-Calvinist because, as Fincham states, it is nearer the truth to describe him as 'an Elizabethan conformist protestant . . . intent on maintaining the unity of the Jacobean ecclesiastical establishment.'[75] In belief he was closer to his predecessor Whitgift than to his successors, the evangelical George Abbot and Arminian William Laud. Bancroft's Canons, however, were rigidly geared to maintaining the exclusive authority of the Church at the outset of James's reign to alleviate the criticism increasingly voiced in Parliament regarding the most common abuses, such as clerical residences, regular preaching and catechizing. The Church of England was to be upheld as the 'true and apostolical church, teaching and maintaining the doctrine of the apostles,' and all those schismatics who were still members of the Church were to be excommunicated. Conventicles, a name which became more common later to describe meeting places of dissenters, were not to be held and 'any sort of ministers and lay persons [who] . . . shall submit themselves to be ruled and governed by them' were to be suppressed. [76] Such commands followed closely after the Hampton Court conference and possibly demonstrated the King's deliberate intention to superimpose his prerogative power on the Church and ensure that any separatists and other Puritan ministers in the Church would not be tolerated.

These Canons led to much controversy among clergy and in Parliament, the result being that about seventy-five ministers were deprived of their livings. James, while supporting the policy behind the Canons, kept close to his coronation oath to maintain the *status quo*, even to the point of not supporting the anti-Calvinist spirit, which

74. Lake, *Anglicans and Puritans?*, 240.

75. Fincham, *Prelate as Pastor*, 291.

76. EHD (1603–1660), 270, 272.

was increasing. That policy, however, was severely criticized in the Parliament of 1621 for taking an extremely anti-Calvinist stance following Puritan criticism of the king's support for the 'Spanish match' rather than pursuing the war against Catholic Spain. In 1622 he ordered stricter control by the bishops over preaching which had to be restricted to the theology prescribed by the Church of England and archbishops and bishops were to be more wary in granting licenses to preachers and lecturers, which were to be recommended only by the bishops. Archbishop George Abbot of Canterbury, himself a moderate Puritan, announced positively in response to James's former directions: 'Now the people bred up with this [Puritan] kind of teaching, and never instructed in the catechism, and fundamental grounds of religion, are ... ready to be filled up with the manuals and catechisms of the popish priests, or the papers and pamphlets of Anabaptists, Brownists and Puritans.'[77]

The Church's authority was also promoted by Archbishop Bancroft and Lancelot Andrewes at a time when Protestantism was declining on the continent, and a new religious sect known as Arminians, described as a 'popish fifth column' and 'liturgical and doctrinal innovators', appeared, whose beliefs appealed to several clergy in the Church. The Presbyterians opposed the growing Arminian beliefs associated with the Dutch theologian Jacobus Arminius of Leyden who believed in the doctrine of the 'real presence' and the importance of rites and ceremonies, music, stained-glass windows, and observance of Church festivals to make the Church a symbol of God's influence on the individual.[78] The movement was also described as a means of softening the hatred in the Church of England towards the Church of Rome. Arminians rejected Calvinism and its predestination and believed in general salvation and that man had his own freewill to act. They also believed that bishops derived their authority by divine order, which was clearly expounded by Archbishop William Laud who had adopted Arminian beliefs and introduced them into the Church. 'Our main crime is,' he stated, 'that we are bishops ... And a great trouble 'tis to them [i.e. Presbyterians] that we maintain that our calling of bishops is *jure divino*.'[79] Arminianism was dismissed at the Synod of Dort in

---

77. Ibid., 283.

78. Tyacke, *English Arminianism*; Parker, *Arminianism and Laudianism*, 20–34.

79. *Works of Laud*, VI (i), 42–43.

1619, which endorsed strict Calvinism and condemned Arminius as
a heretic. Arminians, however, persisted in their belief in the priesthood and the need to enrich ceremonial. To Puritans it savoured of
popery and they resented high churchmen supporting and defending
the king whom they increasingly regarded as their enemy. Moreover,
to exacerbate the situation William Laud, Archbishop of Canterbury,
adopted and advocated the Arminian way, thus creating a division
within the clergy. This situation led Parliament to believe that the
clergy, owing to their loyalty to the Crown, were drawing the nation
back to Catholicism, especially because of Arminian symbolism and
the emphasis on the 'beauty of holiness' in the Church. Not that the
Commons were strongly Puritan, but when tensions between the
Crown and Parliament intensified they became more engaged in opposing the prerogative powers claimed by Charles I in the 1630s when
he governed without it.

Circumstances in the 1630s were frustrating for dissenters and
they intensified their opposition during the following decade down
to the execution of Charles I. Since they had failed to reform the
Church, Presbyterians by that time had assumed a more passive role,
holding prayer meetings and prophesyings. They also served as priests
and lecturers in town corporations but still believed that reform was
possible at parochial level. They stressed the need 'to follow after the
Lord in the purity of his worships.' The Puritan leader Henry Jacob
considered that there was a way by which reconciliation was possible
between dissenters and the Church. Those who held pastorates over
many years, he stated, owed their position to parishioners and not
bishops. Likewise, Presbyterians believed that episcopal authority in
matters of ordination was limited to being a 'civil act,' thus showing
some common ground between Jacob and them. He was an Oxford
graduate and an intriguing reformer intent on combining together
Christian congregations in acts of worship in parish churches. He
feared separatism because, in his opinion, those who had abandoned
the Church weakened the Puritan cause.[80] He was also partly responsible for drawing up the Millenary Petition, and was regarded as a
'semi-separatist' chiefly because he saw possibilities in amalgamating
with the state Church at local level. The prime differences between
Presbyterians and Jacobites (as his followers were called) were two-

---

80. Watts, *Dissenters* I, 51–56; Brachlow, "Henry Jacob's Churchmanship," 228–54.

fold. First, Jacob believed that confessing believers could be admitted to the Church while Presbyterians were more concerned with enforcing discipline within it. To further their cause they issued the *Book of Discipline* in 1586 (later published in 1644 as the *Directory of Church Government*). That was a convenient way of avoiding further conflicts with Parliament. They also believed that 'those who made confession of their faith' should be admitted to communion as a way of 'purifying' local congregations. Secondly, Presbyterianism was established with its hierarchy of officials and meetings similar to the Genevan system. Although the Jacobites also had their pastors, teachers, elders, and deacons, Presbyterians, by giving the senate of elders governing power, denied democracy among members which was a central feature of separatism. It was from the Jacob-Lathrop-Jessey Independent church that the first English Particular Baptist gathering appeared in 1638 under the leadership of John Spilsbury. Henrey Jessey established close relations with William Wroth and assisted him in establishing the first Independent church in Gwent.

Despite their different theological leanings, the mixture of Puritan traditions that emerged in England in the late Elizabethan and early Stuart periods, confronted not only the state Church but also the close links between that Church and Arminianism. In 1629 Charles I, tired of wrangling with Parliament on financial, constitutional, and foreign affairs, dissolved it and chose to govern personally. Thus was introduced the policy of 'thorough' enforcing a strict administration; a policy initiated by Thomas Wentworth (made Earl of Strafford in 1640) and Archbishop Laud, both of them bitter enemies of Puritans. Laud, however, deserves more attention during this decade, particularly in relation to Puritanism. He was a conscientious head of the Church when he was appointed to Canterbury in 1633. It was not yet time to campaign for toleration but despite his anti-Puritan feelings, he did not force them to conform for he was satisfied so long as uniformity was achieved in external matters. His policy, however, was still rigidly uncompromising in many respects and he continually enforced discipline, suppressed Puritan literature and ejected Puritan priests, especially those who disobeyed orders, and forbade private chaplains in gentry houses and corporations from being employed as lecturers and preachers. Any attempt to subvert the *Book of Common Prayer* which caused diversions in formal ceremonials were severely punished and the communion table was moved and placed in a raised position at the eastern end of the Church. Specific reasons were given for this movement, mainly that it prevented people from sitting above God's table or above the priest when consecrating, and that it would avoid 'many prophanations' and abuses—all of which were logistical and not theological reasons.

The Court of High Commission was revived which led to an increase in emigration abroad to the continent and the New World as had occurred in 1620 when the 'Pilgrim Fathers' departed from Plymouth for the Netherlands and America, joined by a group from John Robinson's church in Leiden. Laud was determined to establish uniformity, intent on ending schism and disobedience. The concept of the 'beauty of holiness' that he adopted was, in his mind, present in 'the inward worship of the heart [which is] the true service of God.' When referring to the 'external worship of God in His Church' it is evident that it is 'the great witness to the world that our heart stands right in that service of God.'[81] 'Ceremonies,' he continued, 'are the hedges that fence the substance of religion from all the iniquities which profaneness and sacrilege too commonly put upon it.' He reissued the *Book of Sports*, which caused further serious disruption and Puritans tore down maypoles and other amusements which they considered profane acts on the Lord's Day. Laud considered them to be the greatest dangers to royal authority and, as revisionist historians suggest, Laud was only Charles I's servant and not the initiator of this anti-Puritan policy. It appears that his narrow outlook on religion prevented him from seeking alternative methods of reconciliation with his enemies.[82]

Since the vast majority of the population attended the Church of England the Laudian changes were accepted with little or no opposition. In Wales, the impact of Arminianism was minimal in most areas but vestiges of it appeared in some churches and private chapels of a handful of gentry.[83] In 1637, Rug Chapel of the Holy Trinity, built by the royalist Colonel William Salesbury who, despite his Anglicanism had some Puritan leanings, revealed Arminian decorations and high-church adornment.[84] The altar was placed at the east end of the chancel and fenced with altar rails, candles, reredos, and screen. Similarly, the

81. Reese, *Tudors and Stuarts*, 233.

82. Coward, *Stuart Age*, 148–52.

83. Tyacke, "Puritanism, Arminianism," 71–75; Fincham, "Laudian Style," 161–85.

84. Yates, *Rûg Chapel*, 10–19.

private chapel attached to Llanddwywe parish church in Merioneth, erected in 1615 by Gruffudd Vaughan II of Corsygedol, though earlier in architectural style than Rug, showed distinct Arminian features.[85] Also, during Laud's term of office several Welsh bishops were Arminian, such as William Roberts (Bangor), Roger Mainwaring (St. David's), and Morgan Owen (Llandaff).[86] As in the more conservative areas of England some Catholic rituals continued to survive in remoter parishes and Puritan thought and practice had hardly made any impact on the lives and activities of the vast majority, and radicalization hardly touched the vast majority who accepted the Church as the mainstay of their religious heritage.

In fact, the religious life of Wales in the 1630s revealed a 'conservative conformity' and needs further research. Dr. Lloyd Bowen argues that since much—possibly excessive—attention has been given by historians to the growth of early dissent in Wales of the 1630s, particularly to individual Puritan leaders, the growth of Arminianism may well have been neglected.[87] Prevailing Welsh social and economic conditions and the poverty of the Church hindered the full progress of the Protestant Reformation, which advocated a strong preaching ministry. Illiteracy was widespread, the Bible, translated in 1588 and revised in 1620, was used mainly for public reading in services, and the nature of the Reformation and its literary output—by Edward James, Edmwnd Prys, Robert Llwyd of Chirk, Richard Jones of Denbigh, and others—was more liturgical than devoted to the preaching ministry. Excepting the Puritan centres of Wrexham, Brampton Bryan, and Llanfaches, the language barrier in most other parts of Wales prevented effective Puritan relations being forged between dissenters on both sides of the Welsh border. There is sufficient evidence to prove that in the 1630s churches in several Welsh parishes were renovated and the improved and adorned fabric reflected aesthetic beauty.[88] It may be, therefore, that Arminianism had flourished more than the evidence allows us to believe despite the liturgical and a 'conservative Anglican conformism' that had become a common feature of the Reformation in Wales in the latter half of the sixteenth century. It was what can be

85. RCAHM, VI, *Merioneth*, 76.

86. Bowen, *Politics in the Principality*, 208–9.

87. Ibid., 207–34.

88. Ibid., 213–21.

called 'Prayer Book Protestantism' but Laudianism appealed more to the aesthetic spirit than the sermon.

Laud stood on precarious ground in the eyes of many who considered that he drew closer to Roman practice and ritual. He had been offered a cardinalate, which he flatly refused. He had little to do with a Catholic mission from Rome and Queen Henrietta Maria, Charles I's French Queen, celebrating mass on Christmas Day. His Arminian beliefs, however, were closely associated with those of Rome and there was general opposition to Laud's dealings with the royal Court, which harboured strong Catholic tendencies. Consequently, to defend his position as head of the Anglican Church he strengthened the High Commission Court and punished those who defied conformity and discipline. William Prynne, a lawyer who almost conducted a crusade against Arminianism, was brutally punished by the cropping of his ears, and the priest Henry Burton, an anti-Laudian from Yorkshire, suffered a similar mutilation. And there were others who were pilloried for their refusal to co-operate. It was lack of unity in the Church that forced Laud to adopt such a harsh policy, a unity that was considered necessary to withstand the pressures from Rome. He feared disruption and division in the realm and adopted the same attitude towards the Church as did Elizabeth. But times had changed and the role of dissenting sects had, by the 1630s, became a greater threat. Indeed, by then the Church Settlement of 1559 had lost much of its impetus. In his speech of censure of John Bastwick, Henry Burton, and William Prynne, Laud stated his position: 'For my care of this Church, the reducing of it into order, the upholding of the external worship of God in it, and the settling of it to the rules of its first reformation, are the causes . . . of all this malicious storm . . . the calling of bishops is *jure divino* . . . And this I say in as direct opposition to the Church of Rome, as to the Puritan humour.'[89]

Puritanism, however, was still a force to be reckoned with in Parliament and among gentry landowning families, chiefly in London, the South East, and trade-centred towns. It was also in the 1630s that Puritanism obtained a foothold in conservative frontier areas such as Wales. The seeds of religious dissent were sown in the Principality in the years well before the Civil War. The only prominent Puritan in the late Elizabethan period was John Penry, the 'Brecknockshire firebrand'

89. Works of Laud VI (i), 42–43.

but he seemed not to have had any impact on his native country.[90] Even his intensely written anti-Church treatises in the late 1580s addressed to the Queen and Council in the Marches severely condemning their lethargy in not attending to the prime abuses in the Church probably had very little, if any, impact on his fellow countrymen because of adverse social conditions. Puritan activity, however, appeared at the northern border town of Wrexham in the 1580, mainly because of the influence of Christopher Goodman of Chester and Rowland Puleston of Bersham, possibly a Puritan priest at Wrexham in 1583 wrote a tract entitled *Llyfr o'r Eglwys Gristnogedd* (A book of the Christian Church) which contained Puritan and anti-papist views.[91] Walter Stephens, rector of Bishop's Castle, and Robert Powell, vicar of Llangatwg-iuxta-Neath in Glamorgan, also shared Puritan sympathies as did Stanley Gower, vicar of Brampton Bryan, Herefordshire, and Sir Robert Harley's chaplain. Harley was an ardent Puritan and together with his wife Lady Brilliana, had considerable influence in the areas bordering on Wales. To instruct his monoglot Welsh parishioners in the basic features of the Christian faith, in the first half of the seventeenth century Rhys Prichard, long-serving vicar of Llandingat parish in Llandovery and later Chancellor of St. David's and canon residentiary, composed a large number of popular religious verses that could be read in services.[92] In 1630 the first edition of the 'small Bible' in Welsh was published, financed by two London-Welsh Puritan entrepreneurs Rowland Heylin and Sir Thomas Myddleton. The preface, attributed to Michael Roberts, fellow of Jesus College, Oxford, revealed that there was a slight increase in literacy in the 1630s:

> Yet, neither the wellbeing nor the use of God's word was so public and more common as many devout Christians would have desired. Because ... it could not be delivered afield, nor brought to particular houses and hands because it most completely relates to the liturgy and service of the Church, as it had been at first intended. Now, because we are seeking to search and read the Scriptures especially at home besides doing it publicly and openly in the Church ... And the place where it should verily reside in the heart which is the main of the soul.[93]

90. Jones, "Early Brecknockshire Puritan Firebrand," 23–44
91. Gruffydd, *Gentile Country*, 6.
92. Jones, '*Lanterne to their Feete*,' 5–6.
93. Hughes (ed.), *Rhagymadroddion*, 123.

Prichard composed verses of verses recommending that his flock should purchase the 1630 Bible. Two verses run as follows (in prose translation): 'The Word's a candle which gives you light; The Word is the messenger who will guide you; The Word will lead you to paradise; The Word will bring you directly to heaven': 'Without the Word God cannot be known; Neither His nature nor His holy presence; Nor his Son Christ, nor the Holy Spirit, Nor the virtues of the blessèd Trinity.'[94] Although he was a well-respected rural priest, eager to protect the standards of the Anglican Church, he betrayed strong Puritan tendencies as did Robert Llwyd, vicar of Chirk, who translated into Welsh Arthur Dent's *The Plaine Man's Pathway to Heaven* . . . in 1630.[95]

The failure of Puritanism to make a steady headway in early seventeenth-century Wales was due mainly to adverse social and economic conditions, the remoteness of communities, the lack of many commercial towns—excepting Swansea, Wrexham, and Haverfordwest—where the faith could be fostered among trading families. The 'lecture system' set up in parts of England and Wales between 1620 and 1633, which allowed unbeneficed men to 'teach, preach and catechise', failed to establish itself mainly because Puritan tendencies among many preachers had led to restrictions being imposed and Archbishop Laud, who opposed the scheme, suppressed it in 1633.

William Wroth, rector of Llanfaches in Gwent, after his conversion in 1625, preached extensively in his native area, and in November 1639 established his 'gathered church' at Llanfaches, the first of its kind in Wales, thus laying the foundation of the Nonconformist tradition in the south-eastern borders of the country. It was described as being 'like Antioch the mother of Wales in that gentile country' because of its wide appeal and it was compared with the 'New England pattern' established by John Cotton and others in America.[96] It held its services and cooperated amicably alongside the local Anglican congregation, among which Wroth still ministered, and appointed its own governing elders. Among his supporters at the time were Henry Jessey, Independent minister in London who assisted in the inaugural service together with Walter Cradock, Ambrose Mostyn, Richard Symonds, Richard Blinman, Morgan Llwyd, Henry Walter, Oliver

---

94. Jones, '*Lanterne at their Feete*,' 60.

95. Jones, *Religious Life*, 46, 84, 106–7.

96. Jenkins, *Protestant Dissenters*, 9–12.

Thomas and Vavasor Powell, all of them well-known pioneers of early Welsh Puritanism. The Llanfaches church became the powerhouse of first-generation Congregationalism in Wales. It was a central cog in the Puritan network having established strong connections with dissenters in an area extending from Wrexham, Brampton Bryan, the home of the Puritan Harleys, to Llanfaches.

At the time the Baptist sect was increasing, and a small group, described as extremists, had moved from the Olchon valley in the western parts of Herefordshire in the early 1630s. They were regarded as a small minority 'which schismatically preach dangerous errors, and stir up the people to follow them.' The first leader was John Miles, a Particular Baptist and native of Newton Clifford in the Welsh region of Herefordshire.[97] It was he who established the first Baptist church at Ilston in the Gower peninsula in 1649 and subsequently other churches appeared at Abergavenny, Hay-on-Wye, Carmarthen, and Llanharan. Miles was a dominating figure described a recent historian as 'a Colossus above other Welsh Baptists . . . the most Puritan of Puritans.'[98] His Baptist beliefs differed from the Arminianism with which General Baptists were associated. The stricter Particular Baptists were Calvinistic and believed in the total immersion of believers.

Of other Puritan leaders Walter Cradock, Morgan Llwyd, and Vavasor Powell were to gain prominence.[99] Cradock, a follower of William Wroth, was a noteworthy preacher and moderate political realist. His theology revealed definite comparisons with that of his disciple Morgan Llwyd, who was converted by his preaching at Wrexham, and he was associated with several other Puritan leaders on the Welsh border, such as Richard Symonds, Richard Baxter, Sir Robert Harley, and William Wroth at Llanfaches. In 1635, when serving as curate to William Erbery, vicar of St. Mary's Church at Cardiff, he and Erbery fell foul of William Murray, Bishop of Llandaff, and were brought before the High Commission for their Puritan activities. Cradock—described at the time as 'a bold ignorant young fellow'— was deprived of his licence and Erbery lost his living. Erbery was an enigmatic person; he was no follower of Calvin and after his deprivation in 1638 he adopted radical ideas and joined the sect known as

97. White, "John Miles," 570–90;

98. Jenkins, *Protestant Dissenters*, 30.

99. Nuttall, "Cradock," 118–29; Jones, "Healing Herb," 154–79.

Seekers—forerunners of the Quakers—thus rejecting Presbyterianism and Congregationalism.[100] He also abandoned Cradock and Powell and refused to accept all forms of ecclesiastical organisation. Not surprisingly, he showed some favour towards the Arminians but rejected the Trinity, the visible church of the saints, and all external forms of worship, including the sacraments. Like Morgan Llwyd, Erbery believed that man could associate with God without the formal Church, and for him the Scriptures, sacraments, and church life were irrelevant. He opposed tithes and despised those who were appointed commissioners under the Act for the Propagation of the Gospel in Wales (1650) as careerists and adventurers.[101]

Cradock, on the other hand, clung to his Congregationalism, performing his duties as an itinerant preacher. He rejected Fifth Monarchism, fully supported Cromwell during the Interregnum, and was appointed one of the Puritan Approvers under the Act for the Propagation of the Gospel. Another Approver was the Puritan Oliver Thomas, again a border Welshman from Montgomeryshire, a Presbyterian Calvinist about whom little is known except that he ministered at Oswestry in 1647 and obtained the living of Llanrhaeadr-ym-Mochnant in 1650. He believed that Calvinist doctrine was fundamental to the saving of souls and began to preach extensively and produce catechisms for adults and children, thereby following in the footsteps of Williams Perkins who produced his famous works on regeneration and conversion. His main achievement appeared in the quality of his prose writing, especially in his *Car-wr y Cymry* (1631) [Friend of the Welsh People], a guide for heads of households to enrich spiritual life in their families.[102] 'And regarding things of this world,' he stated when stressing the indispensability of the Bible (referring to the publication of the 1630 Bible) for the spiritual welfare of the individual, 'one must seek and labour for them if one wills and enjoys to satisfy the needs of the body: therefore, to satisfy the needs of the soul searching the Scriptures is necessary.'[103] The Puritan ethos and private devotions relating to the role of the *paterfamilias*, in his view,

---

100. Watts, *Dissenters* I, 184–86.
101. James, "William Erbery," 41–45.
102. Gruffydd, *Gentile Country*, 22–24.
103. Gruffydd, "Anglican prose," 181–82.

served to maintain the unity of the Christian household.[104] Oliver Thomas's associate was Evan Roberts, reputed to be the first Welsh Nonconformist, who published a revised edition of a Welsh translation by Robert Holland, a cleric and native of Conwy, of William Perkins's *Foundation of the Christian Religion* in 1649. It was a work offering profound spiritual guidance to its readers, similar in content to *The Practice of Piety* (*c.*1611) by Lewis Bayly, the Anglican Bishop of Bangor who revealed Puritan traits in what has been acclaimed as a classic among early pietistic works in the English language. The main features of piety in this work were strict sabbatarianism, the doctrine of predestination and preaching the gospel, all of which enhanced Christian discipline.[105]

This background to Welsh Puritanism leads to the conclusion that although it was slow to develop it revealed an ardent desire to improve the spiritual values of the Welsh people and enlighten them in the basic doctrines of the faith. It has been argued that the 'lineaments' of a Welsh Puritan tradition had been established through the connections forged between Puritan centres on the borders from north to south Wales, 'a movement,' R. Geraint Gruffydd comments, 'with a programme [which] stood the test of persecution during the sixteen thirties and bred a generation of leaders that was able . . . to take advantage of the opportunity to evangelise Wales.'[106] It was a movement—the immediate impact of which should not be exaggerated—that enriched its spiritual testimony by means of 'gathered churches' which gradually extended their testimony into other areas in Wales. Walter Cradock, attempting to defend the minority of dissident preachers in Wales stated in 1648, with some exaggeration perhaps, that the Puritan movement was rapidly moving across parts of Wales: 'I have observed . . . in the Mountaines of Wales, the most glorious work that I ever saw in England unlesse it were in London; the Gospel is run over the Mountaines between Brecknockshire, and Monmouthshire, as the fire in the thatch . . .'[107] There were no resident ministers, he continued, but members of 'gathered' churches, who numbered about eight hundred, obtained the services of itinerants

---

104. Hill, "Spiritualization," 443–81.

105. Dodd, "Lewes Bayly," 14–16.

106. Gruffydd, *In that Gentile Country*, 28–30.

107. Cradock, *Glad Tydings*, 50.

who filled them 'with good newes' and encouraged them to tell the 'good newes' to others.[108] True enough, perhaps, but within limited areas, primarily anglicized, for the majority of the population still adhered to the Church of England.

The mid-seventeenth-century Welsh Puritan background, however, requires further examination. Too much emphasis has been placed on the contribution of a handful of prominent individuals labouring in specific areas rather than within a broader context. Although it is appropriate to bestow lavish praise on them there it is also necessary to look at the social, economic, and cultural *milieu* of the age. In the life of Erbery, for example, his connections, not only with Cardiff but also with Bristol and especially Merthyr Tydfil should be examined within the family background as well as the complexity of interrelations and the continuity of the Puritan tradition over generations.[109]

II

Another thorn in the Crown's side in the 1630s was the problem of Scotland and the efforts to enforce uniformity in religious matters on that country. In view of the deep-seated hold that Calvinist Protestantism had on the Scottish nobility the policy adopted was at best contrived. On his accession Charles I revoked all lands royal and ecclesiastical that had been acquired by the nobility since 1542 and those among them who were Catholics were inclined to join the Presbyterians. Although John Knox's spirit was still very much alive in Scotland Charles decided, again heedlessly, to have himself crowned king at Holyrood according to the Anglican rites and ordered Scottish ministers to abandon the Geneva gown for the accustomed surplices. And that was not all, for in 1637 the *Book of Common Prayer* replaced Knox's *Book of Common Order*, and it was imposed without any consultation with Scottish religious leaders. The irreverent assault on the minister of St. Giles, Edinburgh, on 23 July of that year was followed by the National Covenant demanding the withdrawal of the *Prayer Book*. It was a protest against the 'thorough' policies of Laud and Strafford in Scotland and Ulster respectively.

---

108. Ibid.

109. Bowen, 'Seeds and Fruits of Revolution,' *WHR* 25 (2011) 346–73.

Circumstances deteriorated when the Covenanters—now a Scottish army—regardless of their loyalty to the Crown and defiant of Charles's decision to impose his power over the Scots, encamped near the border which led to the Treaty of Berwick in 1639 and the end of the First Bishops' War. The conflict, however, continued while Charles refused to allow the Scottish Parliament and Kirk their independence. This aggressive mood persisted after Strafford returned from Ireland advising Charles to finance an army to suppress the Scots, and the Short Parliament—not an easy one for him—refused the request chiefly because it strongly opposed the King's determination to assert his prerogative power. John Pym, a militant West of England opponent of the Crown's policies, was the most vociferous critic in the Commons against the king's Personal Government and it agencies. Eventually, after the opening of the Long Parliament in 1640 the issues between Crown and Parliament intensified and determined attacks were made, led by the relentless Pym, chiefly on centralized government. The unpopular policies were abolished and those who applied them during the previous decade dismissed. Despite the unmaking of the essential features of his government, as well as the impeachment of Laud and Strafford, Charles stubbornly clung to his prerogative authority over the Church for he had become aware that plans were being discussed in the Commons to impose a new religious settlement. Members of the Commons were not united in their religious alliance but were loyal to the Crown as an institution and opposed toleration and Catholicism, and during Laud's years as Archbishop, respected that 'beauty of holiness' associated with his religious policy. Basically, emphasis was now placed on parliamentary control of religion. Views on the way in which religion should be organised, however, created dissent—Presbyterianism with its Genevan system supported by the Scots, but others opposing it on the grounds that it was too rigid and democratic. Congregationalism appealed to a minority since it allowed universal freedom of worship and conscience. What Parliament did in fact achieve at that stage, however, was military command over the army.

The role of bishops again came to the fore—their power, influence, and fortune within the Church. 'They are not Bishops,' the prolific John Milton stated in *Of Reformation in England* (1641), 'God and all good men know they are not; that have fill'd this Land with late confusion and violence; but a Tyrannicall crew and Corporation of Imposters, that have bluded and abus'd the World so long under that Name.'[110] This relates to the opposition to the office of bishop, and it was decided that episcopacy should be abolished because of its dangers to the state's welfare. This led to the demand for an Erastian state, a Puritan state church, intolerant of all that the national Church, separatists and Catholics, represented. Arminianism was not considered and the 1640 canons were rejected. Erastianism was not totally opposed either for there was a lobby that believed that the traditional Church should be maintained. The plea was heard that the *status quo* should be preserved and episcopacy retained. Thus were established two groups in the Commons, radical and moderate. The radicals, eager to drive forward their own agenda, were intent on depriving the Church of its most basic ceremonial features and imposing observation of the Sabbath. This led to freedom of worship and caused concern among those who considered it to be too radical. It is not surprising, therefore, that the king won good support among those who wished to adhere to traditional worshipping practices in the Church, a decision which again led to strong divisive views voiced in the Commons.

The proposed abolition of Episcopal authority and establishment of an ecclesiastical jurisdiction based on lay control debated in the famous 'Root and Branch' bill of February 1641 failed as did the attempt to have it supervised. All this revealed how unprogressive, even dangerous, parliamentary attempts were to proscribe the Crown's prerogatives and how they failed to prevent increased support for them. The Scottish problem remained but discontent among the royalist army to suppress the Covenanters who professed loyalty to the Crown threatened their position. Charles failed to win over the Scots' support in the army to defend the bishops and he himself feared the threat of an Irish rebellion in October 1641, which, when it happened, brought war closer, especially after the slaughter of a large number of Protestants in Ireland. In view of these dangers Parliament proceeded to strengthen the army again under parliamentary control and Charles's executive power supplanted. In this situation royal support was made up of moderates who defended the Church but that was not sufficient to aid his cause. Pym, however, unprepared to yield power, drew up the 'Grand Remonstrance' in November 1641 detailed the

110. Wolfe, *John Milton I (1624–1642)*, 537.

errors ('evil deeds') of the Crown and recounted the benefits of the Long Parliament. It was an attempt to restore the unity found earlier in the House. However, the need for drastic ecclesiastical reform and the appointment of ministers only increased pressure and divisions within it. Tensions served only to destabilize the Church and its constitution and there were fears that a hated new 'despotism' would arise. The decline of ecclesiastical discipline and government seriously threatened the unity of the whole realm. The 'Grand Remonstrance' succeeded by a narrow margin and placed the king in greater danger of losing his prerogative. The proposal to impeach the Queen for her strong Catholic connections was not fully supported but the five members of the Commons who did approve of it, Pym among them, escaped from the House before the king could arrest them.

The lengthy 'Remonstrance' was the Parliament's final declaration of intent and it decided to assemble 'a general synod of the most grave, pious, learned and judicious divines of this island,' and the Westminster Assembly was convened early in July 1643 to finally settle religious affairs.[111] This led to the publication of the 1644 *A Directory of Church Government* based on Thomas Cartwright's *The Book of Discipline* (1586), and in 1646 the Westminster Confession was formulated and accepted by the assembly. Circumstances then moved on swiftly to a stalemate between Church and Parliament and efforts to achieve a settlement acceptable to both sides failed. Divisions appeared and the ruling sections of society found their unity being destroyed because of religious differences and the political rifts they caused. It cannot be said that the lines of loyalty were rigidly drawn but Parliament obtained most of its support from eastern commercial centres, the wealthy and mainly Puritan classes, while the Crown was supported by the more rural and conservative areas of Wales, the west, the midlands and the north. When war broke out in August 1642 the Puritan loyalties to Parliament were evident. The Scots decided to support Parliament and in the autumn of 1643 Parliament's subscription to the 'Solemn League and Covenant' implied that there would be a religious reformation 'according to the Word of God and the example of the best reformed Churches.' The wording aimed at preserving the 'reformed religion': 'we shall endeavour to bring the churches of God . . . to the nearest conjunction and uniformity in religion, confession

111. EHD (1603–1660), 674 (no. 185).

of faith, form of church government, directory for worship and cat-echising . . . That we shall . . . endeavour the extirpation of popery, prelacy, superstition . . . and whatsoever shall be found to be contrary to sound doctrine and the power of godliness.'[112]

This was a declaration that Presbyterianism, based on Cartwright, would be established by an alliance with Scottish Presbyterianism, but came to an end when the Army forced the expulsion of Presbyterians from Parliament by Pride's Purge in 1648. The role of Independents increased during the Civil Wars and became dominant in the parliamentarian army. While the Presbyterians had endeavoured to establish a state Church Congregationalists, the followers of Henry Jacob, tracing their origins to Robert Browne, the separatist, formed the largest group who served in the New Model Army, but they differed from Presbyterians in that they held separate congregations of believers rather than establishing a state Church, believing that their authority came directly from God.[113] They rejected Presbyterian Erastianism as much as Laud's Arminianism. Strict Baptists followed the beliefs of Congregationalists but differed on the sacrament of baptism in that they accepted adult rather than infant baptism by immersion as the basis of church membership. They believed that baptism was not a means of bestowing grace but an act of faith, which infants could not share. Baptists also were divided between those regarded as General Baptists, associated with the Mennonites (Dutch and Swiss Anabaptists), Dutch Arminians and Particular Baptists who were Calvinists believing in predestination. There has been controversy between historians in the past as to whom religious 'independency' applied but Michael Watts believes that in the two decades of war and republican governments 'the separatists and Congregationalists formed two distinct but collateral branches of the larger tree of Independency.'[114]

This was the era when Oliver Cromwell became leader of the anti-royalist faction and rose to become one of the most prominent public figures in the history of dissent. He was native of Huntingdonshire, and came from minor gentry stock. He experienced religious conversion and was elected Member of Parliament for Huntingdon in 1628 and later for Cambridge in 1640, serving in the Short and Long

112. Ibid., 582–83.
113. Watts, *Dissenters* I, 94.
114. Ibid., 99.

Parliaments. Soon after he was appointed to organise the defence of the eastern counties during which time he revealed his military skills. After achieving two victories in 1643 his rise to power was assured and he became lieutenant general to the Earl of Manchester who commanded the 'Eastern Association.' The climax of his military success came when he led the cavalry at Marston Moor aided by the Scots in 1644 and the other decisive victory at Naseby in the following year. Although he was associated with the Independents his religious connections and beliefs are not clearly known.[115] It does not appear that he was a separatist but rather a Calvinist. The evidence to prove that he intended to form a 'gathered church' for his troops is insufficient but it is certain that he rejected religious intolerance. Although he supported radical sects his true political interests are unclear. Presbyterians and Independents, however, were used by him, after Charles I's execution, to form an alliance but the fanaticism of some Independent groups, especially the Diggers and Fifth Monarchists, caused problems for him.[116]

Following the death of the king in 1649 the Rump of the Long Parliament established the republic, a Council of State was created to replace the old Privy Council and the authority of Parliament and the Commonwealth was supreme. Problems soon occurred in Ireland and Scotland and Covenanters supported the young Prince Charles (later Charles II), but Cromwell and the republican army quashed the Scottish army at Worcester in September 1651, the country afterwards being governed directly from London. Cromwell's supremacy, however, was frustrated by the growth of radical extremists and the disruption they caused in Parliament. The Levellers, led by John Lilburne, favoured the establishment of sovereignty vested in the people. Lilburne was an interesting character;[117] he was imprisoned in 1638 for importing Puritan literature, and then joined the parliamentary army campaigning for the Covenant in 1645. He took a critical view of Cromwell's republic and with other leaders of the movement in 1647 published reforming ideas in such works as *The Case of the Army Truly Stated* and *The Agreement of the People*. Like

115. Morrill (ed.), *Oliver Cromwell*, 13–14, 28–31.

116. Hill, *World Turned Upside Down*, ch. 9, 84–92 *et seq.*

117. Aylmer, *Levellers in English Revolution*, 9–55; Sharp, *English Levellers*; Watts, *Dissenters* I, 117–28; Brailsford, *Levellers and the English Revolution*; ODNB, 33, 773–82.

the Independents Levellers believed in liberty of worship and freedom from arrest and imprisonment. They also strongly believed in democracy while Independents feared the tyranny, which might follow any dissention. They were intent on reconciling democracy with liberty by the use of ancient laws, while Independents believed in divine will which transcended all laws and customs. Levellers also desired to see Parliament dissolved and a new Parliament elected by universal manhood suffrage. In late 1647 they were confronted by the army in the Putney Debates (1647) in London where the New Model Army discussed reconstructing England after the Civil Wars. The involvement of the Levellers in these meetings may have accounted for the lack of a successful outcome. The Diggers, a radical movement that lasted barely a year, were led by Gerrard Winstanley, who aimed at establishing rural communism. This extreme group set up such communities on old Crown and common land in Surrey and the movement spread into midland areas of England.[118] At the same time the Ranters, lacking moral probity and decency, were a group of Antinomians whose existence is not clearly defined, and certainly not as well documented as the Fifth Monarchists. As Christopher Hill states, the period between 1645 and 1653 saw circumstances and radical beliefs change considerably, a time when old values and institutions were questioned and extreme political views were aired. It was a short period, as Hill appropriately maintains, when the 'world was turned upside down.'

The Fifth Monarchists played a much more significant role than these extreme political radicals.[119] They expected the millennium and the coming of Christ, all brought to fruition by the culmination of political events. They also wished to see the Rump of the Long Parliament dissolved and replaced by the 'rule of the saints,' a political structure based on the contents of the Old and New Testaments. Of the leaders in Wales Vavasor Powell and Morgan Llwyd of Merioneth, who held strong Quaker beliefs, became prominent. The Fifth Monarchists believed that four empires existed and had expired—Assyria, Persia, Greece, and Rome—and that the fifth was about to dawn, namely the kingdom of Jesus Christ in all his glory. Verse 11 in chapter 12 of the

118. Dow, *Radicalism in English Revolution*, 74–80; *Oxford Dict. Nat. Biog.*, 59, 762–70. For a comprehensive study of the debates see Mendle, *Putney Debates*, intro., 1–15 *et seq.*

119. For the background to millenarianism see B. S. Capp, *The Fifth Monarchy Men*, ch. 2, 23–45.

Book of Daniel and portions of the Book of Revelation led them to expect that Christ's reign would be in 1656, 1660, or 1666. It was forecast that the demise of the papacy—the Antichrist—was at hand and that Christ's reign would then continue for a thousand years.[120] The movement was part of an apocalyptic crisis of the mind, which was quite common in those days, and it influenced the beliefs of Vavasor Powell, Morgan Llwyd, John Lilburne, and John Bunyan. Morgan Llwyd, in his classic *Llyfr y Tri Aderyn* (Book of the Three Birds) in 1653, described as a 'sharply etched political and religious allegory,'[121] was written to prepare the Welsh people for the coming of Christ's kingdom. The three birds in this work represented the state under Cromwell (eagle), the Anglican Church (raven) and the truth as represented by the godly (the Dove). The saints, according to the Dove, were eagerly preaching the coming of Christ's kingdom: 'But, O! winged Eagle I have an idea that thou art ripe for goodness . . . fly away throughout the thirteen counties of Wales and tell them in every town and village, in every parish and hamlet, in every neighbourhood and family . . . Repent, the Kingdom of the Great King is at hand.'[122] This movement lost much of its impact when *The Instrument of Government* in 1653 created Cromwell Lord Protector of the realm. Extreme radicals rejected him believing that he was associated, especially among moderates, with the Antichrist, an impersonator of the Son of God. They believed, however, that the demise of the Papacy, the conquest of the Turks in the east and a successful war against the Dutch in the early 1650s were essential before the advent of Christ. Doubtless Powell was the most powerful of Welsh Puritans, a powerful and dominating preacher. He was a Radnorshire schoolmaster converted to Puritanism partly by Walter Cradock's preaching and served to appoint godly ministers under the Committee for Plundered Ministers in 1646. Later, in 1650 he was appointed an Approver under the Act for the Propagation of the Gospel. Powell, whose service as preacher extended through Wales and England, was far more politically inclined than the mystic Morgan Llwyd. Walter Cradock was a moderate and had not become

120. For the background to the Papacy as 'antichrist' see Hill, *Antichrist in Seventeenth-Century England*, ch. 1, 1–40.

121. M. Wynn Thomas, *Morgan Llwyd*, 27–30; Knox (ed.), *Reformation, Conformity and Dissent*, 165–79.

122. Jenkins, *Protestant Dissenters*, 83.

involved in millenarianism in that period of religious and political instability. John Owen, vicar of Coggeshall, Essex, a prominent leader of the Independents and well-known preacher who gained Cromwell's favour, shared some of the beliefs of Fifth Monarchists but rejected their expectation that Christ's coming on earth was imminent.[123]

After the dissolution of the Rump by the Army, in July 1653 the Nominated Parliament (also known as Barebones) was convened, thus reducing the power of the Independents. Barebones Parliament was a gathering of orthodox Puritans, and Congregational churches were required to suggest names considered to be suitable. Army officers made their choice supervised by Cromwell himself. It was decided that those nominated were saintly and God-fearing individuals rather than men of landed power. Nevertheless, some radicals managed to become members, such as Thomas Harrison and Praise God Barebones (or Borbon), a Fleet Street leather merchant and Anabaptist who obtained some publicity by giving his name to a Parliament that achieved little if any lasting success. It was dissolved on 12 December 1653, 'It being moved . . . that the sitting . . . will not be for the good of the commonwealth.'[124] It was not a complete disaster, however, and many much-needed reforms were passed revealing its 'broad-mindedness and statesmanship,' such as the Act for the Propagation of the Gospel in Wales (1650), a three-year experiment to improve preaching and Puritan education in Wales.[125] A new religious order was proposed, and tithes and ecclesiastical patronage were to be suppressed. Fanaticism within it, however, soon led to its destruction and the more conservative members considered such decisions to be too radical. The Army called for a new Parliament but in its place the *Instrument of Government*, drawn up by Army officers, persuaded Cromwell to accept the title of Lord Protector on 16 December, 1653, in the absence of Fifth Monarchists who, soon after, expressed their disappointment that an Army leader should come to power instead of Christ. The Act for the Propagation of the Gospel, which was also applied to the north of England, was a formative move to extend

123. Toon, *God's Statesman*. 173; Watts, *Dissenters*, 15–16.

124. EHD (1603–1660), 906–14.

125. Richards, *Puritan Movement*, 79–89; 219–20, 243–45, 270–72; Johnson, "Wales during the Commonwealth and Protectorate," 233–41; Hill., "Propagating the Gospel," 34–59; Roberts, "Welsh Puritanism in the Interregnum," 36–41.

Puritan influence and seventy-one commissioners were appointed, led by Thomas Harrison, to reject ineffective clergy and set up schools, mainly in urban areas. Consequently, a total of 278 were dismissed and Approvers were appointed to replace them with competent ministers. Cromwell's elevation to Lord Protector angered Fifth Monarchists and Vavasor Powell and others preached against him calling him 'the man of sin, the old dragon' and other similar descriptions called 'Scripture ill names.' [126] He was reviled by Vavasor Powell and Christopher Feake, an Independent minister (called a Baptist in this source), known as 'a bold and crafty orator and of a high reputation' among members of the sect who regarded Cromwell as 'the disembleingest perjured villain in this world.'[127] Nevertheless, the Lord Protector continued his policy to 'heal and settle' the kingdom and set about preparing a legislative programme based on religious toleration for all and a system of Triers was established in 1654 to examine candidates for the parish ministry. This was followed months later by the Ejectors to remove unworthy ministers in their respective counties and several non-Anglican Protestants were allowed to serve. It was a policy to improve the quality of the clergy and subsequently the moral condition of the realm described as the 'reformation of manners.' Cromwell's programme was far more robust than that of Barebones yet not entirely successful because the constitution that had set up the Protectorate was challenged. Vavasor Powell forcefully opposed him in *A Word for God . . . against wickedness in high places* (1655), a petition intended to deride the Protectorate. In his preface he condemned the Lord Protector for his contemptuous acts of government and appealed to him to mend his ways: 'Oh, then! that you would lie down in the dust, and acknowledge your iniquity, and return unto the Lord by unfeigned repentance . . . and that you would make hast to do so, lest God's fury break forth like fire upon you, and there being no quenching of it . . .'[128] It showed no mercy towards him as Lord Protector but increasingly made him aware of his sins and transgressions against God and his people. It was supported by 322 signatories drawn mainly from freeholders and artisans in the eastern borderlands of Wales. The petition was circulated in Wales, England and Ireland and it voiced such grievances as the

126. Thurloe, *State Papers* I, 621.

127. Ibid., 641.

128. Thurloe, *State Papers*, 4, 380.

burdens imposed by the government on the saints and the failure of war against Spain. It was concluded that the new government had not received God's blessing and was a complete betrayal of Puritan ideals. It can be argued that the dismissal of Barebones and the Protectorate had placed more burdens on Cromwell's shoulders than he had ever envisaged although John Thurloe, his Secretary of State, described the remonstrance as the work of a crank who, with his followers 'would doe any other thing rather than miss to their end of bringing things to trouble and confusion.'[129] *The Word for God* poses the question: how authentic were the signatories and could they be representative of a 'diminishing social entity' in Wales?

Another sect that became attractive to a small section of society was the Quakers, founded by George Fox, the son of a Leicestershire weaver. It emerged as a religious group intent on 'waiting for the Lord,' and known in the late eighteenth century as the 'Religious Society of Friends.' Prominent though Fox was in the origins of the movement consideration should also be given to his wife, Margaret, who also played a major role in promoting the movement in its early stages.[130] In Wales, following the pioneering work by John ap John of Rhiwabon, they established themselves mainly on the eastern borderlands, parts of Merioneth excepted, the sect rejecting formal worship and a professional ministry, seeking what they considered to be 'the inner light of God.' They were among the most persistent of radicals closely associated with the Fifth Monarchists. They opposed swearing oaths and the payment of tithes to the Church of England. It was the Quaker James Nayler who declared that 'Antichrist is in every man until he be revealed by the light of Christ within.'[131] Thomas Wynne, a Welsh freeholder from Ysgeifiog in Flintshire, made known his conversion to Quakerism after having failed to obtain any satisfaction when seeking spiritual solace:

> then began my Sorrow to encrease, and to be more than I could bear; and this was the time . . . that the Almighty God . . . did break in upon my Soul by his Everlasting Light . . . [I] can do

129. Richards, *Religious Developments*, 235–36; Dodd, "Remonstrance from Wales," 279–85.

130. Kunz, *Margaret Fell* (1994); Wildes, *Voice of the Lord*; Ingle, *First among Friends*.

131. Hill, *Antichrist in Seventeenth-Century England*, 143; Nayler, *Antichrist in Man, Christ's Enemy*, 2.

> no less then give in my Testimony concerning the Operation
> or Working of the Heavenly Power, it wounded as a Sword, it
> smote like a Hammer at the wholy Body of Sin, & in my Bowels
> it burned like Fire, yea, so dreadfully it burned, that it made my
> Bowels boyl, it pierced as a Sword, it broke as a Hammer: And
> then the Pangs of Death I felt in my Members which did make
> me to roar, yea, and to Quake and tremble; for this Fire, when it
> burned, it gave Light . . .[132]

A tense experience indeed, and probably one of the most remarkable descriptions by a layman of the impact Quakerism had on one man. It betrayed a spiritual turbulence in the throes of a guilty conscience seeking deliverance and finding it in extended dramatic episodes in 'the Light of God.'

Fox has been viewed from different angles and seen against the background of his sect as a true radical, a social reformer a divine inspirer and visionary. Nayler was an impetuous Yorkshire man, parliamentary soldier, and preacher, originally an Independent. He was converted to Quakerism by Fox, an extremist demonstrator of religious fanaticism. Like Seekers and Ranters, Quakers were obsessed with sin and shared common objectives such as opposition to tithes and a state ecclesiastical organisation and reform of law, education, and all vestiges of class distinction. The Church was considered the cornerstone of Antichrist and Quakers believed that the denial of the divine being of Christ was its main feature. The conception of the spirit was fostered by the internal light and was not dependent on any visible ceremonial service such as scriptural revelation or religious organisation. That spiritual experience, it was contended, was the true saver, being based on divine regeneration. To them it was the guidance given by the inner life of the spirit which would lead to that revival, the expectation that the individual would be moved by the 'quiet mild voice' to attain salvation. This inward light possessed three attributes, namely, that it was the only experience of God and the means of preserving moral values. It was also the only guide to a perfect moral life, the awakened conscience and enlightened human reason. Quakers opposed Calvinism because they denied that regeneration depended upon the scriptural revelation as such. They were interpreters of the radical tradition, and were convinced that the Spirit

---

132. Wynne, *An Antichristian Conspiracy Detected*, 10.

came without an external agency, as believed by Calvinists, which led to controversy between them and Calvinists who believed that Christ was the Mediator on the cross.

By the mid-1650s Quakers had won followers in almost all areas in England and had established their headquarters at Swarthmoor Hall near Ulverston in Cumbria. Despite his theological writings it is argued that Morgan Llwyd, the mystic who had settled at Wrexham, was not a Quaker. He believed in the worship of the spirit as did the Puritans, for he had realised that the exceptions placed by Quakers on the subjectivity demoted Christ's sacrifice on the cross and the salvation obtained through the atonement.[133]

The threats to Cromwell's power, however, failed to prevent him from making further reforms although the dissolution of his first Parliament in January 1655 caused much disillusionment among his supporters. The next move was a more aggressive military approach with the creation of Major Generals throughout England and Wales. It had not been his intention to strengthen godly ways of life by introducing harsher military means. However, the short rule by eleven Major Generals following a royalist riot—the Penruddock rising—in the west of England was required to restore law and order, improve moral life and administer the counties.[134] This policy was a well-meaning attempt on Cromwell's behalf to restore the country to order, regardless of the degree of success he achieved. They were placed in office not to impose a 'military despotism' or suppress enemies of the state but rather to govern and maintain Cromwell's power. Nevertheless, they did impose a rigorous regime. As individuals, however, they varied with regard to their methods. Charles Worsley (Cheshire, Staffordshire, and Lancashire) and William Boteler (Northamptonshire, Bedfordshire, and Huntingdonshire), for example, were intent on imposing moral standards: 'They are the very bane of the countys,' Worsley said of alehouses in a letter to Thurloe in January 1656, 'these alehouses are the very womb that brings forth al manner of wickedness,' adding that he had destroyed at least 200 of them.[135] He soon set about his task of dismissing unworthy ministers, placing his trust in God: 'I have also

---

133. Hill, *World Turned Upside Down*, 156.

134. Ashley, *Cromwell's Generals*, 121–45; Durston, *Cromwell's Major-Generals*; Roots, "Swordsmen and Decimators," 78–92.

135. Berry, *Cromwellian Major General*, 160.

got a day set for to sit upon the ordinance for ejecting of ignorant and scandalous ministers and schoolmasters, he stated in November 1655, '[and] I have daily more and more encouragement that God will carry on this good work.'[136] The instructions given them emphasized that they were to 'encourage and promote godliness and virtue, and Discourage and Discontinuance all Prophaneness and Ungodliness.'[137] The Puritan ethic of enforcing moral standards—'a campaign of moral rearmament'—throughout the kingdom again became evident during the rule of the Saints and Major Generals. [138] The Puritan 'moral code' was imposed as effectively as possible, regardless of the opposition to such a severe policy in several parts of the realm. Major General James Berry, who was responsible for Worcestershire, Herefordshire, Monmouthshire, and the whole of Wales, became concerned about the problem of alehouses, and his letter to magistrates within his region in December 1655 made his point clearly: 'To see Townes abound w[i]th Alehouses, houses w[i]th drunkards, and the country w[i]th beggars is the reproach of our nation, and indeed Alehouses are become the pest of this Com[m]onwealth, which infest all places and the contagion thereof spreads exceedingly. On Alehouse makes many poore . . . and to what this mischeife will grow (yf not spe[e]dily prevented) the Lorde knows. I beseech you gent thinke of itt and let some stop be put to this spreading Gangreene . . .'[139] Although he was wary of their ability or desire to perform their duties he urged them 'to put on righteousness[s] . . . and you shalbee a terror to euill doers and like dew vpon the tender hearbe, and a refreshing shower vpon the new mowen grasse soe shall youe be to those that feare God . . .'[140]

Cromwell's second Parliament was summoned in September 1656 and in a defence of his religious policies at its opening he declared that 'conscience and liberty' of worship would be maintained:

> If men will profess—be they those under Baptism, be they those of the Independent judgment simply and of the Presbyterian judgment—in the name of God, encourage them, countenance them , while they do plainly hold forth to be thankful to God,

136. Thurloe, *State Papers*, IV, 450; Berry, *Cromwellian Major General*, 160.

137. Berry, *Cromwellian Major General*, 276.

138. Woolrych, 117–18; Fletcher, 209–33.

139. Gwynedd Archive Service, X/QS, 21 December 1655.

140. Ibid.

and to make use of the liberty given them to enjoy their own consciences. For . . . this is the peculiar interest all this while contended for. That men that believe in Jesus Christ . . . are members of . . . Christ and are to Him as the apple of His eye. Whoever hath this faith, let his form be what it will be walking peaceably without the prejudicing of others under another form, it is a debt due to God and Christ, and he will require it, if he may not enjoy this liberty.[141]

Doubtless his desire 'to keep things equal' and to prevent 'any one religion to impose upon another' was commendable, but the threats to his power in political and religious spheres were problems which he found difficult to overcome.

The Major Generals were dismissed early in 1657 and the 'Humble Petition and Advice' (1657–58), a new written constitution compiled by Parliament, offered Cromwell the Crown of England, an offer, tempting though it was, he refused because he believed that it was not God's will that he should restore, leave alone wear the Crown he had so passionately helped to destroy. The heads of the Army did not wish him to wear it for it would lead to the Army's loss of control over the state, and Puritans in the country did not wish it either. His last years saw his relationship with the Army deteriorate and Puritanism declining.

Cromwell died on 3 September 1658, not having accomplished all that he had intended, especially in constitutional matters. His policies in religious affairs, however, were driven by his Puritan conscience. His role as Lord Protector, unpopular though it was in a country which was still broadly loyal to monarchy and the Church of England, revealed his unyielding Puritan beliefs, his total rejection of Laud's religious policy, his campaign for toleration, his opposition to the episcopal system and hatred of Roman Catholics, his resistance to Presbyterianism because of their narrow intolerance, and his faith in the 'rule of the Saints.'

On his son Richard Cromwell's accession as his successor the third Protectorate Parliament that was summoned in January 1659 lasted for only three months and accomplished very little since he was opposed to military rule and planned to disband the army. He was also opposed by Republicans who feared that the Army's power

141. EHD (1603–1660), 1054.

and religious liberty might be destroyed. Richard did not inherit his father's strong character and failed to please Parliament, and in May 1659 he resigned. This gave Charles Fleetwood, John Lambert, senior Army officers, and other staunch Republicans who were members of a 'gathered' church in London, the opportunity to end the Protectorate, and regain their power. On the 7 May they recalled the Rump of the Long Parliament whereby forty-two members were summoned to rule the land. They wished to reduce the Army's influence, which led John Lambert with his troops to dissolving it. The control assumed by General George Monck, commander of the army in Scotland, decided to end all the confusion and marched to London forcing the Rump to allow old conservative members, who had been expelled by Pride's Purge in 1648, to return. In the meantime Fleetwood and others among his supporters recalled the Rump once more on 23 January, 1660, in an attempt to regain their power. Many of its conservative members, however, considered it an opportune moment to turn the clock back and revive the old Presbyterian system. There was no solution to such a confusing situation and Monck, with Presbyterian support, decided to call a 'free Parliament' to establish law and order and invite Charles to the throne. When this Parliament was dissolved in March 1660 the 'Good Old cause' came to an end. The independent Army yielded its power voluntarily to the Convention Parliament (April–December 1660), consisting of members elected after the dissolution of the Rump without coming to any decision as to whether religious toleration would be allowed. It consisted of a small number of radicals, and an equal representation of Episcopalians and Presbyterians, and its first task was to restore Charles to the throne.

Charles was eager to claim his inheritance and he returned to England from Holland, arriving at Dover on 25 May 1660. Extremist leaders were imprisoned, including Vavasor Powell and George Fox, and Quaker and Baptist gatherings were disrupted. John Miles of Ilston went to New England and other leaders were cruelly put to death, some of the most prominent being Colonel Thomas Harrison, the Fifth Monarchist John Carew and the Cornishman Hugh Peter who called for the thorough evangelization of Wales. Several escaped to the continent but the new religious settlement gave very little mercy to those who had been a danger to the Crown and its Church. Charles, however, was inclined to show some measure of toleration to Presbyterianism, but to ensure that a lasting agreement could be made was no easy matter. He was eager to grant a measure of toleration and promised in the Declaration of Breda that he would give 'liberty to tender consciences.' The old rifts that had dominated relations between sectarian groups, however, were still apparent and the 'Good Old Cause,' although ended, did show some signs that a revival might be possible. The Independents desired toleration but the Presbyterians wanted a new comprehensive religious settlement. There were differences between them but Presbyterians obtained some support from the new king who appointed chaplains from among them and offered others ecclesiastical preferments. Charles, in the Worcester House Declaration of October 1661, planned to establish an episcopalian system that would act with the aid of an advisory council formed from cathedral chapters and presbyteries, and changes were to be made to the *Book of Common Prayer*.[142] There is some disagreement, however, whether Charles honestly intended to progress on these lines to please Presbyterians but the strong pro-monarchy Anglican lobby in the House of Commons opposed it. A bill was presented to Parliament but it was voted down by episcopalian members and Independents because they feared that a rise in the fortunes of Presbyterians would spoil any hopes of toleration.

Matters did not auger well for Presbyterians when the Cavalier Parliament was summoned in March 1661 consisting of a preponderance of loyalist Anglican members, which weakened Presbyterianism in terms of membership to sixty. The conference which met at Savoy Palace on 5 April, 1661, consisting of Anglican and Presbyterian leaders with a view to reaching some agreement about the religious problems which divided them, achieved nothing since the Cavalier Parliament had met before its deliberations had ended. Despite the pro-royalist and Anglican membership of this Parliament moderate Presbyterians expected that Charles might graciously show mercy to 'tender consciences,' but that was not to be, especially after the Fifth Monarchist Thomas Venner's rising in London in January 1661 before Parliament had been elected. The persecution which followed lay very heavily on the Baptists, Quakers and Fifth Monarchists and the 'passive disobedience' of the Quakers after the Restoration led to a vehement attack on the Church as stated, for example, in William Simpson's tract: 'Oh

142. Watts, *Dissenters* I, 217–18.

Church of England! This is unto thee, who livest in oppression and cruelty, pride and covetousness; a day of misery is coming upon thee . . . Oppression and cruelty hath been as a staff for thee . . . and thou shalt be left naked . . . and Nations shall be ashamed of thee.'[143]

The series of acts, popularly known as the Clarendon Code, fully realised the ambitions of Anglican leaders from the days of Matthew Parker onwards to those of William Laud, and it forced Puritans to choose between conforming to the Anglican Church, now fully restored, or becoming Nonconformists. The new king's desire to see a comprehensive Church restored was an impossibility and the pro-royalist members of Parliament were eager to see dissenters penalised. The old dissenters, which had persisted in defending their beliefs for almost a century, now saw the danger that lay ahead of them, enduring a severe period of persecution after an intolerant religious settlement. Thus was passed the Act of Uniformity in 1662, which forced Presbyterians to accept episcopacy or be deprived of their livings. They were to accept the *Book of Common Prayer* and reject the 'Solemn League and Covenant' pact with the Scots in 1643. It is estimated that during the years 1660 to 1662 1,909 preachers and ministers were ejected from their livings, most of them from the South East, parts of the South West, and Cumberland. In Wales, likewise, 130 lost their livings, two-thirds of them having departed voluntarily before 1662, the majority from the country's eastern borders.[144] This act followed the Corporation Act in late 1661, which prevented those who refused to renounce the Covenant and to take the sacrament in the Church from holding municipal offices under the Crown. Religious circumstances had changed significantly for during the previous twenty years or so the Church and Puritanism alike had suffered. Much of the Church's structure had been abolished, its morale had weakened and the fabric of several buildings had been defaced. The campaign to establish a Calvinist Church had also been unsuccessful and Presbyterianism had lost much of its impact.

The growth of radical sects, many of them rejecting the old Calvinism, advocated freedom of worship and universal salvation in their private conventicles. The 'gathered churches' of the 1650s were not easily distinguishable for the differences between Baptists,

143. *Short Relation . . . of William Simpson*, 14; Keeble, *Literary Culture*, 38.

144. Jenkins, *Protestant Dissenters*, 42–43.

General and Particular, and Congregationalists were not clear cut. As Christopher Hill notes, the sectarian divisions were indistinct in an age of political and religious turmoil.[145] Dissenting sects, which emerged more clearly in the post 1660 years, were entering into their long period of rehabilitation as Nonconformists.

The time to plant firmly the religious system that moderate Puritans had hoped to realise had come to an end, and the Act of Uniformity, the second in a series of severe penal enactments forced them either to become dissenting sects at home or leave for the continent or America. Despite an arduous period of persecution following 'a narrow, intolerant religious settlement,' the foundation of religious nonconformity—a dominant force in English and Welsh society, culture, and politics of the future—had now been laid.

BIBLIOGRAPHY

Printed Sources

Archer, I. W. and F. D. Price, eds. *English Historical Documents, 1558–1603*. London: Routledge, 2011.

Barlow. W. *The Summe of the Conference . . . at Hampton Court 1603*. London: Norton, 1638.

Baxter, Richard. *Church—History of the Government of Bishops*. London: 1680.

———. *Naked Popery; or the naked falsehood of a book called the Catholike Naked truth*. London: 1677.

Bliss, James, ed. *Works of William Laud*, VI (i). Oxford: Parker, 1857.

Carlson, L. H., ed. *Writings of Henry Browne (1587–1590)*. London: Allen and Unwin, 1962.

Collinson, Patrick, ed. *Letters of Thomas Wood, Puritan 1561–1577*. London: Athlone, 1962.

Coward, B. and P. Gaunt. eds. *English Historical Documents, 1603–1660*. London: Routledge, 2010.

Cradock, Walter. *Glad Tydings from Heaven*. London: 1648.

Fortescue, W. *A Short Relation concerning the Life and Death of William Simpson*. London, 1671.

Gwynedd Archive Service, Caernarfon.

Hughes, G. H., ed. *Rhagymadroddion 1547–1659*. Cardiff: University of Wales Press, 2000.

Hughes, P. L., and J. F. Larkin, editors. *Royal Proclamations of King James I, 1603–1625*. Oxford: Oxford University Press, 1973.

---

145. Hill, "History and Denominational History," 66–68.

Larkin, J. F., ed. *Stuart Royal Proclamations II Royal Proclamations of King Charles I 1625–1646*. Oxford: Oxford University Press, 1983.

Lemon. R., ed. *Calendar of State Papers Domestic 1547–1580*. London: 1856.

McIlwain, C. H., ed. *Political Works of James I*. New York: Russell and Russell, 1965.

Nayler, James. *Antichrist in Man, Christ's Enemy*. London: 1656.

Peel, A., and L. H. Carlson, eds. *Cartwrightiana*, London: Allen and Unwin, 1951.

Peel, R. and H. Leland, eds, *The Writings of Robert Harrison and Robert Browne*. London: Allen and Unwin, 1953.

Sommerville, J. P. *King James VI and I: Political Writings*. Cambridge: University of Cambridge Press, 1994.

Statutes of the Realm. London: Dawsons 1963.

Thurloe, John. *Collection of the State Papers of John Thurloe, 1638–1660*, IV London. 1742.

Williams, David, ed. *Three Treatises Concerning Wales*. Cardiff: University of Wales Press, 1960.

Wolfe, D. M., ed. *Complete Prose Works of John Milton I 1624–1642*. New Haven: Yale University Press, 19153.

Wynne, Thomas. *An Antichristian Conspiracy Detected*. London: 1679.

Secondary Sources: Volumes

Ashley, Maurice. *Cromwell's Generals*. London: Jonathan Cape, 1954.

Aylmer, G. E. *Levellers in the English Revolution*. London: Thames and Hudson, 1975.

Berry, J., and Stephen G. Lee. *A Cromwellian Major General: The Career of Colonel James Berry*. Oxford: Clarendon, 1938.

Bingham, C. *James I of England*. London: Weidenfeld and Nicolson, 1981.

Bowen, Lloyd. *The Politics of the Principality: Wales c. 1603–1642*. Cardiff: University of Wales Press, 2007.

Brailsford, H. H. *The Levellers and the English Revolution*. London: Cresset, 1961.

Bruce, F. F. *The English Bible: A History of Translations*. London: Lutterworth, 1961.

Capp, B. S. *Fifth-Monarchy Men: A Study in Seventeenth-Century English Millenarianism*. London: Faber, 1972.

Collinson, Patrick. *Archbishop Grindal, 1519–1583: The Struggle for a Reformed Church*. London: Cape, 1979.

———. *English Puritanism*. London: Historical Association, 1983.

———. *The English Puritan Movement*. London: Jonathan Cape, 1967.

———. *Godly People: Essays on English Protestantism and Puritanism*. London: Hambledon, 1983.

Coward, Barry. *Stuart Age: A History of England 1603–1714*. London: Longman, 1980.

Daniell, David. *The Bible in English: Its History and Influence*. Yale: Yale University Press, 2003.

Dawley, P. M. *John Whitgift and the English Reformation*. New York: Scribner, 1954.

Doran, S. *Elizabeth I and Religion, 1558–1603*. London: Routledge, 1994.

Dow, F. D. *Radicalism in the English Revolution, 1640–1660*. Oxford: Blackwell, 1985.

Durston, C. *Cromwell's Major-Generals: Godly Government during the English Revolution*. Manchester: Manchester University Press, 2001.

Elton, Geoffrey R. *England under the Tudors*. London: Methuen, 1955.

Evans, A. O. *A Memorandum on the Legality of the Welsh Bible . . .* Cardiff: University of Wales Press, 1925.

Fincham, Kenneth. *Prelate as Pastor: The Episcopate of James I*. Oxford: Clarendon, 1990.

Gardiner, S. R. *History of England 1603–1642*, II *1607–1616*. London: Longmans, Green and Co., 1885.

Gruffydd, R. G. *"In that Gentile Country": The Beginnings of Puritan Nonconformity in Wales*. Bridgend: Evangelical Library of Wales, 1976.

Hill, Christopher. *Antichrist in Seventeenth-Century England*. London: Oxford University Press, 1971.

———. *Society and Puritanism in Pre-revolutionary England*. London: Secker & Warburg, 1964.

———. *The World Turned Upside Down: Radical Ideas during the English Revolution*. Harmondsworth, UK: Penguin, 1975.

Ingle, H. L. *First among Friends: George Fox and the Creation of Quakerism*. Oxford: Oxford University Press, 1994.

Jenkins, Geraint H. *Protestant Dissenters in Wales, 1639–1689*. Cardiff: University of Wales Press, 1992.

Jones, J. G. *Aspects of Religious Life in Wales, c. 1536–1660: Leadership, Opinion and the Local Community*. Aberystwyth, UK: Centre for Educational Studies, 2003.

Jones, R. Brinley. *"Lanterne to their feete": Remembering Rhys Prichard 1579–1644, Vicar of Llandovery*. Porthyrhyd, UK: Drovers, 1994.

Jones, R. Tudur. *Congregationalism in England, 1662–1962*. London: Independent, 1962.

Keeble, N. H. *The Literary Culture of Nonconformity in Later Seventeenth-Century England*. Leicester: Leicester University Press, 1987.

Knappen, M. M. *Tudor Puritanism: a Chapter in the History of idealism*. Chicago: University of Chicago Press, 1939.

Kunz, B. Y. *Margaret Fell and the Rise of Quakerism*. Basingstoke, UK. Macmillan, 1994.

Lake, Peter. *Anglicans and Puritans? Presbyterianism and English Conformist Thought from Whitgift to Hooker*. London: Unwin Hyman, 1988.

———. *Moderate Puritans and the Elizabethan Church*. Cambridge: University of Cambridge Press 1982.

Loades, D. M. *Revolution in Religion: The English Reformation, 1530–1570*. Cardiff: University of Wales Press, 1992.

MacCulloch, Diarmaid. *The Later Reformation in England, 1547–1603*. Basingstoke, UK: Macmillan, 1990.

Matthew, H. G. C., and B. Harrison, eds, *Oxford Dictionary of National Biography*. Oxford: Oxford University Press, 2004.

McGinn, D. J. *John Penry and the Marprelate Controversy*. New Brunswick, NJ: Rutgers University Press, 1966.

McGrath, Patrick. *Papists and Puritans under Elizabeth I*. London: Blandford, 1967.

Mendle, M. T., ed. *The Putney Debates of 1647*. Cambridge: Cambridge University Press, 2001.

Morrill, John, ed. *Oliver Cromwell and the English Revolution*. Harlow, UK: Longman, 1990.

Thomas, M. W. *Morgan Llwyd*. Cardiff: University of Wales Press, 1984.

Nuttall, Geoffrey F. *The Holy Spirit in Puritan Faith and Experience*. Oxford: Oxford University Press, 1946.

———. *The Welsh Saints 1640–1660: Walter Cradock, Vavasor Powell, Morgan Llwyd*. Cardiff: University of Wales Press, 1857.

Pearson, A. F. Scott. *Cartwright and Elizabethan Puritanism 1536–1603*. Cambridge: Cambridge University Press, 1925.

Pierce, William. *John Penry: His Life Times and Writings*. London: Hodder and Stoughton, 1923.

Pollard, A. W. *The Holy Bible . . . An Exact Report . . . of the Authorized Version . . . 1611*. Oxford: Oxford University Press, 1911.

Reese, M. M. *The Tudors and Stuarts*. London: Arnold, 1955.

Richards, Thomas. *A History of the Puritan Movement in Wales, 1639–1653*. London: National Eisteddfod Association, 1920.

———. *Religious Developments in Wales, 1654–1662*, London: National Eisteddfod Association, 1923.

Royal Commission of Ancient and Historical Monuments. County of Merioneth VI. London: H.M. Stationary office (1921) 20–21.

Sharp, A. *The English Levellers*. Cambridge: Cambridge University Press, 1998.

Toon, P. *God's Statesman: The Life and Work of John Owen: Pastor, Educator, Theologian*. Exeter, UK: Paternoster, 1971.

Tyacke, Nicholas. *Anti-Calvinists: The Rise of English Arminianism c.1590–1640*. Oxford: Clarendon, 1987.

Watts, Michael R. *The Dissenters: I From the Reformation to the French Revolution*. Oxford: Oxford University Press, 1978.

Wildes, H. E. *Voice of the Lord: George Fox and the Creation of Quakerism*. Oxford: Oxford University Press, 1994.

Williams, Glanmor. *Reformation Views of Church History*. London: Lutterworth, 1970.

Yates, W. N. *Rûg Chapel, Llangar Church, Gwydir uchaf Chapel . . .* Cardiff: Cadw, 2005.

Articles and Chapters in Books

Bowen, Lloyd. "The Seeds and Fruits of Revolution: The Erbery Family and Religious Radicalism in Seventeenth-Century Glamorgan." *Welsh History Review* 25 (2011) 346–73.

Bracklow, S. "The Elizabethan Roots of Henry Jacob's Churchmanship." *Journal of Ecclesiastical History* 36 (1985) 228–54.

Collinson, Patrick. "John Field and Elizabethan Puritanism." In *Godly People: Essays on English Protestantism and Puritanism*, 335–70. London: Hambledon, 1983.

———. "The Downfall of Archbishop Grindal and its Place in Elizabethan Political and Ecclesiastical History". In *Godly People: Essays on English Protestantism and Puritanism*, 370–97. London: Hambledon, 1983.

Curtis, M. H. "Hampton Court Conference and its Aftermath." *History* 47 (1961) 1–16.

Dodd, A. H. "A Remonstrance from Wales, 1655." *Bulletin of the Board of Celtic Studies* 17 (1958) 279–92.

———. "Bishop Lewes Bayly of Bangor c. 1575–1631." In *Transactions of the Caernarfonshire Historical Society* 28 (1967) 13–36.

Fletcher, Anthony. "Oliver Cromwell and the Godly Nation." In *Oliver Cromwell and the English Revolution*, edited by John Morrill, 209–33. London: Longman, 1990.

Gruffydd, R. G. "Anglican Prose." In *A Guide to Welsh Literature c. 1530–1700*, edited by R. G. Gruffydd, 167–83. Cardiff: University of Wales Press, 1997.

Hague, D. B. "Rug Chapel, Corwen." *Journal of the Merioneth Historical and Record Society* 3 (1958) 178.

Hall, Basil. "Puritanism: The Problem of Definition." *Studies in Church History*, II, edited by G. J. Cuming, 283–96. London: Nelson, 1965.

Hill, Christopher. "History and Denominational History." *Baptist Quarterly* XXII (1967–68) 35–59.

———. "Propagating the Gospel." In *Historical Essays 1600–1750, Presented to David Ogg*, edited by H. E. Bell and R. L. Ollard, 65–71. London: Black, 1963.

———. "The Spiritualization of the Household." In *Society and Puritanism in Pre-Revolutionary England*, 443–81. London: Secker and Warburg, 1964.

Hunt, S. A. "Laurence Chaderton and the Hampton Court Conference." In *Belief and Practice in Reformation England*, edited by S. Wabuda and C. Litzenberger, 207–28. Aldershot, UK: Ashgate, 1998.

James, B. L. "The Evolution of a Radical: The Life and Career of William Erbery (1604–54)." *Journal of Welsh Ecclesiastical History* III (1986) 31–48.

Johnson, A. M. "Wales during the Commonwealth and Protectorate." In *Puritans and Revolutionaries: Essays in Seventeenth-Century History Presented to Christopher Hill*, edited by D. Pennington and K. Thomas, 233–56. Oxford: Clarendon, 1978.

Jones, J. G. "John Penry: The Early Brecknockshire Puritan Firebrand." *Journal of the Brecknock Society (Brycheiniog)* 37 (2005) 23–43.

Jones, R. Tudur. "'The Healing Herb and the Rose of Love': The Piety of Two Welsh Puritans." In *Reformation, Conformity and Dissent: Essays in Honour of Geoffrey Nuttall*, edited by R. Buick Knox, 154–79. London: Epworth, 1977.

Lake, Peter. "The Laudian Style: Order, Uniformity and the Pursuit of the Beauty of Holiness in the 1630s." In *The Early Stuart Church, 1603–1642*, edited by K. Fincham. 161–86. Basingstoke, UK: Macmillan, 1993.

Nuttall, Geoffrey F. "Walter Cradock (1606?–1659): The Man and his Message." In *The Puritan Spirit: Essays and Addresses*, 118–29. London: Epworth, 1967.

Roberts, Stephen. "Welsh Puritanism in the Interregnum." *History Today* 41 (1991) 36–41.

Roots, I. A. "Swordsmen and decimators—Cromwell's Major-Generals." In *The English Civil War and After 1642–1658*, edited by R. H. Parry, 78–92. London: Macmillan, 1970.

Shriver, F. "Hampton Court Re-Visited: James I and the Puritans." *Journal of Ecclesiastical History* 33 (1982) 48–71.

Tyacke, Nicholas. "Puritanism, Arminianism and Counter-Revolution." In *The Origins of the English Civil War*, edited by Conrad Russell, 119–43. London: Macmillan, 1973.

White, B. R. "John Miles and the Structures of the Calvinistic Baptist Mission to South Wales 1649–1660." In *Welsh Baptist Studies*, edited by Mansel John, 35–75. Cardiff: The South Wales Baptist College, 1976.

———. "The Doctrine of the Church in the Particular Baptist Confession of 1644." *Journal of Theological Studies* XIX (1968) 570–90.

Woolrych, Austin. "Cromwell as a Soldier." In *Oliver Cromwell and the English Revolution*, edited by John Morrill, 93–118. London: Longman, 1990.

2

From Ejectment to Toleration in England, 1662–89[1]

David J. Appleby

The Act of Uniformity received the royal assent on 19 May 1662. It laid stringent obligations upon all Church of England clergy, masters and fellows of the universities, schoolmasters, and tutors. They were to affirm that it was illegal to take up arms against the Crown or its representatives under any circumstances whatsoever. They were required to disavow the Solemn League and Covenant. Clergy who wished to retain their livings were ordered to declare publicly that their liturgy would thereafter adhere precisely to the newly revised *Book of Common Prayer*, with its heavy emphasis on ritualised worship. They were, in addition, required to provide the ecclesiastical authorities with proof that they had been ordained by a bishop, or, failing this, to receive such ordination. All persons affected by the Act

1. In this chapter the following abbreviations are used: Bodl.: Bodleian Library, Oxford; BL: British Library; CR: Matthews, *Calamy Revised*; CSPD: *Calendar of State Papers, Domestic*; CSPV: *Calendar of State Papers, Venetian*; ODNB: *Oxford Dictionary of National Biography*; SP: The National Archives (Public Record Office) State Papers.

were obliged to make a public declaration of their unfeigned assent and consent to all its provisions, and to subscribe in writing by 24 August—St. Bartholomew's Day. Any clergyman who failed to adhere to the Act in the smallest particular was to be ejected from his position and prohibited from acting as a minister of the Church of England.[2] The precise and uncompromising language of this legislation was an indication of the temper of many (but by no means all) Cavalier-Anglicans who had reclaimed positions of national and local power in the two years following the Restoration. However, despite its apparent clarity and coherence, the Act of Uniformity was not part of a carefully integrated, state-sponsored plan for the eradication of Puritanism. It was rather the bodged product of an inherently unstable, neurotic, and inconstant political system. Over the next two decades, as the many unforeseen consequences of the Act became obvious and a number of panicky measures were taken to shore it up, the persecution of Nonconformists would fluctuate as different elements within the political establishment struggled for supremacy.

One of the great questions of Restoration history is how moderate Puritans, many of whom had taken huge risks to help facilitate the return of the monarchy, could have been so outmanoeuvred by their detractors as to be ambushed by the Act of Uniformity, and politically loyal clergy ejected *en masse* from the Church of England. In large part, this reverse reflected a miscalculation by a powerful clique of aristocracy and gentry, known to contemporaries as the 'Presbyterian Knot.' These persons mistakenly assumed that after dictating the terms of the King's return they would continue to influence the subsequent direction of Church and State.[3] The constantly shifting sands of Restoration politics made it hard even for those at the centre of power to anticipate future developments, but, even so, far too much faith was placed in Charles II's ability to adhere to his promise to respect tender consciences. Some Presbyterians had been sufficiently naïve as to view the return of a monarch who was technically a covenanted king as an opportunity finally to create 'a truly effective Puritan national church.'[4] Feelings of frustration and betrayal bubbled to the surface as it became

2. 14 Car. II, cap. 4 (Act of Uniformity 1662); Browning, *English Historical Documents*, 377–82; Kenyon, *Stuart Constitution*, 378–82.

3. Hutton, *Restoration*, 105–7, 117–18, 126–27, 153.

4. Miller, *After the Civil Wars*, 131. Charles had taken the Covenant in Scotland in 1650, in order to win military support for his bid to regain the throne.

obvious that the Restoration Church of England would be anything but this. The Presbyterian minister Henry Newcome had participated in Booth's Rising in 1659, and celebrated Charles's return in a thanksgiving sermon in June 1660. But he was soon after demoted from his position at the Collegiate Church in Manchester. On being silenced completely in August 1662, he wrote in his diary, 'It was not God but the king who cast us down.'[5] This view, although often expressed by Nonconformists far from the centre of power, was wide of the mark.

The notion propagated by Cragg and Bosher that Charles and his principal minister, Sir Edward Hyde, had never intended to honour the promises made at Breda, and had simply 'intended to pacify the Puritans until they could safely repress them,' has long since been dispelled.[6] Most historians now accept that Charles sincerely desired a comprehensive settlement, and that he was obstructed by a reactionary majority within the Cavalier Parliament and amongst the provincial gentry as a whole.[7] Others contend that his plans failed for lack of support from moderate Puritans, suspicious that the real objective was to obtain toleration for Catholics.[8] John Spurr has opined that it was Hyde (created Earl of Clarendon in 1661) who attempted to dilute and delay the Act of Uniformity, only to be thwarted variously by Bishop Sheldon, the Duke of York, and the King himself.[9] What is clear is that the character and motivation of the two royal brothers had a large bearing on the treatment accorded Nonconformists between 1662 and 1689.

Considerably more intelligent and personable than his father, Charles II's values had been shaped by the trauma of regicide, defeat and exile. He had emerged from his itinerant existence a manipulative and cynical politician, well versed in the arts of improvisation and expediency. Charles could be energetic and determined where his personal interests were concerned, but lackadaisical where they were not. He assumed that most people's loyalty was motivated by self-interest,

5. Newcome, *Usurpation Defeated*; Newcome, *Diary*, 117.

6. Cragg, *Puritanism in the Period of the Great Persecution*, 5; Bosher, *Making of the Restoration Settlement*, 111, 119.

7. E.g., Nuttall and Chadwick, *From Uniformity to Unity*, 60; Green, *Re-Establishment of the Church of England*, 22, 34–35; Watts, *Dissenters*, 221–22, 247–48; Keeble, *Literary Culture*, 56; Miller, *After the Civil Wars*, 174, 164–68.

8. E.g., Keeble, *Literary Culture*, 56; Watts, *Dissenters*, 222, 247–48.

9. Spurr, *Restoration Church of England*, 42.

although he was sometimes able to recognise constancy and conviction, as shown by his support for Andrew Marvell when the poet was harassed by over-zealous officials.[10] Above all, Charles was pragmatic rather than idealistic. In 1662 the restored monarchy was nowhere near as popular or secure as Cavalier propagandists pretended. By a Privy Council order of July 1660, every church had been required to set up the royal arms; but many had since been defaced.[11] Royal finances were in a desperate state. Charles and Clarendon had already found that to protect and enhance the authority of the Crown they would have to negotiate a path through the vagaries of parliamentary elections, and shifts in faction among the capricious MPs who held the key to the nation's coffers. Both King and Parliament had also to bear in mind the fluctuating moods of a fickle populace, for whom a functioning monarchy was still a novel experience. The passage of the Uniformity Bill shows that the King and his principal minister, although sometimes disagreeing on timing and detail, were as one in their concern with internal security—particularly after the alarm caused by Venner's Fifth Monarchist rising in London in January 1661. Having already set in motion a huge and expensive operation to disband the bulk of the Cromwellian army, Parliament was encouraged to pass the Corporation Act (1661), the Treason Act (1661), and the Licensing Act (1662).[12] As a consequence, the Crown acquired far greater powers than before to intrude in the operation of the magistracy and local government, at the same time as the definition of sedition and treason was broadened, and press controls reintroduced. Charles's financial dependency upon Parliament did not yet allow him to act as he pleased, but if suitable legislation regarding the militia could be passed he saw that he could potentially acquire a greater control over the county lieutenancy and the militia than that enjoyed by any of his forebears.[13]

Charles and Clarendon were reluctant to jeopardise these political gains by acceding to a programme of religious intolerance. Clarendon had remained in regular contact with Presbyterian leaders in particular,

10. Patterson and Dzelzainis, "Marvell and the Earl of Anglesey," 703.

11. SP29/67/90; SP29/57/123.

12. 13 Car. II, st. 2, cap. 1 (Corporation Act 1661); 13 Car. II st.1, cap. 1 (An Act for the Safety and Preservation of His Majesties Person and Government, aka Treason Act,1661); 13/14 Car. II, cap. 33 (Licencing Act 1662).

13. 13/14 Car. II, cap. 2 (Militia Act 1662); 15 Car. II, cap. 4 (Militia Act 1663).

not least because he and the King recognised that the overwhelming majority of Presbyterians were respectable, socially conservative members of society who believed implicitly in the institution of monarchy. Contrary to the lurid allegations of Cavalier journalists such as Roger L'Estrange, there was no grand Puritan conspiracy to throw the monarchy back into the sea. Puritanism was divided against itself. There never had been any love lost between Presbyterian divines and the more radical sects, hence the extent of the Presbyterians' enthusiasm for the Restoration, and their collusion in the framing and implementation of the Act for Restoring Ministers in 1660. Presbyterian ministers similarly had little empathy with the demobilised Cromwellian soldiery, and bitterly attacked Quakers in print and from the pulpit. Quakers in their turn aggravated matters by gate-crashing Presbyterian services and disrupting sermons.[14] However, it was always possible that persecution might drive disparate Puritan constituencies—particularly Presbyterians, Congregationalists, and Baptists—into making common cause. Presbyterians were known to be well connected, with many sympathisers among the social and political elite; including privy councillors such as the Duke of Albemarle and the Earl of Manchester, government officials such as John Birch MP, and numerous army commanders such as Sir Thomas Morgan. Such considerations, coupled with the lack of hard information regarding the numbers, demography and distribution of potential Nonconformists throughout the country caused Charles and Clarendon to proceed with caution. The same uncertainties, by contrast, provoked something of a moral panic among many Cavalier gentry and their representatives in Westminster. It is with good reason that Ian Green has opined that the driving force behind the exclusive and intolerant Restoration religious settlement enshrined in the Act of Uniformity was 'the zeal of the gentry for the episcopal Church of England,' and that the intensity of Cavalier-Anglican feelings during the Uniformity debates of 1662 intimidated the King and demoralised the Puritan clergy.[15] The motivation behind that fervour was largely negative: many influential Cavaliers were still embittered and traumatised by events during the civil wars and Interregnum, and had no taste for toleration, much less a desire for reconciliation. Their

14. Horn, *Quakers Proved Deceivers*; Lye, *Fixed Saint*, 28; *An Exact Collection of Farewell Sermons*, 150; Calamy, *Abridgement* (1713), ii, 158.

15. Green, *Re-establishment*, 200–201.

fear of sedition and thirst for revenge possibly posed a greater threat to the long-term stability of the realm than the activity of any radical group or the disaffection of any Nonconformist. Whether or not this was one of the reasons why Charles II was loath to allow Cavalier-Anglicans to monopolise local or national government is debatable. During most of his reign Charles took care to maintain and encourage rival factions at Court, thereby enhancing his own position. That he intended to govern the Church of England in the same way is indicated by the offer of bishoprics to leading Puritans such as Richard Baxter, Edmund Calamy, and Edward Reynolds, and royal appointments to cathedral chapters.[16] Nevertheless, Charles found it expedient to give way to the Cavalier gentry over the matter of Uniformity. In sacrificing hundreds of politically loyal, religiously moderate Puritan clergy, he undoubtedly smoothed the way for other legislation (notably the Militia Acts), which for him carried a higher priority.

Although there was no single mastermind behind the Act of Uniformity, Gilbert Sheldon, Bishop of London was indisputably the most prominent figure in its conception, formulation, and subsequent enforcement.[17] Brushing aside the aged and infirm primates of Canterbury and York, the energetic Sheldon had quickly emerged after the Restoration as leader of the episcopalian wing of the Church of England and the champion of episcopal government and formal worship. His hostility to religious comprehension had been obvious at the Savoy Conference and in his manipulation of Convocation when it had revised, updated and politicised the *Common Prayer Book* and liturgy.[18] Paradoxically, he had given Baxter a courteous hearing when the latter requested an interview in early 1662, and had permitted the Kidderminster pastor to preach within the London diocese despite being technically in breach of the 1660 Act in so doing.[19] Even more curiously, he led the bishops in the Lords to vote in favour of Clarendon's amendment of the Uniformity Bill, whereby the King was to be given the authority to exempt dissenting clergy from certain clauses.

16. Ibid., ch. 3.

17. See Burnett, *History*, i, 329.

18. Hutton, *Restoration*, 175. Politicised not least by the form of service for the anniversaries of the regicide (30 January) and Charles II's nativity and restoration (29 May).

19. *Reliquiae Baxterianae*, ii, 302.

For those who were likely to suffer the consequences of Uniformity, the passage of Clarendon's amendment in the Commons provided an ominous portent of things to come.

In an effort to bolster support for the amendment Charles offered several important concessions, not least offering his assent to a bill requiring Quakers to take the oaths of Allegiance and Supremacy. It was, of course, well understood that Quakers would refuse to take any such oath on principle, and thus the resulting Quaker Act (1662) duly provided for the banning of any meeting of five persons who had refused to swear. Penalties ranged from fines and imprisonment to transportation for a third offence.[20] The King's promise to the Quaker Richard Hubberthorne that 'you shall none of you suffer for your opinions or religion, so long as you live peaceably' was rendered worthless.[21] Hubberthorne was one among many Friends who would die in prison. Quakers were an obvious and relatively soft target, as their radical notions of religious and social equality, advertised by their seemingly fearless public demonstrations of faith, caused alarm and offence among the wider population, let alone the Cavalier gentry. Of more immediate concern for moderate Puritans was the failure of Clarendon's amendment to the Uniformity Bill, which signified that the King was virtually powerless to protect tender consciences. If the closeness of some votes at various stages of the bill suggests that the Cavalier Parliament was less reactionary than has often been assumed, the final form of the bill shows nevertheless that a majority of MPs were willing to countenance the expulsion of an even larger group of clergy than had been ejected from the Church of England in 1660, and the alienation of a significant proportion of the King's subjects.[22]

The choice of St. Bartholomew's Day for the deadline has often been cited as an example of Cavalier-Anglican vindictiveness, as this was traditionally the date on which the half-yearly tithes were collected. It is certain that many clergy and their families were so dependent upon this source of income that the threat to withhold it was an ideal way to coerce wavering clergy to conform. In any case, provision had to be made for replacement ministers. Ministers' supporters could

20. 13–14 Car. II, cap. 1 (Quaker Act 1662).

21. Quoted in Watts, *Dissenters*, 222.

22. Hutton, *Restoration*, 175; Spurr, *Restoration Church of England*, 42; Seaward, "Gilbert Sheldon," 50.

find ways around the problem, however. Thomas Newnham's parish
ioners on the Isle of Wight deliberately paid their tithes early in order
that he, not his replacement, would benefit. The vestry of St. Lawrence
Pountney simply paid their ejected curate Thomas Wadsworth retro-
spectively.[23] Having said this, 24 August was not originally intended as
the date for the enforcement of the Act. The proposed date for compliance had been put back from Michaelmas, to Midsummer, and belatedly to St. Bartholomew's Day as the debates over the bill had dragged
on.[24] That the ejectment would take place on the anniversary of the
Bartholomew's Day Massacres of 1572 was an inconvenient coinci-
dence for the authorities.

Once the Act had been entered into the statute books, Sheldon's
attitude hardened appreciably. Whereas he had voted for Clarendon's
earlier amendment, he now mobilised the bishops to block a proposal
by Charles, Clarendon and the Earl of Manchester to allow the King
to suspend the Act in individual cases. He was still sufficiently enraged
about this proposal several weeks later to send a vituperative memo to
Clarendon on the subject.[25] Leading Puritan divines such as Baxter,
Bates, Calamy, and Manton also refused to support the proposal. They
recoiled from the suggestion that the Crown be given licence to subvert the authority of Parliament, and were concerned that their assent
might pave the way for the toleration of Catholicism.[26] In any case,
they still clung to the hope that there might yet be genuine comprehension within the Church of England rather than mere indulgence.

The weeks leading up to 'Black Bartholomew's Day' saw feverish
activity in London and the provinces. Some clergy, such as the former
New Model Army officer and parliamentarian navy chaplain Samuel
Kem, embraced conformity wholeheartedly. Kem urged his former
colleagues to disavow the Solemn League and Covenant, which he
claimed had dethroned and beheaded both magistracy and ministry.[27]
Inevitably, there were those who meekly complied with the Act in
order to keep their livings. These earned the contempt of Anglicans

23. CR, 364, 505.

24. Bosher, *Making of the Restoration Settlement*, 250.

25. Bodl. MS Clarendon 77, fo. 319, cited in Sutch, *Gilbert Sheldon*, 86; Spurr, *Restoration Church of England*, 46; Bodl. MS. Carte 32, fo. 3.

26. Keeble, *Literary Culture*, 56

27. Kem, *King Solomon's Infallible Experiment*, 18.

and Nonconformists alike.[28] The Presbyterian minister of Chagford in Devon conformed two days after Bartholomew's Day, but nevertheless found himself locked out of the church by his erstwhile parishioners, who petitioned the patron of the living not to readmit him.[29] A number of others survived by subterfuge; such as the group of Gloucestershire clergy led by William Mew. These ministers read out the declaration of assent to their respective congregations exactly as it was printed, deliberately neglecting to insert their own names when they came to the passage, 'I, A. B., do declare my unfeigned Assent and Consent, etc.'[30] Actions taken against Nonconformist clergy in other areas varied enormously according to the demeanour and efficiency of the local authorities. The diarist Ralph Josselin delivered a farewell sermon and prepared to quit his living; but as nobody came to eject him he simply carried on as if nothing had happened. Although later reprimanded for his failure to wear the surplice, Josselin remained the minister of Earl's Colne in Essex until his death in 1683.[31] The Nottingham ministers William Reynolds, John Whitlock and John Barrett had a very different experience; all three being illegally suspended by the archdeacon of Nottingham several weeks before Black Bartholomew's Day, contrary to the terms of the Act and the orders of the Archbishop of York.[32]

Those Anglican clergy who urged their Puritan colleagues to conform and remain within the Church of England had a variety of motives for so doing. Some were genuinely desirous of maintaining a broad reformed church, whilst others preferred grudging obedience to outright schism. Bishop Burnett's recollection of the Uniformity crisis, however, was that few of the 'episcopal party' sympathised with the plight of their Nonconformist brethren.[33] The mood of most bishops before and after Black Bartholomew's Day (particularly their evident dissatisfaction at the prospect of many Puritan clergy feigning compliance in order to remain in their livings) indicates that ordination services such as those offered by Sheldon at St. Paul's up to 21 August

28. E.g., Bodl. MS Clarendon 77, fo. 157.

29. Bodl. MS Tanner 48, fo. 48 (Seth Ward to Gilbert Sheldon, 27 September, 1662).

30. Calamy, *Abridgement* (1702), 332; *CR*, 349.

31. Josselin, *Diary*, 491.

32. *CR*, 30, 409, 527; Whitlock, *Short Account*, 38; *England's Remembrancer*, 17.

33. Burnett, *History*, i, 329.

were designed to encourage submission and obedience to the revised liturgy and episcopal authority, rather to preserve a broad Church.[34] Almost one thousand clergy (possibly many more, if Josselin's example is at all typical) decided that they could not in conscience comply with one or more of the stipulations in the Act, and prepared to quit their livings.

Churchgoers in hundreds of parishes up and down the nation now began to witness the spectacle of the so-called 'Bartholomean' farewell sermons, by which the dissenting clergy, either individually or in concerted group actions, began to advertise and explain the reasons for their nonconformity. Richard Baxter was a prominent early casualty: despite having been given temporary dispensation by Sheldon, Baxter declared his position almost at once and preached his farewell sermon on 25 May. He claimed later that he had done this in order to comply with a clause in the Act that required itinerant lecturers to cease preaching immediately. However, Baxter was well aware of his celebrity status, and it is clear that he intended to set an example in order to stiffen the resolve of others.[35]

Even before the Act of Uniformity had passed into law, one hostile observer had alleged that Presbyterian ministers were spreading alarm and despondency by claiming 'that persecution is approaching and profaneness and idolatry is coming in like a flood.'[36] Samuel Pepys and the Venetian ambassador independently noted ominous parallels to events that had preceded civil war in 1642; as did the correspondent who wrote to the Duke of Ormonde, Lord Lieutenant of Ireland, on 23 August to warn him that the Nonconformist ministers had grown so insolent that it was quite likely that his army would soon be needed in England.[37] Such nervousness was not mere paranoia: although most plots reported by spies and provincial magistrates proved to be spurious, the fatalities caused by Venner's Rising were a reminder that the government could not afford to take such matters lightly. The authorities were acutely aware that there were thousands

34. *Mercurius Publicus*, 33 (August 14–21, 1662), 554; 34 (August 21–28, 1662), 563.

35. *Reliquiae Baxterianae*, 384.

36. BL MS Egerton 2537, fo. 331.

37. Pepys, *Diary*, iii, 183; *CSPV 1661–64*, 180; Bodl. MS Carte 31, fo. 602 (Goring Rous to James, Duke of Ormonde, 23 August 1662).

of disaffected persons in London and the provinces, linked by myriad networks and coteries. Lists of parliamentarian veterans were drawn up by justices in areas considered particularly at risk. The county trained bands (now firmly under the control of carefully vetted officers and deputy lieutenants) searched houses, confiscated weapons, and arrested former army officers and Commonwealth officials.[38] However, whereas government officials before Black Bartholomew's Day appear most often to have focused on the activities of Quakers and political radicals, the bile of Anglican preachers and their allies in the secular press was more often reserved for Presbyterians. The average Presbyterian was habitually portrayed as a devious hypocrite, who, underneath an outwardly loyal and respectable exterior was 'the traitor in our own hearts.'[39] Since 1660, principally through the vehicle of church services and sermons instituted to commemorate Charles I's execution on 30 January 1649 and Charles II's nativity and restoration on 29 May, Anglican preachers had presented intensely emotive images of the regicide. Presbyterians were repeatedly accused in these sermons of complicity in the judicial murder of the anointed king and royal martyr Charles I 'of blessed memory.'[40] For the journalist John Berkenhead, a former aide to Archbishop Laud, the Uniformity crisis had finally forced Presbyterians to show their true face. He was inspired to write a satire, *Cabala* (1663), in whose pages a committee of leading Presbyterians plotted with the pope to bring down the Church of England, and congratulated one another on the efficacy of their duplicity: 'Brother *Calamy*, Brother *Ashe*, had not we become all things to all men we had gained none.'[41] Another pamphleteer reminded his readers of the sufferings of loyal clergy during the Civil Wars and Interregnum, and named as the principal culprits 'the Brethren of the Presbytery, who now themselves cry out so much of Persecution.'[42]

It was in this highly charged atmosphere that the departing ministers sought to explain from the pulpit why they had chosen to remain true to the laws of God as revealed in Scripture rather than

38. E.g., CSPD 1661–62, 418, 428, 442, 488; SP29/58/139–46; SP29/56/216; SP29/57/235; BL Add. MSS 21922, fos. 249, 250, 253v.

39. Twisse, *England's Breath Stopp'd*, 34

40. E.g., Bury, *The Bow*, 36; Walwyn, *God Save the King*, 8–10; Griffith, *The King's Life-Guard*, 18–30, 44.

41. Berkenhead, *Cabala*, 5, 8.

42. *A Generall Bill of the Mortality of the Clergy of London*, 6.

submit to the laws of man. Richard Baxter, Thomas Lye, and many others preached in London knowing that there were spies within their congregations ready to report any unguarded statements. In the provinces, preachers such as Robert Atkins suffered heckling and intimation during their final hours in the pulpit. The renowned co-author of *Smectymnuus*, Matthew Newcomen defied death threats in order to preach his last sermon, after some thirty years' service in the position of lecturer in Dedham, Essex.[43]

The Act of Uniformity forced Presbyterians to resolve questions of conscience with which many of them had wrestled since the 1640s. One advantage of the comprehensive list of stipulations in the Act was that ministers could declare their opposition to it without needing to specify exactly which clauses they found unacceptable. Nonconformists such as Richard Fairclough, rector of Mells in Somerset considered vestments such as the surplice, bowing at the name of Christ or standing for hymns 'things indifferent.'[44] For many others these were offensive, unscriptural human innovation. George Swinnock declared that 'all worship of God without warrant is like private coyning of mony, *high Treason* against the King of Heaven.'[45] Many of the older Nonconformists had subscribed to the Solemn League and Covenant, and felt unable in conscience to disavow the oath they had taken. Many younger ministers refused to conform on the grounds that having already received their ordination and made their vows to God, they could not submit to a second ordination. The fact that so many glossed over unacceptable clauses of the Act in their farewell sermons, or hid their criticism of the regime behind scriptural metaphor, does not mean that the Bartholomeans were quietist. The very fact that they dissented from the Act of Uniformity at all, however reluctantly, and were prepared to justify their actions in the pulpit was enough to provoke some Cavalier-Anglicans to wonder that 'if some pretend tenderness of conscience against that law, some might pretend tenderness of conscience against any law.'[46] Repeated exhortations for followers to hold fast, to incur fines rather than act against their

43. *Reliquiae Baxterianae*, ii, 302; Lye, *Fixed Saint*, 3; Calamy, *Account*, ii, 215; Essex Record Office D/B5, SB2/9, fos. 17, 116v.

44. Fairclough, *Pastor's Legacy*, 121.

45. Swinnock, *Pastors Farewell*, 62.

46. Thorndike, quoted in Nuttall and Chadwick, *From Uniformity to Unity*, 14.

conscience, and to prepare for harassment and persecution seemed to many detractors a calculated challenge to the authority of the Crown and the legitimacy of Parliament. Resistance was also deduced from the fact that Nonconformist networks continued to function, and followers of Nonconformist clergy had begun to gather at 'conventicles' and listen to illegal preaching rather than attend their parish church as required by law. Even the passive acceptance of persecution could be seen as provocative, as William Assheton complained, 'And still they endeavour to captivate [the people's] Pity, by a bold and impudent insinuation of these two things, *That they are the People of God,* and *That they are persecuted.* For experience shews that the Opinion of Persecution naturally moves men to Pity, and Pity presently turns into Love, and whom men love, they are easily brought to defend.'[47]

Given the restraints already imposed on preachers by virtue of the Treason Act, the veiled, and sometimes not so veiled, criticism of the King and his ministers in so many farewell sermons are instructive. The preamble to the Treason Act did, after all, carry the conclusion that 'the late troubles and disorders did in a very great measure proceed from a multitude of seditious sermons, pamphlets and speeches daily preached, printed and published.' It was treason to 'incite or stir up the people to hatred or dislike of the person of his Majesty or the established government,' to suggest that they were popishly inclined 'by writing, printing, preaching or other speaking.'[48] Whereas Anglican sermons and Cavalier tracts held that Nonconformist defiance furthered the cause of popery, Dissenters retorted that persecution was itself a papist trait.

Despite this battle of words, the physical ejectment of ministers, fellows, and tutors was generally effected with remarkably little trouble, although it was not as clean a break as has sometimes been portrayed. Feelings ran very high in some parishes for some time, and localised demonstrations occurred, particularly in London.[49] The authorities made a great show of mobilising the London Trained Bands and the county militias, and reinforced their patrols with troops from

47. Assheton, *Evangelium Armatum*, sig. [Av].

48. 13 Car. II, st. 1 cap. 1; Browning, *Documents*, 63

49. Pepys, *Diary*, iii, 178; Hyde, *Life*, i, 571; CSPV 1661–64, 185; Bodl. Carte MSS 47, fos. 365v (Sir Edward Nicholas to James, Duke of Ormonde, 13 September 1662), 381v (same to same, 25 October 1662).

the regular army in order to maintain a visible presence in the streets. This had the desired effect, as many departing ministers took pains to urge their followers to avoid physical confrontation.[50] Pepys noted in his diary entry for 30 September, 'for aught I see, they are gone out very peaceably and the people not so much concerned therein as was expected.'[51] Other preachers had been less pliable: Richard Alleine had left his congregation with the parting advice that they should not 'pursue peace, upon tearms dishonourable or prejudicial to *Truth*.'[52] Instead of physical resistance he and many of his colleagues now called on their congregations to prepare for spiritual warfare.[53]

The episcopal authorities were already extremely busy with matters such as building repairs, reclaiming confiscated church property, and dealing with the after-effects of the earlier ejectments of 1660. Ronald Hutton has claimed that the bishops were caught unawares by the sheer numbers of ministers dissenting from the Act of Uniformity, and were hard pushed to provide adequate numbers of replacements.[54] This might explain why partial Nonconformists such as Ralph Josselin could have remained undetected, particularly if they did nothing to draw attention to themselves. Elsewhere, the Lancashire authorities deliberately turned a blind eye to the rather more obvious nonconformity of John Ainger, whilst in Worcestershire the new incumbent of Treddington actually allowed his predecessor to continue to preach.[55] Even where ministers noisily stood their ground and dared the authorities to eject them, the authorities were sometimes slow to react. Joseph Cooper, the curate of Moseley, Worcestershire, had preached a series of eight farewell sermons before Black Bartholomew's Day, but it was not until December that he was physically removed from his living by troopers and imprisoned.[56]

50. E.g., *England's Remembrancer*, 381; Fairclough, *Pastor's Legacy*, 94.

51. Pepys, *Diary*, iii, 210.

52. Alleine, *Godly Man's Portion*, 144.

53. E.g., Alleine, *Godly Man's Portion*, 97; Newcomen, *Ultimum Vale*, 47; Lamb, *Royal Presence*, sig. [B4]; *England's Remembrancer*, 12, 372; *Exact Collection of Farewell Sermons*, 384.

54. Hutton, *Restoration*, 177.

55. CR, 12; Calamy, *Continuation*, ii, 895. See also Seaward, "Gilbert Sheldon," 49–50; Green, *Re-Establishment*, 186–88; Appleby, *Black Bartholomew's Day*, 173.

56. Calamy, *Continuation*, ii, 884.

The most notorious contravention of the Act of Uniformity concerned Edmund Calamy the elder, who felt moved to reoccupy his old pulpit at St. Mary's Aldermanbury on 28 December. There he preached a sermon critical of the times, and was promptly arrested on the orders of Gilbert Sheldon. Formally cautioned and questioned by the lord mayor of London, the aged minister was said to have stated in his defence, 'I hope that what a Popish Priest may do without check, a Protestant Minister may do without imprisonment.'[57] On being told that he was to be committed to prison in Newgate, Calamy assured his interrogator that he was 'ready not to be bound only, but to dye for the Lord Jesus.'[58] A published account of the affair, coupled with several different editions of the offending sermon, soon turned the case into a *cause célèbre*, provoking indignation among Dissenters and increasing the anxiety and anger of Cavalier-Anglicans.[59] For all Calamy's sincerity, his timing was unfortunate: only two days earlier, on 26 December 1662, Charles II had announced his intention to introduce a bill suspending the penal laws against Nonconformists, a first attempt to implement a formal declaration of indulgence.[60] The King was embarrassed by Calamy's actions, allegedly saying to Sheldon when confronted with news, 'I am sure he hath no encouragement to it from my declaration.'[61] However, as the lord mayor had already predicted, it is possible that the incident did have an effect: Cavalier-Anglicans were able to ensure that the King's bill was defeated in the Lords.[62] Despite this, Calamy was released on 13 January, 1663. The Earl of Manchester had taken advantage of the residual Presbyterian influence at court to procure the minister's freedom, on the grounds that he had preached 'with the privity of several lords of the Council, and not in contempt of law.'[63] Calamy was even paid for his sermon.

57. *Master Edmund Calamy's Leading Case*, 14.

58. Ibid., 4; Acts 21:13.

59. Calamy, *Eli Trembling for Fear of the Ark* (Wing C231A). Three further editions were printed in Oxford in 1663 (Wing C231, C232 and C267).

60. Keeble, *Literary Culture*, 56

61. *Master Edmund Calamy's Leading Case*, 13.

62. Ibid.

63. Ibid., 12, 16; *Mercurius Politicus* (1–8 Jan, 1663); Corporation of London, Mayor's waiting book, 2, 13 Jan; SP28/67/39; 44/9, fo. 224, quoted in Hutton, *Restoration*, 194; Pepys, *Diary*, iv, 5–6; CSPD *1663–4*, 10; Guildhall MS 3556.2, cited in Achinstein, *Literature and Dissent*, 2.

Sheldon viewed Manchester and certain other elements at Court as a threat to the re-established Church and state. The residue of the Presbyterian Knot looked towards Manchester. The Earl of Bristol's circle was intent on furthering the cause of Catholics. Former Cromwellians and republicans gravitated towards Anthony Ashley-Cooper, Lord Ashley. Sir Henry Bennett's faction could usually be relied upon to support the bishops, particularly when it caused trouble for Clarendon and his friends. In the middle of this fog of fractious politics, those ministers who had quit their livings saw the prospect of comprehension within a broad Church of England slip further and further away. Moderate Puritans now found themselves marginalised, saddled with the label 'Dissenters', lumped together with radicals and Roman Catholics, and widely advertised as part of the broad threat to the security of the Restoration state.

The experience of the ejected ministers between 1662 and 1689 remains an under-explored field. In his brief survey of ministers' movements after 1662, A. G. Matthews found that only thirty to forty left England altogether.[64] It was widely expected at the time (particularly in Massachusetts) that many ejected ministers and their followers would decamp to America to found new communities there. In the event, only fifteen ministers are known to have made a new home on the other side of the Atlantic. Perhaps more surprisingly, only ten ejected ministers chose to emigrate to the Netherlands. The Dutch had a long-established tradition for providing refuges for English and Scots Puritans, even before Robert Browne and his followers had settled in Zeeland in the 1580s. This trend had become even more pronounced during the times of persecution under Charles I and Laud. Matthew Newcomen was the most notable Bartholomean to move to the Netherlands. Having quit Dedham in December 1662 he accepted an offer to become pastor of the English congregation at Leiden. He immediately moved there with his wife and family, and became a leading member of the community. In March 1666, following the outbreak of the Second Anglo-Dutch War Newcomen was commanded to return to England. That he did not comply was owing to his ill health, and the fact that he had in the meantime become a Dutch citizen.

---

64. All statistics in this paragraph are taken from CR, xiv–xv.

Newcomen would eventually die in Leiden when plague visited the town in 1669.[65]

The vast majority of the ejected ministers remained in the vicinity of their former livings. Edmund Calamy the elder was one of many who began to preach in his own home, a trait later confirmed by the large number of Nonconformists who would be licensed as preachers at their home address in 1672. His old congregation even made an attempt late in 1663 to have him restored to his former living at St. Mary's, Aldermanbury.[66] Henry Newcombe similarly remained close to his old parish, undertaking pastoral work, and visiting private homes to catechise children, repeat sermons, and conduct family prayers. When the authorities ordered him to desist, Newcombe pointed out that the Act of Uniformity did not cover such activity: 'I did not think repeating had been any offence. But the Justice told me it was.'[67] By its very nature, such clandestine spiritual guidance is very difficult for the historian to measure, but it was certainly sufficient to worry the authorities.

Ejected ministers who preached in the homes of sympathetic gentry were slightly safer; in many cases these were prestigious families whom even the most rabid Cavalier-Anglican justice would hesitate to disturb. Some clerics became permanent members of such households. Francis Soreton, formerly rector of Honiton in Devon, entered the household of his long-term patron (and nephew by marriage) Sir William Courtenay.[68] The Puritan gentry, although they had been unable to protect their clergy within the Church of England, proceeded to give succour to many after they had all become Nonconformists, employing ministers as chaplains and tutors, and making financial contributions and bequests. The list of donors includes the familiar names of Puritan families from Yorkshire to Cornwall, such as Holles, Wharton, Russell, Fairfax, Harley, Rich, Barrington, Foley, Barnardiston, and Boscawen.[69] Such patronage was not without some collateral damage,

65. Smith, "Essex Newcomens," 39; Webster, "Newcomen," ODNB.
66. Achinstein, *Literature and Dissent*, 2.
67. Newcombe, *Diary*, 120, 126.
68. CR, 452.
69. Ibid., lvi.

as the Earl of Anglesey found out when he received many reproaches for having chosen a Nonconformist as his private chaplain.[70]

Soon after Black Bartholomew's Day, wild rumours began to circulate regarding Presbyterian plots and gatherings. A correspondent informed Sheldon in September 1662 that 'most of the clergy Presbyters are (as I heare) gone up to London to the Great Rendezvous, where they will endeaver to rally again after this Rout.'[71] A mixture of panic, spite and avarice motivated a large number of would-be informers, whose reports frequently verged on the fantastic. Even the rabidly anti-Puritan journalist and government official Roger L'Estrange declared that he was not mad enough to believe a tenth part of the intelligence he received.[72] Inevitably past associations (which might arise from having been fellow members of a *classis* or association during the 1650s, or having studied together as fellow students at university) did cause Nonconformist ministers to concentrate in certain areas. Birmingham had been a noted hothouse of Puritan feeling during the civil wars. Now many ejected ministers gravitated towards the area described by one as a Nonconformist asylum, encouraged by sympathetic local patrons such as Lady Lucy Graham. Among the Nonconformists who made up the King's Norton group just outside Birmingham were notable divines such as Thomas Bladon and Samuel Fisher, a protégé of Sir George Booth.[73] Notable concentrations in and around London were at St. Giles Cripplegate, Hackney and Stoke Newington. At Stoke Newington Nonconformist ministers could count on the largesse of sympathetic City merchants, who kept country residences there. Further afield some early dissenting congregations were founded in unlikely places such as Wokingham in Berkshire and Mansfield, Nottinghamshire.[74] These extended networks proved particularly worrying to the authorities. There are glimpses of strong connections between London and Bristol, with the arrest of the Dissenting stationer Thomas Brewster at the Bristol fair in February 1663, and a spy's report on 'Mr Hancock of Bristol, lately a Nonconformist and a pestilent fellow,' who was observed preaching

---

70. Bodl. MS Carte 217, fo. 462 (Edward, Earl of Clarendon to James, Duke of Ormonde, 17 August 1662).

71. Bodl. MS Tanner 48, fo. 43.

72. *Intelligencer*, no. 8 (October 19, 1663), 59.

73. Hetherington, "Birmingham and the Ejected," 20, 24–26.

74. CR, xiv–xv.

in London in November 1664.[75] Another strong link can be observed between the capital and the West Country. Ralph Venning, the ejected incumbent of St. Olaves, was reported by an informant to be carrying on a regular correspondence with Devon ministers, by means of the Exeter carrier, who operated from a tavern in Bird Street, London.[76]

The diocese of Exeter was an area of particular tension between Nonconformists and episcopal authority, not least because the zeal of Seth Ward, Bishop of Exeter, for uniformity was second only to that of Sheldon himself. In the weeks following the Great Ejectment Ward seems have been ready to accept Nonconformists back into the Church of England provided they were willing to subscribe to the Act of Uniformity. He wrote to Sheldon in September 1662 to report that he had had meetings with several ejected ministers and was confident that they would eventually be glad to conform in order to receive other livings.[77] By January 1664, however, although his bishop's court had become the most active in England as regards prosecuting ejected minsters for contravening the Act, and depriving others of their livings, Ward had become increasingly irritated by his inability to eradicate nonconformity. Among the many blots on the landscape of his diocese were twenty ejected ministers in Exeter who had 'nothing els to doe but to be gnaweing at the root of Governmt and religion, and to that purpose have many secret meetings and conventicles.'[78] In most cases—such as that of Jonathan Hanmer (deprived of his Tawton living by bishop's sentence in November 1662)—the prosecution was fairly straightforward; but Ward was frequently unjust and inconsistent.[79] Richard Binmore, the ejected rector of Woodleigh, was a particularly unfortunate victim. On being invited to deliver a funeral sermon, Binmore took the trouble to consult some local justices of the peace to ascertain whether this would be permissible. As the justices then assured him (erroneously) that the Act of Uniformity was not intended to prevent the occasional sermon, but rather to prevent 'a more constant stated Preaching,' Binmore preached at the service. He was immediately reported to Seth Ward, who served the justices with

75. CSPD 1663–64, 297.

76. BL MS Egerton 2543, fo. 28.

77. Bodl. MS Tanner 48, fo. 48.

78. Quoted in CR, pp. xiv, xxxviii; Jackson, "Nonconformists," 45.

79. CR, 247.

a certificate of the offence and insisted on a prosecution. The embarrassed magistrates duly ordered Binmore to be taken to Exeter jail, but not before the ejected minister had been permitted an interview with the bishop. Ward subjected Binmore to an abusive, hectoring diatribe, and eventually spared the ejected minister from prison only because 'he should but inrich him to send him to the Goal.'[80] This was in stark contrast to the bishop's treatment of his old college friend Richard Herring, whom he protected from prosecution after Herring was found to have instructed schoolboys in grammar; an illegal act on Herring's part, as he had been ejected from Drewsteignton, Devon in 1660, and more crucially had failed to subscribe to the Act of Uniformity.[81] Similarly, in contrast to his punctilious observance of the law in the case of the wretched Binmore, Ward winked at the occasional sermons of another ejected minister, Samuel Tapper, a Nonconformist who, strange as it may seem, was a regular dinner guest at the bishop's table.[82] Ward's otherwise relentless repression of Dissent continued when he exchanged the see of Exeter for that of Salisbury in 1667, although he was occasionally openly defied by ejected ministers there also. William Brice, formerly of Henley on Thames, candidly admitted that he had preached without a licence, but informed Ward that he 'should make bold to continue to do it, as Opportunity offer'd, unless his Lordship took more Care of the Souls of the poor People, and made better Provision for them.'[83]

The case of John Quick, prosecuted by Ward in December 1663 suggests that Cavalier-Anglicans did have a valid cause for concern in that several Nonconformist preachers clearly enjoyed a large following. Quick, although ejected from his curacy of Brixton near Plympton in 1662, had continued to preach there publicly for over a year before being discovered and jailed. On 19 December 1663 Ward reported to Gilbert Sheldon (who had by then become Archbishop of Canterbury) that Quick had had an audience of between 1,500 to 2,000 listeners on the Sunday when he was arrested and taken down from the pulpit.[84] Leading Puritan preachers, especially in London, had regularly drawn

80. Ibid., 56.
81. Ibid., 259.
82. Ibid., 475.
83. Ibid., 73.
84. Ibid., 402.

crowds of this magnitude before the Act of Uniformity, and several clues in the printed farewell sermons suggest that church pews were packed in the build-up to Black Bartholomew's Day. Whether or not such large audiences followed their preachers after nonconformity is a matter of conjecture. What is evident from Samuel Pepys' diary entries for 29 May 1663 is that services held in London that year to commemorate the restoration of Charles II were very poorly attended.[85] This apathy was sufficiently worrying for the authorities even before they were confronted with the possibility that large numbers of Dissenters had begun to plan direct action. Although, as already stated, many of the so-called plots were nothing of the sort, there were genuine conspiracies—not least the related series of plots known as the Northern Risings—which played a large part in precipitating further repressive legislation.

The Northern Risings took place principally in Yorkshire, Westmorland, and County Durham in October 1663. The rebels' chances of mobilising the populace were ruined by extremely bad weather, and by the fact that their plans had been betrayed to the local authorities, who were ready and waiting for them. Tory accounts of the Rising have often exaggerated the numbers involved in the insurrection. Whig and Nonconformist historians have regularly countered by observing that several of the rebel leaders were informers and agent provocateurs, who enticed many innocent men to take part. There is considerable truth in this, although, as Andrew Hopper has observed, Richard Greaves' painstaking work on radical activity in Restoration Britain in the 1980s inadvertently revived the old Tory case when he concluded that the Risings were 'a potentially large-scale insurrection,' and that they might have succeeded had the plotters made common cause with disaffected Presbyterians in Scotland.[86] As it was, the rebels lacked the suicidal fanaticism of Venner's Fifth Monarchists, and dispersed as soon as it became evident that there were insufficient numbers to achieve their aim. The authorities hunted them down nevertheless, and twenty-six men were condemned to be hanged, drawn, and quartered (two were eventually reprieved). Many more were thrown into prisons across the North and Midlands of England. The

85. Pepys, *Diary*, iv, 163; Appleby, *Black Bartholomew's Day*, 56–58.

86. Greaves, *Deliver Us from Evil*, 6, 228, quoted in Hopper, "Farnley Wood Plot," 282, 284.

fact that ex-parliamentarian soldiers, former Presbyterian army officers and several ejected ministers were implicated seemed to confirm
the Anglicans' fears of a Dissenter alliance. Some ministers—notably
Edward Richardson and Jeremiah Marsden—were clearly involved in
the plotting. The guilt of other Nonconformist clergy seems far less
certain: John Cromwell, arrested and accused of complicity in the
plot, petitioned the King in 1667 to complain that he and three colleagues were still imprisoned in Newark, despite the fact that nothing
had ever been proved against them.[87] Charles II's supporters exploited
the widespread alarm caused by the insurrection by forcing a repeal
of the Triennial Act through Parliament, and clamoured for further
repressive legislation to combat Dissent.

The refusal of Nonconformist ministers and congregations to
curtail their worship had already resulted in thousands being imprisoned across the counties and cities of England. Thomas Palmer, the
former rector of Ashton-on-Trent, Derbyshire, had twice been imprisoned for illegal preaching and attending conventicles before he was
incarcerated in Nottingham in connection with the Northern Rising.[88]
In the absence of specific prohibitions comparable to the Quaker
Act, many attendees at both Presbyterian and Independent religious
meetings had been charged under Elizabethan legislation. Such
measures had snared John Bunyan, and had even led to death sentences being passed against twelve General Baptists from Aylesbury,
Buckinghamshire in 1664 (all of which were commuted by royal
pardon).[89] At the same time, more and more of the farewell sermons
delivered by the ministers who had departed on Black Bartholomew's
Day were being illegally printed and distributed, mainly in pamphlets
and increasingly in huge compendiums. By late 1663, Roger L'Estrange
deduced that there were ten or twelve impressions of the three largest
collections of farewell sermons in circulation, a total of around 30,000
copies. Although his main reason in gathering these statistics was in
order to undermine his rival, John Berkenhead, and acquire the post
of Surveyor of the Press, there is reason to believe that L'Estrange's

87. Hopper, "Farnley Wood Plot," 287–88; *CR*, 147, 339, 410; Hutton, *Restoration*,
205–6.

88. CR, 380.

89. Watts, *Dissenters*, 224; Coffey, *Persecution and Toleration*, 169; Harris, *Restoration*, 76–77.

calculations were substantially correct.[90] In these collections moderate and radical exegesis was inextricably mixed together, together with extremely provocative Biblical references, and discussion of sensitive political topics such as the conflict between divine and secular authority, the limits of kingship, the conflict between faith and obedience, and evocative references to King Jesus.[91] Gilbert Sheldon's exasperation at these developments was evident when he wrote to the Duke of Ormonde in September 1663, 'Tis only a resolute execution of the law that might cure this disease—all other remedies have and will increase it—and 'tis necessary that they who will not be governed as men by reason and persuasion should be governed as beasts by power of force. All other courses will be ineffectual, ever have been so, ever will be.'[92]

The Northern Risings were therefore not seen by Cavalier-Anglicans as an isolated event, but rather the tip of a dunghill of disaffected murmurings, defiance, and sedition. Just as Venner's Rising had enabled the more reactionary elements in Parliament to gain support for the Act of Uniformity, so now the growing sense of moral panic allowed Sheldon and his allies to extend the restrictions of the Quaker Act to Presbyterians, Congregationalists, and Baptists. An attempt had been made to pass a bill through Parliament banning non-Anglican meetings in 1663. It was now revived and passed through the two Houses with ease, opposed only by few voices such as that of Lord Wharton. Other Puritan aristocrats were rather more concerned to ensure that activities in their own houses would be exempt from searches. The Conventicle Act (1664) was, in essence, an extension of the earlier Quaker Act, in that any person of the age of sixteen or above who was found present at any assembly of more than five persons in England, Wales, or Berwick-on-Tweed gathered together for religious worship in form other than that conducted according to the liturgy and practice of the Church of England was liable to a fine of £5. The punishment for a second offence was £10. Those unable to pay such fines were liable to imprisonment. The punishment for a third offence was a fine of £100 or transportation for seven years. Those who

90. L'Estrange, *Considerations and Proposals*, sig. [A3v]; Appleby, *Black Bartholomew's Day*, 139–40, 189.

91. Fairclough, *Pastor's Legacy*, 100; *Third Volume*, 24, 26; *England's Remembrancer*, 122; Swinnock, *Pastor's Farewell*, 49, 61, 62; Lamb, *Royal Presence*, sig. [Cv], E2.

92. Bodl. Carte MS 45, fo. 151 (Gilbert Sheldon to James, Duke of Ormonde, 15 September 1663).

were unable to pay for their own transportation were liable to be sent overseas as indentured servants. Indentured servitude was in essence temporary slavery, and given the poor conditions endured by indentured servants on Barbados and elsewhere it was often tantamount to a death sentence. A number of clauses pushed the Conventicle Act beyond the traditional boundaries of English law: firstly, there was to be no reprieve even for those who repented of their actions; secondly magistrates, constables, and even high sheriffs who failed to enforce the Act were to be punished; thirdly, conviction rested not on the verdict of a jury, but upon the opinion of two justices of the peace or the chief magistrate of any corporation. Members of the House of Lords who offended were liable for a fine of £10 and £20 for the first and second offences, and on a third offence were entitled to stand before a jury of their peers. Ronald Hutton has suggested that the stipulation that the Act should expire after four years might reflect an attempt by certain MPs to ensure the Cavalier Parliament would remain in being; that is, they intended by this to counterbalance the repeal of the Triennial Act, rather than give any hope to Dissenters that their repression would be temporary.[93]

Despite the introduction of significantly more draconian legislation, most latter-day historians consider the persecution of Dissent at this time to have been sporadic. As had been the case since the restoration of the monarchy, the eagerness of local officials to pursue and prosecute Dissenters varied hugely from region to region. If it could be said that persecution was more likely to occur in towns and cities than in the countryside, it could be argued that nonconformity was more likely to be encountered in strength in urban areas. According to Anthony Fletcher, 'the story is rather one of localised battles between particular groups of dissenting congregations and either individual JPs or a few strongly motivated justices.'[94] There is certainly evidence to support this view, but it perhaps underplays the taste for persecution that existed within the wider population. In early modern England justices could only function effectively if a significant proportion of the population were willing to support their initiatives. The injuries and occasional fatalities inflicted by troopers,

93. 16 Car. II cap. 4 (Conventicle Act 1664); Hutton, *Restoration*, 208.

94. Fletcher, "Enforcement of the Conventicle Acts," 245; Coffey, *Persecution and Toleration*, 170; Greaves, *Enemies under His Feet*, 132–33.

militia and members of the public when breaking up Quaker meetings and even those of more conventional Nonconformists suggest that in many areas Cavalier-Anglican justices and deputy lieutenants could be more aggressive because they enjoyed a significant level of popular support—that is, a significant level of grassroots antipathy towards dissenting communities.

Perhaps because it demonstrated his inability to control the Cavalier Parliament, Charles had temporarily lost the will to protect Dissenters in general. He had certainly turned against Quakers, who had been heavily implicated in the Northern Rising.[95] In part the motivation for antipathy towards Dissent was as it had been in previous eras towards Catholics, political as much as it was religious. As Tim Harris has written, 'Protestants did not believe in persecuting people for their religious opinions; that was a popish principle. Nonconformist conventicles were hunted down because they were regarded as nests of sedition—places where "Seditious Sectaries and other disloyall Persons" met "under pretence of tender Consciences" to "contrive Insurrections . . ."'[96]

Just as the Quarter Sessions records of the 1650s are littered with petitions from maimed parliamentarian war veterans and war widows—people who had sealed their adherence to the Good Old Cause with their blood (whether they had originally intended to or no)—so the records from the 1660s are littered with petitions from maimed royalist soldiers and war widows, who had similarly paid a heavy price fighting for the opposing cause. Religion, politics, and ideology were all inextricably intermixed in these competing causes; but it was through religion that they were most often articulated. It was equally evident, not least in the rhetoric of the annual 30 January and 29 May sermons that these religious divisions had now taken on all the attributes of a blood feud.

By 1664 the machinery of repression was firmly in place. Quarter Sessions papers even in areas not particularly known for zealous persecution, such as Kent, show that the justices, deputy lieutenants, militia, and regular army now had considerable experience in the detection and interdiction of disaffected groups.[97] Particularly intense

95. Hutton, *Restoration*, 208.

96. Harris, *Restoration*, 55.

97. E.g. Centre for Kentish Studies, CKS-Q/SB 9, fos. 2–9.

levels of persecution were experienced by Dissenters in London and its hinterlands, Bristol, Chester, Durham, Somerset, and Staffordshire. Prisons in these areas—unhealthy at the best of times—were full of Nonconformists, and some 230 men and women were sentenced to transportation. Hutton has suggested that some magistrates deliberately handed down light sentences for initial transgressions to encourage Dissenters to commit their three offences as quickly as possible, and thus become liable for the worst punishments the courts could inflict. By contrast in places such as Gloucestershire and Norwich persecution was virtually non-existent, and Dissenters were able to conduct their worship with little or no interference.[98] Even within those areas where persecution was heaviest patterns of sentencing were inconsistent. Quakers scorned to use the evasion techniques practised by Presbyterians, Congregationalists, and Baptists at their meetings and thus suffered disproportionately. Richard Baxter admitted that those of his persuasion had benefitted because the Quakers had attracted such attention to themselves.[99]

In 1665 plague crossed the Channel, bringing perhaps the worst visitation since the Black Death of 1348. Over the next two years it spread across England and Wales, mainly through the cloth trade routes. As London citizens began to die in droves, the wealthy and well connected fled. King and Parliament removed to Oxford, leaving George Monck, Duke of Albemarle and his army in charge of London. England was by now at war with the Dutch and, with the economic and political life of the capital seriously disrupted, the authorities were understandably more nervous than usual. The traditional ties between English religious dissenters and the Netherlands gave rise to suspicions of treasonable collaboration, and Albemarle kept his soldiers busy rounding up both Quakers and more conventional Nonconformists. Many of these unfortunate individuals subsequently died of plague in the unhealthy environs of London's prisons; including Richard Flavell, a minister who had come to London after having been ejected from his Gloucestershire living, only to perish in Newgate.[100] Hundreds of arrests were also made in the provinces. Charles appointed his brother, James, Duke of York, to supervise operations in the areas so recently

---

98. Hutton, *Restoration*, 209–10.

99. *Reliquiae Baxterianae*, ii, 436.

100. CR, 201.

affected by the Northern Rising. Predictably, little effort was made to distinguish been radicals and moderates, with the result that peaceable Presbyterian ministers such as Philip Henry found themselves caught in the net.[101]

Whatever else he may have been, Gilbert Sheldon was no coward. He remained working in Lambeth throughout the epidemic. Similarly, at least nineteen Anglican clergy stayed to comfort their London congregations, and eleven of them paid for this devotion with their lives. Several of their colleagues, however, deserted their parishes in panic. Nonconformist clergy who had remained in the city promptly climbed into the empty pulpits, or held prayer meetings in private houses to bring spiritual solace to people by now desperately afraid that judgement day was approaching. Calamy records the names of fourteen such ministers who preached in London during these troubled times, the best known being Thomas Vincent, formerly of St. Mary Magdalen, Milk Street.[102] Several more ministers are known to have been living in London and may also have participated in the work. A number of others, Richard Baxter among them, moved out of the city, taking the plague with them in some cases.[103] Relatively little work has been done to investigate the conduct of Nonconformist clergy (and their episcopalian counterparts, for that matter) in provincial areas affected by the Great Plague, although it has been suggested that matters in the grievously afflicted cloth-working town of Colchester in Essex followed a similar course to London. The former Colchester minister Owen Stockton may well have engaged in pastoral work in the plague-ridden town, for example, and Obediah Grew certainly did so in Coventry.[104] In some cases the courage of certain Nonconformists drew praise even from Anglicans. When the impeccably royalist third Earl of Devonshire, Lord Lieutenant of Derbyshire, received a request that the ejected minister Thomas Stanley be expelled from his residence at Eyam, the Earl replied 'that it was more reasonable, that the whole Country should in more than Words testifie their Thankfulness to him, who together with his Care of the Town had taken such Care,

101. Greaves, *Enemies under His Feet*, 35.

102. CR, 6, 101, 108, 114, 176, 206, 212, 295, 312, 356, 361, 497, 503, 529.

103. Ibid., 149, 168, 412; *Reliquiae Baxterianae*, ii, 448.

104. Dr. Williams's Library, DWL 24.9, fo. 1; CR , 236; Hutton, *Restoration*, 233.

as none else did, to prevent the Infection of the Towns adjacent.'[105] If Nonconformist clergy had demonstrated their worth by preaching and pastoral work in the affected areas, the plague had also worked to their disadvantage. The finances of many merchants who had previously provided financial support for the Nonconformist ministry had been badly affected. Meanwhile, the ecclesiastical authorities were stung by pamphlets deriding those Church of England clergy who had fled from their livings in panic, allowing Nonconformists to take their places. Even a pamphlet such as *A Friendly Letter to the Flying Clergy*, which praised Archbishop Sheldon for remaining at his post, gave a damaging impression of Anglican pusillanimity.[106] This public perception was later reinforced by Daniel Defoe in his fictitious *Journal of the Plague Year*, and even more so by Richard Baxter's published memoirs.[107] The appropriation of the vacant London pulpits, however, was not in itself responsible for the Five Mile Act. Among the items that had been occupying Sheldon's attention even before the Great Plague marooned him in Lambeth Palace had been the results of a questionnaire that he had sent to his subordinate bishops in order to ascertain the state of the ministry within the Church of England. The responses that he received in return included alarming appraisals regarding the potential scope of Nonconformist activities and the extent to which the ejected ministers continued to exercise influence over their former congregations.[108] The various concerns of the Lords and Commons meeting at Oxford in October 1665 also served to fuel their anxieties regarding Dissent, and in particular the need to restrict the movements of ejected ministers. Michael Watts has opined that 'it is possible to justify the Conventicle Act by reason of the Cavalier Parliament's fear of rebellion, but no such excuse can be offered in defence of the Five Mile Act of 1665.'[109] In fact, a deteriorating military situation coupled with political and economic dislocation caused by the worst plague for three hundred years had rendered a fragile state more vulnerable to sedition than ever before. The Cavalier Parliament

105. *CR*, 459.

106. W., *Friendly Letter to the Flying Clergy*, 2–3

107. Defoe, *Journal*, 175, 235; *Reliquiae Baxterianae*, iii, 2–3; CSPD 1665–6, 20; CR, lvi; *Pulpit to be Let*, n.p.

108. Hutton, *Restoration*, 232, 358.

109. Watts, *Dissenters*, 225.

probably had more excuse for anxiety in 1665 rather than less. As ever, Clarendon recoiled from such indiscriminate repression, and so joined the earls of Manchester and Southampton, and Lord Wharton, in opposing the bill.[110]

The preamble to the Five Mile (or 'Oxford') Act declared that many clergy who had refused to subscribe to the various declarations required by the Act of Uniformity had nevertheless continued to preach illegally, and conducted worship at meetings in contravention of the law. Such people were now to be required, as from 24 March 1666, not to live or approach within five miles of any city, corporate town or borough of England, Wales or Berwick-on-Tweed, unless passing through whilst travelling to another destination. The ejected ministers were in addition forbidden to live or come within five miles of any parish, town or place where they had had a ministry since the Act of Oblivion (1660), unless they first took the oath of non-resistance detailed in the Act of Uniformity, with the additional clause that they would not seek any change of government, either in church or state. This became known as the 'Oxford Oath.' The fine for each transgression was to be £40. Any cleric or lay person refusing to take the oath was further forbidden to teach or take on boarders to instruct, on pain of a fine of £40 for each offence. Any two or more justices were henceforth empowered to imprison any found guilty of such offences for a period of six months without bail.[111]

Although relatively few ministers appear to have been prosecuted under the Five Mile Act, it is plain that this new legislation made life much harder for the Nonconformist clergy. Many ejected ministers and their families who were already living in straitened financial circumstances now experienced extreme difficulties in finding willing landlords, or houses at affordable rents elsewhere, even when they could actually find communities far enough away from a city, independent borough, or parish where they had previously preached. 'By this Act,' Baxter wrote, 'the Case of the Ministers was made so hard, that many thought themselves necessitated to break it, not only by the necessity of their office, but by a natural impossibility of keeping it, unless they should murder themselves and their Families.'[112] There were

---

110. Greaves, *Enemies under His Feet*, 35.

111. 17 Car. II, cap. 2 (Five Mile Act 1665); Browning, *Documents*, 382–84.

112. *Reliquiae Baxterianae*, iii, 3.

odd exceptions. Thomas Spademan, the ejected rector of Althorpe in Lincolnshire, was permitted to remain in the parish by magistrates and deputy lieutenants impressed by his proven loyalty and peaceably demeanour.[113] Mansfield, in Nottinghamshire, provided a refuge for a group of eight ejected ministers led by Robert Porter, on whose activities the famous Presbyterian chapel in the town appears to have been founded.[114]

If the Five Mile Act proved reasonably effective in inhibiting moderate nonconformity (as opposed to Quakers and radicals), the Great Fire of London proved to have equally far-reaching consequences. More than two-thirds of the city was destroyed in the conflagration that raged between 2 and 6 September 1666. Although remarkably few people were killed, the Fire had an incalculable effect on the course of Dissent and even on the ultimate stability of the Restoration state. The repression of public preaching that had followed the Act of Uniformity had caused Dissent in all its shapes and forms to rely hugely on the printed word. The printing industry was restricted by law and tradition almost exclusively to London. Weighed down by thousands of kilos of metal type, and needing to stay near the source of the raw materials of their trade, stationers had been less able than most to move their businesses away from the plague-ridden city, and as a consequence suffered from the deaths of many skilled print workers and from the deaths or flight of customers. For an industry notoriously prone to cash flow problems this was serious enough, but worse was to come. The immolation of the neighbourhoods of St. Pauls and Cheapside during the Great Fire destroyed the stock of many of London's booksellers, and the equipment and metal type of most of London's printers. Fate had preserved the business of the royalist stationer Henry Herringman, who proceeded to help colleagues of similar persuasion, but the fortunes of many stationers on whom Dissenters had relied were ruined. The flow of printed farewell sermons had begun to wane even before the Great Fire as the market had become saturated, but now the scarcity of materials, the drastically reduced capacity of the industry, and the soaring cost of book production all served to ensure that the output of Dissenting literature was

---

113. CR, 453.

114. University of Nottingham, "Records of the Old Meeting House, Mansfield," para 1.

severely affected.[115] Valuable collections of books owned by conformist and Nonconformist clergy in the city had also been perished in the flames, as had the libraries of many provincial Dissenters, 'which had been lately brought up to the City'—although at whose behest Baxter neglected to record.[116]

It emerged at the trials of some ex-New Model Army officers in April that radicals had been plotting against the state and that the Dutch had been in contact with a number of disaffected groups to explore the possibility of destabilising the English war effort. In such circumstances it was inevitable that rumours would emerge that an alliance between Presbyterians, France, and the United Provinces lay behind the Great Fire. Within a short space of time, however, the mob and Parliament grew bored with this unlikely notion and shifted the focus of their moral panic onto more traditional scapegoats in the shape of Roman Catholics.[117] Anti-popery, which had been fairly muted since the Restoration (even in the farewell sermons of ejected ministers), was thus rapidly rekindled and would remain an important factor in political calculations until the end of the Stuart dynasty. Due not least to this factor, events over the next few years indicate that persecution temporarily became less onerous for Dissent in many areas of England. This was particular fortuitous for the Dissenting academies, several of which had by now begun to form.

Apart from the clergy ousted from their livings, many heads of university colleges, fellows and tutors had been ejected from Oxford and Cambridge.[118] Since 1662 Oxford had required all students to subscribe to the Thirty-Nine Articles, and to swear the Oath of Supremacy in order to matriculate. Both Oxford and Cambridge had made graduation conditional on the candidate formally subscribing to the doctrine and government of the Church of England. Clearly, this was unacceptable to conscientious Nonconformists. The richest parents could afford to send their children to be educated at Glasgow

---

115. Blagden, *Stationers' Company*, 215–17; Reddaway, *Rebuilding of London*, 25, 54; Bell, *Great Fire of London*, 34, 129, 130, 225–27; *CSPD 1667–8*, 503; Gaskell, *New Introduction to Bibliography*, 37–39.

116. *Reliquiae Baxterianae*, iii, 18. Early modern regimes often seized private libraries in the interests of national security (the confiscation of Sir Robert Cotton's collection in 1629 being a case in point).

117. Porter, *Great Fire of London*, 61; Greaves, *Enemies under His Feet*, 34.

118. CR, xiii–xiv.

or Edinburgh, or perhaps Leiden or Utrecht. For most families, of course, this was not an option. The demand for an alternative, godly university education closer to home thus grew very quickly, as did the desire of several ejected ministers and tutors to provide it. All schools and academies technically required a licence from the episcopal authorities in order to operate. As it was pointless to apply for such a licence, the first dissenting academies naturally led a somewhat discreet existence. Two of the earliest institutions, run by Theophilus Gale and Charles Morton respectively, opened in Newington Green. Further north, Thomas Cole's academy in Oxfordshire operated from at least 1667 (possibly earlier), although it may only have provided a lay education. Other private institutions were founded, possibly slightly later, in Worcestershire and Shropshire.[119] The curriculum at the largest academies covered the complete range of university subjects. Morton's academy, whose alumni eventually including Daniel Defoe and Samuel Wesley, appears to have been particularly well provided with laboratory equipment as well as reading material.[120] Such facilities suggest that although most dissenting academies were discreet, they can hardly have been invisible. There were reasons, of course, why the academies were able to avoid closure during this period.

First and foremost, most Dissenters had proved to be loyal subjects, with many declaring their willingness to defend the realm against Dutch invasion. Similarly, although they were sympathetic towards the efforts of their co-religionists to resist the imposition of prelacy in Scotland, English Presbyterians did not rise in arms to support that resistance when it turned into armed conflict. In the midst of the Galloway Rising of November 1666 the Scottish rebels themselves declared that they were willing to suspend hostilities in order to fight any Dutch troops who dared to land. The government nevertheless still had no hesitation in crushing the insurrection and exacting

119. Material for this paragraph has been obtained from: Parker, *Dissenting Academies in England*; McLachlan, *English Education Under the Test Acts*; Ashley Smith, *Birth of Modern Education*; and the online resource of the Dr. Williams's Centre for Dissenting Studies, *Dissenting Academies Project*. I am grateful for Mark Burden's helpful comments, following his conference paper "Reading the Bible at the Dissenters Academies 1660–1720," which was delivered at the *King James Bible Conference*, University of York, 8 July 2011.

120. Girdler, "Defoe's Education," 575.

brutal retribution.[121] The events of the Galloway Rising appear to have gone some way towards restoring Charles II's confidence in moderate English Dissent, as he now initiated a series of reconciliatory measures. Imprisoned Dissenters found themselves invited to petition for pardon and release, and orders were issued for the freeing of notable figures such as the Quaker leader George Fox. John Bunyan was not yet favoured, and remained in Bedford gaol; although he had, of course, used the time to write and publish many of his most famous works, such as *Grace Abounding* (1666). As ever, such toleration may well have been Charles's natural inclination, but there were also now political and economic imperatives. The escalating cost of the war against the Dutch (who had now allied themselves with France) had placed huge pressures on over-stretched royal finances, and measures were even then being taken to expand and modernise the tax-gathering apparatus. There was every indication that unprecedentedly high levels of taxation, and innovations such as the Hearth Tax were reducing the government's low level of popularity still further and generating widespread disquiet.[122] The King was well aware that such domestic conflicts undermined his capacity to wage war against the Franco-Dutch alliance. Given that many Presbyterians were entrepreneurs and employers, toleration was beneficial to the economy and, by extension, to the war effort.

The monarchy's need to widen the base of its moral support became even more urgent in the blaze of criticism (principally from outraged Cavalier-Anglicans) that followed an unprecedented military disaster in the Medway in June 1667. The Dutch navy's success in destroying the English fleet at anchor and calmly towing away the English flagship, the *Royal Charles*, was a shuddering blow to national prestige and the political nation's confidence in the royal government. Faced with the necessity of salvaging the dented reputation of the Crown, Charles sacrificed Clarendon to public opinion.

The brief abatement of religious persecution during the late 1660s and early 1670s has sometimes been ascribed to Clarendon's political demise and the coming to power of that religiously heterodox

---

121. Greaves, *Enemies under His Feet*, 73; Hutton, *Restoration*, 264; Harris, *Restoration*, 118–19.

122. E.g., *My Lord Lucas His Speech*, 2–4.

inner council of royal advisers known as the Cabal.[123] However, apart from indications that the tide of events had already been flowing in favour of toleration, Clarendon had regularly demonstrated a willingness to include moderate Nonconformists in the political nation. More specifically, he had consistently opposed most of the penal legislation, which was (much) later ridiculously and erroneously labelled the 'Clarendon Code.' It is true that no member of the Cabal was an orthodox Anglican. Lord Clifford had consistently supported freedom of worship for Catholics and Nonconformists, and was already well on the way towards becoming a Roman Catholic himself. Sir Henry Bennett, Lord Arlington, in his capacity as Secretary of State, had often collaborated with Sheldon during the early years of the Restoration. Ostensibly Anglican during his lifetime, Arlington would declare himself a Catholic on his deathbed. The Duke of Buckingham and Lord Ashley (soon to be Earl of Shaftesbury) were both known to be sympathetic to Dissent. Why Buckingham had become a sympathiser is difficult to explain: despite his orthodox Anglican upbringing within the royal household, the Duke's closest confidant, secretary, and legal adviser for most of his political career was the notorious radical John Wildman. The fifth member of the Cabal, the Duke of Lauderdale had recently overseen the suppression of Presbyterian resistance in Scotland, but as John Maitland, the plain covenanting colonel, he had once fought alongside Fairfax and Cromwell. It was perhaps more predictable, then, that once the furore following the Galloway Rising had died down, Lauderdale threw his weight behind a policy to ensure that 'peaceable dissenters [in Scotland] may be endeavoured to be reclaimed,' presenting these proposals to the King in September 1667.[124] This strange mix of ministers, and indeed the policy of toleration itself, suited Charles's preferred political strategy of divide and rule. He had continued to maintain a balance between several opposing factions at court, and his policies at this time suggest that he was happy to countenance a similar religious heterodoxy among provincial ruling elites in the country at large. In this way, as all sides naturally looked to him to resolve their inevitable disputes, Charles now sought to reaffirm the role of the Crown not simply as the font of authority and justice, but also as the guarantor of unity and peace. The

123. E.g., Watts, *Dissenters*, 226.
124. Quoted in Greaves, *Enemies under His Feet*, 82.

Cabal was therefore a catalyst for toleration only in as much as it was a central arena for the power struggles resulting from this strategy. It was never a unified group of tolerationists with a common agenda to ease the burden of persecution.

At the same time as these changes were taking effect in government, Nonconformist clergy suddenly became more militant in their public worship. In fire-ravaged London, ejected ministers began to defy the Five Mile Act, preaching openly in their old neighbourhoods. Richard Baxter later recalled the mood of his London colleagues at this time: 'The Churches being burnt, and the Parish Ministers gone (for want of places and maintenance) the *Nonconformists* were now more resolved than ever, to preach till they were imprisoned.'[125] This appears to have encouraged brethren in other areas to follow suit, particularly in Bristol where the congregation at Broadmead enjoyed 'liberty for about four years after, in some good measure', and in Yarmouth, where the ejected town lecturer William Bridge resumed preaching, and some hundreds of Congegationalists founded a regular meeting hall.[126] Leaders among the Nonconformist laity also began to find the confidence to reassert themselves, mounting so many successful bids for places as magistrates, aldermen and other positions in the capital that, in the estimation of Gary De Krey, by 1669–70, 'the Anglican royalist monopoly on office-holding in London had been decisively broken.'[127]

This renewed political activism on the part of Dissent brought unwelcome consequences. The King could not afford to allow the laws to be flaunted with such impunity, even if he personally disapproved of the penal legislation. In 1668 and again in 1669 royal proclamations were issued, ordering religious meetings of Dissenters in London to cease forthwith.[128] These proved counterproductive not least because they were almost completely ignored. Conformist MPs were still the majority interest in the Commons, but felt increasingly besieged as the visible presence of Dissent had grown to such an extent that it now posed a threat to Anglican control of the capital. Among the many incidents that aggravated their anxieties were the so-called Bawdy

125. *Reliquiae Baxterianae*, iii, 19.

126. Porter, *Great Fire of London*, 170; *CSPD* 1675–6, 18, 275; *CSPD* 1676–7, 155; Watts, *Dissenters*, 245.

127. De Krey, *London and the Restoration*, 99.

128. *Proclamation*, 1668 (Wing C3340); *Proclamation* 1669 (Wing C3217).

House Riots, which took place during the Easter of 1668. Riots were fairly common in early modern England, but the disorder on this occasion was particularly ferocious and long-lived, and notable for the huge number of rioters involved. Unusually also, otherwise respectable Nonconformists had seemingly joined in with the normal holiday mobs of apprentices in attacking the brothels. Perhaps even more alarming to Cavalier-Anglicans was the discovery that the King had no wish to renew the 1664 Conventicle Act, and was, on the contrary, desirous of sponsoring a toleration bill. With its renewal actively obstructed by Charles's supporters in the Commons the Conventicle Act duly expired on 1 March 1669. When, in November, MPs attempted to draw up new penal legislation to replace the Act (and proposed to delay supplying the royal coffers with money until its progress was assured) Charles prorogued the session. He and certain members of the Cabal were meanwhile conducting secret negotiations with Louis XIV in an effort to raise money by shadier means. The moderately secret aspects of the treaty would prove controversial in themselves: England was to ally with Catholic France, help Louis conquer the Netherlands and receive certain Dutch territories and other spoils of war as a reward. The most secret undertakings, known only to Charles, Clifford, Arlington and the Earl of Arundel, were far more ominous: that Charles should himself convert to Catholicism and obtain legal toleration for English Catholics. In return Louis agreed to supply £150,000 and to send French troops to England to help put down the anticipated domestic resistance. Charles's inclination for toleration had degenerated to little more than a lever to gain political and financial advantage.

By the time Parliament reconvened in February 1670, England was officially part of a triple alliance with the Netherlands and Sweden against France, but MPs seem already to have had wind of Charles's dealings with Louis. They remained reluctant to vote the King an adequate supply of money, preferring instead to investigate the inept handling of the recent Dutch war and corruption in government. These initiatives were largely supported by Presbyterian sympathisers in the House such as John Birch. Cavalier-Anglican MPs, however, were also still intent on pushing English religion back onto the path mapped out by the 1662 settlement, and renewed their efforts to put through legislation to replace the old Conventicle Act. In this they were seconded by allies in the Lords led, as ever, by Gilbert Sheldon. Anthony Fletcher has observed that the new Conventicle bill 'had a mixed reception and a rough passage.'[129] John Birch attacked the proposed legislation, outlining the harm it was likely to do to the national economy. Surprisingly, he found a supporter in Sir Robert Howard, an MP with impeccable Anglican credentials who had served in the royalist army in the civil wars. Howard equated the proposed legislation with the persecution carried out by the Duke of Alva in the Netherlands; a rather extreme comparison, which was seized on by the proponents of the bill. Replying to Howard, Henry Coventry declared flatly that there 'never was there a more merciful bill that punishes neither with blood or banishment a people that have punished us with both of these.'[130] With no money as yet received from his cousin Louis, Charles was forced to give his assent to this Second Conventicle Act, in return for promises that Parliament would thereupon vote him an adequate supply of money and desist in their efforts to impeach his beleaguered government officials.

Despite some caveats introduced in the Lords, allowing the King some future room for manoeuvre, the Second Conventicle Act (1670) imposed severe new restrictions on non-Anglican worship. The new Act was aimed not so much at rank and file Nonconformists as at their ministers, together with those who provided meeting venues and magistrates who omitted to prosecute them. Ordinary people found guilty of attending an illegal conventicle were now to be fined five shillings for their first offence, and ten shillings for each offence thereafter. If any proved too poor to pay the fine, and had insufficient possessions to make up the difference, their fine was to be transferred to the wealthier worshipers arrested at the same meeting. Preachers and owners of meeting places were to be fined £20 for a first offence, with a penalty of £40 for each offence thereafter. Added incentives were given to informers, who stood to collect a third of the fines resulting from each incident. In an era that was something of a golden age for snitching, this legislation allowed some particularly vile individuals to present themselves as agents of the public good, whilst spreading anxiety and disharmony within local communities. As Richard Greaves has noted, 'informers were not only persons of obnoxious character

129. Fletcher, "Enforcement of the Conventicle Acts," 236.

130. Quoted in Witcombe, *Charles II and the Cavalier House of Commons*, 100–101.

but doubly offensive because they could not be cross-examined.'[131] In an ominous departure from earlier legislation, the 1670 Act allowed a single justice of the peace to convict offenders without trial. A confession, the testimony of two sworn witnesses, or 'notorious evidence and circumstance of the fact' were now held to be sufficient evidence for conviction. Only those whose fine was liable to exceed ten shillings were to be allowed the right to trial by jury. Magistrates who failed in their duty with regard to the Act were to be fined £100. Unlike the first Conventicle Act, the Act of 1670 was declared to be permanent.[132]

The new legislation compelled justices to take action where many had previously not done so. Moreover, their performance was increasingly being monitored by bishops and deputy lieutenants, overwhelmingly Cavalier-Anglican in temperament (the sponsor of the Act, Sir John Bramston, was a notably active deputy lieutenant in Essex). Nevertheless, there are indications that despite the additional pressure placed on justices, the application of the Act was distinctly patchy. There were certainly magistrates with an appetite for persecution, such as Sir Daniel Fleming in Westmorland, Sir Roger Bradshaigh in Lancashire, and Robert Thoroton in Nottinghamshire. Believing, like their Suffolk colleague Edmund Bohun, that the aim of nonconformity was 'the destruction of the monarchy and the bringing in of a republic,' such men fined and imprisoned with an almost psychopathic energy.[133] However, such zealots frequently found themselves isolated, and obstructed by fellow justices, jurymen and petty constables less eager to persecute their neighbours. There is some disagreement among historians as to whether this new Conventicle Act was easier to enforce in urban areas. However, an informer opined at the time that whilst it was relatively easy to suppress conventicles in rural areas (because he believed that country people tended to be more dependent on the local gentry and the culture of deference was still quite strong), 'in corporations it will never be carried through by the magistrates or inhabitants, their livelihood consisting altogether in trade, and this depending one on another, so that when any of these

---

131. Greaves, *Enemies at His Feet*, 155.

132. 22 Car. II, cap. 1 (Conventicle Act 1670); Kenyon, *Stuart Constitution*, 383–84.

133. Fletcher, "Enforcement of the Conventicle Acts," 238–42.

shall appear to act in the least measure, their trade shall decline, and . . . their credit with it.'[134]

Many justices remained disinclined to utilise informers. One justice in London even bound over an informer for intruding into his chambers.[135] This continued reticence, despite the strictures of the 1670 Act, might have arisen from the justices' personal religious sympathies, or from considerations of trade; it might also have reflected caution in the face of widespread public anger. Some 12,000 Dissenters were reported to have attended conventicles in London in May 1670, and many were clearly determined to resist unto blood. Street violence became more prevalent, especially in the capital, and Dissenters frequently gave as good as they got. As the clashes became more frequent, many arrests were made. Ejected ministers and old Cromwellian officers were observed travelling into London to lend their support, giving the government and the Cavalier-Anglican community cause to fear yet again that civil war was imminent.[136] In the face of needlessly harsh repression, the various Dissenting communities were beginning to make common cause, and were being driven to such a pitch of frustration and desperation as to make conflict inevitable. Not for the first time, several figures close to the centre of power, such as Arlington's protégé Joseph Williamson felt that persecution was counterproductive, as it served only to radicalise and alienate hitherto peaceable people.[137]

As far as the King's own thoughts can ever be gleaned, the text of the Declaration of Indulgence (1672) suggests that he was just as frustrated as Williamson. The time had come, Charles now declared, for the Crown 'to make use of that supreme power in ecclesiastical matters which is not only inherent in us but hath been declared and recognised to be so by several statutes and acts of Parliament.'[138] Assuring Anglicans that the existing doctrine and government of the Church of England would remain inviolate, he summarily suspended the penal laws against Dissenters and Catholics, and ordered that

134. CSPD 1675–6, 1; Stater, *Noble Government*, 111; Fletcher, "Enforcement of the Conventicle Acts," 245; Watts, *Dissenters*, 245–46.

135. Watts, *Dissenters*, 245–46.

136. De Krey, *London and the Restoration*, 110–11; Greaves, *Enemies at His Feet*, 157–59.

137. CSPD 1671, 496.

138. Kenyon, *Stuart Constitution*, 407.

those currently imprisoned under such laws be released. After twelve years of almost continuous imprisonment, even John Bunyan was now freed. Charles proposed to allow all Dissenting sects henceforth to meet and worship publicly, and Catholics to do so privately. As ever, there was heart-searching within Nonconformist ranks, as they agonised over the legality of the suspending power and the concessions given to Catholics; but the fact that 1,434 Nonconformist pastors chose to accept the King's invitation to apply for preaching licences shows that most had now come to accept that the breach with the Church of England was insuperable. Some indication of the demographics of moderate nonconformity (the Quakers having refused to participate) can be gleaned from the details of those clergy who now applied for a licence: 854 applicants declared themselves to be Presbyterians, 375 Congregationalists, with 202 describing themselves as Baptists and three of indeterminate denomination. Almost two-thirds of those licensed had been ejected under the Acts of 1660 and 1662. A. G. Matthews has rather pessimistically deduced from this that fewer Nonconformist clergy persevered with their ministry after 1662 than has sometimes been claimed.[139] On the other hand, the fact that around one-third of the licensed preachers had commenced their ministry after Black Bartholomew's Day suggests that nonconformity had thrived in adversity.

The King's repeated efforts to ease the condition of Dissenters over the first twelve years of his reign indicate that he was genuinely in favour of toleration. The timing of the Declaration of Indulgence, however, reveals that this enthusiasm was driven by political opportunism as much as altruism. Well aware of the furore his initiative would provoke, Charles had issued the Declaration on 15 March 1672, whilst Parliament was in recess. In doing so, he had partially fulfilled the secret undertakings made to Louis to advance the Catholic cause in England. Two days later, in compliance with another clause of the Secret Treaty of Dover, Charles broke the Triple Alliance and joined his cousin in declaring war on the Netherlands.

War, as ever, proved ruinously expensive. By February 1673 it became necessary to recall Parliament in order to obtain a fresh supply of money. The House of Commons returned in a fine rage, but for once the energies of the Anglican majority were not directed against

139. CR, xv.

Dissenters. Certainly, the House lost no time in informing the King that he had been 'very much misinformed' in assuming that he had any right to suspend legislation regarding ecclesiastical matters. After intimating that they would vote him a generous supply for the war MPs made it clear that no money would be forthcoming until he backed down over the issue of Indulgence.

Charles's initial determination to stand firm was punctured by the intervention of the French ambassador, who informed him that Louis XIV had far more interest in the Dutch war than in English Catholics. No secret payments would arrive from Versailles until Parliament was placated and the war properly financed. At the same time a sea change was occurring in the Commons: in an effort to call the King's bluff over a general indulgence, a bill was tabled which proposed relief for Protestant Dissenters, at the same time as another was introduced to reassert the principle that Catholics be excluded from office. Under pressure from all sides, Charles acknowledged defeat. The Declaration of Indulgence was withdrawn in March.[140] It was unthinkable for Charles to allow himself to appear sympathetic to popery, so he had little option but to give his assent to the anti-Catholic bill, which duly passed into law as the Test Act (1673).[141] This had serious and immediate repercussions: unwilling to take the required declaration repudiating the doctrine of transubstantiation or to renounce the Mass, Lord Clifford resigned from the government, and the Duke of York was forced to relinquish the office of Lord Admiral. At the same time as he was forced into humiliating retreat over the Declaration of Indulgence, therefore, Charles had been confronted by Nonconformist enthusiasm (not least that of the Earl of Shaftesbury) for the Test Act. The King thereby not only lost his appetite for universal toleration, but also from this point on began to view Dissenters as opponents rather than potential allies. Meanwhile, beyond Whitehall, celebratory bonfires were lit to mark the withdrawal of the Declaration of Indulgence in towns and cities as far apart as London, York, Ipswich, Nottingham, and Manchester; indicating that there was still a significant level of antipathy towards Dissent within the general

140. Jones, *Country and Court*, 178; Witcombe, *Charles II and the Cavalier House of Commons*, 132–35; Kenyon, *Stuart Constitution*, 408–10, Harris, *Restoration*, 63–64.

141. 25 Car. II, cap. 2 (Test Act 1673); Kenyon, *Stuart Constitution*, 461–62.

population.[142] In addition to these developments the misfortunes of Dissenters were compounded in that the bill for their relief had foundered amidst wrangling between the Lords and Commons. With no legal protection in place to compensate for losing the King's goodwill, Dissent had been rendered more vulnerable to persecution than ever.

Over the next two years some Dissenting communities continued to enjoy a degree of *de facto* toleration. In many cases this was because justices hesitated to enforce the penal laws. Many magistrates (some no doubt disingenuously) pleaded that they were unsure as to whether or not the withdrawal of the Declaration of Indulgence had invalidated the preaching licences issued under its auspices. Where the authorities did attempt to clamp down many Nonconformists reverted to the kind of pugnacious behaviour that had greeted the 1670 Conventicle Act. One informer was chased by a huge crowd of Presbyterians through Norwich and badly beaten. Another died in Great Yarmouth after receiving similar treatment.[143] If such violence seems incompatible with godliness, it should be borne in mind that with one report an informer could devastate the lives of many peaceable and otherwise law-abiding people. Cotton Mather's later claim that the penal laws of Charles II's reign had caused 'the ruine of threescore thousand families' during the period may have been an exaggeration; but it is certain that the pain, misery and bereavement inflicted on the Nonconformist community was very considerable.'[144] Greaves has observed a clear link between surges of radicalisation and intense periods of religious repression.[145] It is hardly surprising that the weight of evidence also indicates that religious conviction tended to translate into civil disorder and disaffection during such times.

The hardened attitude at Whitehall was made manifest in a fresh royal proclamation in February 1675, which reminded local magistrates that they were still required to suppress conventicles and prosecute those still pretending to preach under licence.[146] Presbyterians in Bristol responded by collaborating with Congregationalists and Baptists in order to stage so many meetings in different venues that

142. Miller, *After the Civil Wars*, 74.
143. Greaves, *Enemies at His Feet*, 226.
144. Mather, *Magnalia*, I, iii, 238.
145. Greaves, *Enemies at His Feet*, 227.
146. Ibid.

the city authorities were soon overwhelmed. The justices complained that they and the constables were exhausted, and that there was no time to devote to more routine matters of law and order.[147] Yarmouth justices were initially more successful in curtailing the activities of Congregationalists and Presbyterians in their town, but over the next twelve months the Nonconformists regrouped so well that the town was reputed to be completely in their power.[148] However, with the disintegration of the Cabal and the rise of Thomas Osborne, Earl of Danby, a particularly intolerant strain of Anglicanism now began to influence the direction of royal policy.

Danby set out to convince Charles that Dissenters were less numerous than he feared, and that the state had adequate military resources to overpower them if needs be. To this end, he commissioned the efficient Henry Compton, Bishop of London, to undertake a nationwide survey. The Compton Census of 1676 certainly provides some indication of the demographics of both Dissent and Catholicism, revealing them to have constituted around 5 percent and 1 percent of the population respectively.[149] It also reveals the central government's continuing taste for surveillance, and insights into the attitudes of the Anglican clergy. Census returns from incumbents of church livings in Sheldon's own archdiocese of Canterbury range from the lazy and tolerant to those keenly interested in the activities of their parishioners; the latter invariably hostile to Dissent.[150] Such zealousness reflected Danby's own thinking. During the years he was in power the Lord Treasurer promoted a policy of narrow Anglicanism in both church and state, the central plank of which was the repression of popery and Dissent. But despite the fact that he set up a tightly organised party of Court supporters in Parliament Danby never endeared himself to Charles II. Independently minded Cavalier-Anglican MPs found his methods repugnant and were suspicious of his true motives. If his great rival Shaftesbury daily performed a delicate balancing act (attempting to maintain street credibility with Dissenters whilst simultaneously cultivating moderate Anglicans in Parliament), Danby attempted an even more complicated trick: attempting to steer Charles away from

147. *Broadmead Records*, 98, 101–2, 109, quoted in Watts, *Dissenters*, 231.
148. Watts, *Dissenters*, 245.
149. See Whiteman, "Compton Census of 1676," 78–116.
150. E.g., Canterbury Cathedral Archives, CCA-DCb-H/Z, fos. 34, 40.

Louis XIV and towards a Dutch alliance whilst at the same time using propaganda, patronage and coercion to ensure that Anglicans dominated all positions of national and local significance. The schemes of both men would be overtaken by the events of 1678.

In August that year the thoroughly vile Titus Oates claimed to have unearthed a popish plot to kill the King. Oates' allegations, and the mysterious death of the magistrate to whom they were first disclosed, led to a nationwide orgy of anti-popery which proved beyond the government's ability to control. As it had become increasingly obvious that Charles II would die without legitimate issue, and that his openly Catholic brother would succeed him, more and more Anglicans had gradually come to question the direction taken by the Court—and Danby in particular. With this in mind, MPs began to introduce measures to safeguard the Church of England, passing the Second Test Act (1678) specifically to exclude Catholic peers from sitting in the House of Lords.[151] Charles gave his assent, but then dissolved Parliament, hoping that fresh elections would produce a more pliable Commons. In the event, the country returned a very similar mix of representatives, but with more Anglican MPs willing to cooperate with their Dissenting colleagues. Taking their lead from Shaftesbury, the new alliance in the Commons introduced a bill to exclude James, Duke of York from the royal succession. This was completely unacceptable to Charles, who dissolved Parliament in July 1679. The next parliament proved equally recalcitrant, and promptly revived the Exclusion Bill. The bill was voted through the Commons and went up to the Lords in October 1680. But the Lords (no doubt mindful of their own hereditary rights) proved unwilling to disrupt the succession and the bill was defeated. The King, emboldened by this victory, then felt free to withhold his assent from a bill which *had* passed through both Houses; one which would have repealed the old Elizabethan law so often used against Dissenters. Parliament was dissolved before it could dispute the matter. Charles's last parliament, which met in Oxford in 1681, lasted only a week. With a large subsidy from Louis, a good income from custom duties, and belatedly learning the benefits of fiscal discipline, Charles now saw no need to share power.

---

151. 30 Car. II, st. 2, cap. 1 (Second Test Act 1678); Kenyon, *Stuart Constitution*, 465–66.

Dissenters had been vociferous in their support of Exclusion, and in so doing had lost the friendship of the King. This would prove unfortunate, as a political backlash was underway which would result in an intense and sustained period of persecution. A recognisable Tory interest had emerged on the streets of several English cities during the Exclusion Crisis. Tory mobs were more concerned with asserting the divine right of kings and burning effigies of Jack Presbyter than they were with the finer points of Anglican doctrine, but above all they and the gentry behind the demonstrations were determined that Dissent should be equated with treason. During the last months of the First Civil War, Thomas Fairfax had stationed troops of the New Model Army around the Bodleian Library in Oxford to preserve the precious books contained within; by contrast, the University authorities now ordered works by authors such as Milton, Hobbes, Owen, and Baxter to be taken out of the Library and publicly burned.[152] Anglican preachers, who had long singled out Presbyterians for excoriation during the annual 30 January commemorations, exhibited unprecedented levels of ferocity. In 'all their sermons,' Burnett wrote, 'popery was quite forgot, and the force of their zeal was turned almost wholly against the dissenters.'[153] Anglican clergy who failed to express such extreme views—or worse, maintained contacts with Nonconformists—found themselves ostracised and attacked as traitors to the Church. This had an effect on secular law enforcement, as a revealing statistic from Middlesex shows: whereas in 1679 some 70 percent of people arrested for recusancy had been Catholics, by 1683 they would only account for 6 percent.[154] Needless to say, the proportion of Dissenters prosecuted grew alarmingly during the same period.

Sheldon had died in 1677, leaving Sir Leoline Jenkins (appointed Secretary of State in 1680) and the new Archbishop of Canterbury, William Sancroft, to carry on his work. Using an ecclesiastical commission as a vehicle of personal patronage, Sancroft manipulated preferment within the Church. Meanwhile, Jenkins, an efficient bureaucrat, whose abstemious, Puritan-like demeanour belied his ruthless Tory-Anglican soul, did his best to ensure that 'disaffected' people in political or judicial positions around the country were detected

152. Spurr, *Post–Reformation*, 169.
153. Burnett, *History*, ii, 290, 168.
154. Miller, *Popery and Politics*, 191.

and removed. Two hundred and seventy two justices were dismissed in 1680 alone.[155] A similar trend is evident in a swathe of dismissals from bodies under direct royal control, such as the Royal Navy and the Customs service. Towns, cities, and livery companies were cowed into submission by threats to recall their charters. No case was more notorious than that of London, where the recall and revision of the Corporation's charter gave Charles increased powers to interfere in the city's government. In December, the King intervened personally to ensure the suspension of a prominent alderman of the Corporation of London for attending a conventicle. The level of surveillance was already very evident in provincial cities. In Nottingham, in May 1682 John Sherwin, one of the city sheriffs, was reported for attending Independent and Presbyterian prayer meetings. All the while, Jenkins sifted information from informers regarding the efforts of certain justices and mayors to obstruct efforts to prosecute Nonconformists.[156] Even the poor were subjected to scrutiny. In February 1682 an order was issued by Middlesex Quarter Sessions that the overseers of the poor within their county give no financial relief 'except to those conformable to the Church of England.' The justices ordered that weekly payments were to be made immediately after morning service, ensuring that any absentees lost their allowance. Middlesex petty constables who failed to submit the names of all those poor attending mass or conventicles were liable to a fine of five pounds.[157]

Suspected meeting houses were broken into and ransacked. Following a search of the premises owned by the Surrey minister Nathaniel Vincent, Colonel Peter Rich reported back to Secretary Jenkins that 'we went round the place and find that almost every seat adjoining the sides of the conventicle has a door like the sally port of a fire ship to escape by and in each door a small peep-hole, like taverns' and alehouses' doors, to ken the person before they let them in.'[158]

A trap was set for Vincent, who was arrested on returning to the meeting house, and later sentenced to three months in prison.[159] As ever, Quakers did not trouble to engage in evasive techniques, and

155. Spurr, Post-Reformation, 167.

156. CSPD, 1682, 60, 80, 84, 101, 193, 251, 238, 574, 583.

157. Ibid., 59.

158. Ibid., 75–76.

159. CR, 502.

suffered heavily as a result. Some 400 Quakers are estimated to have died in prison during the so-called 'Tory Reaction' of the 1680s, in the company of many more conventional Nonconformists, including several leading ministers.[160]

Matters were aggravated still further in 1683 by the discovery of the Rye House Plot, a design conceived by a splinter group of Dissenters to kill the King and the Duke of York as they journeyed from Newmarket. Shaftesbury had died in exile in Amsterdam the previous January and the Earl of Argyll had fled, but other leading Whigs were rounded up and put on trial, including Arthur Capel, Earl of Essex. The King's illegitimate son, the Duke of Monmouth was also implicated, but received a royal pardon. Most suspects were almost certainly innocent, but Essex allegedly committed suicide in prison, whilst Algernon Sidney and Lord Russell were publicly executed. Anglican paranoia in the provinces grew to new heights. In Northamptonshire that month no less than fifty-one 'ill-affected' members of the gentry were presented by the grand jury and bound over to keep the peace. Similar action was taken in Cheshire in September against twenty-eight gentlemen, including the Earl of Macclesfield.[161] Unsurprisingly, dissenting academies were subjected to intense pressure during this period. Richard Frankland, an ejected minister, had set up his academy in Rathwell, North Yorkshire, in 1670. In 1674 he had been necessitated to move the institution to Westmorland. During the 1680s official harassment forced him to relocate on no less than five occasions.[162]

Despite the very real dangers, there was resistance to the oppression, not only from Dissenters, but also from moderate Anglicans increasingly worried by gathering evidence of arbitrary government, and concerns regarding the disruption of commerce. Informers were still regularly beaten up and sometimes imprisoned by justices.[163] Despite the threat to their charters, it is noticeable that among the thirty places in London reported to have hosted conventicles in 1682

160. Spurr, *Post-Reformation*, 168.

161. Harris, *Restoration*, 322.

162. Sell, *Church Planting*, 27 (a reference I owe to the kindness of Alan Sell); Dr. Williams's Centre for Dissenting Studies, *Dissenting Academies Project*; Handley, "Frankland," *ODNB*.

163. CSPD, 1682, 272.

were several livery company halls, such as those of the Haberdashers, the Cordwainers, and the Lorimers. Many leading ejected clergy risked their liberty to preach at these venues, including Matthew Mead, Daniel Bull, Thomas Jacomb, John Owen, and Richard Baxter.[164] Resistance reared its head in familiar areas, including Taunton, which was described by an informer as a rebellious town, full of obstinate and presumptuous magistrates and natives, who vowed that 'they'll see bloody noses ere they'll desert conventicles.'[165] In Southwark an angry crowd attacked a company of the King's foot guards, who were attempting to arrest a preacher.[166] If the unexpected death of Charles II in February 1685 did not immediately bring a change in royal policy it may conceivably have averted a descent into armed confrontation.

As Duke of York, James had helped enforce the government's repressive religious policies during the early 1680s, especially in Scotland. He was in addition acutely aware that many Dissenters had actively supported attempts to exclude him from the succession. He soon had a further excuse to dislike them. After landing in Dorset in June the Duke of Monmouth presented himself as the Protestant alternative to his uncle. Promising, among other things, to repeal all penal laws against Dissent, he gathered a force of around 4,000 volunteers and headed north. The crushing defeat of Monmouth's rag-tag army at Sedgemoor led to a punitive manhunt through the West Country. Several Nonconformist ministers were arrested, although only two were definitely implicated in the Rising. The first, John Hickes, would die in the mass executions held at Taunton. The second, Robert Ferguson, was an inveterate troublemaker who had been involved in the Rye House Plot. He escaped the noose for the umpteenth time, and, ironically, eventually became a Jacobite and lived to a ripe old age.[167] Other ejected ministers were seized in Exeter, among them Joseph Hallett and the peripatetic Nathaniel Vincent. Vincent's presence so far from Surrey was sufficiently suspicious for him to be taken to London for further examination. His explanations must have been satisfactory as he was eventually released.[168] After Monmouth and the Earl of Argyll, taken in Scotland, the most high-profile victim of the

164. Ibid., 609–10.
165. Ibid., 197–98.
166. Harris, *Restoration*, 305.
167. CR, 193–94, 260
168. Ibid., 243, 503.

government's retribution was Dame Alice Lisle. John Hickes had been found in an old priest's hole in her house, and as the widow of a notorious regicide and a known friend and protector of ejected ministers, Lady Lisle had little chance. The tone at her trial was set by the infamous Judge Jeffreys, who bullied testimony out of reluctant witnesses, calling one 'a lying Presbyterian rogue.'[169] The elderly gentlewoman was duly found guilty and was the first 'rebel' to be executed.

The vast majority of Dissenters had not risen in arms in 1685, and having dealt with the risings, James appears to have been reassured by the numerous declarations of support that came in from all religious denominations. Unfortunately, although not as selfish and unprincipled as his brother, the new king was conspicuously lacking in political nous. James's overriding ambition was to obtain religious and political equality for his fellow Catholics, something that could only be achieved by breaking the Tory-Anglican grip on the levers of power. The way he went about this, however, reveals his utter ineptitude as a politician. In some ways he was unlucky: Louis XIV's revocation of the Edict of Nantes in October 1685 caused thousands of Huguenot refugees to flee to England, bringing with them rumours of a renewed Counter-Reformation, and a coordinated assault on European Protestantism. In other respects James's actions were simply idiotic: he managed to alarm both Whigs and Tories by keeping a large standing army in being long after Monmouth's Rising, and openly flaunted the law by granting a large number of commissions in that army to Catholics. He began to dispense with the penal laws in order to insert increasing numbers of Dissenters and Catholics into positions of power. Next, having promised on several occasions to respect the integrity of the Church of England, James began to exert his influence as its supreme governor, attempting to interfere not only with regards to preferment but, more significantly, in matters of doctrine. Finally, in April 1687 he issued a Declaration of Indulgence which went much further than Charles's had done fifteen years before.

That James's ultimate ambition was the rehabilitation of the Catholic faith was evident at the beginning of the second paragraph of his Declaration, where he declared 'We cannot but heartily wish, as it will be easily believed, that all the people of our dominions were

---

169. CR, 452; Trench, *Western Rising*, 234–37.

members of the Catholic Church.'[170] If James hoped by such candour to have gained the trust of the political establishment he was being incredibly naïve. The Declaration did more than propose a suspension of the penal laws; it proposed to give all non-Anglicans full civil rights. The rage of the Tories was hardly assuaged by the promise that in due course Parliament would be given the opportunity to ratify these freedoms. Presbyterian, Congregationalist, and Baptist leaders, aware that they had been freed from persecution only by default, were divided amongst themselves as to whether to signify their acceptance. The fact that very different policies were then being followed in James's other kingdoms undoubtedly gave them pause for thought: in Ireland the Earl of Tyrconnell was rapidly catholicising the Irish establishment; in Scotland, after a tussle with the Scottish Parliament James had given Catholics and Quakers freedom of worship, but had frozen out Presbyterians. And he was soon busily acquiring further power in England by pruning the county Lieutenancy and the Quarter Sessions benches of potential opponents and replacing them with Catholics and Dissenters. In April 1688 he reissued the Declaration of Indulgence, this time demanding that it be read out in every church. This provoked outright resistance from the leading bishops, and James sent seven of them, including Sancroft and Compton, to the Tower. Whilst awaiting trial the bishops were visited both by Anglican supporters and concerned Nonconformist clergy. To the huge embarrassment of the King the bishops were eventually acquitted. The experience had clearly had an effect even on the previously irascible Sancroft, who now began to make overtures towards the more conservative Nonconformists with a view to forming a united Protestant front against any further royal encroachments.

In practice, Dissenters now temporarily enjoyed the best of both worlds: they were free to meet and worship, and even to hold office under the auspices of James's Declaration of Indulgence, whilst relations between the more orthodox Nonconformist ministers and the Church of England authorities were becoming increasingly cordial. James was not a young man, and thus it was assumed that the problems caused by his pro-Catholic policies were only temporary. The heir to the throne, his daughter Mary and her husband Prince William of Orange, were both firm Protestants, and had already indicated their

170. Kenyon, *Stuart Constitution*, 410–12.

support for a wide liberty of conscience. All was thrown into doubt in June 1688, when James's second wife, Mary of Modena, gave birth to a son. Suddenly Anglicans and Dissenters were faced with the prospect of a permanent Catholic royal dynasty.

Although it was some months before William and Mary landed in Torbay it was evident from public propaganda and private negotiations conducted during the intervening period that invasion was inevitable. The pair arrived at the head of 20,000 seasoned troops, and (whether by chance or providence) managed to land on the auspicious Protestant red-letter day of 5 November. No fighting took place as the Anglo-Dutch army advanced on London. James's royal army melted away as his officers either absconded or changed sides. James, realising that his position was hopeless, attempted to escape, only to be captured. On 21 December a clerical deputation led by Bishop Compton met William to thank him for the nation's deliverance. The deputation included several Nonconformist leaders, whom Compton introduced as 'brethren' of the Church of England. Two days later James was again allowed to escape overseas, this time successfully. When the newly elected Convention Parliament met in January 1689, it was thus able to declare the throne vacant, and duly invited William and Mary to reign as joint monarchs.

England had had a taste of arbitrary government, and the Convention Parliament was determined to ensure that it would never happen again. The Declaration of Rights seriously curtailed future monarchs' freedom of action, and added the specific proviso that the monarch could not be of the Roman Catholic faith, nor, indeed, married to a Catholic. All that was left was to work out a lasting religious settlement for the nation's Protestants.

Two parallel strategies were followed over the next few months: comprehension and toleration. Both strands could trace their ancestry back to bills considered by the Exclusion Parliament of 1680. In hindsight, it is surprising that so much time was spent on a comprehension bill: from January to March 1689 a selection of Anglican clergy under the chairmanship of the Tory Earl of Nottingham hammered out a set of proposals with the Lords. These served only to annoy Tory MPs and dismay Dissenters. Much as they had been willing to work with Nonconformists in the recent past, the Tories were not prepared to allow them equal access to civil and political office. For Dissenters, the terms under which comprehension was to be offered presented many of the same obstacles which had faced the original Bartholomeans in 1662; most particularly, the requirements to be ordained by a bishop and to adhere to the Common Prayer Book in every detail. They also suspected that comprehension was a ruse to divide Dissent by enticing the more moderate Presbyterian clergy back into the Church, and excluding all others. Anglican clergy for their part resented the proposal that anyone could be admitted into the ministry of the church who had only subscribed to thirty-six of the Thirty-Nine Articles of the Church of England (the missing three articles pertaining to the government of the Church). They also feared the disruption a godly faction might cause once admitted; as one wag put it, 'A Church that grows numerous by taking in Dissenters, may be no stronger than an Army that fills up its Company with Mutineers.'[171] The comprehension bill, to everybody's relief, was laid aside.

Amidst fears that it too would fail, the Earl of Nottingham presented the toleration bill to the Lords on 28 February. By 24 May 1689 it had successfully navigated its way through both Houses and received the royal assent. It is important to note that the Toleration Act (1689) did not repeal the legislation of the previous decades, but rather offered exemption from most of its penalties. Under the terms of the Act, all Dissenters who took the new Oath of Allegiance, and subscribed to the 1678 Test Act were free to engage in public worship, provided their meeting places had been registered with the local justices. Presbyterian and Congregationalist clergy were allowed to exercise their ministry free of the penalties of the Uniformity and Five Mile Acts provided they additionally subscribed to the relevant thirty-six of the Thirty-Nine Articles. Concessions were made to Baptist ministers (who were not required to subscribe to the article on infant baptism) and to Quakers (who were allowed to declare their allegiance rather than swear an oath). The Act pointedly excluded Catholics, non-Trinitarians and atheists.[172]

For Dissenters, the Toleration Act brought to an end to decades of uncertainty, fear and suffering. John Spurr has rightly pointed out that the Act was not 'the long-delayed admission of a prized civil right,' but

---

171. M., *Letter from the Member of Parliament*, 5; quoted in Spurr, "Church of England," 943.

172. 1 Will. & Mar. cap. 18 (Toleration Act 1689); Browning, *Historical Documents*, 400–403.

rather a 'grudging concession.'[173] As with all compromises, both sides had their regrets and grumbles and these would continue to rumble on in some cases for generations. There would always be a residue of die-hard Cavaliers who would regard Dissenters as Cromwell's whelps and Charles I's murderers, and would never be reconciled to the idea that toleration be extended to religious fanatics. There remained loopholes in the law through which it was possible for such people to vent their spite: Dissenting academies, for example, remained vulnerable to judicial harassment, as the Act had failed to remove the requirement for the staff of the academies to obtain an episcopal licence to teach.[174] This brought further problems for tutors such as Richard Frankland. Although he had been able to return to Rathwell in Yorkshire in 1689, and had a properly registered meeting house, he had to fight off several attempts over the next decade to close his academy.[175]

Dissenters were now free to associate and worship. Nevertheless, they remained second-class citizens, officially barred from civil and political employment. The struggle for equality would continue throughout the next century. Although equality was eventually achieved, later commentators have sometimes conveyed a sense of regret that the chance was missed in 1662, and more crucially in 1689, to bring English Protestantism under one roof. The chance was never there. The Church of England was from its inception a political institution. After the Restoration it became even more emphatically an arm of the state. By 1689, therefore, the cause of religious reformation was probably more likely to be advanced by remaining peacefully outside the Church than by becoming embroiled in fresh political controversy within it.

BIBLIOGRAPHY

Primary Sources (manuscript)

The National Archives (Public Record Office, Kew, London)
SP29/56 Letters and papers, Secretaries of State: June 1662
SP29/57 Letters and papers, Secretaries of State: July 1662

173. Spurr, *Post-Reformation*, 189.

174. Watts, *Dissenters*, 264.

175. *ODNB*

SP29/58   Letters and papers, Secretaries of State: August 1662
SP29/67   Letters and papers, Secretaries of State: January 1667

British Library, London

Add. MSS 21922   Letter book of Sir Richard Norton, deputy lieutenant of
          Hampshire: 1660–1662
MS Egerton 2537   Correspondence of Sir Edward Nicholas: 1660–1661
MS Egerton 2543   Correspondence of Sir Edward Nicholas: 1661–1669

Bodleian Library, Oxford

MS Carte 31   Correspondence of James, Duke of Ormonde: 1660–1662
MS Carte 45   Papers on ecclesiastical affairs in Ireland: 1660–1685
MS Carte 47   Correspondence of James, Duke of Ormonde: 1652–1683.
MS Carte 217   Correspondence of James, Duke of Ormond: 1662–1690
MS Clarendon 77   Clarendon State Papers
MS Tanner 48   Correspondence and miscellaneous papers.

Canterbury Cathedral Archives

CCA-DCb-H/Z   Compton Census for the Diocese of Canterbury: 1676.

Centre for Kentish Studies, Maidstone

CKS-Q/SB 9   Kentish Quarter Sessions papers: 1663–65.

Dr. Williams's Library, London

DWL 24.9   Papers of Owen Stockton: 1630–1680.

Essex Record Office, Chelmsford

D/B5 SB2/9   Colchester Borough Quarter Sessions, examinations and
          recognizances: 1647–1687.

Primary Sources (printed)

(Wing catalogue numbers have been given where multiple editions
are known to exist.)

A Generall Bill of the Mortality of the Clergy of London. London: 1662 (Wing G495).
Alleine, Richard. *The Godly Man's Portion and Sanctuary.* London: 1664 (Wing A989).
An Exact Collection of Farevvel Sermons, Preached by the Late London-Ministers.
    London: 1662 (Wing E3632).
Assheton, William. *Evangelium Armatum.* London: 1663.
Baxter, Richard. *Reliquiae Baxterianae.* Edited by M. Sylvester. London: 1696.
Berkenhead, John. *Cabala.* London: 1663.
Bury, Arthur. *The Bow.* London: 1660.
Calamy, Edmund (1600–1666). *Eli Trembling for Fear of the Ark.* London: 1662 (Wing
    C231A).
Calamy, Edmund (1671–1732). *An Abridgement of Mr Baxter's History of His Life
    and Times. With an Account of Many Other of those Worthy Ministers Who were
    Ejected.* London: 1702.

————. *An Abridgement of Mr Baxter's History of His Life and Times. With an Account of Many Other of those Worthy Ministers Who were Ejected.* 2nd ed. 2 vols. London: 1713.

————. *A Continuation of the Account of the Ministers . . . Who were Ejected and Silenced.* 2 vols. London: 1727.

England and Wales, Sovereign. *A Proclamation against Numerous Conventicles.* London: 1669 (Wing C3217).

————. *A Proclamation for Inforcing the Laws against Conventicles and for Preservation of the Publick Peace against Unlawful Assemblies of Papists and Non-conformists.* London: 1668 (Wing C3340).

England's Remembrancer, Being a Collection of Farewel-Sermons Preached by Divers Non-Conformists in the Country. London: 1663 (Wing E3029).

Fairclough, Richard. *A Pastor's Legacy, to His Beloved People.* London: 1713.

Griffith, Matthew. *The King's Life-Guard: An Anniversary Sermon Preached to the Honorable Societies of Both the Temples on the 30th of January 1664/5.* London: 1665.

Horn, John. *The Quakers Proved Deceivers.* London: 1660.

Intelligencer, no. 8. London, October 19, 1663.

Kem, Samuel. *King Solomon's Infallible Experiment for Three Kingdoms' Settlement.* London: 1660.

Lamb, Philip. *The Royal Presence, or God's Tabernacle with Men.* London: 1662.

L'Estrange, Roger. *Considerations and Proposals in Order to the Regulation of the Press.* London: 1663.

Lucas, Lord John. *My Lord Lucas His Speech in the House of Peers.* London: 1671.

Lye, Thomas. *The Fixed Saint.* London: 1662.

M., M., *A Letter from the Member of Parliament.* [London?]: 1689.

Master Edmund Calamy's Leading Case. London: 1663.

Mercurius Publicus 33. London, August 14–21, 1662.

Mercurius Publicus 34. London, August 21–28, 1662.

Newcome, Henry. *Usurpation Defeated and David Restored.* London: 1660.

Newcomen, Matthew. *Ultimum Vale, or The Last Farewel of a Minister of the Gospel to a Beloved People.* London: 1663.

A Pulpit to be Let. London: 1665.

Swinnock, George. *The Pastors Farewell, and Wish of Welfare to His People, or A Valedictory Sermon.* London: 1662.

The Third Volume of Farewel Sermons, Preached by some London and Country Ministers. London: 1663 (Wing T914C).

Twisse, Robert. *England's Breath Stopp'd.* London: 1665.

W., J. *A Friendly Letter to the Flying Clergy Wherein is Humbly Requested and Modestly Challenged the Cause of their Flight.* London: 1665.

Walwyn, William. *God Save the King.* London: 1660.

Whitlock, John. *A Short Account of the Life of the Reverend Mr. William Reynolds.* London: 1698.

Sources and Calendars

Browning, A. *English Historical Documents 1660–1714.* London: Eyre and Spottiswoode, 1966.

Burnett, Gilbert. *A History of My Own Time.* Edited by Osmund Airey. 2 vols. Oxford: Clarendon, 1897.

Defoe, Daniel. *A Journal of the Plague Year.* Edited by L. Landa. Oxford: Oxford University Press, 1990.

Josselin, Ralph. *The Diary of Ralph Josselin 1616–1683*, edited by Alan Macfarlane. Oxford: Oxford University Press, 1976.

Calendar of State Papers, Domestic, Charles II. Edited by M. A. E. Green *et al.* 28 vols. London: HMSO, 1860–1939.

Calendar of State Papers, Venetian, 1661–1664. Edited by A. B. Hines. London: HMSO, 1932.

Hyde, Edward, Earl of Clarendon. *The Life of Edward, Earl of Clarendon, Lord High Chancellor of England.* 2 vols. Oxford: Oxford University Press, 1857.

Kenyon, John P. *The Stuart Constitution 1603–1608: Documents and Commentary.* Cambridge: Cambridge University Press, 1966.

Matthews, A. G. *Calamy Revised.* 1934. Reprint. Oxford: Clarendon, 1988.

Mather, Cotton. *Magnalia Christi Americana, or the Ecclesiastical History of New-England*, vol. I, Third Book ('Polybius'). 2nd ed. Hartford, CT: Silas Andrus & Son, 1853.

Newcome, Henry. *Diary of the Revd. Henry Newcome.* Edited by R. Parkinson, vol. 18. Manchester, UK: Chetham Society, 1849.

Pepys, Samuel. *The Diary of Samuel Pepys.* Edited by R. Latham and W. Matthews. 11 vols. London: Bell and Sons, 1970.

Secondary Sources

Achinstein, Sharon. *Literature and Dissent in Milton's England.* Cambridge: Cambridge University Press, 2003.

Appleby, David J. *Black Bartholomew's Day: Preaching, Polemic and Restoration Nonconformity.* Manchester, UK: Manchester University Press, 2007.

Ashley Smith, Joe W. *The Birth of Modern Education: The Contribution of the Dissenting Academies, 1660–1800.* London: Independent, 1954.

Bell, W. *The Great Fire of London in 1666.* London: Bodley Head, 1951.

Blagden, C. *The Stationers' Company: A History 1403–1959.* London: Allen Unwin, 1960.

Bosher, Robert S. *The Making of the Restoration Settlement.* Rev. ed. London: Black, 1957.

Coffey, John. *Persecution and Toleration in Protestant England, 1558–1689.* Harlow, UK: Longman, 2000.

Cragg, G. R. *Puritanism in the Period of the Great Persecution.* Cambridge: Cambridge University Press, 1957.

De Krey, Gary S. *London and the Restoration 1659–1683.* Cambridge: Cambridge University Press, 2005.

Dr. Williams's Centre for Dissenting Studies. "Dissenting Academies Project." Online: http://www.english.qmul.ac.uk/drwilliams/academies/legislation.html.

Fletcher, Anthony. "The Enforcement of the Conventicle Acts 1664–1679." In *Persecution and Toleration: Papers Read at the Twenty-Second Summer Meeting and the Twenty-Third Winter Meeting of the Ecclesiastical History Society*, edited by W. J. Sheils, 235–46. Oxford: Blackwell, 1984.

Gaskell, Philip. *A New Introduction to Bibliography.* Oxford: Clarendon, 1972.

Girdler, Lew. "Defoe's Education at Newington Green Academy." *Studies in Philology* 50.4 (1953) 573–91.

Greaves, Richard L. *Deliver Us from Evil: The Radical Underground in Britain 1660–1663*. Oxford: Oxford University Press, 1986.

———. *Enemies under His Feet: Radicals and Nonconformists in Britain 1664–1677*. Stanford CA: Stanford University Press, 1990.

Green, Ian M. *The Re-Establishment of the Church of England 1660–1663*. Oxford: Oxford University Press, 1978.

Handley, Stuart. "Frankland, Richard (1630–1698)." *Oxford Dictionary of National Biography*. Oxford University Press, online edition, 2004. No pages. Online: http://www.oxforddnb.com/view/article/10085.

Harris, Tim. *Restoration: Charles II and His Kingdoms 1660–1685*. London: Allen Lane, 2005.

Hetherington, R. J. "Birmingham and the Ejected of 1662." Unpublished essay: Birmingham Central Library, 1957.

Hopper, Andrew, "The Farnley Wood Plot and the Memory of the Civil Wars in Yorkshire." *The Historical Journal* 45.2 (2002) 281–303.

Hutton, Ronald. *The Restoration: A Political and Religious History of England and Wales 1658–1667*. Oxford: Oxford University Press, 1985.

Jackson, P. W. "Nonconformists and Society in Devon 1660–1689." PhD thesis, University of Exeter, 1986.

Jones, J. R., *Country and Court: England 1658–1714*. London: Arnold, 1978.

Keeble, Neil H. *The Literary Culture of Nonconformity in Later Seventeenth-Century England*. Leicester, UK: Leicester University Press, 1987.

McLachlan, Herbert. *English Education under the Test Acts*. Manchester, UK: Manchester University Press, 1931.

Miller, John. *Popery and Politics in England, 1660–1688*. Cambridge: Cambridge University Press, 1973.

———. *After the Civil Wars: British Politics and Government in the Reign of Charles II*. Harlow, UK: Longman, 2000.

Nottingham, University of, Manuscripts and Special Collections. "Records of the Old Meeting House, Mansfield." No pages. Online: http://www.nottingham.ac.uk/manuscriptsandspecialcollections/collectionsindepth/nonconformistchurches/oldmeetinghouse.aspx.

Nuttall, G. and O. Chadwick. *From Uniformity to Unity, 1662–1962*. London: SPCK, 1962.

Parker, Irene. *Dissenting Academies in England*. Cambridge: Cambridge University Press, 1914.

Patterson, Annabel, and Martin Dzelzainis. "Marvell and the Earl of Anglesey: A Chapter in the History of Reading." *Historical Journal* 44.3 (2001) 703–26.

Porter, Stephen. *The Great Fire of London*. Stroud, UK: Sutton, 1996.

Reddaway, T. *The Rebuilding of London after the Great Fire*. London: Arnold, 1940.

Seaward, Paul. "Gilbert Sheldon, the London Vestries and the Defence of the Church." In *Politics of Religion in Restoration England*, edited by Harris *et al.*, 49–73. Oxford: Blackwell, 1990.

Sell, Alan P. F. *Church Planting: A Study of Westmorland Nonconformity*. Eugene, OR: Wipf and Stock, 1998.

Smith, C. Fell. "The Essex Newcomens." *Essex Review* ii (1893) 35–40.

Spurr, John. "The Church of England, Comprehension and the Toleration Act of 1689." *English Historical Review* 104.413 (1989) 927–46.

———. *The Post-Reformation 1603–1714*. London: Longman, 2006.

————. *The Restoration Church of England, 1646–1689*. New Haven, CT: Yale University Press, 1991.

Stater, Victor L. *Noble Government: The Stuart Lord Lieutenancy and the Transformation of English Politics*. Athens, GA: University of Georgia Press, 1994.

Sutch, V. D. *Gilbert Sheldon, Architect of Anglican Survival 1640–1675*. The Hague: Nijhoff, 1973.

Trench, Charles Chenevix. *The Western Rising: An Account of Monmouth's Rebellion*. London: Longmans, Green and Co., 1969.

Watts, Michael R. *The Dissenters: From the Reformation to the French Revolution*. Oxford: Clarendon, 1978.

Webster, Tom. "Newcomen, Matthew (d. 1669)." *Oxford Dictionary of National Biography*, Oxford University Press, online edition, 2004. No pages. Online: http://www.oxforddnb.com/view/article/19995.

Whiteman, Anne, "The Compton Census of 1676." In *Surveying the People: The Interpretation and Use of Document Sources for the Study of Population in the Later Seventeenth Century*, edited by Kevin Schurer and Tom Arkell, 78–116. Oxford: Leopard's Head, 1992.

Witcombe, D. T. *Charles II and the Cavalier House of Commons 1663–1674*. Manchester, UK: Manchester University Press, 1966.

3

From Ejectment to Toleration in Wales, 1662–89[1]

Eryn M. White

There is sound evidence to substantiate the suggestion that the vast majority of the population in Wales welcomed the restoration of the Established Church and had never been other than reluctant, coerced converts to the Puritan regime.[2] It has also sometimes been taken for granted that Puritanism reached Wales through England and was therefore not strictly speaking a movement native to the country.[3] Even so, there were signs of home-grown enthusiasm, even if it was in the main heavily influenced by ideas and developments from across the border. The doyen of the study of Welsh Puritanism, Thomas Richards, pointed to the importance of the borderlands of Wrexham, Radnorshire, Breconshire, and Monmouthshire for the nurture of

---

1. In this chapter the following abbreviations are used: DWB: Dictionary of Welsh Biography; NLW: National Library of Wales.

2. Williams, *Welsh and Religion*, 47–49; Jenkins, *Foundations of Modern Wales*, 173–74.

3. For example, Williams, *History of Modern Wales*, 110.

early Dissent.[4] It was certainly in those areas that the first generation of leaders emerged, including Morgan Llwyd, Vavasor Powell, Walter Cradock, William Erbury, and William Wroth. Walter Cradock had declared confidently of this border area that 'the Gospel is run over the Mountaines between Brecknockshire, and Monmouthshire, as the fire in the thatch.'[5] Puritanism was initially more readily received in urban and border regions where greater knowledge of English allowed an easier reception for the new ideas, which had yet to be discussed extensively through the medium of Welsh, either through sermons or in print. Yet, it was perhaps the experiences of the subsequent generation in the period between ejectment and Toleration, which did most to determine the future character of Welsh Nonconformity.

This period has frequently been called the 'heroic' or 'golden' age of Dissent in Wales.[6] Thomas Richards suggested that this time of persecution in effect served to purify the cause from any trimmers who had only professed adherence because of the benefits that might ensue during the Commonwealth period; it thus 'restored Puritanism to itself.'[7] Certainly, it was unlikely that any but the most committed, and sometimes the most contrary, would persist in their profession of faith after 1662 in the light of so many hindrances. That formidable old Puritan, Colonel John Jones of Maesygarnedd, who was executed as a regicide before having to witness the effects of the penal laws, once insisted that 'the more the Saints are tryed, the more their luster will appeare.'[8] That Dissent survived this testing time confirmed that it was no temporary fad, but a set of beliefs that had contrived to strike deep roots amongst certain sections of society. It also emerged with a firmer sense of its identity, as a more intrinsically Welsh movement with a history and heroes in which it would take great pride in years to come. Although links with their brethren across the border were maintained to some extent, especially with Bristol,[9] the Welsh congregations were

---

4. Richards, *Puritan Movement*, 25–28.

5. Cradock, *Glad Tydings*, 50.

6. Richards, *Wales under the Penal Code*, xi; Williams, "Crefydd dan gysgod erledigaeth," 12; Jenkins, "Friends of Montgomeryshire," 17; Jenkins, *Foundations of Modern Wales*, 193–94.

7. Richards, *Wales under the Indulgence*, 232.

8. Quoted in Richards, *Puritan Movement*, 270.

9. Richards, *Wales under the Indulgence*, 42–43; Williams, "Crefydd dan gysgod erledigaeth," 15–16.

more isolated than in the past and forced to fall back on their own strength. In order to survive, dissenting groups had to be resourceful and some of the methods and strategies adopted proved to have a long-term significance. For all these reasons, this proved to be a vitally important formative period for Welsh Nonconformity.

Tracing the history of Welsh Dissent during the time when it was forced underground after 1662 is by no means straightforward. Dissenters were understandably wary of committing the names of their ministers and members to paper, so that even the earliest churches have scant records of this period.[10] The Ilston Church Book, for instance, contains a register of its Baptist members for 1649–50, 1650–57 and then from 1718.[11] The records of Cilgwyn Independent Church in Cardiganshire stop in 1659 and recommence in 1692.[12] A number of churches were officially established in the wake of the Toleration Act so that their records in effect began then, with the occasional retrospective glance back over the preceding period. The Rhydwilym Baptists' Church Book, for example, was started after Toleration but listed its existing members in 1689 and referred back to those who had been baptised from 1667 onwards.[13] The Independents at Llandeilo Mynydd Bach, near Swansea, began their register with a list of names of some of those who had been 'members of the Church of Jesus Christ' in the time of Charles II.[14] In addition, although the Independent cause at Pant-teg started its records in 1690, some individuals buried in the 1720s and 1730s were described as having been received as members forty years or more previously by Stephen Hughes at Pencader, dating back to a time when that membership would perforce have been illicit.[15]

Despite these gaps in the records, glimpses do emerge which provide an indication of the survival of the Puritan cause beyond the restoration and ejectment. The account by Edmund Calamy, along with the work of Joshua Thomas in the eighteenth century and Thomas

10. Owens, "Cofrestri'r Ymneilltuwyr," 31–49.

11. NLW, NLW MS 9108–9D; see also Owens, *Ilston Book*.

12. Jones, "Llyfr Eglwys y Cilgwyn," 22–31.

13. NLW Deposit MS 127A; see also Owens, "Trichanmlwyddiant Rhydwilym," 54–56.

14. NLW MS 371B; see also Jones, "Llyfr Eglwys Mynydd Bach."

15. NLW MS 12362; see also Jones, "Llyfr Eglwys Pant-teg," 18–70.

Rees in the nineteenth century, remain crucial in tracing the careers of the ministers ejected between 1660 and 1662 and the fate of their congregations. The volumes of Thomas Richards's meticulous research published in the 1920s also provide a store of invaluable information along with the foundation for most subsequent historiography. His work on the ejected ministers has to some extent been further updated by the research published by R. Tudur Jones and B. G. Owens in 1962. Yet, there are still uncertainties and contradictions. For instance, Calamy lists ten ministers and one candidate for orders who were expelled from parishes within the county of Cardiganshire by August 1662, Thomas Rees has ten ministers and itinerant preachers from the county, Thomas Richards names seven who were ejected under the Act of Uniformity, and Jones and Owens suggest thirteen were lost in total.[16] The fact that some ministers chose to conform quite quickly and that several departed before August 1662 has made it difficult to come up with a definitive list in many counties.

Even with these difficulties, the geographical pattern of ejectment does help to map the strengths and weaknesses of Dissent in Wales. Counties where Puritanism had made a mark had the highest number of ejected clergy by 1662, namely, Glamorgan, Breconshire, Montgomeryshire, Cardiganshire, Pembrokeshire, and Denbighshire. Glamorgan was considerably in the lead with twenty-three of the total 130 ejected ministers. This number may signal both the underlying strength of Puritanism and the deep resentment of it among those restored to power, after the virtual dictatorship over the county of Colonel Philip Jones and his small cohort of supporters under the Commonwealth.[17] Monmouthshire might have been expected to have produced more than ten ejected ministers, bearing in mind that it was the location of what is acknowledged as the first dissenting gathered church in Wales, at Llanfaches in 1639.[18] However, the county also had the strongest tradition in Wales of Catholic loyalism, with the Compton Census listing 541 Catholic Dissenters for Monmouthshire, a figure which Thomas Richards suggested still underestimated the

16. Calamy, *Account, II,* 716–9; Rees, *History of Protestant Nonconformity,* 124–27; Richards, *Puritan Developments,* 488, 495, 498; Jones, "Ymneilluaeth Gynnar," 103–4; Jones and Owens, "Anghydffurfwyr Cymru," 8.

17. Jones and Owens, "Anghydffurfwyr Cymru," 8; Williams, "Dissenters in Glamorgan," 497–98; Jenkins, *Making of a Ruling Class,* 109–21.

18. Jones, "Piwritaniaeth gynnar," 4–26; Jenkins, *Protestant Dissenters,* 12–13.

actual strength of the old faith in the area.[19] It also becomes clear that the Puritan gospel had failed to penetrate the north-west of the country to any great degree. The three counties of the north-west—Anglesey, Caernarfonshire, and Merionethshire—mustered only nine ejected ministers between them and one of those conformed quite speedily and took up another benefice.

Some thirty-four of the 130 listed as ejected felt able to conform subsequently, leaving less than a hundred committed dissenting ministers throughout the country. Some ministers had been ejected, not necessarily because of their objections to the Act of Uniformity, but largely in order to make it possible to restore those who had been removed by the Puritan measures of the 1650s and who were now regarded as the legal incumbents. Some of those displaced in this manner were appointed to livings elsewhere as they fell vacant, so technically cannot be considered Dissenters in any real sense. The most incongruous name to appear on the list of the ejected was that of Thomas Vaughan, removed from the parish of Llansanffraid in Breconshire in 1662.[20] He was the twin brother of Henry Vaughan, the poet, and thus belonged to a branch of the distinguished Vaughan family. Having fought on the royalist side in the civil war he was removed as rector of his native parish of Llansanffraid under the Propagation Act in the 1650s. It is not certain when he was reinstated, but his ultimate ejectment owed nothing to any Puritan beliefs as he was a staunch Anglican. It may rather have been his interest in the study of alchemy that made him seem unsuitable. Of those who did then accept royal supremacy and the *Book of Common Prayer*, a proportion may well have done so out of necessity or convenience rather than conviction. The prospect of the loss of income, coupled in many cases with the need to provide for a family, must have been a major consideration. It is impossible to know in most cases whether their ministry continued to be affected by Puritan tendencies, although there are indications that some were not entirely reconciled to the new order. In Cardiganshire, Thomas Evans was removed from the parish of Llangeitho in 1662 under the Act of Uniformity, but was restored to his living in 1668. For all that

19. Richards, *Religious Census*, 82–99, 106–7; Morgan-Guy, "Religion and Belief," 159–62.

20. DWB, 1003; Jones and Owens, "Anghydffurfwyr Cymru," 85–86; Jennifer Speake, "Thomas Vaughan."

he seemed to have satisfied the church authorities of his willingness to conform, it would appear that he had not in fact abandoned his dissenting beliefs. Evans was accused before the consistory courts in 1671 of regularly preaching at a conventicle at Llangeitho in which some forty or fifty worshippers from four parishes gathered to hear him.[21] Llangeitho would, of course, later emerge as the epicentre of the Methodist Revival in the eighteenth century.

It is not always easy to determine the fate of those dismissed from their parishes since many disappear from all records thereafter. Among them is Jenkin Jones of Llanddeti, whose disgruntled reaction to the restoration and his ejection from Cadoxton, Glamorgan, was to fire a bullet through the door of the parish church in defiance of 'the whore of Babylon.' This behaviour was not uncharacteristic of the man who was said to have greeted the outbreak of civil war with a sword in one hand and the Bible in the other. Jones was apparently imprisoned in Carmarthen in 1660 for some time, but what became of him afterwards remains something of a mystery.[22]

The ejected ministers frequently played a crucial role in maintaining some semblance of worship within the pockets of resistance which emerged after 1662, despite the fact that they were in reality all too few in number. As might be expected, areas such as Wrexham where Puritanism had already established a hold emerged as strongholds of Dissent. The tendency was to focus on continuity, with dissenting worship persisting in areas where it had previously gathered some support and where dissenting ministers remained at work. The Five Mile Act of 1665 forbade ejected ministers from preaching or teaching within five miles of their former livings. If it had been rigorously applied, it should have served to eradicate the influence of former pastors and to undo the bonds of loyalty between them and their former flocks. However, several deprived clergy stayed put or moved only a short distance from their previous sphere of activity, enabling them to maintain a connection with their followers. Samuel Jones was removed from Llangynwyd, Glamorgan, but remained in the parish at his home at Brynllywarch, both preaching and teaching in the vicin-

---

21. NLW, SD/CCCd/G/2; Jones, "Ymneilltuaeth Gynnar," 104–5.

22. Rees, *History of Protestant Nonconformity*, 111–14; Jenkins, *Protestant Dissenters*, 44.

ity throughout the period when the Clarendon Code was in force.[23] Marmaduke Matthews did not budge from the town of Swansea, continuing to shepherd his flock there for years to come.[24] William Jones was ejected from Denbigh in north Wales only to be identified in 1675 as the minister of the gathered church of Presbyterians in the town.[25] After being removed from Llanfair Dyffryn Clwyd, Denbighshire, Jonathan Roberts remained in the vicinity, obtaining a licence to preach at his house there under the Indulgence granted to Dissenters in 1672.[26] Others moved but a little way, to comply with the letter of the law but not its spirit. Peregrine Phillips left Llangwm and Freystrop to settle at Dredgman Hill, near Haverfordwest, and was the leading figure amongst Pembrokeshire Independents.[27] In the Vale of Glamorgan, Joshua Miller moved from St. Andrews Major to nearby Wenvoe and John French from Wenvoe to Cardiff, not too far distant.[28] In Caernarfonshire, Ellis Rowlands, former rector of Clynnog Fawr, seems to have maintained some activity in the area, based at Caernarfon, receiving copies from Philip Henry in 1666 of the Welsh version of Richard Baxter's *Call to the Unconverted* to distribute.[29] Philip Henry himself, having been ejected from Worthenbury in Flintshire, moved over the border to Whitchurch in Shropshire in 1667 possibly to avoid criticism that he was contravening the Five Mile Act. After some years of reticence, the Indulgence of 1672 seemed to reinvigorate him and he became active again in both counties.[30] Given some of these examples of continued activity, it is strange that Bishop George Griffiths of St. Asaph could categorically state that there were no ejected ministers whatsoever in his diocese in 1665. The possible explanation is that he was thinking only of those removed in August

23. Jones, "Samuel Jones."

24. DWB, 621.

25. Underhill, *Records of Broadmead*, 513.

26. Jones and Owens, "Anghydffurfwyr Cymru," 75.

27. Wright, "Peregrine Phillips."

28. Jones and Owens, "Anghydffurfwyr Cymru," 28, 60–61.

29. Lee, *Diaries of Philip Henry*, 193, Richards, *Religious Developments*, 507; Richards, *Wales under the Indulgence*, 44.

30. Greaves, "Philip Henry"; Nuttall, "Nurture of Nonconformity," 18–25.

1662 under the Act of Uniformity and disregarded those already departed, but it hardly gives an accurate impression of the situation.[31]

Other ministers were more inclined to uproot themselves and settle elsewhere. London and its environs in south-east England proved attractive to some, especially perhaps to those from more anglicised parts of the country or those who did not have strong ties to the areas where they had ministered. Christopher Jackson had moved to Pembrokeshire during the period of the Propagation Act but chose to remove to London after he was ejected from Lampeter Velfrey in 1660.[32] Charles Price, a former itinerant preacher from Radnorshire, having lost his living at Cardigan in 1662, wound up as a Congregationalist minister in Hammersmith.[33] Richard Taylor, formerly of Holt in Denbighshire, established himself as a dissenting minister in Barking.[34] Richard Steele was a native of Cheshire who had been ejected from the living of Hanmer in Flintshire. Although he remained at Hanmer initially, keeping in close contact with Philip Henry, after the passing of the Five Mile Act of 1665 he preferred to move to London.[35]

Some ministers took up some other profession, which may have allowed them to continue to preach at the same time. Two entered the medical profession. Nicholas Cary, having been removed from his benefice in Monmouth town, moved to London where he became a doctor specializing in ailments of the eyes and ears.[36] John French combined work as a doctor with preaching after he left Wenvoe for Cardiff in 1662.[37] Rather more turned to teaching, which was often compatible with preaching. Among them was William Thomas, described by Calamy as 'of Eminent Piety and Learning,' who set up a school in Swansea having lost his living at St. Mary Hill, near Bridgend.[38] One of

---

31. Richards, *Religious Developments*, 511–12.

32. Calamy, *Account*, II, 717; Jones and Owens, "Anghydffurfwyr Cymru," 40.

33. Richards, *Religious Developments*, 508; Jones and Owens, "Anghydffurfwyr Cymru," 69–70.

34. Calamy, *Account*, II, 716; Richards, *Religious Developments*, 507; Jones and Owens, "Anghydffurfwyr Cymru," 82–83.

35. Rees, *History of Protestant Nonconformity*, 134–35; Nuttall, "Nurture of Nonconformity," 11–12.

36. Calamy, *Account*, II, 473; Jones and Owens, "Anghydffurfwyr Cymru," 14.

37. Rees, *History of Protestant Nonconformity*, 138–39; Jones and Owens, "Anghydffurfwyr Cymru," 28.

38. Calamy, *Account*, II, 85; Rees, *History of Protestant Nonconformity*, 137.

the intended outcomes of the penal legislation against Dissenters was to bar them from university education, thus making it more difficult to develop an informed ministry. Necessity thus gave birth to the invention of the dissenting academy to provide the sort of instruction that Dissenters could not receive elsewhere. The earliest such institution in Wales would seem to be the academy founded by Samuel Jones at Brynllywarch farmhouse in Llangynwyd, near Bridgend, Glamorgan, in c.1668.[39] Jones had been ejected from his living at Llangynwyd in 1662 but, despite the Five Mile Act, remained in the parish, his spacious farmouse at Brynllywarch providing a suitable location for an academy. Amongst the pupils were James Owen, who went on to head the dissenting academy at Oswestry and Rees Price, the father of the radical philosopher, Richard Price. Even Thomas Mansell, son of Sir Edward Mansell of Margam, a member of one of the most wealthy and influential families in Glamorgan, was sent there in the 1670s.[40] Other Anglican families who became aware of the level of scholarship at the academy followed suit.[41] A native of Denbighshire, Samuel Jones had himself been educated at All Souls and Merton, Oxford, before being appointed a fellow of Jesus College, so was evidently well qualified to undertake the instruction of his pupils.[42] Calamy described him as 'a great philosopher, a considerable master of the Latin and Greek tongues, and a pretty good Orientalist.'[43] The curriculum at Brynllywarch seems to have included tuition in science as well as in the more traditional classical languages. Bishop Hugh Lloyd of Llandaff was sufficiently impressed with Jones's scholarship to have attempted to persuade him to conform so that he might accept a church living once more. Jones responded with a series of queries, including whether unfeigned assent could be given to the complete content of any book, other than the Bible, and whether it was not therefore hypocrisy to support the *Book of Common Prayer* in the way the Act of Uniformity demanded.[44] He did not waver in his commitment to the

39. Owen, *Ysgolion a Cholegau*, 1–6; Jones, "Fame and obscurity," 41–65.

40. Jenkins, *Making of a Ruling Class*, 121.

41. Jones and Roderick, *History of Education in Wales*, 31.

42. DWB, 511–12.

43. Calamy, *Account*, III, 501.

44. Rees, *History of Protestant Nonconformity*, 232–33; Jones, *Grym y Gair*, 96; Jones, *Congregationalism in Wales*, 53–54. .

dissenting cause, registering Brynllywarch as a meeting house under the terms of the 1672 Indulgence and training pupils to preach. His was also one of the earliest academies to receive support from the Congregational Fund set up in 1690. After Jones's death in 1697, the academy moved to Abergavenny under the tutorship of Roger Griffith. As was the case with a number of early dissenting academies, it was to move location to suit the convenience of subsequent tutors until eventually settling more permanently at Carmarthen, where it established itself as a renowned institution, which educated several prominent figures in Welsh life.[45]

Samuel Jones's academy at Brynllywarch is acknowledged as the first to be established in Wales. It has, however, sometimes been claimed that as an educational establishment it was actually preceded by the school set up by Rees Prydderch (or Protheroe) near his home at Ystradwallter, near Llandovery in Carmarthenshire, after he was ejected from his position as a schoolmaster. It was stated that Prydderch had been engaged in teaching for forty years by the time of his death in 1699, which, if accurate, would predate the restoration.[46] Such traditions cannot easily be substantiated, although Prydderch was definitely cited before the consistory court in 1674 as an unlicensed schoolmaster.[47] However, early he embarked on his career, his contribution to Nonconformist education was obviously considerable, including instructing William Evans, who later became the first tutor of Samuel Jones's former institution when it moved to Carmarthen in 1704.

Some former ministers were lost to their former flocks for various reasons. Although never ordained or beneficed, Vavasor Powell was one of the more influential Welsh Puritan preachers of the 1640s and 1650s who survived to see the end of the Commonwealth. He was closely associated with the despised Propagation Act, under the authority of which a number of Anglican clergy had been removed from their parishes, and had been accused by his enemies of corruption during the 1650s. Since he was regarded as the 'metropolitan of the itinerants,'[48] it is no surprise that he should have been a prime target

45. See Roberts, "Nonconformist Academies," 13–35; Davies, Hoff Ddysgedig Nyth.

46. Rees, Protestant Nonconformity, 286; Roberts, "Nonconformist Academies," 43–44; Owen, Ysgolion a Cholegau, 12–13; Jones, Congregationalism in Wales, 97.

47. SD/CCB/8.

48. Griffith, Strena Vavasoriensis, title page.

for retaliation by resentful Anglicans and royalists. He was arrested in Shrewsbury shortly after the restoration for refusing to take the oaths of supremacy and allegiance and spent most of the decade after the restoration in captivity. Powell refused to be cowed and seemed to relish the opportunities afforded by his various appearances in court to air his views and to debate with his accusers. Upon his arrest for holding a conventicle in Merthyr Tydfil in 1668, he argued that, since the law stated that such a meeting was 'in pretence of religious worship', and since they were really worshipping rather than pretending to do so, the law could not apply.[49] He justified disobedience to the authorities in his confession of faith: 'As it is unlawful for Rulers to command any thing that God hath forbidden, and to compel men to obey the same, or to forbid any thing that God commands; so it is lawful for the servants of God to disobey such commands.'[50]

Housed in harsh conditions in the Fleet Prison, he contrived to write his *Bird in a Cage Chirping* in 1661, in which he defended the achievements of the Propagation Act in the 1650s and his own involvement with it, whilst urging his Welsh friends to keep the faith. He was transferred to Southsea Castle, near Portsmouth, for a further five years before being released in November 1667, when he took up his old role of itinerant preacher with his customary gusto. However, a year later he was arrested once more for unlawful preaching and sent back to the Fleet where he died in August 1670 aged fifty-three.[51]

The other pioneering figure who survived into the 1660s was the closed communion Baptist John Miles, who had been ejected from Ilston in Gower. His influence was far-reaching, with the church at Ilston in 1649 the first of a number of Baptist causes he helped found. Under his guidance, another group of Baptists split from the Independent congregation at Llanigon, Breconshire, in 1650 to form a church in the area of Hay.[52] Further offshoots sprang up at Llanharan, Llantrisant, Carmarthen, and Abergavenny.[53] Possibly in 1663, and certainly by 1666, he and some of his followers had emigrated to

49. Bagshaw, *Life and Death*, 136.

50. Ibid., 43.

51. Ibid., 123–91; Jones, *Vavasor Powell*, 166–88; Jones, "Sufferings," 77–89; Roberts, "Vavasor Powell."

52. NLW MS 9108; Davies, "Episodes," 16–17; Jones, "Religion in Post-Restoration Brecknockshire," 15.

53. White, "John Miles," 35–71.

Rehoboth in Massachusetts, before moving south to found the town of Swansey where Miles died in 1683.[54] Some of the causes associated with him withered on the vine, especially that at Carmarthen, but the remnants of the Ilston and Swansea Baptists, joined by some of the Llantrisant Baptists, were amongst those who survived to form a church in 1689. His former colleague, Thomas Proud, who was ejected from Cheriton in Glamorgan, was excommunicated in 1662 for not bringing his children to church for baptism.[55] It was the issue of infant baptism that made the Baptists targets for persecution, which in turn must have been one of the major incentives for emigration to America. The resulting loss of Miles and other Baptists undoubtedly weakened the leadership of the closed-communion Baptists, who remained largely separate from those other Baptists who were willing to receive at communion those who had not been baptised as adults.

Inevitably also some of the leading figures died out, but as they were lost, others came to the fore. Surely one of the most remarkable was Henry Maurice, set to work by the Triers in 1658 in his native Caernarfonshire, in Llannor and Deneio, which included the town of Pwllheli on the Llŷn peninsula. On the face of it, his Puritan credentials appeared unimpeachable. When Stephen Hughes prepared an anthology of Rees Prichard's work for publication in 1659, it was to Henry Maurice he turned for notes to explain some of the more colloquial south Wales dialect words for readers in the north. Maurice was also invited by Hughes to add a brief word to the reader at the close of the book.[56] Yet in later life Maurice spoke with regret of his many sins and shortcomings during this time.[57] When 1660 dawned, he was removed to make way for the previous incumbent, now deemed legally entitled. Yet, although his name appears on the list of those ejected as a result, he was appointed as vicar of Bromfield, near Ludlow, in March 1661. Although he also received the rectorship of Mellteyrn in April 1661 he remained at Bromfield rather than return to Caernarfonshire. It has been suggested that his retreat from his native land may be a sign of a troubled conscience, preferring to be seen to conform to the Anglicanism he had previously rejected where he was less well

54. Roberts, "John Miles."
55. SD/CCCm/2.
56. Prichard, *Rhan o waith*, 158–59.
57. Rees, *History of Protestant Nonconformity*, 209, 215.

known,[58] but it may simply be that he was offered a convenient benefice through family connections. The other possible reason for keeping his distance was that he sought to keep his troubles with debt and the shame attached to this from his acquaintances in Wales. Whatever kept him at Bromfield, it was there that he bowed to the terms of the Act of Uniformity in 1662.

By 1668 he had been promoted to the rectorship of Church Stretton in Shropshire, with its attendant salary of £140, and all seemed set fair for a safe career in the Church. The only cloud on the horizon would seem to be his inability to handle his finances, which saw him land in Shrewsbury gaol for a short interval.[59] Despite these financial difficulties, he nevertheless resigned his secure living in 1671 to devote himself to the dissenting cause. How this conversion back to his former Puritan principles took place remains unclear, although it has been suggested that an outbreak of the plague in the area in 1670 may have had some impact.[60] In his change of heart, he was evidently able to rely on the wholehearted support of his wife, Elin, despite her being the daughter of the royalist gentry family of the Glynnes of Gwynfryn in Caernarfonshire.[61] By the time of the 1672 Indulgence he was resident at Much Wenlock and took out three licenses in the vicinity, as well as another in Church Stretton.[62] With something of the careless attitude he displayed to money, he disregarded the strict terms of these licenses and took it upon himself to embark on a preaching tour in mid and north Wales. As Calamy declared, on the basis of evidence provided by James Owen, who knew Maurice well, 'His natural Temper was brisk.'[63] Sadly, Maurice's original diary, which covered six months of this busy year of 1672, has been lost, but extracts relating to the summer of 1672 were reproduced by Thomas Rees in 1883 and have therefore been preserved. These include the reference to his first visit to Breconshire and Radnorshire, where he was made welcome by various groups of Dissenters.[64] During September, he and his wife

58. DWB, 622–23.

59. Calamy, *Account*, II, 568–69; Richards, "Henry Maurice," 29.

60. Davies, "Episodes," 27.

61. Richards, "Henry Maurice," 26.

62. Richards, *Wales under the Indulgence*, 126–27, 163.

63. Calamy, *Account*, II, 571.

64. Rees, *History of Protestant Nonconformity*, 212–13.

were travelling through north west Wales, where Maurice was troubled by 'the remembrance of my former evils committed here, and my voidness of pity at heart at the observation of the sinful and miserable estate of my relations, and others in this country.'[65] His flouting of the terms of Indulgence licences continued when he attempted to preach in some of the parish churches in Llŷn, including his former church from which he was barred by its curate, Richard Owen. Undeterred by this, he attempted the same at the church of Llanarmon the following Sunday, only to have to resort to preaching in the churchyard.[66]

By the end of the year, with the Indulgence still in force, Maurice had been invited to take care of the Independent groups that had been inspired by Vavasor Powell in Breconshire, including the dispersed church centred around Llanigon. With them came some of the open communion Baptists who remained separate from the closed communion Baptists of Olchon and Llanigon and the Arminian Baptists in Radnorshire led by Henry Gregory. Along with Henry Williams of Montgomeryshire, Maurice also helped oversee the remains of Vavasor Powell's followers in Radnorshire, a mixture of Independents and Baptists.[67] Maurice emerged as one of the leading Welsh Dissenters for the next ten years, until his death in 1682 at the age of forty-eight.[68] He was more than likely the 'Morrice' that Bishop William Lucy complained about in 1673 for preaching without a licence and attracting some two to three hundred followers, which was probably an underestimate of his flock within the diocese of St. David's.[69] Not surprisingly, Maurice became a target for the church authorities once the Indulgence ended. He ignored summons to appear before the consistory court in 1673 and was excommunicated as a result in 1674.[70] It was an acknowledgement of his position at the forefront of Welsh Dissent that in 1675 he was asked by Edward Terril of Bristol for an account of the state of the cause in Wales, as someone who was obviously considered in a position to know. The resulting account is useful as further evidence

65. Ibid., 215.

66. Ibid., 215–18.

67. Underhill, *Broadmead*, 511–18.

68. Calamy, *Account*, II, 567–72; Richards, "Henry Maurice," 15–67; Jones, "Post-Restoration Brecknockshire," 44–46; Parry, "Prelates and Preachers," 50–51.

69. Richards, "Henry Maurice," 50.

70. SD/CCB/8. Jones, "Post-Restoration Brecknockshire," 55–56; Williams, "Crefydd dan gysgod erledigaeth," 7.

of the geographical spread of Dissent and its areas of relative strength, although Maurice tended to highlight the Independents and to gloss over the presence of Arminian Baptists.[71] Maurice described himself as the 'pastor elect' (meaning that he had been chosen by the congregation) of the gathered church 'which commonly meets at Llanigon.'[72] After his death in 1682, his congregations in Brecon and Radnor were overseen by Rhys Prydderch, the schoolmaster of Ystradwallter, along with his own flock in north Carmarthenshire.[73]

Henry Maurice's report in 1675, along with the list of licenses sought under the Declaration of Indulgence of March 1672 to March 1673, provide evidence of the geographical spread of dissenting ideas some ten years after the Act of Uniformity. Anglesey apparently remained something of a wilderness for Dissent, with no licenses being sought there and Maurice reporting that there was no church to be found on the island.[74] The north-west in general remained relatively weak, with the Quakers emerging as the only thriving group in Merionethshire.[75] In Caernarfonshire, there was evidently some activity on behalf of the Independents and Presbyterians and two ejected ministers received licenses: Ellis Rowlands in Clynnog and John Williams in Llangian.[76] In the north, it was Wrexham and Denbigh that had emerged as the most notable centres and here the Independents dominated.[77] The south looked far stronger, receiving 136 of the 185 licenses granted. Yet only six licenses were allotted to Breconshire, although possibly this number might have been greater after Henry Maurice had spent more time nurturing the groups there. Glamorgan yet again dominated the south, with forty-two licenses, and Monmouth followed close behind with thirty-nine. The town of Swansea figured prominently, with Daniel Higgs, Stephen Hughes, Marmaduke Matthews, and Lewis Thomas all obtaining licenses to preach. In the south-west, the number of licenses for Carmarthenshire seems lower than anticipated at eleven, compared to thirteen in Cardiganshire. In

71. Underhill, *Broadmead*, 511–18.

72. Ibid., 512,

73. Davies, "Episodes," 31.

74. Underhill, *Broadmead*, 511.

75. See Williams, "The Quakers of Merioneth," 122–56, 312–39.

76. Richards, *Wales under the Indulgence*, 144–46.

77. Ibid., 146–49.

Cardiganshire the foundations of what would come to be known as the Cilgwyn church had emerged in the vicinity of Cellan, Lampeter, and Llangybi. Pembrokeshire played host to Peregrine Phillips's congregation of Independents.[78] The limitations of the usefulness of the licenses sought under the terms of the Indulgence is evident in the instance of the Rhydwilym closed communion Baptists, who sought no freedom under the Indulgence, but who are mentioned by Henry Maurice as drawing members from Carmarthenshire, Cardiganshire, and Pembrokeshire and being under the leadership of William Jones. These Baptists were among those Dissenters who distrusted the issuing of the Indulgence, fearing that it would simply provide the authorities with the names and locations of those they should persecute. The most extreme fears that the Indulgence would end in a wholesale massacre of Dissenters were not realised.[79] But some misgivings were not entirely misplaced as, once the Indulgence was withdrawn, the authorities were in a better position to identify some of the diehard opponents of the Church and to pursue them as a result. Conversely, the Indulgence also galvanized some individuals into action, including Philip Henry and Henry Maurice, who both made substantial contributions thereafter. What does become clear from both sources is that it was the Independents who had the strongest following throughout the country, receiving 126 of the 183 licences, leading Thomas Richards to proclaim Wales 'the most Independent part of the British Isles.'[80]

It is, nonetheless, difficult to gauge just how successful the efforts of dissenting ministers were in this period, but all evidence indicates that their followers comprised a very small minority of the population. Thomas Rees overstates the case when he suggests no fewer than 15,000–16,000 Dissenters throughout Wales. He based this number on the returns from Llandaff and St. Asaph to Archbishop Shelden's enquiry in 1669, calculating that these underestimated the actual figures and assuming an even distribution of Dissenters throughout the whole of the country.[81] Figures drawn from the 1676 census suggest that there were 4,193 Dissenters in Wales, as opposed to 153,046 who conformed to the Anglican Church and a mere 1,072 Catholics.

78. Underhill, *Broadmead*, 511–18; Richards, *Wales under the Indulgence*, 109.

79. Lee, *Diaries of Philip Henry*, 253.

80. Richards, *Wales under the Indulgence*, 228–29.

81. Rees, *History of Protestant Nonconformity*, 176.

With the addition of the Welsh parishes situated within the diocese of Hereford, the total numbers of Dissenters stands at 4,221, with 154,796 conformists and 1,085 Catholics.[82] Whiteman's analysis of the census adjusts these figures slightly to a total of 4,248, including the Welsh parishes in the diocese of Hereford, or around 1.15 percent of the population.[83] As might be expected, over half of the Dissenters (2,401) were to be found within the vast, sprawling diocese of St. David's, which covered most of south-west and mid-Wales. Llandaff in the south-east included 905, whilst numbers declined in the two northern dioceses, with 463 in St. Asaph and a mere 247 in Bangor. It would appear, however, that the returns quite substantially underestimated the numbers of Dissenters in various areas, with some churches being omitted completely, such as the thriving congregation at Merthyr in Glamorgan and the church associated with Samuel Jones at Llangynwyd, Monmouthshire. An estimate of the numbers of Nonconformists in Monmouthshire sent to Archbishop Sheldon in 1669 suggested a total of 360 members, for instance, compared to the 103 recorded in 1676.[84] So considerable a decline in a relatively short space of time seem unlikely, so that the actual numbers must surely have been greater than the census indicates, although probably not massively so. Thomas Richards concluded that bishops and incumbents sought to downplay the strength of Dissent, although Anne Whiteman proposes that they did indeed strive to be accurate.[85] In any case, the situation was inevitably complicated by the number of people who were inclined towards Dissent but who nevertheless continued to attend church in order to avoid prosecution, a proportion in each parish church not readily calculated by incumbents or historians. Official figures must surely tend to be lower than the real number of adherents, who were after all for the most part attempting to conceal their presence from the authorities. Even with the problematic nature of the evidence, the 1676 census gives an indication of the continued strength of the dissenting cause, with the Independents emerging again as the largest group.

82. Richards, *Religious Census of 1676*, 44.

83. Jenkins, *Protestant Dissenters*, 58.

84. Williams, "Crefydd dan gysgod erledigaeth," 10–11.

85. Richards, *Religious Census of 1676*, 47–63; Whiteman, *Compton Census*, xxx-vii; Jenkins, *Protestant Dissenters*, 57–58.

Where church clergy were aging, poorly qualified or inactive, opportunities presented themselves for the Dissenters to extend their activities and the number of their followers. In both urban centres where Dissent manifested itself most strongly, Wrexham and Swansea, elderly clerics may have been ill equipped to counter the challenge to their parochial authority. In 1667, the vicar of Swansea was Morgan Hopkin, who, at the age of eighty-two, had first been appointed to the parish sixty years previously.[86] Surrounded as he was by some of the most effective preachers of the time, it is perhaps little wonder that Swansea became a dissenting stronghold. The vicar of Wrexham since 1662 was William Smith, described by Bishop William Lloyd as 'a Presbyterian in the late times and still halts on that foot.'[87] By 1682, Smith was elderly and infirm, with his duties falling to a curate who seemed barely capable of fulfilling them. In stark contrast, the Independents in the town were ministered to from 1668 onwards by the more energetic and well-educated John Evans, who had married Katherine, the widow of Vavasor Powell.[88] Smith's death and the dismissal of the curate allowed for the appointment of more able replacements, who might be better placed to attract parishioners back to the Church.[89]

Even without the continued presence of dissenting ministers, parishioners themselves might show dissatisfaction with the changes implemented with the restoration. Anthony Stephens had been removed from the parish of Northop in Flintshire in 1660 to make way for the return of the lawful incumbent John Williams.[90] Nothing is known of Stephens after this, but in his absence his former parishioners at Northop were not easily persuaded to conform themselves. By 1663, Archibald Sparke was described as the vicar of Northop and he encountered considerable hostility within the parish. Five members of the congregation insulted him in church in April, throwing away his *Book of Common Prayer* and he was again attacked in church in June of the year.[91]

---

86. Richards, *Religious Census*, 80–81.

87. Quoted in Richards, *Religious Developments*, 389.

88. Rees, *History of Protestant Nonconformity*, 146–47; Jones, *Vavasor Powell*, 180–81.

89. Richards, *Wales under the Penal Code*, 40–41.

90. Richards, *Religious Developments*, 375; Jones and Owens, 81.

91. NLW, Wales 4/986/7; Griffiths, "Restoration St. Asaph," 28–29.

What the reaction to such tension was depended to a large extent on the attitude of the bishops in the four Welsh dioceses of St. Davids's, Llandaff, Bangor, and St. Asaph. Bangor was the diocese with probably the fewest Dissenters and successive bishops were able to take a firm line without encountering much difficulty. The other three dioceses all had their centres of dissenting activity: Wrexham in St. Asaph, various groups in Glamorgan and Monmouthsire in Llandaff, as well as congregations in Brecon and Radnor and the town of Swansea in St. David's. In 1660, William Roberts of Bangor was the only pre-Commonwealth bishop who survived to reclaim his diocese. The other vacant sees needed to be filled and some care was taken to supply men with local connections, but who would be staunchly loyal to the restored regime. Hugh Lloyd, the new Bishop of Llandaff, had been a cleric in the diocese since 1617, although little is known of his history during the Commonwealth period.[92] George Griffiths at St. Asaph was from Anglesey and had previously served as a clergyman in the diocese.[93] The remaining see of St. David's was granted to William Lucy, a native of Hampshire who had been archdeacon of Brecon, presumably as a reward for his continued loyalty during the 1650s.[94] Although a number of Englishmen were appointed to Welsh sees, including Henry Glemham and Isaac Borrow in St. Asaph, there was also a far higher proportion of Welshmen serving as bishops in Wales than there would be during the eighteenth century. William Roberts was succeeded in Bangor by Robert Morgan and later by Humphrey Lloyd and Humphrey Humphreys, whilst William Lloyd was appointed to St. Asaph, another William Lloyd and Francis Davies to Llandaff and William Thomas to St. David's.[95] None of them was particularly tolerant of Dissent, although some adopted a harsher stance than others. Probably the most uncompromising enemy of Dissenters among them was William Lucy who earned the epitaph on his memorial at Christ's College, Brecon, of having been a vigorous opponent of schismatics and heretics.[96] In 1670 he published an attack on sectaries in his *A Treatise of the Nature of the Minister* and

92. Spurr, "Hugh Lloyd."
93. Griffiths, "Restoration St. Asaph," 9.
94. Parkin, "William Lucy."
95. Jones, *Grym y Gair*, 92–93; Williams et al., *Welsh Church*, 65–66.
96. Parry, "Prelates and Preachers," 47–49.

frequently bemoaned their temerity to Archbishop Shelden. After his death in 1677, however, he was followed by the more tolerant William Thomas, who, after his translation to Worcester in 1683 was succeeded by Lawrence Womack and later John Lloyd, who in both cases were hardly in post long enough to make any lasting impact.[97]

Bishop William Lloyd of St. Asaph has been regarded as rather more tolerant, because of his willingness to engage in debate. Lloyd came from a family with Welsh roots and had acquired a number of benefices in Wales, including the post of dean of Bangor.[98] He was appointed in 1680 and took up residence in April 1681, giving every indication of being committed to meeting the challenge presented by this somewhat impoverished see. The diocese included the north-eastern borderland where Puritan influences had been planted by Morgan Llwyd at Wrexham and continued to infiltrate into Flintshire, Denbighshire, and Montgomeryshire. His initial approach to the persistence of Dissent within his territory was to attempt to negotiate and, if possible, to convert.[99] To this end, he arranged to meet the leading Quakers Charles Lloyd and Thomas Lloyd in Welshpool during his first visitation. More daringly, a two-day public meeting was convened at Llanfyllin, Montgomeryshire, in September 1681, with the Bishop imposingly accompanied by leading clerics and justices of peace. Four days later a further debate was held with the more moderate Presbyterians—James Owen, Philip Henry, and Jonathan Roberts—in the town hall at Oswestry. Lloyd also met with the 'Conventiclers' of Wrexham and their minister John Evans in December 1681. After lengthy discussions with the Quaker Richard Davies, Lloyd suspended for the time being the serving of the writ that would have imprisoned Davies.[100] On these occasions, neither side managed to convince the other of the rightness of their cause, but Lloyd did make a favourable impression on many of the Dissenters nonetheless. He seemed to have particular respect for Philip Henry, who was no fervent advocate of separatism and may have found more common ground with

97. Jones, "Eglwys Loegr a'r Saint," 93.

98. Mullett, "William Lloyd."

99. Richards, *Wales under the Penal Code*, 40–45; Hart, *William Lloyd*, 40–53; Jones, "Anglicans and Dissenters," 90–93; Jones, "Eglwys Loegr a'r Saint," 99–103; Williams *et al.*, *Welsh Church*, 67.

100. Davies, *Account*, 207–9.

the Bishop than some of the other Dissenters. James Owen's brother, Charles, described Lloyd as an 'excellent and Learned Prelate, being a declared Enemy to Persecution' who 'studied to reduce the Dissenters in his Diocess, by mild and Christian Methods.'[101] Lloyd's willingness to engage in such discussions must have seemed a quite remarkable innovation to Dissenters more used to the hostility of ecclesiastical authorities. Thomas Richards attributes Lloyd's approach to his 'large-hearted humanity,'[102] which may indeed be the case. However, his attitude appeared to harden when it became apparent that persuasion alone was not succeeding in solving the problem of Dissent. R. Tudur Jones interprets this as a change in tactics rather than a change of heart, suggesting that Lloyd had never been any great friend of the Dissenters and had always believed that they needed to be eradicated, one way or another.[103] Tindal Hart, Lloyd's biographer, argues that the Bishop did 'sing a very different song' in 1683, in the wake of the discovery of the Rye House Plot.[104] Any suspicion of sympathy with those who did not conform to the Established Church might well have had serious repercussions at the time and it is suggested that Lloyd sought to convince Archbishop Sancroft of his zeal in pursuit of Dissent. It was certainly likely that, in the furore over Catholic plots, Lloyd may have considered that the time for patient persuasion was past. Whether his previous conciliatory appearance was a complete sham it is difficult to judge, but he certainly seemed to repent somewhat of his harsher attitude on the eve of Toleration.[105]

It is often only through their opposition to the restored Church that Dissenters appear at all in historical records after 1662. The very persecution that drove Dissenters to secrecy also provides some evidence of their existence, although, unfortunately, not all the relevant church or civil court records have survived. The Act of Uniformity continued to claim some victims amongst those who, when confronted with the issue, could not accept royal supremacy or the *Book of Common Prayer*. The penal legislation passed in the 1660s, which became known as the Clarendon Code, included both Conventicles

101. Owen, *Some Account*, 29.
102. Richards, *Wales under the Penal Code*, 40
103. Jones, "Anglicans and Dissenters," 93–94; Jones, *Grym y Gair*, 101–3.
104. Hart, *William Lloyd*, 47.
105. See below.

Acts, the Quaker Act, the Five Mile Act and the Test and Corporation Acts. Collectively, these laws made adherence to their faith exceedingly difficult for Dissenters, which was, of course, the aim. In addition, they could still fall foul of the Established Church's requirements regarding attendance and payment of dues. It was the ecclesiastical courts within each diocese that had the responsibility of ensuring regular attendance at services and payment of the parishioners' financial dues towards the upkeep of the fabric of their church.[106] Within the Welsh dioceses, the responsibility for maintaining discipline fell to the consistory or bishop's courts, in the absence of any archdeacon's courts. However, the truth is that the ecclesiastical courts lacked teeth by this period and found it difficult to enforce attendance or to require those they admonished to carry out their penance.[107] A number of cases therefore resulted in excommunication of the offender for non-appearance to answer the charges. The only way to compel someone to bow to the court was by recourse to the secular arm of the law. An appeal to the Court of Chancery could result in a writ empowering the sheriff to arrest the offender as one who had been excommunicated for over forty days.[108] Yet, the separate court system in Wales seems to have thrown up some difficulties for the authorities, which may have afforded some offenders a little extra breathing space. The Court of Great Sessions, set up by the second Act of Union in 1543, was held twice a year, in spring and autumn, in the four different circuits in the country. Bishop William Lloyd of St. Asaph complained that writs issued by the Court of Chancery could only be enforced after receipt by the judges who visited the country for a week each time the Sessions were assembled. This situation inevitably led to delays in prosecution.[109] Nevertheless, R. Tudur Jones suggests that the fear of the proceedings of the consistory courts amongst Dissenters should not be underestimated whilst the possibility of referring offenders to the secular authorities remained.[110] The relief felt at the lifting of such sanctions by the Indulgence of 1687, after a period of more severe per-

---

106. Morgan, "Consistory Courts," 5–24; Morgan, "Cases of Subtraction of Church-Rate," 70–72.

107. Morgan, "Prosecution of Nonconformists," 29–30; Jones, *Grym y Gair*, 93–94 .

108. Jones, "Religion in Post-Restoration Brecknockshire," 50–51.

109. Richards, *Wales under the Penal Code*, 33–34.

110. Jones, "Anglicans and Dissenters," 81–82.

secution, is evident in the verse of Richard Pugh, miller of Tredwstan, Breconshire, who with more enthusiasm than eloquence rejoiced that writs and excommunication could no longer be wielded as weapons against Dissenters:

> *Hwbwb! Hobob! llys yr Esgob a fu dop-dop a ni'n hir:*
> *Maen' hwy 'rwan yn lled egwan; cerddent alan oll o'r tir.*
> *Ymaith fradwyr a goganwyr, ffyrnig dreiswyr chwerwon chwyrn*
> *'Does mo'ch ofn arnaf weithian; torwyd llawer ar eich cyrn.*[111]
> [Hip, hip! Hip, hip! The Bishop's court was on top for some time
> Now they are quite feeble; all banished from the land.
> Hence traitors and revilers, fierce, bitter, severe tyrants
> I don't fear you any more; your horns have been cut back.]

The most severe punishment at the disposal of the ecclesiastical courts was excommunication, which hardly represented a meaningful threat to those who already refused to conform to the Church and to attend its services. Stephen Hughes was excommunicated in 1667 for preaching at a conventicle at Llanstephan. He was then summoned before the court of the Brecon archdeaconry in 1670 for keeping school without a licence and excommunicated again for contempt when he failed to appear.[112] He nevertheless carried on with his educational and publishing activities, even in collusion with Bishop William Thomas of St. David's, seemingly without great concern and without major repercussions.[113] The sentence of excommunication might preclude someone from holding office but Dissenters already faced those sorts of sanctions. Ironically, it was often only in death that excommunication became a real problem, since an excommunicant could not leave property by will or be buried in consecrated ground. It was the refusal of Christian burial to an individual who died outside the communion of the Church that might cause real distress to their surviving relatives.[114] It is not surprising that Baptists continued to recount with horror the story of the 'pious maid' buried in secret in the churchyard of Llanfihangel Brynpabuan, Breconshire, only to be exhumed at

111. Thomas, *Hanes y Bedyddwyr*, 42–44.

112. SD/CCCm/2; SD/CCB/6.

113. Williams, "Dissenters in Glamorgan," 471; Williams, "Stephen Hughes," 25; Evan and Rees, "Independents in Llanybri and Llanstephan," 29.

114. For significance of Christian burial, see Cressy, *Birth, Marriage and Death*, 379–473.

the command of the local incumbent and interred at a crossroads in the manner customary for a suicide or felon. She may have been the Catherine Edwards of Llysdinam whose exhumation was recorded by the vicar of the neighbouring parish, Llanafan Fawr, in 1668.[115]

Reprisals against Nonconformists were not just the business of ecclesiastical courts, however, but involved the civil authorities as well. The penal legislation known as the Clarendon Code was intended to be oppressive, designed to make it nigh on impossible for Dissenters to continue to practice their faith. The effects of the legislation were aggravated by the way the law was applied in some cases. Goods could be distrained to pay fines incurred for non-attendance at church or holding conventicles. It was not uncommon for the property seized to be grossly undervalued to ensure that even more property had to be taken to pay the fines. Such practices could lead to real hardship, as well as the trauma of having one's home invaded and ransacked in search of items of any value. Persecution was particularly acute during 1660–67, 1670–71, and in the first half of 1680s when fears regarding papist activities were at their height. Several active Dissenters found themselves constantly harassed by the local authorities, sometimes egged on by church officials as well. Peregrine Phillips, for instance, was presented several times in Pembrokeshire for refusing to attend church and for holding conventicles.[116] William Jones, the founder of the Baptist cause in Pembrokeshire, spent four years in Carmarthen prison for preaching.[117] Resistance over a lengthy period could be both costly and wearing. Thomas Gwyn of Pantygored, one of the more substantial members of the Llanigon church, contested the decision to excommunicate him in 1685. He was evidently outgunned and forced to bow to the church authorities, promising to conform on pain of the payment of £100.[118] Once the Toleration Act was passed, however, his home was licensed as a dissenting meeting house. Some magistrates were fierce in their determination to root out Dissent, although perhaps not 'the immense majority' of them that Thomas Richards

115. Richards, *Wales under the Penal Code*, 21; Jones, "'Anabaptists' of Llanafanfawr and Llysdinam," 75.

116. Jones, "Disaffection and Dissent," 213–16.

117. Rees, *History of Protestant Nonconformity*, 162.

118. SD/CCB/13; SD/CCB/G/87; Jones, "Post-Restoration Brecknockshire," 60–61; Williams, "Crefydd dan gysgod erledigaeth," 7.

claims.[119] Sir Matthew Price of Newton Hall, Montgomeryshire, actively pursued Dissenters like Vavasor Powell.[120] Preaching at Merthyr Tydfil in 1668, Powell was also confronted by Sir John Carne, who laid his hand upon his sword and claimed it served as his authority to act.[121] David Maurice of Penybont, Montgomeryshire, was known as an arch-persecutor and his ultimate fate of drowning when thrown from his horse into the Tanant river was regarded as nothing less than just retribution.[122]

In these troubled times, many Dissenters took comfort in a sense that Providence was at work in their favour and against their persecutors. Henry Williams, Ysgafell, who acted as pastor to the Independents of Montgomeryshire, suffered considerable persecution at the hands of the county authorities. It was said that whilst he was in prison, a raid on his house to seize some of his goods involved his pregnant wife being mistreated and his elderly father being killed in a struggle with the officials. All of his stock was rounded up to pay his fines, seemingly condemning the remaining household to misery and penury. Yet, one field of wheat remained untouched and its crop was so abundant as to sustain Williams and his family through the coming year. As a result, the field, some three miles west of Newtown, became known as '*Cae'r Fendith*' or 'the field of the blessing.' To add to the sense that this was an intervention by Providence, it was stated that some of the persecutors who had abused Williams and his family came to an untimely end.[123] Similarly, Charles Edwards recounted how the officer who had ordered his arrest in 1666 not long after quarrelled with his family and died of a violent fever 'in the heat of Anger.' Edwards also claimed that most of those men who had stormed his house on the occasion of his arrest had died in the prime of life within two or three years of this event.[124] A similar fate was said to have fallen the men who seized the last cow belonging to Henry Gregory, leader of the Arminian Baptists in Radnorshire. Gregory was reported to have

119. Richards, *Wales under the Penal Code*, 25.

120. Griffiths, "Restoration St. Asaph," 32.

121. Bagshaw, *Life and Death*, 138.

122. Thomas, *Hanes y Bedyddwyr*, 286; Jenkins, "Friends of Montgomeryshire," 21.

123. Thomas, *Hanes y Bedyddwyr*, 286–87; Rees, *History of Protestant Nonconformity*, 159–60.

124. Edwards, *Afflicted Man's Testimony*, 21–22.

comforted his wife over the loss of the beast by declaring, 'Providence, I doubt not, will again, by some means, procure us another cow.'[125] Such resignation and faithfulness in the light of suffering was also held up as an example, as in the detailed account of Vavasor Powell's many trials and tribulations, including spending years in close confinement in a malodorous cell next to the dunghill in the Fleet prison.[126]

The records of prosecution have inevitably been used to draw attention to the early pioneers of Nonconformity, but Walter Morgan suggests that the numbers accused may have been exaggerated. He cautions against assuming too readily that all those who came before the church courts were truly Dissenters, since act books do not include full details of the cases and failure to attend or to pay church-rate might well stem from other causes.[127] It is also the case that persecution was by no means carried out with consistent rigour in all areas and over the whole of the period. There were intervals of relative respite: between the lapse of the first Conventicles Act in December 1667 and the passing of the second in May 1670, during the period of the Indulgence between March 1672 and March 1673, and again after the granting of the Indulgence under James II in 1687. Much may have depended on the attitude of Anglican clergy locally and the extent to which they resented the activities of dissenting ministers in their parishes. It was also the case that many of the gentry in their capacity as justices of the peace showed little enthusiasm for hunting down Dissenters, either because of a distaste for hounding individuals for their faith or a simple disinclination to expend the energy required.[128] It is perhaps worth noting that, in the past, previous generations of magistrates in Wales had seemingly been quite prepared to suffer witches to live and had frequently needed to be goaded into bringing Catholic recusants to book.[129] Persistent, proactive persecution of religious Dissenters of whatever shade of opinion had therefore hardly been a characteristic of the country's civil authorities at any time. Philip Jenkins has demonstrated that former radicals formed a

125. Rees, *History of Protestant Nonconformity*, 160–61.

126. Bagshaw, *Life and Death*, 123–91.

127. Morgan, "Cases of Subtraction of Church-Rate," 87; Morgan, "Prosecution of Nonconformists," 31–32.

128. Fletcher, "Enforcement of the Conventicle Acts," 245–46.

129. Williams, *Council in Wales*, 85–105; Suggett, *History of Magic and Witchcraft*, 134–36.

substantial proportion of officials in each county in Wales and many retained some of their previous sympathies.[130] There were a number of reasons, therefore, why the local authorities might be slow to move against Dissenters in their jurisdiction. The Quakers in Cardiganshire reported that the justices of peace gave them little trouble and Sir John Vaughan of Trawscoed, one of the most prominent landowners in that county, was known to be far from severe in his attitude.[131] Sir Rice Williams of Edwinsford, Carmarthenshire, tended to be tolerant also. Justices of Peace in Flintshire were said to have been moderate and civil towards Philip Henry, even, somewhat ironically, inviting him to take on the role of high constable in 1680.[132] In Glamorgan the mighty Mansell family of Margam was inclined to give some succour to Dissenters, as were the Hobys of Neath. Bussy Mansell of Briton Ferry, despite being one of the pillars of the Commonwealth regime in Glamorgan, had found it possible to conform, yet not to the extent that he was disposed to root out those who had once been his allies.[133] It was reported that the deputy-lieutenant of south Wales, Sir Edward Mansell, treated Vavasor Powell 'very civilly and mildly' when he was arrested in the county in 1668.[134] Such attitudes may explain why some of the gentry in the Vale of Glamorgan complained in 1664 that conventicles 'abound in the western parts, and that we could not well remedy the same without giving some disgust to the deputy lieutenants and justices of the peace of those limits,' presumably a reference to the Mansell cousins.[135] West Glamorgan did indeed emerge as something of a haven for Dissenters in a way it could hardly have done without a certain tolerance, if not active sympathy, from the local gentry. It has also been pointed out that Lord President of the Council of Wales, who had supervision of all justices of peace in the country, from 1672 was the Duke of Beaufort, the descendant of a staunchly Catholic family who had converted to Anglicanism and tended towards toleration where possible.[136] Even so, with the heightened climate of persecution

130. Jenkins, "Old Leaven," 818–19.

131. Evans, "Quakers of Cardiganshire," 22; Williams *et al.*, *Welsh Church*, 67–68.

132. Nuttall, "Nurture of Nonconformity," 22.

133. Williams, "Dissenters in Glamorgan," 479; Johnson, "Bussy Mansell," 23–26.

134. Bagshaw, *Life and Death*, 140.

135. Quoted in Jenkins, *Making of a Ruling Class*, 121.

136. Morgan, "Prosecution of Nonconformists," 51.

in the 1680s, a warrant was issued in 1684 for 103 parishioners from the Swansea and Llangyfelach area to appear before the court of Great Sessions for absenting themselves for church services for over three weeks.[137] The list was headed by Stephen Hughes and also included Samuel Jones. Not all those listed were necessarily Dissenters, but the names of some had also appeared previously on the Ilston Church Book, so their religious tendencies can be assumed to have remained unchanged.[138] But what is perhaps most notable is the suggestion that many of these individuals had regularly avoided arrest over a substantial period, which again suggests a certain lack of alacrity in the pursuit of such offenders.

Some individual Dissenters also had family connections or gentry patronage that helped them escape the attentions of the local authorities. William Jones of Denbigh was given shelter by the Trefor family of Plas Teg, Flintshire.[139] Peregrine Phillips, the Independent 'apostle of Pembrokeshire', was apparently protected from worse persecution by two prominent local families: the Owens of Orielton and the Perrotts of Haroldston.[140] His landlord, Sir Herbert Perrott, went so far as to leave him £5 in his will, describing him as his 'loving friend.'[141] Samuel Jones's father-in-law, Rice Powell of Goitrehen, was a Glamorgan gentleman who maintained his commitment to the Puritan cause and his support for Jones.[142] Bishop William Lucy of St. David's complained to Archbishop Sheldon that wealthy individuals ('greate purses') actively maintained fanatics in his diocese and also inveighed against the way Stephen Hughes seemed to be sheltered from harm by some of the 'leading men' of the county of Glamorgan.[143] Hughes's father had been a respectable merchant and mayor of Carmarthen and he himself was well-connected through marriage, giving him a certain status which may have guarded him from more extreme persecution, despite Bishop Lucy's animus against him. Similarly, Calamy reported

---

137. NLW, Margam and Penrice MS 6029.

138. Hugh, "Annibyniaeth," 20–23.

139. Calamy, *Account*, II, 713–14; Jones and Owens, "Anghydffurfwyr Cymru," 48.

140. *Dictionary of Welsh Biography*, Owens, "Rhydwilym Church," 93–94.

141. Wright, "Peregrine Philips."

142. Jones, "Samuel Jones."

143. Richards, *Wales under the Penal Code*, 32–33; Jenkins, "Apostol Sir Gaerfyrddin," 11–12; Williams, "Stephen Hughes," 25.

of Henry Maurice, who had gentry connections in Caernarfonshire: 'He was taken but once, and then he was Bail'd; and upon Appearance made, was discharg'd by the Favour of some Gentlemen, who were Justices of the Peace, and his Friends and Relations.'[144]

There are suggestions that such friendly intervention was not unusual within counties where bonds of family ties and old acquaintanceship were frequently felt more keenly than the demands of office.

Loopholes could also at times be found to help evade the letter of the law. Swansea, for instance, came to be regarded as a 'city of refuge' for Dissenters since, as a borough without parliamentary representation, it was considered to be technically exempt from the conditions of the Five Mile Act.[145] Although a ruling in a case in 1678 contradicted this reading of the Act, Swansea had by then already established itself as 'the Welsh Bristol.'[146] Puritan influences had long been at work in the vicinity, with John Miles founding the first Baptist church in Wales at Ilston in 1649, the remnants of which in Neath, Baglan, Aberafan, and Newton Nottage came under the care of Lewis Thomas after the restoration.[147] The result was a cluster of ejections in the surrounding parishes, in addition to Marmaduke Matthews in Swansea itself.[148] Throughout the period when the penal code held sway, Swansea remained a haven for ejected ministers with four of them, William Thomas, Daniel Higgs, Stephen Hughes, and Marmaduke Matthews living and operating in the town with seeming impunity. Calamy reported that Matthews 'went from House to House to instruct the Inhabitants of the Town . . . He preach'd at a little Cappel at the end of the Town by the Connivance of the Magistrates.'[149] In 1672 the houses of Matthews, Daniel Higgs, and Stephen Hughes were each licensed for preaching and Lewis Thomas was also granted a license to preach in the house of the Baptist, William Dykes.[150] By 1675, Daniel Higgs

144. Calamy, *Account*, II, 570.

145. Richards, *Wales under the Penal Code*, 37–38; John, "Braslun," 14.

146. Jones, "Older Dissent of Swansea and Brecon," 139.

147. NLW 9108D; Bassett, *Welsh Baptists*, 41; Morgan, *Wales and the Word*, 6.

148. These included Daniel Higgs, Thomas Proud of Cheriton, and John Miles of Ilston. Morgan Jones of Llanmadog and Evan Griffiths of Oxwich were also ejected but later conformed. Jones and Owens, "Anghydffurfwyr Cymru," 28, 32–33, 45, 58–60, 73; John, "Braslun," 14.

149. Calamy, *Account*, II 732–33.

150. Evans, "Stephen Hughes," 33.

had seemingly taken charge of the Swansea Independents who had first been gathered together by Ambrose Mostyn.[151] Higgs had been ejected twice, from his former living at Rhosili in 1660 and then from Porteynon in 1662, both on the nearby Gower peninsula.[152] William Thomas had moved to Swansea to set up a school after losing his living at St. Mary Hill.[153] All these men were regarded as highly capable preachers and pastors and, under their influence, the town became one of the largest centres of dissenting activities in Wales, with 292 adherents listed in the 1676 census, compared to 1,500 conformists, the highest total in any Welsh parish, with a further 132 in the Gower.[154] Glanmor Williams suggests an even higher figure in reality of some 300–400 Dissenters in the town and surrounding area.[155]

Worshippers also had to resort to a number of evasive tactics to avoid detection. In Cwmystwyth, coloured clothes were hung on bushes to signal whether or not it was safe to assemble.[156] Some Dissenters held their meetings in the surely less than congenial surroundings of local caves. In Carmarthenshire, for instance, Stephen Hughes's congregation worshipped in a cave at Cwm Hwplyn near Pencader and Rees Prydderch's followers at Craig yr Widdon cave near Llandovery.[157] Tradition states that the Hay Baptists worshipped in the mountains under the Darren Ddu rock, near Olchon.[158] Several groups formed in locations near county boundaries, enabling them to flee into a neighbouring county jurisdiction where the same sheriff's writ would not run. This practice continued even after the second Conventicles Act specifically forbade it.[159] The Baptist cause at Rhydwilym, for example, emerged in the borderland of Carmarthenshire and Pembrokeshire.

151. Underhill, *Broadmead*, 514; Jones, *Congregationalism in Wales*, 71.

152. Richards, *Religious Developments*, 436, 442, 498.

153. Richards, *Religious Census of 1676*, 80; Jones and Owens, "Anghydffurfwyr Cymru," 85.

154. Richards, *Religious Census of 1676*, 78–81; Jones, "Older Dissent of Swansea and Brecon," 124–25; John, "Braslun o ddechreuadau Ymneilltuaeth," 14.

155. Williams, "Stephen Hughes," 25.

156. Jenkins, "Protestant Dissenters," 51.

157. Rees, *History of Protestant Nonconformity*, 224; Roberts, "Nonconformist Academies in Wales," 43.

158. Bassett, *Welsh Baptists*, 44.

159. Richards, *Wales under the Indulgence*, 43; Morgan, "Prosecution of Nonconformists," 51.

There was thus a good deal of co-operation between different counties, such as between the Independents in north Monmouthshire and Breconshire. Throughout, however, it was the Baptists and Quakers who encountered the greatest hostility: the Baptists for their attitude to infant baptism and the Quakers for the way they challenged the social norms.

Perhaps the most remarkable achievement for the Baptists during this period was the success in founding the new church of Rhydwilym in the south-west of the country. Although the origins of its foundation are not completely clear, it is apparent that William Jones played a vital role. He may well be the same William Jones who was appointed to the living of Cilymaenllwyd by the Provers in 1650 only to be ejected from it in 1660, but he was certainly the individual who journeyed to Olchon to be baptised by Thomas Watkins in either 1666 or 1667.[160] Jones was faithful to the tenets that John Miles had established at Olchon, espousing closed communion, immersion, personal election and the laying on of hands and the church at Rhydwilym reflected Miles's influence as a consequence. The tradition that William Jones came under the influence of Jenkin Jones of Llanddeti whilst imprisoned in Carmarthen is less easy to substantiate.[161] It is known, however, that he started to baptize converts in the south-west from 4 August 1667, beginning with Griffith Howell of Rushacre, so that by the time the church was formed on 12 July 1668 there were thirty members having received baptism at his hands. Jones and Griffith Howell were declared elders of the church, with Morgan Rhydderch and Llywelyn Jones as deacons. Thomas David Rees was made an additional elder in 1669. Despite all the difficulties of the time, Rhydwilym continued to recruit steadily, forming a gathered church with members drawn from the three surrounding counties of Pembrokeshire, Carmarthenshire and Cardiganshire. The members of Rhydwilym laid low and sought no freedom under either of the royal Declarations of Indulgence, possibly fearing identifying themselves for fear of future reprisal. As a result, although the church book dates back to 1667, it is sketchy on any detail regarding the early years.[162] By the advent of Toleration, the church

---

160. Thomas, *Hanes y Bedyddwyr*, 319; Owens, "Rhydwilym Church," 95–96; Bassett, *Welsh Baptists* 44; Jenkins, *Protestant Dissenters in Wales*, 64–65.

161. Owens, "Rhydwilym Church," 95.

162. NLW, NLW Deposit MS 127A.

amounted to 113 members from thirty-eight parishes who finally felt free to announce their presence to the world, sending William Jones and Griffith Howell to represent them at the London Association in 1689. Although the church had previously met in various locations, its centre was now established as Rhydwilym in the parish of Llandysilio in Pembrokeshire, located near the Carmarthenshire border. The burgeoning of the cause at Rhydwilym led to further branches in the area during the later seventeenth and early eighteenth century, including Glandŵr in 1696 and Cilfowyr in 1704, thus helping to establish a tenacious Baptist presence in the north of Pembrokeshire.

Quakers remained the most reviled of dissenting groups and experienced the most acute persecution, which ultimately had the effect of reducing their numbers. While some leniency might often have been displayed towards the more socially acceptable Independents and Presbyterians, the Quakers were deemed more dangerous and intolerable. They were also specifically targeted by the government in the Quaker Act of 1662. The Quakers kept fuller records of their privations than other dissenting groups, with some four hundred of them listed as having suffered in some form during the period between restoration and Toleration,[163] although it has also been suggested that the term 'Quaker' was used very loosely in some areas and may indicate Dissenters more generally.[164] Five of them died in gaol in Wales during this period, through illnesses aggravated by the filthy and uncomfortable conditions in which they were kept. Others languished in prison for years in conditions similar to that of Welshpool gaol where they had to endure a shower of urine and excrement from the chamber above.[165] Although the social standing of Charles and Thomas Lloyd of Dolobran may have provided some measure of shelter from the worst excesses, there is no doubt that Montgomeryshire Quakers suffered considerably, as demonstrated by the petition they sent to the Quarter Sessions in 1662.[166] Merionethshire Friends also experienced a great deal of hostility from ecclesiastical and civil authorities. Opposition seemed unrelenting in most counties, yet a small number of Friends survived in many areas. The Quakers maintained

163. Rees, *History of Protestant Nonconformity*, 171.

164. Morgan, "Prosecution of Nonconformists," 33.

165. Jenkins, "Friends of Montgomeryshire," 18.

166. Davies, *Account*, 40–42; Griffiths, "Restoration St. Asaph," 32–33.

a presence in Monmouthshire, building a meeting house at Pont-y-moel in 1679, under the patronage of the Richard Hanbury, a connection to the powerful Hanbury family.[167] Groups of Quakers clung on to their beliefs in parts of Glamorgan as well, including at Cardiff and Swansea.[168] Yet, for some tormented Quakers the only solution seemed to be the refuge offered by William Penn's settlement in Pennsylvania. Emigration to America depleted the numbers of Welsh Quakers substantially, especially in Merionethshire, which supplied half of the Quaker emigrants to Pennsylvania.[169]

The difficulties in continuing to worship inevitably had an effect on the nature of the dissenting congregations. Some dissenting ministers took on a wider mission than in the days when they had been confined to specific parishes. Since they were few in number, there was a common awareness that they would have to serve several groups of Dissenters across an extensive area. There would probably have been a general consensus in favour of Vavasor Powell's guidance on the definition of the visible church: 'It is a Gospel-Ordinance for Saints to gather themselves together into Christian societies, or particular churches, that they may the better perform such duties as they owe unto the Lord, and to one another: and it is the duty of all believers, if possibly and conveniently they can, to joyn themselves unto some such Church, and being joyned, to continue members thereunto, unless some necessary and good reason occasion the contrary . . .'[170]

But these were exceptional times and the ideal of gathering together regularly was immensely difficult to achieve when the law forbade meetings of more than five in number. The result was the emergence of a rather different kind of church, with many of those congregations identified as a single church, such as Llanigon in Breconshire and Rhydwilym in Pembrokeshire, in essence consisting of a number of different centres. R. Tudur Jones suggests that the 'county church' emerged as an entity during this period simply because of the restrictions that hampered the development of individual congregations.[171] These churches were in reality several separate gatherings, connected

167. Morgan-Guy, "Religion and Belief," 157.

168. Williams, "Glamorgan Quakers," 57–63.

169. Williams, "Quakers of Merioneth," 122.

170. Bagshaw, *Life and Death*, 36. See also Gibbard, *Elusen i'r Enaid*, 34–42.

171. Jones, "Trefniadaeth Ryngeglwysig," 24–30.

chiefly by having a pastor in common, who had to take on duties over a wide area because of the scarcity of ministers. Stephen Hughes, for instance, was said to have had to ride eight or ten miles between preaching engagements with his various congregations in Carmarthenshire on a Sunday.[172] Each congregation met at several different locations to avoid any routine that might alert the authorities to their presence. This system must have placed a considerable burden on church elders and deacons to help sustain the separate communities and individual believers who were at times located at some distance from their minister. It was a situation that made it difficult for either a Presbyterian or an Independent organisation to develop properly.[173] The need for a number of what were in effect separate centres of worship to be grouped together under a single minister made it difficult to implement a proper Independent system of government, as each church was in reality a loose federation of different congregations. A firm Presbyterian structure was also hard to achieve because the need for secrecy demanded an element of flexibility, with alternating and irregular meeting places. This flexibility included considerable co-operation between Dissenters of differing views. The lines between Presbyterians and Independents in particular were blurred and they frequently came together to worship. Presbyterianism did not have such a strong presence as Congregationalism in Wales, although it had some extremely capable supporters in Philip Henry and Samuel Jones, Llangynwyd.[174] Vavasor Powell's evangelical work had also led to mixed congregations of Baptist and Independents in Montgomeryshire and Radnorshire.[175] There are suggestions that groups of closed and open communion Baptists, such as existed in Radnorshire, might also be prevailed upon to join forces temporarily during this time of trial.[176] It was only after Toleration when public worship became possible once more that denominational lines were more emphatically redrawn.

Another fundamental difficulty faced by ejected ministers was how to maintain themselves and their families after the loss of their stipend. Some were fortunate enough to be men of means and were

172. Calamy, *Account*, II, 718.

173. Davies, "Episodes," 30.

174. Richards, *Wales under the Indulgence*, 180–94.

175. Bassett, *Baptists*, 37.

176. Matthews, "Bedyddwyr Maesyfed," 1–13.

able to sustain themselves without their benefices. Stephen Hughes, after being removed from his parish of Meidrim, returned to his father's house at nearby Carmarthen. John Hughes was a successful silk merchant of Puritan tendencies who was doubtless willing to provide for his son. However, Hughes also made an advantageous marriage, probably around 1665, to Catherine, daughter of John Daniel, mayor of Swansea, gaining a wife who supported him financially and shared his faith. Hughes moved to her home in Swansea where he remained for the rest of his life.[177] Not all were as fortunate however, and many of the Dissenters came from the middling sorts of society who did not always have sufficient resources to survive without a regular income from some profession. Marmaduke Matthews was said to have 'live'd above the World, and depended wholly upon Providence for the support of himself and his Family.'[178] Providence assisted him through the means of well-wishers but chiefly through his children, including Mordecai Matthews, who had been removed from Llancarfan, Glamorgan, to make way for the restoration of the previous incumbent in 1660. Unlike his father, he was content to conform and received the living of Reynoldston in the Gower in 1661. Part of his income from the Church seems to have gone towards maintaining his dissenting father in his activities, however.[179] Some ministers were the recipients of patronage by the gentry, such as William Jones who, as mentioned previously, was given shelter on the estate of the Trefor family of Plas Teg, Flintshire, after having been removed from Denbigh.[180] Ambrose Mostyn, who had been one of the pioneers of Puritanism in its two major strongholds of Swansea and Wrexham, found refuge for a while at the house of Lord Saye and Sele in Oxfordshire, where he acted as chaplain.[181] Teaching and other occupations helped sustain others, but many had to rely on the good will of their families and contributions from their followers. This may well have accustomed members to the necessity of such contributions, which became a regular way of life

177. Calamy, *Account*, II, 718; Williams, "Stephen Hughes," 22, 25; Evans, "Stephen Hughes," 31–40.

178. Calamy, *Account*, II, 732.

179. Jones and Owens, "Anghydffurfwyr Cymru," 56–57.

180. Calamy, *Account*, II, 713–14; Rees, *History of Protestant Nonconformity*, 131; Jones and Owens, "Anghydffurfwyr Cymru," 48.

181. Rees, *History of Protestant Nonconformity*, 57; Jones and Owens, "Anghydffurfwyr Cymru," 64,

after Toleration as the Dissenters licensed their meeting houses and formed their churches.

Preaching and maintaining some form of worship were the most constant demands on ministers and the most obvious means of being of service to their followers. Yet, in addition to preaching, ejected ministers also strove to keep the cause alive through the use of print. Many of the works produced were moderate enough to avoid controversy and to prove palatable to a wider audience than devout Dissenters. Indeed, some publications represented important milestones in the history of print through the medium of Welsh. The development of print culture in Welsh had been severely hampered by the licensing laws that limited the establishing of printing presses to London, Oxford, and Cambridge until 1695.[182] The majority of Welsh books were produced in London as a result, in printing houses where the workers would have had no knowledge of the Welsh alphabet or ability to spot errors in the printed text. Authors of early Welsh books often issued heartfelt and sometimes despairing apologies for these mistakes, attributing them to the difficulties of printing outside Wales. Such an apology appeared in the foreword by Stephen Hughes of his edition of Rees Prichard's work in 1659, for instance.[183] Books published in Oxford might have had something of an advantage, as there were generally Welsh-speaking students glad to earn a little extra cash by proof reading Welsh works for printers. In the light of all these difficulties, it is perhaps not surprising that only around 108 Welsh titles appeared between 1546 and 1660.[184] It was only in the eighteenth century, with the development of presses within Wales and growing demand created by increasing literacy rates, that publication in Welsh became more viable and efficient.

Judging by the content of Welsh publications from the post-Restoration period, it would seem that the longstanding concern about the need to instruct the inhabitants of Wales in Protestant doctrine had by no means been satisfactorily resolved. Residual loyalty to Catholic practices had plagued generations of committed reformers from the reign of Elizabeth I onwards. Converting the Welsh to the Protestant cause had always been a slow process, hampered by illiteracy

---

182. Parry, "From Manuscript to Print," 263–76; Llwyd, *Printing and Publishing*, 93–95.

183. Hughes, *Rhan o waith*, sig A4v.

184. Jenkins, *Literature, Religion and Society*, 34.

and a continuing shortage of Welsh-medium materials, despite the great leap forward provided by the translation of the Scriptures.[185] The period of Civil War and Commonwealth had to some extent distracted from that ongoing campaign, even with the good intentions of the Propagation Act of 1650,[186] but concerned individuals took up the work of instilling Protestant doctrine once more after the restoration. Religious issues formed the subject matter of the overwhelming majority of books published in Welsh between 1662 and 1689. Yet the emphasis appeared to be more on the need to resist the Catholic faith than to combat the threat of Dissent, which one might have supposed would have seemed more immediate in the light of recent events. There may have been a number of reasons behind this focus, including the active involvement of Dissenters such as Stephen Hughes and Charles Edwards in Welsh-medium publications at the time. Another factor was the possible disquiet caused by the publication in London of *Allwydd neu Agoriad Paradwys i'r Cymru* ('The Key to Paradise for the Welsh'), by John Hughes in 1670. The preface stated that the work was primarily directed to the author's friends in Monmouthshire and Breconshire, areas where Catholic loyalties lingered, especially under the patronage of the Earls of Worcester (later Dukes of Beaufort) from Raglan Castle.[187] In addition to a calendar of saints days, with special attention to Welsh saints, it contained prayers such as the Lord's Prayer, the Ave Maria, and the Miserere in Welsh. It also included guidance on how to read and pronounce words in Welsh and Latin, the latter purportedly in order to shame the English whose pronounciation of Latin was said to be abysmal! In effect, it was a devotional manual for Catholics that might offer practical help in enabling them to maintain their worship in Welsh. Its very existence, and the perceived demand for it, would have been a cause for concern for Welsh Protestants at all points on the religious spectrum.

In addition, there was a more general fear that Catholicism might take advantage of the schisms within Protestantism to reclaim some of those left confused or disillusioned by the changes to church services before and after the Act of Uniformity. Such concerns were fuelled further by the general sense of panic by the early 1680s over

185. See White, *Welsh Bible*, 39–52.

186. Jenkins, *Protestant Dissenters*, 17–28.

187. Hughes, *Allwydd neu Agoriad Paradwys*, i; Geraint Bowen, "Allwydd neu Agoriad Paradwys," 80–160.

the Popish Plot and Rye House Plot. The authorities felt it necessary to translate into Welsh Charles II's declaration to his subjects in 1683 regarding the recent plot against him and his government.[188] Also translated was a work by Thomas Comber, which took the form of a debate between a devout Protestant and a Catholic priest, with the Protestant emerging triumphant.[189] Fear of Catholicism also motivated Thomas Jones, the Welsh printer based in London, to publish *Y Gwir er Gwaethed Yw* ('The Truth no matter how bad') (1680), a collection of anti-Catholic verses.[190] The preoccupation with the perceived Catholic threat percolated through a number of publications aimed at boosting religious knowledge, including John Thomas's devotional manual of 1680 which took the opportunity of condemning papists for hiding the gospel from the common people by insisting on prayers in an unfamiliar language.[191]

The exception to the general rule that there was little overt criticism of dissenting ideas in print in this period was, as might perhaps have been anticipated, attacks on the Quakers. Rondl Davies, vicar of Meifod, Montgomeryshire, was indignant not just because of the influence of the Friends in his locality, but also because his daughter, Prudence, had fallen in love with a Quaker blacksmith. An outraged sense of social status as well as defence of religious orthodoxy therefore lay at the heart of his *Profiad yr Ysprydion* ('Trial of the Spirits') (1675), denouncing all those who did not conform to the Anglican Church. Although his false prophets included Catholics, Presbyterians, and Independents, he spared his greatest ire for the Quakers, for their emphasis on the intangible inner light and their lack of deference to their social superiors.[192] The other blast against Quaker doctrine came from the pen of William Jones, in response to Thomas Wynne's *The Antiquity of the Quakers Proved out of the Scriptures of Truth* (1677). Wynne was a barber-surgeon from Caerwys, Flintshire, but had previously earned his living as a cooper. His work searched the Bible for

188. *Traethiad Mawrhydi y Brenin*, passim.

189. Comber, *Teg Resymmeu*, passim. A translation of *The Plausible arguments of a Romish priest, answered by an English Protestant*, the Welsh title refers instead to 'a Protestant of the Church of England,' which may have been a more acceptable rendition for a Welsh audience.

190. Jones, *Y Gwir er Gwaethed Yw*, passim; Jenkins, *Thomas Jones*, 22–26.

191. Thomas, *Ymarferol Athrawiaeth Gweddi*, passim.

192. Davies, *Profiad yr Ysprydion*; Jenkins, "Friends of Montgomeryshire," 19.

instances of individuals trembling before the Lord which were then construed as early signs of Quaker activity. Although most of the book was written in English, there was a section in Welsh targeted at the author's 'dear brothers and sisters of the land of my birth,' urging them kindly to turn to the true light of faith.[193] The Anglican clergyman William Jones, writing anonymously in response, dwelt in particular on Wynne's social origins, as indicated by the full title of his volume: *Work for a Cooper, Being An Answer to a Libel, Written by Thomas Wynne the Cooper, the Ale-man, the Quack, and the Speaking-Quaker* (1679). The tone was deeply contemptuous and dismissive of Wynne's audacity, with a particularly vitriolic section in Welsh responding directly to Wynne's address to his Welsh readers:

> Yspys oeddem er ystalm fod y Bendro arnat; ond nis gwybuom dy fod o'th gôf, nes gweled dy bappyr anhirion. Tydi a wyddit fod y Cymru wedi eu dyscu yn Ffydd a Ffyrdd yr Arglwydd lawer cant o flynyddoedd cyn i'r Wiber ddodwy yn dy Siolyn, na bod erioed sôn am Gwaceriaeth yn y byd; ac a wyddit ma'i nad Cyscu yr oeddem pan beraist ti inni Ddeffro.[194] [It was known to us for some time that you suffered from giddiness, but we did not know that you were out of your mind, until we saw your unkind paper. You know that the Welsh were taught in the faith and ways of the Lord many hundreds of years before the viper laid its egg in your shawl, or there was ever mention of Quakerism in the world, and you know that we were not sleeping when you caused us to wake.]

Wynne rightly guessed the identity of his attacker and produced a further work in reply in 1679.[195] Another work that might be considered a defence of Quaker practices was the publication by George Fox and others, *A Battle-Door for Teachers & Professors to Learn Singular and Plural*, which appeared in 1660. This was a justification of the use of 'thou' through grammatical rules and scriptural precedent. It included a section in Welsh, entitled 'The Welch Battle-Door,' insisting that to use the plural form when addressing an individual was 'incorrect Welsh.'[196] After Toleration a larger number of polemical works appeared, as dissenting groups had greater freedom to publicize their

193. Wynne, *Antiquity of the Quakers*, 19–20.
194. Jones, *Work for a Cooper*, 30.
195. Wynne, *Antichristian Conspiracy Detected*.
196. Fox *et al.*, "Welch Battle-Door," 1–8.

ideas and as Anglicans strove to defend the tenets of their church. In particular, the issue of infant baptism became a matter of controversy with publications both for and against the Baptist stance appearing in the 1690s.[197] These included James Owen's *Bedydd Plant or Nefoedd* ('Children's Baptism from Heaven') in 1693 in defence of infant baptism and, in response, a translation of Benjamin Keach's *Light Broke Forth in Wales* in 1696.[198]

Such arguments in print were an indulgence only really possible after Toleration, however. Prior to 1689, the focus of most dissenting literature, as of Welsh-medium publications in general, was on producing instructive, improving guides to the principles of the Protestant faith. The most active contribution in this area came from Stephen Hughes, the ejected minister of Meidrim in Carmarthenshire, who had settled in Swansea after marrying a native of that town. Whilst some ejected ministers strove to continue to minister to their flocks, some took to teaching and others were engaged in publishing, Hughes managed to combine all three during the 1670s and 1680s. Perhaps the best remembered and most feted of those who could not conform, he became known as the 'Apostle of Carmarthenshire' but his influence was felt far more widely than that county alone. Part of the reason for his considerable influence was the highly successful collaboration with Thomas Gouge, the founder of the Welsh Trust in 1674.[199] Gouge, who had been expelled from his living at St. Sepulchre in London, had much in common with Hughes in terms of religious views and attitudes. Despite having no direct connection with Wales, he had become aware of the need to fund publications in Welsh by reading the biography of Joseph Alleine of Taunton, who had expressed similar concerns. Alleine may have been motivated through a link with Samuel Jones, who had been ordained by the Presbyterians at Taunton.[200] In 1671–72, Gouge travelled to the Welsh borders to judge for himself and became convinced of the crying need for a supply of Bibles in Welsh. It was this which prompted him to establish his charity, which attracted support from members of the Welsh community

197. Jenkins, *Literature, Religion and Society*, 174–78; Jenkins, "Goleuni Gwedi Torri Allan," 92–96.

198. Jenkins, "James Owen versus Benjamin Keach," 57–66.

199. Jones, *Charity School Movement*, 277–89.

200. Calamy, *Account*, II, 721; Jones, "Samuel Jones."

in London, especially those who had flourished financially and whose consciences might be moved to help their less fortunate compatriots.

Part of the Trust's aim was to establish schools, along the same lines as what had been achieved under the terms of the Propagation Act in the 1650s. By 1675, 2,225 pupils were being taught at eighty-six schools in the country.[201] These schools were wound up when the Trust ended with the death of Gouge in 1684 and it is hard to estimate their influence. The decision to teach in English must have limited their impact, but would probably not have been so much of an issue in some areas of Radnorshire and Monmouthshire where English-speaking pupils might well have benefited.[202] Yet, it is interesting to note that the counties with the highest number of schools tended to be those closest to Stephen Hughes's sphere of influence: Carmarthenshire, Pembrokeshire and Glamorgan. Breconshire and Radnorshire, where there were substantial number of Dissenters, had only two and three schools respectively. The counties of Merionethshire and Montgomeryshire had no schools, Anglesey only one and Caernarfonshire four. The south of the country was obviously the area that received most attention, therefore, and possibly the area where English-medium schools were more practicable.

Despite using English as a medium of instruction in school, Gouge and his Trust were persuaded of the value of supplying religious literature in Welsh. The Trust operated partly by buying up existing copies of Welsh books so that they might be distributed as needed and partly by backing further publications. By 1675 thirty-two Welsh Bible and 479 Welsh New Testaments, which were 'all that could be had in Wales or London' were acquired, as were five hundred copies of *Holl Ddyledswydd*, the translation of Richard Allestree's *The Whole Duty of Man*.[203] At the same time, the Trust also oversaw a new edition of *Ymarfer Duwioldeb*, the Welsh version of Bayly's *Practice of Piety* which had already been republished twice since Rowland's Vaughan's translation had first appeared in 1629. Two and a half thousand copies were printed and distributed free among the poor and among school pupils. Stephen Hughes became Gouge's chief contact in Wales and advised him regarding the choice of publications. Most of the works

201. Jones, *Charity School Movement*, 284.

202. White, "Popular Schooling," 318–19.

203. Jones, "Two Accounts," 72–73; Llwyd, "Printing and Publishing," 99–101.

produced under the aegis of the Trust were broadly acceptable to all devout Protestants and were, as Calamy suggested, not aimed to recruit readers to the dissenting cause but 'contain such practical duties as all good Christians are and must be agreed in.'[204]

Hughes's other main collaborator in this venture was Charles Edwards, the Oxford-educated former vicar of Llanrhaeadr-ym-Mochnant on the Denbighshire-Montgomeryshire border. Edwards had lost this comfortable living prior to the restoration in 1659, in circumstances that remain unclear, although he tends to attribute it to the fact that he had incurred the displeasure of some of the wealthier members of the community.[205] He took the oath of allegiance required under the 1662 Act and afterwards: 'I lived very [p]rivately, and as inoffensively as I could. For pe[a]ce sake I o[f]ten went to hear the Conformists in publick, and seldom joyned in private Worship with [a]ny greater number than the Law allows of, and never medled with any designs to disturb the Government . . .'[206]

This meekness did not spare him the attentions of the authorities, however, and he was arrested and conveyed to gaol in 1666. He claimed that the raid on his house to take him captive was responsible for the death of one of his children who had been terrified by the experience. It also cost him the company of his remaining family, since his wife parted from him, keeping the children with her. It was this traumatic turn of events that led Edwards to Oxford and then London, where he devoted his energies to the publishing of improving literature in Welsh. By the time he came into contact with Hughes, he had already produced the first version of his best-known work, *Ffydd ddi-ffuant* ('Unfeigned faith') in 1667. This first edition relied heavily on the work of John Foxe and had little to say about Wales specifically. By the time the second edition appeared in 1671, Edwards had evidently read more widely and had been influenced by Bishop Richard Davies's letter to the Welsh people, which formed the preface to the first Welsh translation of the New Testament in 1567. This work presented Edwards with the argument that the Christian gospel had first been received in the British Isles by the ancestors of the Welsh through Joseph of Arimathea before the influence of Roman Catholicism had

204. Calamy, *Account*, II, 10.
205. Edwards, *Afflicted Man's Testimony*, 6–7.
206. Ibid., 8.

been brought to bear. Edwards leant increasingly towards an inter-pretation of Christian history that concentrated on the destiny of the Welsh people and this is what was contained in the third edition of his work, with a slightly altered title, *Y ffydd ddi-ffuant* ('The unfeigned faith') in 1677.[207]

Edwards's mastery of the Welsh language, combined with Hughes's determination to produce work that would be accessible to the ordinary reader, led to a series of successful titles. There was a tendency towards producing translations of English books whose content had already proved effective since this seemed a quick way of disseminating sound religious guidance. The known dissenting be-liefs of Gouge, Hughes, and Edwards were bound to make their works subject to scrutiny and they probably had to tread very carefully to avoid any material that might be considered contentious or proselytis-ing. They turned to the work of moderate Puritans such as Richard Baxter, William Perkins, Arthur Dent, and Lewis Bayly.[208] Edwards had already revised the translation of Bayly's *The Practice of Piety* for publication by the Trust in 1675. The focus was on useful content, conveyed in readable prose. Older works were frequently revised by Edwards and he was responsible for overseeing the printing, cutting down substantially on the number of errors in the final editions. In this process, Hughes and Edwards also worked with another dissenter, Richard Jones, former master of Denbigh School,[209] who may have been known to Edwards as a fellow native of Denbighshire. Jones had already been responsible in 1659 for the Welsh version of *A Call to the Unconverted* by Richard Baxter. More of his works were published under the patronage of the Trust and in one of the composite vol-umes edited by Hughes, *Tryssor i'r Cymru* ('A Treasure for the Welsh') which appeared in 1677. This volume contained Jones's translation of Richard Baxter's *Now or Never*, a translation by Robert Llwyd of Arthur Dent's *A Sermon of Repentance* and a new edition of the Puritan Oliver Thomas's original work *Drych i dri math o bobl* ('A mir-ror to three kinds of people') which first appeared in 1648.[210] Hughes

207. See Morgan, "Charles Edwards," 213–30; Morgan, *Charles Edwards*, 9–62; Thomas, "Puritan Writers," 190–209.

208. Jenkins, "Apostol Sir Gaerfyrddin," 12; Jenkins, "A lleufer dyn," 207–16.

209. Calamy, *Account*, II, 543–44; Davies, "Richard Jones," 173–74.

210. Hughes, *Tryssor i'r Cymru*.

was responsible for editing six works during the lifetime of the Welsh Trust, three of them composite volumes containing three separate works. In addition to *Tryssor i'r Cymru*, 1677 also witnessed the publication of *Cyfarwydd-deb i'r Anghyfarwydd* which contained Oliver Thomas's *Carwr y Cymru*, Vavasor Powell's *Ymddiddanion rhwng Crist a'r Publican* (a translation of *Saving Faith set forth in Three Dialogues*) and Robert Holland's translation of William Perkins's *An Exposition of the Lord's Prayer, Agoriad byrr ar Weddi'r Arglwydd*. The volume of William Perkins's catechism translated by Richard Jones which Hughes had edited in 1672 was bound with two more of Jones's translations: *Rhodfa Cristion* (Henry Oasland's *Christian Daily Walk*) and *Amdo i Babyddiaeth* (Richard Baxter's *A Winding Sheet for Popery*).[211] Thomas Gouge's own works were also selected, with Richard Jones translating his *Christian Directions* as *Hyfforddiadau Christianogol* in 1675 and William Jones of Denbigh producing *Gair i Bechaduriaid a Gair ir Sainct* (A Word to Sinners, and a Word to Saints) and *Principlau neu Bennau y Grefydd Ghristianogol* both in 1676. These composite volumes illustrate the way Hughes combined tried and tested works with new translations, which he judged would prove effective. The patronage of the trust was crucial in printing this stream of publications and in ensuring that a proportion were allocated to the most needy. Charles Edwards, as proofreader of Gouge's *Hyfforddiadau Christianogol*, claimed in his foreword that Providence was feeding the Welsh through the English in the same way as it had done by providing honey for Samson from the lion's mouth. Contributions from England had made it possible to print three thousand copies of the work for 'our countrymen.'[212] Even so, Hughes apparently spent a third of what he and his wife had put by on publishing *Tryssor i'r Cymru* and *Cyfarwydd-deb i'r Anghyfarwydd* in 1677. He must also have been put to considerable expense travelling to collect subscriptions as well as journeying to London to keep in touch with the Trust and the printers.

Throughout, Hughes displayed a keen sense of which works would appeal to readers as well as prove instructive. That was why he prepared for the press the verse of Rees Prichard, commonly known as Vicar Prichard. The vicar of Llandovery in Carmarthenshire in the mid-seventeenth century, Prichard's homely verses had been kept

211. Hughes, *Catechism*.
212. Gouge, *Hyfforddiadau*, 2.

alive in folk memory and conveyed simple, pious messages in an easily memorised format. Hughes had edited a printed collection of Prichard's work in *Gwaith Mr Rees Prichard* in 1659 and was to oversee the publication of three further, fuller editions in 1672 and yet another, even more comprehensive one, in 1681. It was the 1681 edition which was first given the title by which Rees Prichard's work would become better known: *Canwyll y Cymry* or 'The Welshman's Candle,' a title drawn from a line of Prichard's work. Some fifty editions of the collection appeared by 1820, demonstrating its long-term popularity as a means to greater knowledge of the Bible and the Protestant gospel.[213] Hughes's judgement also proved well founded in his decision to prepare a translation of John Bunyan's *Pilgrim's Progress*: *Taith y Pererin*, which appeared in 1688. It was a work without precedent in Welsh and Hughes was concerned that the unfamiliar medium of fiction might prove disconcerting to the readers. Despite his reservations, it was a runaway bestseller, for its time. For the Dissenters in particular the image of the hero struggling to keep the faith through all manner of trials must have struck a chord. Forty-one editions appeared by 1934, making it one of the most popular books in Welsh, after the Bible itself.[214] It was also yet another collaboration with Charles Edwards, since Hughes was assisted to complete the work by Edwards, Iaco ab Dewi and one other anonymous translator.

Hughes's greatest achievement was surely the 1678 edition of the Welsh Bible, published with the backing of the Welsh Trust and printed by the royal printers. This gave rise to the quite extraordinary scenario of an officially sanctioned publication of the Bible being edited by a man who had suffered excommunication from the Established Church. This was not achieved without some unwillingness on the part of Bishop Humphrey Lloyd of Bangor and Bishop William Lucy of St. David's, who died in 1677 before the Bible appeared, to be replaced by the more amenable William Thomas.[215] Thomas, as precentor of St. David's, had already encouraged the printing of Rees Prichard's work in 1672, earning him a dedication from Hughes. As bishop, he continued to realise the value of such publications.[216] Although Hughes

---

213. White, *Welsh Bible*, 50–51.
214. Jenkins, *Literature, Religion and Society*, 129.
215. Jones, *Charity School Movement*, 286.
216. Jenkins, *Literature, Religion and Society*, 57–58; Jones, *Grym y Gair*, 106.

was the main editor of the Bible, it was Charles Edwards, who was more conveniently based in London, who corrected the proofs.[217] Eight thousand copies were produced, with seven thousand sold at a price of 4s. 2d., whilst the remaining thousand were distributed free to the poor. Gouge and Hughes had collected the names of subscribers beforehand to help meet the £2,000 cost of printing, the first time that such a practice had been used for a Welsh publication. Despite the involvement of prominent Dissenters who had met with persecution for their faith, the edition was well-received and helped supply an obvious need among both Anglicans and Dissenters. This was perhaps again the consequence of Hughes's conciliatory personality. Calamy said of him that 'His Moderation and lively Preaching, recommended him to the Esteem of the sober Part of the Genry, by whose Connivance he often preach'd in publick Churches.'[218] Although Calamy can hardly be regarded as the most dispassionate observer,[219] Hughes's career bears out this assessment of his moderate attitude. He proved remarkably able to bring together people of contrasting beliefs and attitudes in support of a common goal.

Hughes had hoped to complete a further edition of the Bible, this time without including the Apocrypha or the *Book of Common Prayer*. This was purportedly in order to cut down on costs, but it may also have suited Hughes's dissenting beliefs. He was to die in 1688 before seeing the work through to completion and it was yet another ejected dissenter, David Jones, formerly incumbent of Llandysilio, Carmarthenshire, who edited the 1689–90 edition, ten thousand copies of which were printed and which indeed did not contain the *Book of Common Prayer*.[220] Charles Edwards survived his friend, returning to his native Denbighshire after their collaboration ended. But, judging by the evidence of his memoir, *An Afflicted Man's Testimony concerning his Troubles* (1691), he became mentally rather unstable by the end of his life and nothing is known of his fate after the autobiography ends in July 1691. Thomas Richards is rather less than complimentary about Edwards, seeming to regard him as lacking the resolution displayed by

---

217. Edwards, *Afflicted Man*, 9, 12.

218. Calamy, *Account*, II, 718.

219. Wykes, "Calamy's Account," 387–88.

220. Jones and Owens, "Anghydffurfwyr Cymru, 42–43; White, *Welsh Bible*, 70.

other Dissenters.[221] Yet this perhaps fails to take into consideration the broader, long-term contribution of his labours on the Bible, in proof-reading the books produced by the Welsh Trust and in producing a classic of Welsh literature in *Y ffydd ddi-ffuant*. There is no denying that Welsh-medium print culture in the latter half of the seventeenth century would have been immeasurably poorer without the contribution of these Dissenters. Between 1660 and 1689, some ninety-six books appeared in Welsh, only ten of them between 1660 and 1669 owing to the upheavals of that decade.[222] The subsequent increase during the 1670s and 1680s was almost solely a result of the work of Dissenters like Stephen Hughes, Charles Edwards, Richard Jones, and William Jones, who were driven by their concern to spread religious knowledge through the medium of the only language most of the people of Wales could understand. In terms of print culture in Welsh, it could therefore be argued that the period of persecution brought unintended benefits as it drove men like Charles Edwards to seek new ways of making a contribution to the spread of religious knowledge.

All the various measures taken to try to provide support for dissenting groups and to avoid persecution would not be necessary much longer, however. The Declaration of Indulgence issued by James II in 1687 effectively brought persecution of Dissenters to an end. Intense fear of Catholicism brought about a greater sense of unity between Anglicans and Dissenters, at least for a while. In 1688, Bishop William Lloyd of St. Asaph was one of the seven bishops sent to the Tower of London for opposing James II's second declaration of Indulgence. In the same year, he met James Owen in Oswestry and indicated that William of Orange was on his way. He seemed to be seeking some sort of rapprochement and emphasised the bond between their two sides as fellow Protestants: 'You and we are Brethren: we have indeed been angry Brethren, but we have seen our folly: and we are resolved if ever we have it in our power again, to show you that we will treat you as Brethren.'[223] That promise was not kept in full as Nonconformists were not afforded complete equality, but life would undoubtedly be far easier for them in the future.

---

221. Richards, *Religious Developments*, 280–81; Richards, *Wales under the Indulgence*, 118–19.

222. Jenkins, *Literature, Religion and Society*, 34–35.

223. Jones, *Grym y Gair*, 109.

Some of the ministers deprived of their positions in 1660–62 lived long enough to see their congregations registered as Protestant dissenting meeting houses under the terms of the Act of Toleration. Peregrine Phillips oversaw the construction of a meeting house at Haverfordwest before he died in 1691.[224] William Jones ushered the Rhydwilym Baptists into the new age of Toleration, although little is known of his subsequent history.[225] Philip Henry recalled St. Bartholomew's Day 1662 as 'that fatal day' on which he died by law, yet the congregation he had nurtured in Broad Oak, Shropshire, failed to become a church since Henry's attitude remained firmly non-separatist.[226] Stephen Hughes died in 1688 but the early Independent churches in Carmarthenshire looked to him as their founder and he was remembered with respect well into the eighteenth century.[227] The larger county churches now splintered into smaller, localized affairs, which could usually trace their origins back to the causes maintained during the years of persecution. The gathered church of Breconshire of which Henry Maurice had been pastor divided into separate causes such as Tredwstan, Troedrhiwdalar, Maesyronnen, Brecon, Llanwrtyd, and Llangynidr. However, the ministers could not have succeeded to the extent they did in keeping the dissenting cause alive without the commitment of devout laymen, whose membership of the dissenting movements often required considerable fortitude. Their role has perhaps been somewhat neglected since little is known of them compared to the ejected ministers. Most of them belonged to the stalwart, pious middling sorts of society, although a few had some claims to slightly higher status.

This period was therefore crucial to the development of a distinctive tradition of Nonconformity in Wales. It furnished the emerging denominations with a heroic past which they would increasingly seek to reclaim through works like Joshua Thomas's eighteenth-century history of the Baptists and Thomas Rees's *History of Protestant Nonconformity in Wales* in the nineteenth century. It has been suggested that there is an element of injustice in hailing as heroes the ejected Dissenters in Wales, when far more Anglican clergy were

---

224. Rees, *History of Protestant Nonconformity*, 227.
225. DWB; Owens, "Rhydwilym Church," 104.
226. Lee, *Diaries and Letters*, 145; Nuttall, "Nurture of Nonconformity," 25–26.
227. NLW MS12382, 129, 136.

deprived by law under the Commonwealth.[228] The truth is of course that different brands of the Christian faith have always identified their separate heroes: one believer's martyr is often another's heretic. The dominance of Welsh Nonconformity in the nineteenth and twentieth centuries, culminating in the disestablishment of the Welsh Church, led to a prevailing interpretation of history that emphasised the role of Dissent. There has possibly been a natural tendency to dwell on the extent of the suffering, but, although none of the Dissenters were burnt at the stake for their faith, several endured very real privations, including periods of imprisonment, and many others were subject to constant harassment. Perhaps more crucial in the long term than this image of the period as an heroic age of endurance is the fact that Welsh Dissent developed a far greater sense of its own identity, as a result of being more isolated than in the early years of the seventeenth century. Moreover, it could also be argued that the relatively small number of ejected ministers had a disproportionate influence on Welsh culture in general at this time, far beyond what their counterparts achieved in England. This can largely be attributed to the remarkable contribution of Stephen Hughes and Charles Edwards, who played such a prominent role in Welsh publishing at a time when print culture in Welsh was still in its early stages. The other long-lasting legacy, apart from the churches themselves, was arguably the development of the dissenting academies, again probably far more significant in Wales than in England, despite being smaller institutions. The reason for the particular importance of the presence of the academies in Wales was that the country remained without a university until the founding of the university college at Aberystwyth in 1872. The academies therefore provided an opportunity for higher education without the prospect of having to travel to Oxford or Cambridge. The growth of Carmarthen Academy in the eighteenth century in particular meant that a number of leading figures in Welsh life were able to receive a good grounding in the classics, history and theology, relatively close to home. In turn, the alumni of the larger academies often established smaller institutions and private schools, which spread some of those standards of learning more widely. They followed the lead of universities in England and grammar schools in Wales by not using the Welsh

228. It is calculated that 544 out of 752 clergy were deprived between 1645 and 1652. James, "1662 and Before," 52–54.

language as a medium of instruction, which may have caused some difficulties for some students.[229] The impact of the academies is therefore difficult to measure, but they certainly added to the educational opportunities available within Wales.

The early Puritan causes, which had first emerged in the 1640s and 1650s, thus survived the hard frost of the age of persecution and proved to be remarkably hardy. The significant factor for the future was that Dissent contrived to do more than merely retain some of its existing congregations, and, as the history of Rhydwilym demonstrated, was able to recruit new members and establish new causes. It is easy to be wise after the event and to interpret the survival of dissenting groups during this period as the foundation of the later remarkable growth of Nonconformity in the country. It would, however, have been difficult to foresee such a development from these early beginnings. Dissent remained very much a minority affair for many years after the advent of Toleration. That toleration came in the form of an act of Parliament rather than a declaration that might easily be revoked must have given reassurance to those who had been wary of Indulgences in the past. Even so, there may have been a long-term psychological impact that tended to hamper the immediate growth of the new denominations. When the Nonconformists emerged blinking into the light in 1689 after years of lurking in the shadows, it is possible that the resulting sense of relief may have left them content simply to have attained their freedom and less inclined to evangelize actively. It may also have taken some time for them to let down their guard and relax in the knowledge of their safety from further persecution. As a result, rather than being denounced as hot-headed militant radicals, they came to be mocked as 'y Sentars Sychion' ('the dry Dissenters') by the early eighteenth century.[230] It was the evangelical revival in the mid-eighteenth century that helped ensure their reawakening and sparked the remarkable growth of Nonconformity into the nineteenth century, in a way that could hardly have been foreseen by either the dissenting minority or their persecutors in the seventeenth century.

---

229. White, "Popular Schooling," 321–32.

230. See, for example, Jenkins, "Apostol Sir Gaerfyrddin," 7; Jones, *Grym y Gair*, 154.

BIBLIOGRAPHY

Manuscript Sources

National Library of Wales (NLW)

NLW 371B (Llandeilo Mynydd Bach)
NLW MS 9108–9D (Ilston)
NLW MS 12382 (Pant-teg)
NLW Deposit MS 127A (Rhydwilym)

Penrice and Margam MS 6029.

Great Sessions Records: Wales 4/986/7.

Church in Wales Records:
Consistory Court Records:
Archdeaconry of Brecon (SD/CCCB) 1660–89
Archdeaconry of Cardigan (SD/CCCd) 1660–89
Archdeaconry of Carmarthen (SD/CCC) 1660–89

Printed Sources:

Bagshaw, Edward. *The life and death of Mr. Vavasor Powell, that faithful minister and confessor of Jesus Christ*. London: 1671.

Comber, Thomas. *Teg Resymmeu Offeiriad Pabaidd wedi ei hatteb gan Protestant o Eglwys Loegr*. Translated by W. J. London: Clavell, 1686.

Cradock, Walter. *Glad Tydings from Heaven: To The Worst of Sinners on Earth*. London: 1648.

Davies, Richard. *An Account of the Convincement, Exercises, Services and Travels of Richard Davies*. London: Sowle, 1710.

Davies, Rondl. *Profiad yr Ysprydion, Neu Ddatcuddiad Gau Athrawon: A rhybudd iw gochelyd*. Oxford: Hall, 1675.

Edwards, Charles. *An Afflicted Man's Tesimony concerning his Troubles*. London: 1691.

———. *Ffydd Ddi-ffuant. Adroddiad o Helynt y Grefydd Gristnogol Er dechreuad y byd hyd yr oes hon*. Oxford: Hall, 1667.

Fox, George, John Stubs, and Benjamin Furley. "The Welch Battle-Door." In *A Battle-Door for Teachers & Professors to Learn Singular and Plural*, 1–8. Reprint. Menston, UK: Scolar, 1968.

Gouge, Thomas. *Gair i Bechaduriaid a gair ir sainct*. Translated William Jones. London: Maxwell, 1675.

———. *Hyfforddiadau Christianogol. Hyfforddiadau Christianogol. Yn dangos Pa fodd i rodio gyda Duw ar hyd y Dydd*. Translated Richard Jones. London: Maxwell, 1675.

———. *Principlau neu Bennau y Grefydd Ghristianogol, A agorir fel y gallo y gwannaf eu deall*. Translated William Jones. London: Maxwell, 1676.

Griffith, Alexander. *Strena Vavasoriensis*. London: 1654.

Hughes, John. *Allwydd neu Agoriad Paradwy i'r Cymru*. [London:] 1670.

Hughes, Stephen, ed. *Catechism Mr Perkins*. London: Darby, 1672.

———. *Cyfarwydd-deb i'r Anghyfarwydd*. London: Dawks, 1677.

————. *Tryssor i'r Cymru*. London: Dawks, 1677.

Jones, E. D. "Llyfr Eglwys Mynydd Bach." *Y Cofiadur* 17 (1947) 3–6.

Jones, J. M., ed. "Llyfr Eglwys y Cilgwyn." *Y Cofiadur* 1 (1923) 22–31.

Jones, M. G. "Two Accounts of the Welsh Trust, 1675 and 1678(?)." *Bulletin of the Board of Celtic Studies* 9 (1939) 71–80.

Jones, Thomas. *Y Gwir er Gwaethed Yw*. London: Jones, 1680.

Jones, William. *Work for a Cooper: Being an Answer to a Libel, Written by Thomas Wynne the Cooper, the Ale-man, the Quack, and the Speaking-Quaker*. London: 1679.

Keach, Benjamin. *Goleuni Gwedi torri allan Ynghymry, Gan ymlid ymmaith dywyllwch*. Translated by Robert Morgan. London: 1696.

Lee, M. H. *Diaries and letters of Philip Henry*. London: 1882.

Owen, Charles. *Some Account of the Life . . . of . . . James Owen*. London: 1709.

Owen, James. *Bedydd Plant or Nefoedd: neu Draethawd am Natur a Diben Bedydd*. London: Colins, 1693.

Owens, B. G. *The Ilston Book: Earliest Register of Welsh Baptists*. Aberystwyth, UK: National Library of Wales, 1996.

Prichard, Rees. *Rhan o waith Mr Rees Prichard*. London: Brewster, 1659.

Thomas, John. *Ymarferol Athrawiaeth Gweddi*. London: 1680.

Thomas, Joshua. *Hanes y Bedyddwyr*. Carmarthen, UK: Ross, 1778.

Traethiad Mawrhydi y Brenin iw holl garedic ddeiliaid ynghylch y Cydfrad twyllodrus a ddatcuddwyd yn ddiweddar yn erbyn ei ardderchawg Berson, ar Llywodraeth. London: Assigns of John Bill, Harry Hills and Thomas Newcomb, 1683.

Underhill, E. B., ed. *The Records of a Church of Christ Meeting in Broadmead, Bristol*. Bristol: 1847.

Whiteman, Anne, ed. *The Compton Census of 1676: A Critical Edition*. Oxford: Oxford University Press, 1986.

Wynne, Thomas. *An Antichristian Conspiracy Detected, and Satans Champion Defeated: Being a reply to an Envious & Scurrilous Libel, without any Name to it, Called, Work for a Cooper*. [London:] 1679.

————. *The Antiquity of the Quakers Proved out of the Scriptures of Truth*. London: 1677.

Secondary Sources

Bassett, T. M. *The Welsh Baptists*. Swansea, UK: Ilston House, 1977.

Bowen, Geraint. "Allwydd neu Agoriad Paradwys i'r Cymry, 1670." *Transactions of the Honourable Society of the Cymmrodorion* (1961) 80–160.

Cressy, David. *Birth, Marriage and Death: Ritual, Religion, and the Life-Cycle in Tudor and Stuart England*. Oxford: Oxford University Press, 1997.

Davies, Cynthia Saunders. "Richard Jones o Ddinbych: Crefftwr o Gymro." In *Agweddau ar Dwf Piwritaniaeth yng Nghymru yn yr Ail Ganrif ar Bymtheg*, edited by J. Gwynfor Jones, 167–202. Llanbedr Pont Steffan, UK: Mellen, 1992.

Davies, Dewi Eirug. *Hoff Ddysgedig Nyth: Cyfraniad Coleg Presbyteraidd Caerfyrddin i Fywyd Cymru*. Swansea, UK: Penry, 1976.

Davies, Pennar. "Episodes in the History of Brecknockshire Dissent." *Brycheiniog* 3 (1959) 11–65.

Evan, J. Hopkin, and Eiluned Rees. "The Independents in Llanybri and Llanstephan." *Carmarthenshire Antiquary* 44 (2008) 28–50.

Evans, Gethin. "The Quakers of Cardiganshire." *Ceredigion* 16.3 (2011) 17–61.

Evans, Non, "Stephen Hughes: The Family Man." *Carmarthenshire Antiquary* 37 (2001) 31–40.

Fletcher, Anthony. "The Enforcement of the Conventicle Acts 1664–1679." In *Persecution and Toleration: Studies in Church History 21*, edited by W. J. Sheils, 235–46. Oxford: Blackwell, 1984.

Gibbard, Noel. *Elusen i'r Enaid: Arweiniad i Weithiau'r Piwritaniaid Cymreig, 1630–1689*. Pen-y-bont ar Ogwr, UK: Llyfrgell Efengylaidd Cymru, 1979.

Greaves, Richard L. "Philip Henry." *Oxford Dictionary of National Biography 2004–11*. www.oxforddnb.com.

Griffiths, G. Milwyn. "Restoration St. Asaph: The Episcopate of Bishop George Griffith, 1660–1666." *Journal of the Historical Society of the Church in Wales* 12 (1962) 9–27; 13 (1963) 27–40.

Hanes ac Egwyddorion Annibynwyr Cymru. Abertawe, UK: Undeb yr Annibynwyr Cymraeg, 1939.

Hart, A. Tindal. *William Lloyd 1627–1717: Bishop, Politician, Author and Prophet*. London: SPCK, 1952.

Hugh, R. Leonard. "Annibyniaeth yng Ngorllewin Morgannwg." *Y Cofiadur* 18 (1948) 3–58.

James, J. W. "1662 and Before." *Journal of the Historical Society of the Church in Wales* 11 (1961) 25–56.

Jenkins, Geraint H. "'A lleufer dyn yw llyfr da': Stephen Hughes a'i Hoff Awduron." In *Agweddau ar Dwf Piwritaniaeth yng Nghymru yn yr Ail Ganrif ar Bymtheg*, edited by J. Gwynfor Jones, 167–202. Llanbedr Pont Steffan, UK: Mellen, 1992.

———. "Apostol Sir Gaerfyrddin: Stephen Hughes c.1622–1688." In *Cadw Tŷ mewn Cwmwl Tystion: Ysgrifau Hanesyddol ar Grefydd a Diwylliant*, 1–28. Llandysul, UK: Gwasg Gomer, 1990.

———. *The Foundations of Modern Wales 1642–1780*. Oxford: Oxford University Press, 1987.

———. "The Friends of Montgomeryshire in the Heroic Age." *Montgomeryshire Collections* 76 (1988) 17–30.

———. "'Goleuni Gwedi Torri Allan Ynghymry': Her y Bedyddwyr yn ystod y 1690au." In *Cadw Tŷ mewn Cwmwl Tystion: Ysgrifau Hanesyddol ar Grefydd a Diwylliant*, 86–102. Llandysul, UK: Gwasg Gomer, 1990.

———. "James Owen versus Benjamin Keach: A Controversy over Infant Baptism." *National Library of Wales Journal* 29 (1975) 57–66.

———. *Literature, Religion and Society in Wales 1660–1730*. Cardiff: University of Wales Press, 1978.

———. *Protestant Dissenters in Wales 1639–1689*. Cardiff: University of Wales Press, 1992.

———. *Thomas Jones yr Almanaciwr 1648–1713* Cardiff: University of Wales Press, 1980.

Jenkins, Philip. *The Making of a Ruling Class: The Glamorgan gentry 1640–1790*. Cambridge: Cambridge University Press, 1983.

———. "'The Old Leaven': The Welsh Roundheads after 1660." *The Historical Journal* 24.4 (1981) 807–23.

Johnson, A. M. "Bussy Mansell (1623–99), Political Survivalist." *Morgannwg* 20 (1976) 9–36.

John, Stanley. "Braslun o ddechreuadau Ymneilltuaeth yn Abertawe." *Y Cofiadur* 48 (1983) 2–27.

Jones, D. R. L. "Fame and Obscurity: Samuel Jones of Brynllywarch." *Journal of Welsh Religious History* 1 (1993) 41–65.

———. "Samuel Jones." *Oxford Dictionary of National Biography* 2004–11. www .oxforddnb.com.

Jones, E. D. "Llyfr Eglwys Pant-teg." *Y Cofiadur* 23 (1953) 18–70.

———. "Ymneilltuaeth Gynnar yng Ngheredigion." *Ceredigion* 4 (1961) 96–112.

Jones, Francis. "Disaffection and Dissent in Pembrokeshire." *Transactions of the Honourable Society of the Cymmrodorion* (1946–47) 206–31.

Jones, Gareth Elwyn and Roderick, Gordon Wynne. *A History of Education in Wales.* Cardiff: University of Wales Press, 2003.

Jones, J. Gwynfor. "Piwritaniaeth gynnar yng Nghymru a sefydlu Eglwys Llanfaches, 1639." *Cofiadur* 55 (1990) 4–26.

Jones, Owain, "The 'Anabaptists' of Llanafanfawr and Llysdinam." *Brycheiniog* 18 (1978–79) 71–77.

Jones, M. G. *The Charity School Movement: A Study of Eighteenth Century Puritanism in Action.* Cambridge: Cambridge University Press, 1938.

Jones, Philip Henry, and Eiluned Rees, eds. *A Nation and its Books: A History of the Book in Wales.* Aberystwyth, UK: National Library of Wales, 1998.

Jones, R. Tudur. *Congregationalism in Wales.* Edited by Robert Pope. Cardiff: University of Wales Press, 2004.

———. *Grym y Gair a Fflam y Ffydd: Ysgrifau ar Hanes Crefydd yng Nghymru.* Edited by D. Densil Morgan. Bangor, UK: Canolfan Uwch-efrydiau Crefydd yng Nghymru, 1998.

———. "The Older Dissent of Swansea and Brecon." In *Links with the Past: Swansea and Brecon Historical Essays,* edited by Owain W. Jones and David Walker, 117–41. Swansea, UK: Davies, 1974.

———. "Relations between Anglicans and Dissenters: The Promotion of Piety, 1670–1730." In *A History of the Church in Wales,* edited by David Walker, 79–102. Penarth, UK: Historical Society of the Church in Wales, 1976.

———. "Religion in Post-Restoration Brecknockshire 1660–1688." *Brycheiniog* 8 (1962) 11–65.

———. "The Sufferings of Vavasor." In *Welsh Baptist Studies,* edited by Mansel John, 77–89. Cardiff: South Wales Baptist College, 1976.

———. "Trefniadaeth Ryngeglwysig yr Annibynwyr." *Y Cofiadur* 21 (1951) 3–63.

———. *Vavasor Powell* Swansea, UK: Penry, 1971.

Jones, R. Tudur, and B. G. Owens. "Anghydffurfwyr Cymru 1660–1662." *Y Cofiadur* 32 (1962) 3–93.

Jones, Richard. *Crynwyr Bore Cymru 1653–1699.* Abermaw, UK: Jones a'i Feibion, 1931.

Llwyd, Rheinallt. "Printing and Publishing in the Seventeenth Century." In *A Nation and its Books: A History of the Book in Wales,* edited by Philip Henry Jones and Eiluned Rees, 93–107. Aberystwyth, UK: National Library of Wales, 1998.

Matthews, D. Hugh. "Bedyddwyr Maesyfed yn yr 17eg Ganrif: Gwers mewn Goddefgarwch." *Trafodion Cymdeithas Hanes Bedyddwyr Cymru* (1986) 1–13.

Morgan, D. Densil. *Wales and the Word.* Cardiff: University of Wales Press, 2008.

Morgan, Derec Llwyd. *Charles Edwards.* Caernarfon, UK: Gwasg Pantycelyn, 1994.

———. "Charles Edwards (1628–1691?): Awdur *Y Ffydd Ddi-ffuant.*" In *Y Traddodiad Rhyddiaith,* edited by Geraint Bowen, 213–30. Llandysul, UK: Gomer, 1970.

Morgan, Walter T. "An Examination of the Churchwardens' Accounts and of Some Disputes Concerning Them before the Consistory Courts in the Diocese of St. David's." *Journal of the Historical Society of the Church in Wales* 8 (1958) 58–81.

———. "Cases of Subtraction of Church-Rate before the Consistory Courts of St. David's." *Journal of the Historical Society of the Church in Wales* 9 (1959) 70–91.

———. "The Prosecution of Nonconformists in the Consistory Courts of St. David's." *Journal of the Historical Society of the Church in Wales* 12 (1962) 28–54.

Morgan-Guy, John. "Religion and Belief, 1660–1780." In *The Gwent County History Volume 3: The Making of Monmouthshire, 1536–1780*, edited by Madeleine Gray and Prys Morgan, 146–73. Cardiff: University of Wales Press, 2009.

Mullett, Michael, "William Lloyd." *Oxford Dictionary of National Biography 2004–11*. www.oxforddnb.com.

Nuttall, Geoffrey. "The Nurture of Nonconformity: Philip Henry's Diaries." *Transactions of the Cymmrodorion* 4 (1998) 5–27.

Owen, Geraint Dyfnallt. *Ysgolion a Cholegau yr Annibynwyr*. Abertawe, UK: Undeb yr Annibynwyr Cymraeg, 1939.

Owens, B. G. "Cofrestri'r Ymneilltuwyr." *Trafodion Cymdeithas Hanes Bedyddwyr Cymru* (1968) 31–49.

———. "Trichanmlwyddiant Rhydwilym." *Trafodion Cymdeithas Hanes Bedyddwyr Cymru* (1968) 50–59.

———. "Rhydwilym Church 1668–89: A Study of West Wales Baptists." In *Welsh Baptist Studies*, edited by Mansel John, 92–107. Cardiff: South Wales Baptist College, 1976.

Parkin, Jon. "William Lucy." *Oxford Dictionary of National Biography 2004–11*. www.oxforddnb.com.

Parry, Charles. "From Manuscript to Print II: Printed Books." In *A Guide to Welsh Literature c. 1530–1700*, edited by R. Geraint Gruffydd, 263–76. Cardiff: University of Wales Press, 1997.

Parry, Edward. "Prelates and Preachers: Anglicanism and Dissent in Breconshire, 1621–1721." *Brycheiniog* 35 (2003) 37–65.

Rees, Thomas. *History of Protestant Nonconformity in Wales, from its Rise in 1633 to the Present Time*. 2nd ed. London: Snow, 1883.

Richards, Thomas. "Henry Maurice: Piwritan ac Annibynnwr." *Y Cofiadur* (1928) 15–67.

———. *A History of the Puritan Movement in Wales*. London: National Eisteddfod Association, 1920.

———. *The Religious Census of 1676*. London: The Honourable Society of the Cymmrodorion, 1927.

———. *Religious Developments in Wales (1654–1662)*. London: National Eisteddfod Association, 1923.

———. *Wales under the Indulgence (1672–1675)*. London: National Eisteddfod Association, 1928.

———. *Wales under the Penal Code (1662–1687)*. London: National Eisteddfod Association, 1925.

Roberts, H. P. "Nonconformist Academies in Wales (1662–1862)." *Transactions of the Cymmrodorion* (1929) 13–35.

Roberts, Stephen K. "John Miles." *Oxford Dictionary of National Biography 2004–11*. www.oxforddnb.com.

———. "Vavasor Powell." *Oxford Dictionary of National Biography 2004–11*. www.oxforddnb.com.

Speake, Jennifer. "Thomas Vaughan." *Oxford Dictionary of National Biography 2004–11*. www.oxforddnb.com.

Spurr, John, "Hugh Lloyd." *Oxford Dictionary of National Biography 2004–11*. www.oxforddnb.com.

Suggett, Richard. *A History of Magic and Witchcraft in Wales*. Stroud: Tempus. 2008.

Thomas, M. Wynn. "Seventeenth-Century Puritan Writers: Morgan Llwyd and Charles Edwards." In *A Guide to Welsh Literature c.1530–1700*, edited by R. Geraint Gruffydd, 190–209. Cardiff: University of Wales Press, 1997.

White, B. R. "John Miles and the Structures of the Calvinistic Baptist Mission to South Wales 1649–1660." In *Welsh Baptist Studies*, edited by Mansel John, 35–76. Cardiff: South Wales Baptist College, 1976.

White, Eryn M. "Popular Schooling and the Welsh Language 1650–1800." In *The Welsh Language before the Industrial Revolution*, edited by Geraint H. Jenkins, 317–41. Cardiff: University of Wales Press, 1997.

———. *The Welsh Bible*. Stroud, UK: Tempus, 2007.

Williams, David. *A History of Modern Wales* London: Murray, 1950.

Williams, Glanmor. "Crefydd dan gysgod erledigaeth: Anghydffurfwyr de-ddwyrain Cymru, 1660–88." *Y Cofiadur* 47 (1982) 3–19.

———. "The Dissenters in Glamorgan, 1660–c.1760." In *Glamorgan County History Volume IV: Early Modern Glamorgan*, edited by Glanmor Williams, 468–99. Cardiff: Glamorgan County History Trust, 1974.

———. "Stephen Hughes (1622–1688): 'Apostol Sir Gâr,' 'the Apostle of Carmarthenshire.'" *Carmarthenshire Antiquary* 37 (2001) 21–30.

———. *The Welsh and Their Religion*. Cardiff: University of Wales Press, 1991.

Williams, Glanmor, William Jacob, Nigel Yates, and Frances Knight. *The Welsh Church from Reformation to Disestablishment 1603–1920*. Cardiff: University of Wales Press, 2007.

Williams, J. Gwynn. "The Quakers of Merioneth during the Seventeenth Century." *Journal of the Merioneth History and Record Society* 8 (1977–80) 122–56, 312–39.

Williams, M. Faye. "Glamorgan Quakers 1654–1900." *Morgannwg* 5 (1961) 49–75.

Williams, Penry. *The Council in the Marches of Wales under Elizabeth I*. Cardiff: University of Wales Press, 1958.

Wright, Stephen. "Peregrine Philips." *Oxford Dictionary of National Biography 2004–11*. www.oxforddnb.com.

Wykes, David L. ""To let the memory of these men dye is injurious to posterity": Edmund Calamy's *Account* of the Ejected Ministers." In *The Church Retrospective: Studies in Church History 33*, edited by R. N. Swanson, 379–92. Woodbridge, UK: Boydell, 1997.

Part Two: **THEOLOGICAL**

4

The Doctrinal and Ecumenical Significance of the Great Ejectment[1]

Alan P. F. Sell

It was only to be expected that the Great Ejectment would become part of the folk memory of those in the Christian traditions most affected by it. As the Presbyterian Samuel Palmer observed in 1775, 'The Protestant Dissenters, of all denominations, have ever been wont to revere [the memories of the ejected], as the fathers of their interest, and the worthy pattern of their conduct.'[2] Hear, for example, the Congregationalist, Thomas Binney, writing of the ejected ministers in 1835:

1. In this chapter the following abbreviations are used: CR: Matthews, *Calamy Revised*; DWB: *The Dictionary of Welsh Biography*; ODNB: *The Oxford Dictionary of National Biography*; SI, Charles Surman's Index of Dissenting Ministers at Dr. Williams's Library, London, and online; WTW: Taylor and Binfield, eds, *Who They Were*.

2. Calamy, abridged by Palmer, *The Nonconformist's Memorial*, iv. Palmer immediately adds, 'Those who have differed the widest from the generality of them in their doctrinal sentiments have spoken of their piety and zeal with rapture.' For Palmer (1741–1813) see ODNB, SI. See further, Seed, "History and Narrative identity."

They were placed in a position in which it was to be shown whether they would submit to man or obey God. They chose the latter alternative. They determined to appeal from earth to heaven, and to cast themselves, their wives, and their little ones, on *Him* who feeds the fowls of the air and the beasts of the forest. The day fixed for the trial of their resolution and their constancy at length came,—the day fearfully anticipated but firmly met; it dawned upon them in the possession of that, which, but for conscience, they might have continued to retain,—it closed over them beggars and outcasts. '*This was the beginning of sorrows*.'[3]

Passing over the excess of quasi-homiletic passion which permits Binney to overlook the fact that a small minority of the ejected passed their 'beggarly' days in the stately homes of their well-to-do friends, I observe that to this day there remains a remnant who were taught in Sunday School to look with pride upon those of 'our people' who stood by their principles no matter what the cost. My impression is that nowadays, while there is considerable and welcome scholarly interest in sixteenth- and seventeenth-century Dissent (and this on the part of persons who may or may not be attached to any of the Dissenting traditions or even to the Christian faith), the denominational folk memory of the period is rapidly fading. To the extent that this is so, I deeply regret it. Nearly seventy years ago George Phillips, my Professor of the History of Doctrine, declared that 'To our great detriment we have almost lost historical sense, which is one of the most serious causes of our weakness.'[4] It is not that I advocate wanton denominational triumphalism, and Phillips certainly would not have done so; rather, I believe that in the doctrinal principles for which the Dissenters stood are to be found incentives to revitalized proclamation of the gospel, and to fresh ecumenical endeavour in our own time.

Just as socio-political circumstances called forth the conscientious responses of the early Dissenters, so the commemorations of their stand have been contextually influenced. As Ernest Payne rightly observed, 'The Church can never separate herself from the historical conflicts of the day, nor from the political, social and ideological

---

3. Binney, *Dissent Not Schism*, 31. For Binney (1798–1874) see ODNB, SI.

4. Phillips, "Freedom in Religious Thought," 41. For Phillips (1893–1967) see SI; Sell, *Enlightenment, Ecumenism, Evangel*, 259; Sell, *Nonconformist Theology*, 4, 141.

influences which mould her members.'[5] A review of Ejectment commemorations will underline the point.

COMMEMORATING THE GREAT EJECTMENT

If Binney's panegyric was composed as Dissenters were reaching the
crest of a post-Evangelical Revival wave and becoming more denomi-
nationally conscious and organized, the heirs of the ejected who lived
throughout the eighteenth century had neither the organization nor the
favourable circumstances required to commemorate their forebears in
any official or public way. Their remembrance was low-key, even private. Hence, it is not easy to find any references to the Ejectment at its
Jubilee in 1712, its centenary in 1762, or its sesquicentenary in 1812.
Possible reasons for this are not hard to seek.[6] First, denominational
lines were not clearly drawn, and there was corresponding ministerial
fluidity. In the wake of the Ejectment some ministers came over from
the Church of England, while others conformed to it. Among the latter
was Thomas Secker who had been educated at the Dissenting academies
of Timothy Jollie at Attercliffe and Samuel Jones at Tewkesbury.[7] Having
failed to receive a call to the Dissenting cause at Bolsover, he turned first
to medicine, conformed in 1721, and managed thereafter to become
Archbishop of Canterbury.[8] Secondly, the establishment of churches
and the gaining of licenses was an early preoccupation of the newly
tolerated. Thirdly, there were those throughout the eighteenth century
who wished to turn back the clock of toleration, or at least to make life
difficult for Dissenters. Certainly the climate at the 1712 Jubilee was
not conducive to celebration. On the contrary, in the previous year, in

5. Payne, *Fellowship of Believers*, 9. For Payne (1902–1980) see ODNB.

6. The considerations following may go some way towards supplying reasons in
support of Hora's bald, unexplained, assertion that in 1862 'no tradition of commemorating the Ejectment existed; no similar celebrations were held in 1762.' See
Hora, "Robert Vaughan," 411. She immediately adds that 'the ejected ministers had
never been held up as models for contemporary Nonconformists to emulate.' See,
however, Samuel Palmer's observation from which I set out, and remarks in such
works as Calamy's *The Nonconformist's Memorial*, Neal's *History of the* Puritans,
Bogue and Bennett's *History of Dissenters*, and in the writings of authors as various
as Samuel Chandler, Joseph Priestley, and Andrew Fuller. They all thought that the
ejected ministers were more than worthy of emulation.

7. For Jollie (1659/60–1714) and Jones (c.1681–1719) see ODNB, SI.

8. See Hester, *Attercliffe*, 31. For Secker (1793–1768) see ODNB.

the course of the Sacheverell riots, meeting houses had been robbed and burned; also in 1711 the Occasional Conformity Act, whereby Dissenters had been permitted to qualify for government and public office if on occasion they took communion in the parish church, was repealed; in 1714 the Schism Act (repealed in 1719) seriously threatened the activities Dissenting academies by making non-conforming teachers liable to three months' imprisonment; in the following year Jacobite mobs vandalized eleven meeting houses in Staffordshire and six in Lancashire, thereby fomenting the fear of capitulation to Rome—a fear which took cultural expression in more than one way.[9] In the wake of the Jacobite uprising in 1745, which further fuelled fears of a Roman Catholic take-over of the country a public commemoration of the fiftieth anniversary of the Ejectment might well have been literally inflammatory. As if all this were not enough, the Dissenting interest was weakening in the land. The poles of the debate are represented by the differing diagnoses offered, and remedies prescribed, by Strickland Gough (more rational liberty required) on the one hand, and his respondent, Philip Doddridge (more genuine evangelical experience needed), on the other.[10] With hindsight F. J. Powicke noted that evidence of Dissenting decadence is seen in the fact that,

> after 1715 the formation of new Churches almost ceased for the
> next fifty years . . . There was little or no grasp on the thought
> of a Church as constituted by the living spirit of Christ in the
> midst, but there was a fanatical grasp on the supposed form of
> sound words and form of worship removed as far as possible
> from the Prayer Book, while, with this, there went a pharisaic
> rancour which poisoned the springs of brotherly love . . . Each
> Church stood in isolation—withering often on its own feet.[11]

9. See, for example, Mourby, "Why do the English Hate Opera?" A pamphleteer of 1727 felt it unsafe to have 'Popish singers' in England, and contended that 'it would be a great Security to the Protestant interests' if an Act of Parliament required 'all Foreign Singers, Dancers and Tumblers, to abjure the Devil, the Pope and the Pretender, before they appear in Publick.' Ibid., 126. Handel was pilloried for writing opera, which, being Italian, was deemed Catholic, so he turned to oratorios—that is, to 'operatic music without the opera.' I owe the reference to Dr. Karen Sell.

10. See Gough, *An Enquiry*, and Doddridge, *Free Thoughts*. For Gough (d. 1752) and Doddridge (1702–51) see ODNB, SI. Others who entered the fray included Isaac Watts (1674–1748) and Abraham Taylor (fl. 1720–40), for both of whom see ODNB, SI. For Taylor see Sell, *Hinterland Theology*, ch. 3.

11. Powicke, "English Congregationalism in its Greatness and Decline," 302, 303, 309. For Powicke (1854–1935) see SI, WTW.

Meanwhile many other ways of punishing Dissenters were devised, among them the ploy of the Corporation of London whereby persons elected to serve as sheriff who refused to take up office were to be fined £400. On grounds of conscience Dissenters were not willing to serve because the Corporation Act opened the office to Church of England communicants only; thus from 1730 to 1767 a number of Dissenters were elected, refused to serve, and were fined. The proceeds—£15,000 in one period of six years—went towards the building of the Mansion House. Numerous attempts were made to improve the legal position of Dissenters, to no immediate avail; and when rumbles of the French Revolution were felt in England, the Dissenters were again represented as agents of disruption—none more so than Joseph Priestley who added strictly illegal anti-trinitarianism to his Dissent. In July 1791 his Birmingham house was vandalized by the mob, many of his papers, much of his scientific apparatus was destroyed, and he sought safety across the Atlantic.[12]

By the beginning of the nineteenth century the denominational boundaries as we have come to know them were beginning to be drawn. The evangelicalism of both Calvinistic and Arminian Methodism had brought numerical gains to the Congregationalists and to those Baptists most inclined to receive them, namely, the Particular Baptists who stood in the line of Andrew Fuller's evangelical Calvinism, and the evangelical Arminian General Baptists of the New Connexion (1770), led by Dan Taylor. The orthodox Presbyterians of Old Dissent were now in a minority (largely north-eastern). The majority of their co-religionists had become Congregationalist, the remainder, together with more rationalistic General Baptists, had become, or were on the way to becoming, Unitarian. Home and overseas mission was a preoccupation of Baptists no less than Congregationalists, and non-hierarchical advisory union for a variety of purposes was increasingly seen to be required; hence the formation of the Congregational Union of England and Wales in 1831, and of the Baptist Union of Great Britain and Ireland in 1832, in succession to a series of assemblies held from 1813 onwards.

With considerably increased numbers, and with organization in place, the Baptists and Congregationalists were well placed to commemorate the Bicentenary of the Great Ejectment in 1862, and they

12. For Priestley (1733–1804) see ODNB.

threw themselves into a variety of preparatory activities with enthusiasm. This expressed itself in more than one way. Under the leadership of the Congregationalist, Edward Miall (1809–81),[13] some of the more radical Nonconformists had founded the Anti-State Church Association in 1844. The members of this body, more delicately renamed the Liberation Society in 1853, flew the flag of political Dissent and crusaded for the disestablishment of the Church of England, often couching their objective in terms of doing that Church a profound favour. No doubt some of the crusaders drew encouragement from Joseph Thompson, the American Congregationalist, who exhorted the English Nonconformists thus: 'Like their brethren in America, they must go beyond Dissent, and assume the name, and fulfil the mission of ABOLITIONISTS.'[14] It is not impossible that their aspirations were further fuelled by 'A Fraternal Address' sent at the behest of the American Congregational Union to its English counterpart. Signed by Thompson, William Ives Buddington and David B. Coe, and dated—significantly—4 July 1862, it dangled before its recipients the following carrot: 'In the United States we know nothing of "dissent" because we have no "establishment";—nothing of "religious toleration" as a privilege, because we everywhere enjoy religious freedom as a sacred constitutional right.'[15] Needless to say, such language was not calculated to impress most members of the Church of England, a number of whom suspected that the Bicentenary commemorations would be nothing more than a front for the Liberation Society's cause.[16] Views such as those later expressed by James Guinness Rogers concerning Congregational Dissent gave them some excuse: 'It is not co-extensive with political dissent, for there is a numerous and increasing body of politicians who object to Erastianism . . . but who have no sympathy with the theological doctrines or ecclesiastical arrangements of Independent Churches. But it is, in its essence, political Dissent, for the root-principle of its whole constitution is incompatible with the existence of a State Church.'[17]

13. For whom see ODNB, SI.

14. Thompson, "The Bicentenary of Nonconformity," 197.

15. Thompson et al., "A Fraternal Address," 370.

16. All of which engendered a pamphlet war. See Larsen, "Victorian Nonconformity"; Taylor, "The Bicentenary of 1662."

17. Rogers, The Church Systems, 621. For Rogers (1822–1911) see ODNB, SI.

Other Nonconformists, less stridently political and more in favour of a historical-doctrinal approach, were nonplussed at the bolder agitations of some of their friends. But even they reveal a certain ambivalence in their writings and utterances. This is true even of Samuel Martin (1817–78), of whom is said that 'Nobody could be so holy as Samuel Martin looked,' and of whom it is written that 'his constructive spirit and emphasis on positive and fundamental doctrines made him desire urgently the unity of all Christian people.'[18] Martin, the minister of Westminster Chapel, London, occupied the Chair of the Congregational Union in the Bicentenary year. He referred to the Church of England thus:

> We are not her enemies because we defend vigorously our own churches. We could not say, Destroy her, but do say, Reform her; break her bondage to the State; purify her liturgy from heresy; let her prelates be true bishops; give more liberty to her clergy, and relieve them of a subscription which does not secure uniformity of creed and worship, and which . . . in some cases appears to involve declension from truth and uprightness. Until the so-called Church of the nation is completely reformed, and entirely Protestantized, we must stand outside chafing her by our Nonconformity, and provoking her by our Dissent . . . Our Nonconformity . . . is to us a moral necessity . . . We are Nonconformists for Christ's sake.[19]

The Bicentenary Chairman's Address at the Baptist Union Assembly was given by Charles Stovel, described by Ernest Payne as 'a formidable personality,' and by Joseph Angus as one for whom 'all questions were momentous; every field of conflict was a Thermopylae; every struggle was for life.'[20] Stovel begins by reminding his hearers that those who are individually united Christ are thereby united with all who are his. He refers to the situation of Baptists in Europe, to American slavery (to which he was determinedly opposed), and to the need at home for the removal of the civil disabilities that constrain Nonconformists. He then comes to the Bicentenary. He does not wish the 'celebration' to 'resuscitate wrongs done to Dissenters which charity should forget,' but he waxes hot against the *Book of Common Prayer* because it 'expresses

18. Peel, *Congregational Two Hundred*, 187–88. For Martin (1817–78) see also ODNB, SI.

19. Quoted by Waddington, *Congregational History to 1880*, 365, 368.

20. Payne, *The Baptist Union*, 108. For Angus (1816–1902) see ODNB.

and assumes the Papal fraud of sacramental grace, and the citizens of England are still compelled to foster the clergy who subscribe to all it contains.[21] He proceeds to reaffirm the separatist line: 'The churches comprised in this Union have withdrawn from the world, and openly denounced its corruptions';[22] but he soon returns to his main bugbear, thundering that 'The infirmities of the Commonwealth, however great soever, bear no comparison with the perfidy which revived and re-enforced subscription to this sacramental fraud.'[23] Ending on a lyrical note, we may suppose that he sent his hearers home happy: 'Descending like a seraph from before the eternal throne, [truth] sees herself insulted and abused; yet, strong in her resource, she means to reign. She has embodied herself in the Sufferer of Golgotha, and she smiles now at all adversity. Her very glance is terrible to those who love her not; but comforting her children against all hostility, she saith: Unto you that fear my name shall the Sun of Righteousness arise, with healing in His wings.'[24]

In the following year, from the Chair of the Congregational Union, Enoch Mellor (1823–81)[25] looked back on the Bicentenary year and lamented that 'In celebrating the Bicentenary . . . we have unhappily been brought into collision with some of our brethren in the Church of England. We but meant to visit with loving memory the shrines of those noble heroes, and lo! We had scarcely started before we were met by armed men. The pilgrimage became a battle—a battle we never sought, and which when offered we could not shun . . . [W]e intended to honour them, and we have accomplished our purpose.'

Returning to the Bicentenary year itself, we find that the *Evangelical Magazine* entered into the commemorative spirit by utilising an anonymous donation of 50 guineas as prize money in an essay competition open to Baptist and Congregational ministers. Candidates could choose one of three topics: 'The nature and constitution of the Church in New Testament times'; 'The development of church organization from the Reformation to 1662'; and 'The advantages that would result from a true representation, based on Scripture principles, of

21. Stovel, "The Chairman's Address," 137.

22. Ibid., 139.

23. Ibid., 140.

24. Ibid., 141.

25. For whom see SI; Peel, *Congregational Two Hundred*, 201–2.

the entire body of Church members (ministerial and lay so-called) in England and Wales, for the purposes of fraternal Christian conference and co-operation, with suggestions for the attainment of such a representation, and for safeguards against its abuse.' The prizewinner on the first subject was the Baptist, Joseph Angus; the Congregationalist, John Waddington,[26] was successful on the second topic, and his fellow Congregationalist Austin E. Lord managed to comprehend the third title, and won on that.[27] The essays by Angus and Waddington were published during 1662.

The most significant inter-denominational Bicentenary activity, however, occurred under the auspices of the impressively-named Central United Bartholomew Committee, which brought Baptists and Congregationalists together, and had its office at 10 Broad Street Buildings, London. The Committee publicized its *Objects and Plans*, making it clear that while Dissenters should do well to thank God for those who 'held for us the Thermopylae of freedom against an overwhelming host,'[28] the Committee's contribution to the commemorative proceedings was intended to be balanced and non-inflammatory. It published *A Summary of the Public Proceedings which issued in the Act of Uniformity*, and eleven tracts followed, under the titles: *The First Protest*; *The Book of Sports*; *The Star Chamber and High Commission*; *The Ejection of the Episcopalians*; *The Savoy Conference*; *The Act of Uniformity*; *The Farewell Sunday*; *The Effects of the Ejectment*; *On the Prayer Book*; *On Clerical Subscription*; and *The Act of Toleration*. These sold at two pence each. Much more substantial was the Committee's collection of *Documents relating to the Act of Uniformity of 1662*, to which Peter Bayne[29] supplied an Introduction.

The Committee did not overlook the public platform. It arranged a series of four lectures: 'The story of the Ejectment' by Thomas McCrie, 'Fidelity to conscience' by Alexander Maclaren, 'Nonconformity in

---

26. For Waddington (1810–80) see ODNB, SI.

27. See *Evangelical Magazine*, 1852, 498.

28. Quoted by Waddington, *Congregational History 1850–1880*, 373. Waddington reproduces the full text of the letter (ibid., 372–76) signed by the Chairman, Samuel Morley (1809–86) (Congregationalist), the Treasurer, Samuel Morton Peto (1809–89) (Baptist), and the Secretary, Samuel Cox (1826–93) (Baptist): two businessmen and a minister, united as much in commemorative endeavour as by their Christian names. They are all in ODNB.

29. For Bayne (1830–96) see ODNB.

1662 and 1862' by R. W. Dale, and 'The design and effects of the Act of Uniformity' by Robert Halley. All of this activity notwithstanding, a writer in *The Baptist Magazine*, remarking on the fact that 'The Baptists . . . have not, so far as we are aware, taken any separate denominational action,' feared that 'the United Committee, deriving but little strength from the Independent body, will show in the end but very feeble results. Yet some good must always arise from the enlightenment of the public mind.'[30] From across the Atlantic Joseph P. Thompson observed that 'for reasons that are not very clear to us on this side of the water, the Congregational Conference appointed by the [Congregational] Union to make arrangements for this celebration, have declined the proposals of the Baptists for a united commemoration, and have decided that "for practical purposes, it is desirable for the Congregational body to promote a denominational rather than a combined movement."'[31]

Undeniably, the Congregationalists engaged in multifarious activities—many of them costly—with considerable zeal.[32] Joshua Wilson was asked by the Congregational Union Council to propose a series of commemorative projects, many of which came to fruition. A series of six lectures, delivered during the Union's Autumn Assembly, was published under the title, *St, James's Hall Addresses*. The speakers included R. W. Dale and Robert Vaughan,[33] the latter of whom had, just one year previously, been commissioned by the Union to write the official Memorial Volume—a fresh account of *English Nonconformity*. This substantial work of 486 pages duly appeared in 1862, and in it Vaughan took a long run at his subject from paganism, through early British Christianity to the Anglo-Saxons, and onwards. A monument to the ejected ministers was erected at Bunhill Fields, where so many Dissenters are buried, and plans were put in hand for the building of the Memorial Hall to house the offices of the Union. This imposing building, commemorative of the ejected ministers, was erected in Farringdon Street on the site of the old Fleet Prison in which some

---

30. Anon. reviewer, *The Baptist Magazine* 54 (1862) 577–78.

31. Thompson, "The Bicentenary of Nonconformity," 196.

32. See Peel, *These Hundred Years*, 236–41.

33. For Dale (1829–95) and Vaughan (1795–1868) see ODNB, SI; Peel, *Congregational Two Hundred*, 205–6.

of Congregationalism's Separatist forebears had been incarcerated.[34] It cost in excess of £70,000, and was formally opened on 19 January 1875.

Without question, Wilson's challenge regarding the erection of new chapels had the most lasting effect in the country at large. He urged that fifty new chapels be opened on Bartholomew's Day 1862, and that on the same day the foundation stones be laid for a further fifty. Under the leadership of such prominent businessmen as Samuel Morley, George Hadfield, and Wilson himself Chapel Building Societies were organized for London, England and, for a reason shortly to be explained, Lancashire. Great efforts were made to secure funds for the building programme, and work began. At Shrewsbury land was purchased in 1862 for £750, and on it was built the Abbey Foregate Church and Sunday School.[35] At Hatherlow, in neighbouring Cheshire, under the leadership of the scholar-pastor William Urwick, additions were made to the chapel which more than doubled the space available for the Sunday School; and, for good measure, Urwick prepared his edited volume, *Historical Sketches of Nonconformity in the County Palatine of Cheshire* (1864).[36] New buildings included those of Clapton Park, Highbury Quadrant, and City Temple in London; the John Robinson Memorial Church, Gainsborough, Lincolnshire; Grange Congregational Church, Bradford; and Clifton Road Church, Brighton.[37]

Particular credit must go to the Lancastrians. Lancashire was regarded as a special case, in that approximately one third of the ejected ministers had connections with the county, among them Thomas Jollie and Henry Newcome;[38] and the bicentenary fell during the Cotton Famine, when almost 250,000 people were unemployed and 500,000 were in receipt of relief.[39] Despite this, nearly £20,000 was raised and twenty-seven chapels were erected in the county, among them those at Ashton in Makerfield; St. George's Road, Bolton;

34. On my first visit, as an intending ministerial candidate, to The Memorial Hall in 1952, I well remember savouring the irony of the fact that the archives of the Union were stored in the cells which had once housed the Separatists.

35. Elliot, *Shropshire*, 295–96.

36. Powicke, *Cheshire County Union*, 193. For Urwick (1826–1905) see ODNB, SI. Urwick was at Hatherlow from 1851–74; Powicke served there from 1886 to 1916.

37. R. T. Jones, *Congregationalism in England*, 196–97.

38. For Jollie (1629–1702) and Newcome (1627–95) see ODNB, SI.

39. Robinson, *Lancashire Congregational Union*, 50–51.

Hollinwood, Oldham; Hope, Oldham; Ancoats, Manchester; Stubbins; and Waterloo, Liverpool; and assistance was also given to some causes in north Cheshire.[40] In the country at large some £250,000 was raised, and 365 chapels were erected by 1867—this at a time when many Nonconformists were viewing the advance of Anglo-Catholicism and ritualism in the Church of England with great suspicion. Hence Geoffrey Nuttall's dry remark, 'The bicentenary of the Ejection of 1662 was ironically celebrated all over the country by the erection of pseudo-Gothic chapels. Gradually the building is lengthened; then transepts appear . . . finally chancels return, liturgically differentiated by steps, sometimes even, as at Mere, Wilts., with an apsidal termination. An inevitable consequence was the removal of the pulpit from the centre back to a lateral, and often to a corner position . . . One wonders who the architects of these churches are, or have been.'[41]

Two commemorative enterprises of the educational variety may be noted, both of them in Wales. In 1862 the Baptists opened Bartholomew College in Llangollen for the training of ministers. The first enrolment was of six students. The College was later known as the North Wales Baptist College, and it removed to Bangor in 1892.[42] In the bicentenary year Samuel Morley, M.P., and others, laid plans to open a new Memorial College in Brecon. Since 1838 the College's home had been a mansion formerly owned by David Blow,[43] minister of Glamorgan Street Church in the town. The project cost almost £12,000, of which Morley contributed £1,250. He laid the foundation stone on 13 June 1867, and the opening ceremony took place on 15 September 1869. These events are recorded in a volume on the Congregationalism of Brecon and Radnor, itself published to commemorate the 250th anniversary of the Ejectment.[44]

Over and above the more or less official commemorative activities, numerous independent publications flowed from the presses,

---

40. Ibid., 52–53. Cf. Nightingale, *Lancashire Congregational Union*, ch. 6.

41. Nuttall, "Reconstruct to Hear the Word!" 254. In a somewhat strident footnote he adds, 'At Mere the pulpit remains central, *in* the apse! [Horror of horrors!] The liturgical purpose of an apse was for procession round the altar. No one wants to process round a pulpit.' For Nuttall (1911–2007) see Sell, "Geoffrey Nuttall in Conversation."

42. Roberts, "Nonconformist Academies in Wales," 63.

43. For Blow (d. 1878) see SI.

44. Thomas and Jones, eds., *Brecon and Radnor*, 212.

some more polemical than others. Robert Vaughan emerged as an incisive pamphleteer with his answer to the Revd. George Venables' tract, *How Did They Get There?* entitled, *I'll Tell You: An Answer to How Did They Get There?* Venables posed two questions, the first of them concerning the Cromwellian period: 'How did this medley of so-called Dissenters, not a few of whom had not been ordained in any way whatever, come into possession of the emoluments, and parsonages of this horrible thing—the Church?'[45] Secondly, 'Why *not more* than two thousand of them became sufferers under the Act?'[46] To the first question Vaughan replied that they got there because, not for the first time, 'The State had given church property into new hands.'[47] Vaughan's reply to the second question was that Nonconformist behaviour was more consistent than Venables allowed: 'The Nonconformist says now what the Nonconformist said then; viz.—I cannot accept religious office on the condition of professing to believe what I do not believe, or to approve what I do not approve.'[48] Vaughan challenges Venables as to the cogency of his reasoning and the reliability of his history, regretfully concluding (as if the Liberation Society had not given so much as a nudge) that the episcopalians have 'forced the Bicentenary Celebration into the shape of a direct discussion on the broad ground of difference between Church and Dissent. All I would say is—If this *must* be the course of things, let it so be. Nonconformists will, I doubt not, acquit themselves intelligently, candidly and successfully, in relation to it.'[49] Venables' tract reached its thirty-seventh thousand, Vaughan's its sixth.

Less pugilistically, the urbane Congregationalist, John Stoughton, published his more substantial work, *Church and State Two Hundred Years Ago*—a book welcomed by a reviewer in the following terms: 'While the "sin of conformity" is retorted by the "sin of schism," we turn with delight to a publication which maintains a calm and Evangelical tone, and presents so pleasing a contrast to the storm which rages around.'[50] Those who wished to study a longer span of

45. Venables, *How Did They Get There?* 5–6.

46. Ibid., 6.

47. Vaughan, *I'll Tell You*, 6.

48. Ibid., 8.

49. Ibid., 31.

50. Anon., Review in *The Baptist Magazine* 44 (1862) 372–73. For Stoughton (1807–97) see ODNB; SI.

years across four volumes could turn to Joseph Fletcher's *The History of the Revival and Progress of Independency*, which was reprinted in 1862.[51] No other writer attained the circulation of Frederick Smeeton Williams,[52] of whose eight-page tract, *Bicentenary Nonconformist Memorial. The Story of Black Bartholomew*, 55,000 copies were sold before the year was out.

A cursory glance over some of the magazines and lectures of the day reveals interestingly different emphases among the writers. Thus, a writer in the Strict Baptist *Earthen Vessel*, facing up to the current Christian disarray, is anxious on the one hand, to remind readers that even in the darkest times God 'has often granted times of refreshing, seasons of holy joy'; and on the other, to make it plain that 'it has not been the religion of Jesus Christ which has brought in these floods of sorrow into a world; but man's pride, contending for the supremacy in civil government, in common prayer-books, in ordinances of man's invention, and in forms as opposed to vitalizing powers—from hence has the conflict arisen.'[53] A different note is sounded in another Strict Baptist magazine, *The Gospel Herald*. The writer refers to the dismay expressed by some Evangelical clergymen at the prospect of bicentennial activities, for the arrangements being made appear to them to be disruptive of the increasingly close fellowship that they enjoy with Nonconformists. The writer, however, thinks that the Nonconformists in question have paid 'too much deference . . . to the priestly claims of the State-favoured brethren on the platforms and in the Committee rooms of the Bible Society, the Evangelical Alliance, and other kindred institutions . . . Dissenters . . . have manifested too much *obsequiousness* in their intercourse with the State-Clergy . . . and [are] too willing to cast aside their distinctive principles to secure the honour of Episcopal countenance and friendship.'[54] Even-handed in judgment, the writer thinks it unsurprising that 'the Bicentenary Movement should have excited feelings of hostility in the bosoms of a clergy, who, with all their excellencies, cannot but be galled with a consciousness that *they themselves*, by a determined adhesion to the Prayer Book and Ritual of their own Church, can bear but little affinity with those noble

---

51. For Fletcher (1816–76) see ODNB, SI.

52. For Williams (1829–86) see SI.

53. Anon., "The Bi-centenary Scales Fairly Adjusted," 102.

54. Anon., "The Bicentenary of the Bartholomew Ejectment," 123.

confessors, who preferred freedom of conscience to the fetters of dishonourable complicity with acknowledged error.'[55] The concluding hope is that 'the proceedings of the Bicentenary year will be the means of reviving the good old spirit of uncompromising Nonconformity.'[56]

Thomas Goadby[57] contributed a three-part article to *The General Baptist Magazine*. He discusses 'Puritans and the Act of Uniformity', 'The story of the two thousand'; and in the third part, 'The spirit and purpose of the Bicentenary', he reminds his readers that 'Our attachment to the great principle of liberty of conscience is far older than 1662. We have never placed ourselves under the shadow of any ecclesiastical synod or establishment.'[58] The Baptists are not Nonconformists because they have never conformed; they are not Dissenters because they have never assented to state-imposed formularies [surely that is in part why they *are* Dissenters?]. On the contrary, 'The Scriptures are our rule and law.'[59] The Church of England claims to be a comprehensive Church, but in ejecting the Puritans it demonstrates the hollowness of the claim. A master of the *tu quoque* argument (as befits a prizeman in logic and philosophy of the University of Glasgow), Goadby declares that Baptists position *vis-à-vis* the Church of England is one 'we are driven to by the sad schism of her ecclesiastical exclusiveness'[60]—a view shared by many others.

From across the Atlantic there came further reflections on the Ejectment. 'Why is this horrible story raked up again?' asked J. M. Cramp (1796–1881)[61] from the Baptist heartland of Nova Scotia's Annapolis Valley. He answered his own question thus: 'strict justice demands that the story shall be frequently told, so that our children and our children's children may be sufficiently informed on the subject, and well guarded against any attempt to introduce opinions or

55. Ibid. The same point is made in *The Baptist Magazine*, 54 (1862) 578.

56. Ibid., 124. *The Gospel Herald* also gave space to the ejected ministers, Francis Holcroft (1628/9?–1692) and Joseph Oddy (bapt. 1628/9, d. 1687), and to an article on the texts used in farewell sermons by ejected ministers. Holcroft is in ODNB and for both see CR.

57. For Goadby see Carter, *Midland Baptist College*; Goadby, *Not Saints But Men*; Shepherd, *Northern Baptist College*, 112–16.

58. Goadby, "The Black Bartholomew Commemoration. III," 298.

59. Ibid.

60. Ibid., 301.

61. For whom see ODNB; *Dictionary of Canadian Biography online*.

practices which may tend to revive the disorders and repressions of the seventeenth century.'[62] He does not wish to excite hostility towards the Church of England; after all, 'It is well known that great numbers of the truest friends of the Church are dissatisfied with her present position,'[63] and 'The civil equality of all sects is now nearly attained in Great Britain.'[64] He ends by calling upon Jesus to return, 'for now the voice of thy bride calls thee, and all creatures sigh to be renewed.'[65]

The *Parousia* being still delayed, the National Council of Evangelical Free Churches saw fit in 1912, on the occasion of the 250th anniversary of the Great Ejectment, to reprint the address that Alexander Maclaren had given in 1862 under the auspices of the Central United Bartholomew Committee. Arguing throughout that their fidelity to conscience constituted the predominant reason for honouring the ejected ministers, he drew towards his conclusion thus:

> The future of England will be to that Church which shall know how to reconcile most perfectly the rights of the individual and the power of society; the claims of free thought and the claims of definite dogmatic truth. A Church on the so-called multitudinist theory will not do it; for of the two terms of the antithesis it reduces one, the element of dogmatic truth, practically to zero. An Established Church, be-articled, and be-liturgied, and be-bishoped will not do it. Narrow Dissenterisms will not do it. But Churches which take the Bible for their creed, and Christ for their sole master, and all their members for brethren, ought to do it. They may do it if they will be true to themselves, to their principles, to their ancestry. Shame on them if they fail.[66]

Maclaren's paper was published by the National Council of Evangelical Free Churches in a volume entitled, *The Ejectment of 1662 and the Free Churches*. The publisher's name, taken in 1896 in pref-

62. Cramp, *The Great Ejectment*, 26, 27.

63. Ibid., 28. A number of Nonconformist authors quoted the Church of England scholar, Julius Charles Hare (1795–1855) with approval. Hare had delivered a sermon at St. Peter's, Brighton, in 1841 in which he appealed for catholic unity among Christians, and countered the view that uniformity of practice leads to uniformity of will, on the ground that Acts of Uniformity have proved divisive and injurious to freedom. See, for example, E, S.S.,"The late Rev. Julius Charles Hare."

64. Cramp, *The Great Ejectment*, 32.

65. Ibid., 35.

66. Various, *The Ejectment of 1662*, 34. For Maclaren (1826–1910) see ODNB.

erence to the National Free Church Council, formed in 1892, itself suggests that H. Elvet Lewis was not too wide of the mark when, in his introductory chapter he rejoiced that 'Fifty years ago, when the Bicentenary commemoration was held, Nonconformists stood more apart from each other than they do today,'[67] though he might have noted that the addition of the adjective to the body's revised name, while in one sense positive, was also designed to make it clear that Unitarians, though Free Church people, were not welcome as members.[68] The other chapters in the book concern the relations of the churches of Old Dissent with the Ejectment: the Presbyterians (A. H. Drysdale), the Congregationalists (Henry W. Clark), and the Baptists (W. T. Whitley); while George Eayrs traces the link from some of the ejected clergy to the Wesleys and Methodism, and Lewis himself covers the Ejectment in Wales.

The religious press duly noted the anniversary. Interestingly, *The Christian World's* closest issue to Black Bartholomew's Day gave precedence to a major report of the death of General Booth of the Salvation Army, and devoted its first leading article to a memorial tribute to him. The second leading article is entitled, '1662 and 1912,' and in it statistics are placarded in a somewhat triumphalist manner:

> This week-end Nonconformists everywhere will be celebrating [not, more graciously, commemorating] the Ejectment of 1662 under the Act of Uniformity that came into force on August 24 of that year. This year's statistics of the Free Churches of England and Wales show a membership of 2,143,991, exclusive of the Salvation Army, with 9,275 ministers, 53,864 local preachers, 403,636 Sunday-school teachers, and 3,383,076 Sunday-school scholars. The nominal Anglican church membership is 2,342,153—the Nonconformists undoubtedly have the larger effective membership. Even these figures do not indicate the measure of the failure of the unrepealed Act of Uniformity. The world membership of the Anglican Church in 1909 was 3,905,957, but the world membership of churches of Nonconformist origin was 21,693,391.[69]

There follows a brief account of the Ejectment, and the leader concludes by noting with evident satisfaction that 'To-day Nonconformists,

67. Ibid., 4.

68. See Jordan, *Free Church Unity*, 49–50

69. Anon., "1662 and 1912," 10.

proscribed in 1662, hold the most responsible positions in the Government, and are the King's trusted counsellors.'[70] In the same issue it is noted that the (anachronistically named) National Free Church Council has published 'An Order of Commemoration Service for Sunday Schools.' It is said, perhaps predictably, to include a reading of the story of Daniel in the fiery furnace, as well as catechetical questions on Nonconformity.[71]

On the following day *The Baptist Times and Freeman* published 'The day of St. Bartholomew,' by J. G. Greenhough, Principal of Midland Baptist College.[72] Greenhough draws parallels between the massacre of the Huguenots in Paris on that day 340 years before, and the events of 1662. He finds that 'The Great Ejectment ultimately wrought, not the ends which pride, bigotry, and uncharity sought, but the ends which Divine justice planned. Instead of re-establishing the Anglican Church in the splendour, power, and unity of which the Bishops dreamed, it speedily weakened and demoralised the Church and virtually established Nonconformity as a mighty and ever-increasing religious and moral force in the land.'[73] As for the ejected themselves, the Presbyterian majority among them learned the importance of toleration, and gradually came to agree with the Congregationalists that 'the Church always suffers from its adulterous connection with the secular power, and is always spiritually mighty when it uses spiritual weapons alone.'[74] Greenhough stops short of advocating the disestablishment of the Church of England.[75]

---

70. Ibid.

71. *The Christian World*, 22 August 1912, 4.

72. For John Gershom Greenhough (1843–1933) see *The Baptist Handbook*, 1935, 320.

73. Greenhough, "The Day of St. Bartholomew," 621.

74. Ibid.

75. There is an interesting conjunction of items in *The Times*, 1 October 1912, 4. We learn that on the previous evening a service was held at Clapham Congregational Church to commemorate the Great Ejectment, the jubilee of the Church, and the ministry of James Guinness Rogers, who served there from 1865 to 1900. Albert Spicer, M.P., was present, and a window in memory of Rogers was unveiled. Rogers was an ardent advocate of the disestablishment of the Church of England. We further learn that on 8 October the Bishop of Llandaff was to preside at protest meeting in Cardiff against the disestablishment of the Church in Wales, at which the Bishops of St. Davids and St. Asaph were to speak. On 18 October, 10, *The Times* gave a full report of a speech given by Principal Thomas Rees of Bala Bangor Independent

On 29 August *The British Weekly* gave two columns to notes of a sermon preached by the Congregationalist C. Silvester Horne at Church Stretton on the previous Sunday.[76] The story of the ejected, he declares, is one 'of which every patriot is justly proud.' It is to the honour of the Christian ministry, and to that of the villages from which so many of them came. Victories were won for freedom of association and freedom of speech, and the truth of the Sermon on the Mount was demonstrated, namely, the victorious power of meekness. Towards the end he reminds his hearers that 'The Act of Uniformity is still the law of the land, though modified by toleration acts which have drawn its fangs. Some day it will disappear before the uprising of a nobler Church, a united Protestant Church, priestless, democratic, free, founded on the eternal simplicities of the Gospel, and the service of Humanity . . . We have to complete [the ejected ministers'] testimony in order to conserve their gains.'[77]

To George W. Macalpine, 'The one great service which the Act of Uniformity rendered to the Church of Christ was that it drove out into the wilderness a large number of godly and consecrated men who there came to recognize that religious liberty was essential to the well being of the Church—that a Free Church in a Free State was the grand ideal towards which the Church of Christ must ever advance.'[78] While he wanted such a church to be united, he was no advocate of any uniformity that would threaten liberty, for the Church is a body of believers united to Christ, and 'the only uniformity imposed by the New Testament is that of conformity to the image of God's Son.'[79]

The major commemorative events were well publicized in *The Times*. On 19 September advance notice was given of the forthcoming Free Church commemorative activities, and fuller information was supplied on 3 October. The following day Principal W. B. Selbie of Mansfield College, Oxford, preached a commemoration sermon in the

---

College at the annual Assembly of the Congregational Union as he moved a resolution of thanks to the Government for introducing the Welsh Disestablishment Bill. For Rees (1869–1926) see DWB online, SI, WTW.

76. The adjacent two columns are almost entirely occupied by an illustrated advertisement for the Mulcuto safety razor, the makers of which had 20,000 sticks of shaving soap to give away at the rate of one per razor.

77. Horne, "The Ejected Ministers," 524. For Horne (1865–1914) see SI, WTW.

78. Macalpine, "A.D. 1662," 115.

79. Ibid., 116.

Memorial Hall.[80] There followed tea and speeches by the Chairman of the Congregational Union, Principal Walter F. Adeney of Lancashire Independent College, and the Revd. Thomas Jackson, Chairman of the Primitive Methodist Conference. 500 persons marched to the Martyr's Stone at Smithfield, where they were addressed by the Baptist, the Revd. F. B. Meyer[81] and the United Methodist, the Revd. George Eayrs. In the evening Albert Spicer chaired a meeting addressed by C. Silvester Horne, Richard Roberts, and Thomas Phillips.

The 1912 address from the Chair of the Congregational Union was delivered by Adeney (1849–1920)[82] under the title, 'The more excellent way.' He looks back to the bicentenary of 1862 which was 'the one national event which impressed my boyhood, and to my father's lecture at Reigate on that occasion I trace an indelible consciousness of the necessity of Nonconformity and of the duty of maintaining those great truths and duties that were illustrated in the heroic conduct of the ejected ministers.'[83] Like Cramp before him, he mentions this because 'we can hardly begin too soon the training of young people in the history of the Free Churches.'[84] He hopes that during the anniversary year special attention will be paid to the children in our homes, churches, and Sunday schools (Adeney was a tireless worker for the National Sunday School Union).

Adeney makes it clear that he does not wish to defend the 'sternly uniformitarian' attitudes of the Puritans, but he cannot fail to note that 'the dream of Uniformity has not been realised even within [the Church of England's] own shrunken fold. Ritualists and Evangelicals have proved to be more irreconcilable than those whilom rivals and opponents, but now friends and brothers, Presbyterians and Congregationalists.'[85] He further points out that the 'English Act of Uniformity did not even aim at uniformity—in any large and national application of the idea. It was frankly and brutally separatist; it was meant to be so.'[86] That Adeney was a man in whom the old fires still burned is clear from the following remarks:

80. For Selbie (1862–1944) see ODNB, SI, WTW.

81. For Meyer (1847–1929) see ODNB.

82. For whom see SI; Sell, *Hinterland Theology*, ch. 9 and *passim*.

83. Adeney, "The More Excellent Way," 36.

84. Ibid.

85. Ibid., 38.

86. Ibid., 37.

> We have no desire to be graciously permitted to return to the
> Established Church, either as her whipped children creeping
> in at a back door, or even as respectable exiles welcomed home
> with generous admissions that we should never have been os-
> tracised. These 250 years have not been lived in vain. We have
> come to see the utter unchristianity of the control of Church
> affairs by the arm of the State, to see that it is a usurpation of
> the rights of Christ and a dishonour to His body that not one
> line of the obligatory Book of Prayer can be altered without the
> consent of Parliament, and that the chief places in the pastoral
> office should be filled at the dictation of the First Lord of the
> Treasury—even though we might imagine a time when that
> Minister of State should happen to be a Baptist.[87]

In his Introduction to *The Ejectment of 1662* Elvet Lewis wrote,
'fifty years lie between us and the Tercentenary; and those of us who
live to-day are anxious that those who live then shall see a still closer
union between the Free Churches of this land . . .'[88] Two world wars
had intervened between the 250th anniversary of the Ejectment and
its tercentenary in 1962; the way of life of most people had changed
radically in numerous ways—notably in opportunities for education
and health care; the colonies were *en route* to independence; and the
mainline British churches were facing post-War re-building on the
one hand and declining numbers on the other. The World Council
of Churches had been formed in 1948, and the British Council of
Churches was working hard in this land, though its activities were often regarded by local churches as optional extras to their normal pro-
grammes. The Presbyterians, now more of Scottish, Irish, and Welsh
extraction than of Old Dissent, and the Congregationalists were in
conversation regarding unity, but of the idea of a national federation
of Free Churches such as was mooted by P. T. Forsyth and others before 1920, little was now heard.[89] This was the climate in which the
tercentenary of the Great Ejectment was commemorated with some
enthusiasm.

A Joint Commemoration Committee was convened comprising
official representatives of the Baptist Union, the Presbyterian Church
of England, and the Congregational Union, with observers from the

87. Ibid., 45.

88. Lewis in Various, *The Ejectment of 1662*, 4. For Lewis (1860–1953) see DWB
online, ODNB, SI.

89. For Forsyth (1848–1921) see ODNB, SI, WTW.

Methodist Church and the Free Church Federal Council. Howard S. Stanley, General Secretary of the Congregational Union,[90] was appointed secretary, and it was decided that the emphasis of the occasion should be upon the principles at issue three hundred years before, and that the objective should be to show how far those principles were still operative and relevant. By March 1960 the committee was able to announce its intentions in the following terms: 'We believe ourselves justified in drawing public attention to the tercentenary of this Great Ejectment because it constituted an important landmark in English religious and social history; because from it flowed some of the main streams of historic Nonconformity; because it was bound up with certain convictions to which testimony must still be borne; and because the commemoration of 1662 will focus attention upon certain issues which still confront our Churches.'

The committee regrets the bitterness of past controversy, welcomes the progress made towards full religious liberty for Nonconformists and the increasing co-operation with the Church of England, not least that through the British Council of Churches, and concludes that 'the particular contributions which we can make towards the achievement of such closer relationships are, in part at least, based on a fellowship of convictions with those who were ejected.'[91] A second *Bulletin* followed in November 1961, in which relevant publications were listed and two events were advertised: a service at the City Temple on Bartholomew's Day 1962, and a meeting at the Royal Albert Hall on 23 October of the same year.

The press, both religious and national, paid such attention as might have been expected to the tercentenary. On 6 January 1962 *The Guardian* sounded a discordant note under the headline, 'The Great Ejectment Dispute.' This was a reference to the fact that what we might call 'the Unitarian problem' which had haunted earlier Free Church dealings had raised its head again because the offer of the Unitarians to share in the tercentenary preparations had been declined. Howard Stanley said that although, historically, the Unitarians were concerned with the events of 1662, and although their contribution to the struggle for religious liberty and to intellectual and social progress was valued, 'ours is a religious and not a historical celebration' and

90. For Stanley (1901–75) see SI, WTW.
91. Anon., *Bulletin One*.

that the statement of the commemorative theme was designed to 'help not worsen the relations between the Churches.' There is clearly an element of special pleading here, for there was no question that the occasion was historical as well as religious: indeed, it could not have been the latter had it not been the former; and when Stanley gave as evidence of the committee's success the fact that Archbishop Ramsey had accepted an invitation to attend the service to take place in the (Congregational) City Temple, and that his predecessor, Archbishop Geoffrey Fisher had asked for an invitation, it must have been crystal clear to the Unitarians with which churches the committee did not wish to worsen relations. The Unitarians were, however, invited to take an 'honoured place' along with other church representatives who would be attending the service, but this they declined on the ground of their exclusion from the tercentenary arrangements.[92]

The writer of the editorial in *The Baptist Quarterly* regrets that Baptist church members are not, for the most part, clear as to the significance of the Ejectment, with the result that 'Enthusiasm among Baptists for marking the tercentenary of 1662 can, at best, be designated as "patchy"'[93] (though it was the inspiration for a Baptist Union Tercentenary Fund with a target of £300,000). The editor's view is that the occasion raises afresh two pertinent questions: 'Do I believe that Church and State ought to be separated? Do I believe that within any act of worship there should be freedom in the Spirit for prayer?'[94] *The Congregational Quarterly* for August 1962 carried a number of articles relating to the tercentenary. The first was a characteristically gracious and well informed greeting from Michael Ramsey the Archbishop of Canterbury who, *inter alia* thanked God for the witness of a number of Congregationalists, among them P. T. Forsyth, sometime minister at Emmanuel Congregational Church, Cambridge, where Ramsey's father had served as a deacon. G. W. Pibworth reminded his Strict Baptist readers of the provisions of the Act of Uniformity and challenged them in the following terms: 'What are *we* prepared to give up for our Lord and His cause? "Freedom to Worship" was the watchword of those who went before us. And so often, we who have that freedom to the full neglect it! Our fathers risked fine, imprisonment,

92. See ibid.

93. Anon., "Editorial," 241.

94. Ibid., 242.

transportation to meet in the assembly of God's people; there are many professed Christians to-day who count it a cross, very often, even to be expected to *attend* two or three services a week!' *The British Weekly* for 6 September reported on tercentenary addresses given in various parts of the country.

A torrent of other publications flowed from the presses. Anglicans and Dissenters (including Roger Thomas the Unitarian) contributed to a volume edited by the Congregationalist Geoffrey F. Nuttall and the Anglican Owen Chadwick entitled, *From Uniformity to Unity*. The Independent pushed the boat out with *Rooted in Faith*, a lucid account of three centuries of Nonconformity by the Presbyterian F. G. Healey; a short popular work by Erik Routley entitled, *The Story of Congregationalism*, and the more substantial work, *Congregationalism in England* by R. Tudur Jones.[95] As if this were not enough the Press published a series of twenty-eight *Heritage Biographies* of significant Nonconformists from Robert Browne (1550–1633) to Benjamin Waugh (1839–1908). In a way that would have delighted Cramp and Adeney, the Congregational Union published a series of Sunday School lessons by its Secretary for Children's Work, Constance M. Parker, entitled, *The Congregational Road*. These were used in many churches, and we still possess the large posters that our Sedbergh deacon, the artist Marjorie Anderson, and Karen Sell drew to illustrate them. A number of one-act plays were published for the use of church dramatic societies, and Robert Duce published *Fire in the City*—a play in three acts.[96] From the Congregational Historical Society there came a special supplement, *1662 and its Issues*, and an essay competition. Candidates could choose to write on one of the following subjects: '1662–1962, the panorama of Congregationalism'; '1662–1962, has Nonconformity justified itself?'; 'The abiding significance of Congregationalism.' Interestingly, the total numerical value of the prizes of £25, £15 and £10 was less than that of one of the three 50 guinea prizes offered in 1862, and significantly lower in purchasing power. Not to be outdone, the Epworth Press published *1662—and After: Three Centuries of Nonconformity*, a thoughtful volume by the eminent Methodist scholar, John T. Wilkinson.

95. For Routley (1917–82) and Jones (1921–98) see SI, WTW.
96. For Duce (1908–88) see SI.

It was only to be expected that the Ejectment would provide the theme of the Annual Assembly addresses of the President of the Baptist Union and the Chairman of the Congregational Union. On 30 April the former, William Dodds Jackson,[97] spoke on 'Our Heritage and Opportunity,' while on 14 May the latter, W. John F. Huxtable, took 'The Tradition of our Fathers' as his theme. He argued that while there was much justification for the Dissenting protests of the past, Congregationalists should nevertheless face up to the challenge of God's will for unity, however difficult the road ahead might be; and they should not allow denominational pride to become a stumbling block to ecumenical progress.[98]

Back in 1862 John Corbin,[99] the minister at Park Chapel, Hornsey, gazed into the future and speculated that 'When the Congregationalists of 1962 hold their Union meetings in London, it may be that, *in their own Memorial Hall*, some Vaughan or Stoughton of that age will recount the successive steps of a century of progress; and raise to God a song of praise for what their fathers of this age were enabled to accomplish.'[100] In the event, the Tercentenary Union Meetings were held in Westminster Chapel, while the first of the two most important public events of the year, a service of worship, took pace on Bartholomew's Day in the City Temple, now rebuilt following war damage and opened in 1958; while the second, a Rally, filled the Royal Albert Hall on 23 October.

The City Temple service received widespread coverage *via* television. The congregation included representatives of all the Free Churches, the Moderator of the International Congregational Council, Norman Goodall, Mrs. George F. Kahlenberg, Moderator of the General Council of the Congregational Christian Churches in the United States, and, as already mentioned, Archbishops Ramsey and Fisher. R. D. Whitehorn (Presbyterian) conducted the service; the lessons were read by Archbishop Ramsey and Leonard Griffith, the minister of the City Temple; the Baptist, Ernest Payne, offered the prayers; hymns of Baxter, Watts, and Doddridge were sung; and the sermon was preached by H. F.

97. For Jackson (d. 1980) see *The Baptist Handbook*, 1980–81, 287–88.

98. See Huxtable, *The Tradition of our* Fathers; also his article, "The Obedience of the Dissenter." For Huxtable (1912–90) see ODNB, SI, WTW.

99. For Corbin (1811–90) see SI.

100. *The Congregational Year Book*, 1863, 67.

Lovell Cocks,[101] the former Principal of Western College, Bristol and current Moderator of the Free Church Federal Council.

Lovell Cocks took Hebrews 13:7–8 as his text: 'Remember your leaders, those who spoke to you the word of God; consider the outcome of their life, and imitate their faith. Jesus Christ is the same yesterday and today and for ever.'[102] He first welcomed the fact that Anglicans and Free Church people were commemorating the Ejectment together. He recalled the service held the previous May to commemorate the tercentenary of the *Book of Common Prayer*, during which Archbishop Ramsey had said that 'two Englands, Church and Chapel, were created by 1662 . . . two Englands, two cultures, embittered and aloof, became the pattern of our history.' Yet by God's overruling providence Nonconformists had contributed much to the development of democracy and, through the Nonconformist Conscience—and despite its 'blind spots'—to civic responsibility. Indeed, 'the moral and spiritual health of the community still depends on the sales-resistance of the Christian pilgrims of every denomination as they pass through the Vanity Fair of our affluent society.'[103] He grants that we do not believe everything that our forebears in the faith believed, and unlike those who celebrated the bicentenary of the Ejectment,

> We no longer campaign for the disestablishment of the Church of England . . . But we notice that many Anglicans are uneasy about a system under which the Prime Minister of the day nominates the diocesan bishops and no change can be made in the law and liturgy of the Church except by Act of Parliament. The 1662 establishment now seems to them as it has always seemed to us, a secular usurpation of spiritual authority which on the face of it is a denial of the Crown Rights of the Redeemer. Here, at any rate, the Nonconformists of 1662 are winning their case.

For all the glories of the *Book of Common Prayer*, Nonconformists continue to protest against the imposition of uniformity in worship and the exclusion of free prayer—'a heritage we hold in trust for the Church Universal.' As for episcopacy, Nonconformists have always recognised the necessity of oversight, but:

101. For Cocks (1894–1983) see ODNB, SI, WTW; Sell, *Commemorations*, ch. 13.

102. For the text of the sermon see Cocks, "We Must Sacrifice our Prejudices."

103. For its report on the service *The Times* drew its headline from Cocks' words. See Anon., "Vanity Fair of our Affluent Society."

> we should be more ready to see in episcopacy an eloquent wit-
> ness to the continuity of the Church through the centuries and
> the unity of her faith were it not for the claim that it constitutes
> that unity and continuity, so that ordination by bishops stand-
> ing in historical succession from the Apostles is the only way
> in which the Church may be assured of a valid minister of the
> Word and Sacraments. To us, as to the men of the Ejectment,
> such a theory conflicts with our understanding of the biblical
> doctrine of divine grace.

He underlines the fact that the primary concern of the ejected 'was not that *they* should be unfettered but that the Word of God should not be bound.' All Christians are already one in Christ, 'But the unity must be made manifest to the world . . . No Christian fellowship, whether local church or world-wide communion that clings to a Laodicean independence, believing itself to be rich and in need of nothing, can be truly free for Christ and His Gospel.' He concludes by challenging his hearers to imitate the faith of their forebears by submitting to continuing reformation, ever listening to what the Spirit has to say to the churches: 'So shall be in very deed *Free* Churches, obedient to Him whose service is perfect freedom—Jesus Christ, the same yesterday, today and for ever.' I have quoted at some length from Lovell Cocks' sermon because no other single tercentenary address so ably encapsulates and balances the historical-sociological-theological considerations to which attention was drawn in the tercentenary commemorations.

Free Church people from all over England and Wales flocked to the Royal Albert Hall for the Rally on 23 October 1962, at which the devotions were led by John Huxtable and addresses were given by Ernest Payne, the General Secretary of the Baptist Union of Great Britain and Ireland, and Howard S. Stanley,[104] the General Secretary of the Congregational Union. Stanley welcomed the fact that the Ejectment was being commemorated in a better spirit than that which prevailed in 1862 and even in 1912, but observed that the Free Churches were not only still separated from the Church of England, but also from each other. He attributed this to the fact that the convictions of the ejected had too often been expounded in negative terms. While it is still necessary to dissent from the control of the Church by the secular government, he argued, the positive High Churchmanship

---

104. For a report of the occasion see Anon., "Churches' Disunity 'Rebuking Fact.'"

of Free Churchpeople, namely, that Christ alone is Lord of the Church, must be emphasized. This is a point to which I shall return shortly.

From a number of standpoints it is possible to make good the claim that the Ejectment was a significant event in the life of England and Wales. Thus, to the nineteenth-century historian, Herbert Skeats, 'The passing of the Act of Uniformity, considered as an enactment instigated by the State Church, was a fatal blunder; considered as an essential element in the development of the Free Churches of England, it was the most happy event that could have taken place.'[105] As to the blunder, a number of Anglicans would have agreed. Reflecting on the Act of Uniformity as early as 1675, Shaftesbury addressed *A Letter from a Person of Quality to his Friend in the Country* (probably composed for him by John Locke) which contains the following sober judgment: '*Bartholomew day* was fatal to our Church, and Religion, in throwing out a very great Number of *Worthy, Learned, Pious and Orthodox Divines*, who could not come up to [some] things in that Act.'[106] Nearly two centuries on, in his address of 10 December 1840 to the Chichester Diocesan Association Julius Charles Hare, preaching in St. Peter's Church, Brighton, on 'The unity of the Church' (Ephesians 4:4–6), declared that 'All hope of unity was blasted by that . . . most disastrous, most tyrannical, and most schismatical Act of Uniformity; the authors of which, it is plain, were seeking not unity but division'[107]—a judgment reiterated, as we saw, by W. F. Adeney in 1912. Hare further remarked that while the Act

> bore the name of Uniformity on its forehead: can there have been any who persuaded themselves that a Uniformity so enforced could be a means to Unity? The only Unity that could have ensued from it would have been that of a dead level: and full of woe as have been the consequences of this Act in its failure, they would have been still more terrible had it succeeded. Therefore even we, who love and revere our national Church above every earthly institution, may bless God that it did not succeed.[108]

105. Skeats and Miall, *History*, 58.

106. Shaftesbury, *A Letter*, 2.

107. Hare, *The Mission of the Comforter*, I, 247. Hare dedicated his sermon to Henry Edward Manning, Archdeacon of Chichester.

108. Ibid., 249.

With regard to the theological and spiritual calibre of many of the ejected ministers—and, it must be confessed, with some exaggeration—a writer in *The British Quarterly Review* of 1862 declared that the 'immediate result' of the Act 'was to thrust the piety of the land out of the Established Church.' He concluded that the Act left the Church of England substantially as it is today, but 'at the cost of seeing half the nation disown its authority.'[109] Again, many have said that the significance of the Act resides in the demonstration once and for all that religious uniformity is not achieved by parliamentary legislation. Yet again, there is view expressed by Archbishop Ramsey at the service held to commemorate the tercentenary of the *Book of Common Prayer*, namely, that the Act enshrined the socio-cultural distinction between Church and Chapel in law, and subsequent Acts reinforced the position and seriously curtailed the ability of Nonconformists to participate in professional or civic life. Though this does not excuse the punitive measures, we might observe that one consequence of them was to direct Nonconformists into business and industry— otherwise we might not have had the spate of church building in the years around 1862, not to mention the town of Saltaire, named after Titus Salt its founder; nor would we have had the cigarettes or the benefactions of W. D. and H. O. Wills of Bristol.[110] Such businessmen and pioneering industrialists became wealthy, and many of them possessed philanthropic zeal and political clout. The Anglican, Hensley Henson, affirmed that in the wake of the Ejectment 'Religious dissent for the first time became both considerable and respected.'[111] Finally, we may note the opinion of the Methodist, Gordon Rupp, that the ejected ministers 'made England safe for the Evangelical Revival. They ensured that the Methodist movement was able to grow up in a new kind of freedom, to establish forms of worship, proclamation, and piety such as in the seventeenth century could only have emerged in bitter strife and amid forcible proscription.'[112]

It is relatively easy to make and justify the claims just noted, but what shall we say of the doctrinal significance of the Great

109. Anon., Review of Girdlestone, 319, 322.

110. If the Congregationalists went for their customers' lungs, the Quakers went for their teeth (Cadburys, Frys, Rowntrees), and exercised stewardship over their money (Barclays, Lloyds).

111. Henson, Puritanism, 204.

112. Rupp, "Clerical Integrity," 148.

Ejectment? In my opinion one of the most important results of 1662 is that the ejected ministers, now associating with those Baptists and Independents who had never taken livings from which they could be ejected, made more than a numerical difference to the Dissenting ministry; they considerably strengthened its intellectual calibre. Many of them, especially the Congregationalists and the minority of Baptists, but over time some of the Presbyterians, acknowledged their indebtedness to the Separatists of the preceding century, especially as far as pneumatology and ecclesiology were concerned. If, as seems to be the case, the Congregationalist Lemuel Tuke was the only physical ministerial link between the ejected ministers and the Separatists, for he had been both,[113] in terms of doctrine and polity the line is clear, as Alexander Mackennal rightly saw. Referring to the ejected Congregationalists, he wrote,

> The Independents were not enamoured of the name Separatist or Brownist, and that not simply because it was an offensive title, carrying a stigma with it.[114] They were not true Separatists; had they been so, they would not have sat in the Westminster Assembly, nor entered into Cromwell's purpose of founding a National Church . . . [Nevertheless] [a]ll they knew of Congregational Independency, gathered Churches, discipline, the association of the members with the ministers in church government, the desire for toleration, had been formulated for them by Browne, and Barrowe, and John Robinson, and Henry Jacob, and Henry Ainsworth.[115]

113. See Nuttall, "The First Nonconformists," 165–66.

114. That is, the stigma of sectarianism. The ejected had lived through the more disturbing antics of some of the Commonwealth sectaries. If Gordon Rupp is to be believed, there was also a temperamental distinction between the Separatists and the ejected Puritans: 'The Puritans were no longer what they had been in their beginning—their leaders were no longer angry young men with fire in their bellies—like Penry, Greenwood, Barrow—but milder, middle-aged men who had to take care of their stomachs.' Rupp, "Clerical Integrity," 146. As for Mackennal himself, he declared: 'Let me frankly confess—I do not like Robert Browne . . . He was a man offensive to his opponents and objectionable to his friends; he betrayed the causes to which he attached himself; and I do not wonder at the heat with which English dissenters have always repudiated the nickname "Brownists." But . . . he produced an admirable and complete doctrine of the Church, which at once determined the whole future of Congregationalism.' *The Evolution of Congregationalism*, 69. For Browne (1550?–1633) see ODNB. For Mackennal (1835–1904) see ODNB, SI.

115. Mackennal, *The Evolution of Congregationalism*, 123. For Barrow (d. 1593), Robinson (c.1575–1625), Jacob (1563–1624), and Ainsworth (c.1569–c.1622) see ODNB, SI.

The Fraternal Address sent by the American Congregationalists to their English counterparts in 1862 made the same point: 'Though the Pilgrim Exodus that brought religious freedom and Church purity to these shores, preceded by forty-two years the [Ejectment] . . . both were prompted by the intolerance of the same ecclesiastical corporation, and each by moral influence furthered the aims of the other.'[116] It is also very important to remember that some of the ejected Congregationalists—Thomas Goodwin and William Bridge; and some who were not in pastorates from which they could be ejected—John Owen and Philip Nye, among them, had composed the *Savoy Declaration of Faith and Order* in 1658—a document which, as they declared, sought a middle way between Presbyterianism and strict Brownism.[117] The *Declaration* reveals clear indebtedness to broadly Separatist ecclesiology, as we shall see. Hence Geoffrey Nuttall's puzzlement: 'it is strange,' he writes, 'that in some quarters there should be a desire to eject [Browne, Smyth and Robinson] from their accepted and honoured place in Congregationalism's origins';[118] hence also Ernest Payne's insistence that 'Congregationalist and Baptist origins alike run back into Separatism.'[119]

The evidence for all of this will emerge as we proceed as, I hope, will the fact that the term 'Separatist catholicity' denotes a fact, even if, as A. J. Grieve said, 'It is one of the divine paradoxes that separatism and catholicity meet in the Congregational way.'[120] For the present I would simply add that the importance of the Separatist-ejected link is that, unlike the Methodists, who did with greater or lesser degrees of reluctance, secede from the Church of England, the Separatist harbingers of Old Dissent never opted into it.[121] As the Congregational historian Bernard Lord Manning put it,

116. Thompson, *et al.*, "A Fraternal Address," 369.

117. For Goodwin (1600–80), Bridge (1600?–70), Owen (1616–83) and Nye (1595?–1672) see ODNB, SI.

118. Nuttall, *Visible Saints*, 7. For his careful tracing of the links, familial and other, between the Separatists and the ejected see "The Emergence of Nonconformity."

119. Payne, "Baptist-Congregational Relationships," 96.

120. Quoted by Surman, *Alexander James Grieve*, 47. For Grieve (1873–1952) see also SI, WTW.

121. The motivation of the Methodists was evangelistic, that of Old Dissent was ecclesiological. The latter were proposing an alternative understanding of the church which would preserve Christ's sole Lordship over it.

We of the Three Dissenting Bodies never 'left the Church.' From the moment when, at the Reformation, the mediaeval Church began to spit up, there were churchmen who stood in this country for a Church after the Calvinistic pattern, and hoped to make such a Church the Church of England. Of those men we are the descendants. We did not take ourselves off in a fit of pious ill-temper as a result of some small difference with Anglicans—in 1662 or at any other date . . . Our specific form of churchmanship is at least as old as the historic Anglican Settlement. I should claim that it is even older, that it goes back to Geneva—to say nothing of the New Testament.[122]

DISTILLING THE 'MESSAGE' OF THE GREAT EJECTMENT

Before going further it is necessary to ask ourselves what we are doing when we reflect upon such an event as the Ejectment, its antecedents, and its aftermath. In a word, we are doing what our forebears did when they commemorated the Ejectment: we are engaging in an act of distillation. The fact that distillation has occurred is readily seen if, recalling the principal provisions of the Act of Uniformity, we set down the nineteenth- and twentieth-century objections to them. These, as summarized by Gordon Robinson, were:

(1) The authority of the visible Church in matters concerning its Faith and Order is distinct from and not subordinate to the civil authority; (2) the revelation of God recorded in the Scriptures is the supreme standard within the Church in matters of Faith and Order; (3) the historic episcopate is not a divinely required constituent of the visible Church, and the validity of the exercise of the functions of spiritual oversight and of the minister of the Word and Sacraments by ministers duly ordained otherwise than by a bishop, but agreeably to the will of God as recorded in the Scriptures, should be recognised; (4) the orderly public worship of God should not be required to follow the patterns laid down by a particular book.[123]

122. Manning, *Essays*, 132, 145. Cf. Manning, *The Making of Modern English Religion*, 93–94. Every ecumenist should read B. L. Manning's *Essays*—at least twice. For Manning (1892–1941) see ODNB, WTW. For a notable misconstruing of the principle of Dissent as separating from 'a great national Church' because of 'very slight differences of opinion' and hence denying the principle of the Reformation, see the remarks of Edward Harold Browne, Bishop of Winchester, in *The Chronicle of Convocation*, 12 May 1887.

123. Robinson, "A Fellowship of Convictions," 1. Robinson here summarizes

Omitted from this list is any reference to the requirement that the oath taken regarding the Solemn League and Covenant of 1643 be abjured. The oath concerned the determination of the English and the Scots to uphold the Reformed faith, and the covenant ensured Scottish military support of English anti-Royalist endeavours. A number of the Presbyterians who suffered ejectment were greatly concerned by the requirement to abjure the oath, either because they stood by it, or because they felt it sinful to go back on such an oath, or both.[124] The fact that Robinson does not include it in his list suggests that distillation has occurred: what was important to many of the ejected was, in the different circumstances following the deaths of those who had taken the oath, no longer a neuralgic issue. The commemorations of 1862, 1912, and 1962 were silent on the matter, and I am not aware of anyone who wishes to resurrect the theme in 2012. Again, so exercised were many of the Dissenters of 1862 concerning the disestablishment of the Church of England that of the associated traditional complaints regarding the contents of the Prayer Book relatively little was heard. The Baptist Charles Stovel was almost a lone platform voice in hammering perceived sacerdotalism; and by 1962 Lovell Cocks, while noting the continuing Dissenting objection to the legal imposition of a prayer book and extolling the gift of free prayer, was nevertheless able to speak without embarrassment of the glories of the *Book of Common Prayer*.

Healey, *Rooted in Faith*, 73 ff. and 117 ff., which book he is reviewing. For Robinson (1903–76) see ODNB, SI, WTW; Sell, "A Valued Inheritance."

124. We should note that while some English seventeenth-century Presbyterians were content to think in Scottish fashion of an hierarchy of church courts, others, in the line of Thomas Cartwright, thought in terms of autonomous congregations each of which was supplied with minister, elders, and deacons. Some of the latter regarded the Scottish idea as 'an exotic novelty.' See Nuttall, *The Holy Spirit*, 11, 12. In the event, the majority of the Presbyterian churches of Old Dissent had become Congregational by the end of the eighteenth century, while a significant number of them, together with many of the General Baptist churches and a handful of Congregational and Particular Baptist churches, had become Unitarian by the early nineteenth century. Thus, the Presbyterian Church *of* England, with which the majority of English and English-speaking Welsh Congregational churches united in 1972 to form the United Reformed Church, was constituted in 1876. It comprised the remnant of orthodox Presbyterian churches of Old Dissent (most of them in north-east England), the churches of the Presbyterian Church *in* England (ex-Church of Scotland, but sided with the Free Church of the 1843 Disruption), and the churches of the United Presbyterian Church of Scotland (the Seceder tradition) that had been established on English soil.

There are two main reasons why distillation occurs. First, those of the Dissenting traditions, like those of any other tradition, have had to respond to changing times and circumstances. Thus whereas in 1862 the Liberation Society was crusading with a view to the disestablishment of the Church of England; and whereas in 1912 George Macalpine opined that 'The one great service which the Act of Uniformity rendered . . . was that it drove out into the wilderness a large number of godly and consecrated men who there came to recognize that religious liberty was essential to the well being of the Church—that a Free Church in a Free State was the grand idea to which the Church of Christ must ever advance,'[125] the fact is that some of the ejected ministers, at least up to the time of their ejectment, were content with an establishment sufficiently flexible to permit the practice of their polities, while the Presbyterians—in some cases to the end of the seventeenth century, were hoping for an established Church conducted on Presbyterian lines. Not surprisingly, the anonymous reviewer in *The Baptist Magazine* for 1862 remarked upon 'the amusing anomaly of commemorating [the ejected ministers'] expulsion upon a principle utterly foreign to their views and practice, and endeavouring to do honour to their memory by condemning one of the most prominent of their tenets.'[126] Gordon Rupp echoed the point in 1962.[127] There is, however, something to be said in explanation, if not in full justification, of the ejected ministers of Congregational persuasion. When, during the Interregnum, it was possible for them to lead churches according to their own polities in parish churches—and even in Westminster Abbey—and to receive tithes for so doing, and all of this, they hoped, with an ultimate view to the establishment of a godly kingdom such as that conducted by their co-religionists on the New World, we can perhaps understand why they would not have objected to the continuance of such a plan. We may also presume that they were in sympathy with Cromwell's objective of ensuring that every parish in the land was served by a preacher and pastor of integrity. Such explanations notwithstanding, the Congregationalist, H. W. Clark trounced his forebears in 1912 in uncomfortably Olympian fashion. He contended that the most important things about the Act of

125. Macalpine, "A.D. 1662," 115.

126. Anon., Reviews, 376.

127. See Rupp, "Clerical Integrity—1662," 147.

Uniformity was that 'it linked together a Presbyterianism only super-ficially and by accident Nonconformist and an Independency which, though essentially and truly Nonconformist, had already fallen in no small measure from its earliest high estate.'[128] Clark did, however, acknowledge that some Congregational ministers remained outside Cromwell's system, as did most Baptist pastors. These were especially opposed to receiving tithes, and therefore many of them were pas-tors of the tent-making sort. Clark also observed, with some justifica-tion, that 'the real and original Nonconformist stream—the stream flowing most directly from the original Nonconformist sources of the early Separatist days—had so to say gone *round* the whole crisis [of the Ejectment], and had now to receive into itself the confluent streams of those Presbyterians and Independents expelled from the Established ranks.'[129] It remains to add that while in 1962 Lovell Cocks could affirm that the Nonconformists were not currently urging the disestablishment of the Church of England, he did note the uneasiness that some Anglican ministers experienced over the governing of the Church's order and worship by the state.

The inevitability of distillation notwithstanding, it remains pos-sible to trace a line from the ejected—indeed, from the Separatists—to the present day of those who deny the necessity of Episcopal ordina-tion (of which more in due course), and who dissent from the view that in spiritual matters concerning the worship and ordering of the Church it is the prerogative of the monarch or the parliament to leg-islate. I am bound to say that I have neither heard nor read a cogent theological repudiation of this view, though I have heard a number of pragmatic-*cum*-instrumentalist justifications of the establishment, unique in the Anglican communion, that is the Church of England.[130]

Secondly, distillation occurs not only because times and circum-stances change; it is also the case that we do not believe everything that our forebears in the faith believed, and we believe some things differently. For this reason subsequent distillations can, and some-times do, misrepresent the position of the forebears. Even the authors of the objectives of the Central United Bartholomew Committee of

128. Clark, *History of Nonconformity*, II, 35. Cf. Clark, in Various, *The Ejectment of 1662*, 62–63, 69–70. For Clark (1869–1949) see SI; *The Times*, 12 July 1949, 7.

129. Clark, "The Ejection of 1662," 232.

130. See further Sell, *Testimony and Tradition*, ch. 11.

the 1662 suggested that 'If Dissent may be rightly regarded as the
protest of Individualism against Multitudinism [and this was clearly
how they regarded it], we . . . have abundant reasons for a thankful
commemoration . . .' [131] In fact, this is a distillation of the anachronis-
tic and inaccurate kind, for the witness of the ejected was not in the
name of individualism—'they were not concerned about the rights of
individuals within the Church; so far as the individual was affected
they laid more stress on his duties and responsibilities than on his
rights.' [132] Positively, they stood for the Crown Rights of the Redeemer
in His Church.

Again, if we were to advocate agreement with all of our Separatist
and Dissenting forebears we should at once find ourselves in a contradictory position, for they were by no means in sweet harmony on
all conceivable points of doctrine and polity, and sometimes they
showed themselves capable of changing their minds. John Robinson,
for example, having at one time persuaded himself that the Church
of England was utterly given over to Antichrist, later came to see that
there were some Christians within it, and recalled that he himself had
been converted whilst in that Church. Some were more inclined to
give a place to consultative synods than others. Again, whereas Robert
Browne placed church discipline in the hands of all the church members, Henry Barrow and John Greenwood [133] restricted its exercise to
the elders. Even when they were in broad agreement, the Separatists'
heirs likewise revealed differences of emphasis:

> For William Greenhill [134] it was a doctrine of Holy Scripture
> which precluded conformity to the ceremonies. For John
> Owen a doctrine of the Holy Spirit precluded use of the
> liturgy. For John Howe [135] a doctrine of grace precluded re-
> ordination: of grace not only as received at ordination but
> as manifest in a ministry of many years. It is still possible to
> ground Nonconformity in and one, or in more than one, of
> these doctrines; but what made Baxter [136] a Nonconformist was

---

131. Quoted by Waddington, *Congregational History 1850–1880*, 374.

132. Selbie, "The Religious Principle of Congregationalism," 33.

133. For Greenwood (d. 1593) see SI, ODNB.

134. For Greenhill (1591–1671) see ODNB, SI.

135. For Howe (1630–1705) see ODNB, SI.

136. For Baxter (1616–91) see ODNB.

precisely the 'burning desire after the peace and unity of the churches.'[137]

The upshot is that George Gould wrote nothing less than the truth when, in 1862 he asserted that 'neither the Presbyterians, nor Independents, nor Baptists of the present day, can pretend to hold all the opinions of the Nonconformists of 1662.'[138] Fifty years on, Elvet Lewis concurred. Referring to the ejected ministers he wrote, 'Their views . . . are not always one with ours; on some points they are even opposed.'[139] In 1962 Lovell Cocks resumed the point.

To take a crucially important example: we can no longer, with integrity, regard the Bible in exactly the same way as our forebears did, and in particular we cannot justifiably hold that one only form of church polity is prescribed therein. It is often said that the rise of modern biblical criticism associated with the 'higher criticism' that emanated from nineteenth-century Germany is responsible for this, and certainly this gave great impetus to fresh approaches to Scripture and caused much fearful trembling in certain Christian quarters. We might, however, recall that as early as 1661 the Englishman, Edward Stillingfleet, who went on to become Bishop of Worcester, declared that 'our Saviour hath determined no more of Church Government then [*sic*] what is applyable to a diversity of particular forms, and so hath not by any Law or practice of his own determined [the necessity] of any one form.'[140] By contrast, one of the reasons why the bolder Separatists were inclined to call the Church of England 'Antichrist' was because of their conviction that Christ had indeed laid down one pattern for church order, and that to deviate from it was to repudiate the Church's Lord, and hence to place oneself in grave danger. Thus a Separatist-Congregational covenant of the 1560s includes the following testimony: 'I have now joined myself to the Church of Christ wherein I have yielded my selfe subject to the discipline of Gods Word as I promised at my Baptisme, which it I should now again forsake and joyne my self with the traditioners, I should then forsake

---

137. Nuttall, "The First Nonconformists," 185–86. He quotes Baxter's letter of 5 February 1652/3 to John Drurie; Dr. Williams's Library, London, MSS. 59.6.94. For Baxter (1615–91) see ODNB.

138. Gould, "Sixteen Hundred and Sixty-Two," 69–70.

139. Lewis, "Introduction" in Various, *The Ejectment of 1662*, 3.

140. Stillingfleet, *Irenicum*, 229; cf. 182.

the union wherein I am knyt with the body of Christ, and joyne my selfe to the discipline of Antichrist.'[141] Somewhat more restrained, the Congregationalists of the *Cambridge Platform* (1648) were no less convinced that 'The partes of Church-Government are all of them exactly described in the Word of God . . . Soe that it is not left in the power of men, officers, Churches, or any state in the world, to add, or diminish, or alter, anything in the least measure therein.'[142] Similarly, John Owen came to be persuaded that 'Congregational Churches alone suited unto the ends of Christ in the institution of his church,' and 'No other church-state of divine institution'[143] When we come to the nineteenth century, however, we find R. W. Dale articulating the opposite view as if it were a truism: 'it is obvious that if every Church must be built on the exact model of the Church at Corinth, at Ephesus, or at Antioch, we are in hopeless difficulties. The plans have been lost, and the specifications destroyed.'[144] In our own time, and in relation to a traditionally troublesome issue, the report of the Anglican-Reformed International Commission declares in no uncertain terms that 'The particular ministerial structures which are now embodied in our different communions cannot claim the direct authority of Scripture. The New Testament cannot be held to prescribe a three-fold ministry of bishops, priests and deacons, a Presbyterian or congregational form of government, or the primacy of the see of Rome. All attempts to read off one divinely authorized form of ministry from the New Testament are futile.'[145]

I must grant that while, when seeking to relate to or learn from the past, a measure of distillation is inevitable for the reasons given, it carries with it the peril of distortion, and in particular of distortion by attenuation. We recall that Howard Stanley, when speaking at the Albert Hall Rally of 1962, observed that Nonconformist principles could sound negative rather than positive. This was inevitable given that the Act of Uniformity said, You will do this, and the ejected ministers said, No we will not. But the negatives turned upon a number of positives which did not always emerge clearly on the commemorative

141. Quoted by Peel in Various, *Congregationalism through the Centuries*, 21–22.

142. Walker, *The Creeds and Platforms of Congregationalism*, 203.

143. These are two chapter headings in Owen, *An Inquiry into the Original Nature . . . and Communion of Evangelical Churches*, in *Works*, XV.

144. Dale, *Essays*, 31.

145. Anon., *God's Reign and Our Unity*, 48–49.

occasions, and which receive less that their just deserts in most ecumenical dialogue reports. Our task is to elucidate the pneumatological positives which not only underpin and, indeed, imply the Separatist and Ejectment negatives, but which also have wider ecumenical implications. The ejected ministers and their Separatist forebears were rooted in doctrines that collectively answer the question, Who are the saints, and whence do they come? The answer to this question restores ecclesiology to its basis in pneumatology, and opens the way to a fresh understanding of catholicity and the ecumenical task. Indeed, I believe that only when we have answered this question shall we be able to take the necessary radical steps towards the manifestation of the unity that the Father has already given us in Christ by his Holy Spirit.

It is my conviction that now that almost all of the anti-Nonconformist impediments have been removed (albeit the Act of Uniformity remains of the Statute Book) the way is clearer than it has ever been for serious inter-confessional reflection upon the doctrinal and ecumenical implications of the sixteenth- and seventeenth-century events. In what ecclesiastical climate are we called upon to distil what we can from those events? We can safely say that is it one that would have staggered those whom we commemorate. I can readily recall that whereas the tercentenary commemorative events of 1962 took place at a time of ecumenical enthusiasm and hopefulness, we are now assured by some that we live in an 'ecumenical winter.' By 'we' I mean we of the West and especially of these islands; for we should not overlook the fact that in matters ecumenical things move at different paces around the globe. Those who speak of an ecumenical winter have in mind the dismal fact that attempts to draw denominations into closer union have not been an unmitigated success, and that those few efforts that have in large part succeeded have left behind one or more remnants comprised of those who felt that they could not in conscience proceed. In my view this is not the whole story: there are numerous local expressions of ecumenical service and worship, many of them involving ministry shared by representatives of more than one Christian tradition; there are joint study groups and dialogues, and a good deal of common service, sometimes undertaken in fellowship with those of other faiths or none. Some may, indeed, feel a little jaded. They have been around the houses many times over the neuralgic issues of baptism, eucharist, and ministry, for example. They are beyond the point at which they are thrilled to be in the same room with Christians of other tribes with a view to sharing with, and learning from, them. They have been doing this for more than a century—at least, our mainline traditions have, and for some of us it feels as though we have! Indeed, the Ejectment itself reminds us forcibly that the attempt to adjust divergent church orders is a centuries-old pursuit. I grant, of course, that to meet with those of other traditions with a view to sharing our insights and receiving theirs as far as we can is infinitely preferable to the hurling polemical brickbats at one another from afar; and, since times and attitudes change, it is entirely likely that this mutual sharing will need to be undertaken by each successive generation. I nevertheless believe that, when taken in its context of a heritage of witness from Separatism onwards, the Ejectment poses a challenge to all Christians whatever their denominational allegiance that is more radical than the fostering of mutual sharing and learning. It profoundly raises the question of the relation of ecclesiology to pneumatology, and requires us to engage in an exercise of lateral thinking, so that instead of focussing in ecumenical discussion upon what we have to learn from others and what we have to offer them, we probe more deeply and ask, What has the God of all grace actually done?[146] The answer in a sentence is that on the ground of the Son's saving work, the Father has called out one church by the Spirit, uniting the saints on earth with the saints in heaven, because all are united with Christ. We have to act, not simply to discuss and learn; and we shall see what we have to do when we pay due attention to what God has first done.

So to the complex of doctrinal convictions which informed the stance taken by Separatists and ejected alike. They are all aspects of the work of God the Holy Spirit; they all concern what the old divines would have called the matter of the church; taken altogether they answer the fundamental question, Who are the saints and whence do they come?[147]

146. I have posed this question in Sell, *Enlightenment, Ecumenism, Evangel*, ch. 11.

147. I have discussed these doctrines with reference to Calvin's ecclesiology in Sell, "Rectifying Calvin's Ecclesiology."

THE WORK OF GOD THE HOLY SPIRIT VIS-À-VIS THE MATTER AND POLITY OF THE CHURCH

Two preliminary points must be borne in mind as we approach the pneumatological doctrines at issue, namely, election, regeneration, justification, adoption, and sanctification. First, these terms do not label a temporal sequence of successive stages in the saint's experience. They are all indicative of ways of talking about the one saving act of God the Holy Spirit. God is the God of prevenient grace, who acts before we do. Secondly, I take my starting-point from the *Westminster Confession* (suitably distilled) of 1647, (a) because both Presbyterians and Congregationalists were involved in its authorship; and (b) because since the doctrinal sections of the Congregationalists' *Savoy Declaration of Faith and Order* (1658) and the *Second London Confession* (1677) of the Particular Baptists largely follow *Westminster*, we are here concerned with what may be regarded as the mainline teaching of historic orthodox Dissent which gave the ejected ministers their positive pneumatological foundation.

First, according to the confessions, God effectually calls the saints 'by his Word and Spirit, out of that state of sin and death in which they are by nature, to grace and salvation by Jesus Christ.'[148] Although the call is effectual, the saints are drawn to Jesus Christ in such a way that 'they come most freely, being made willing by his grace.'[149] In his lucid and unduly neglected study, *Saints in Christ Jesus*, Owen E. Evans, observes that of the sixty occasions in which the substantive *hoi hagioi* is used of church members in the New Testament, thirty-nine occur in the Pauline epistles.[150] Thus, for example, from Romans 1:7 we learn that Christians are, according to some versions, 'called to be saints.' This, however, is ambiguous, and might wrongly be taken as implying that they are called to become saints at some unspecified date in the future. Hence the preferred rendering is that they are 'saints by calling'—saints now because they have been called.[151] We might also note that on a number of occasions Paul places *hoi hagioi* side by side

148. *Westminster Confession*, X.i.

149. Ibid.

150. Evans, *Saints in Christ Jesus*, 29. It would be well if all ecumenists read my teacher's work, for whom see Sell, "A Valued Inheritance"; Sell, *The Bible in Church, Academy and Culture*, ch. 7.

151. Cf. ibid., 43.

with *en Christô*.[152] The idea of election is ineradicable from the Bible and from the various types of writing flowing down from orthodox Dissenters and Nonconformists. Thus Thomas Watson, the pithiest of Presbyterians, who published *A Divine Cordial* in 1663, the year following his ejectment, declares that 'God, by the outward call, blows a trumpet in the ear; by the inward call, He opens the heart . . . The ministers of God are only the pipes and organs; it is the Spirit blowing in them, that effectually changes the heart.'[153] We find the concept of election in many of the local covenants and confessions of faith devised by Congregationalists and Baptists, so that, for example, in 1766 the Congregationalists of Hinckley affirmed their belief in 'God the Father as choosing His people to Salvation through the sanctification of the Spirit and belief of the Truth.'[154] Again, the Dissenters sang about God's call. Clearly alluding to Jesus's words, 'You did not choose me: I chose you' (John 15:16), Josiah Conder writes,

> Tis not that I did choose Thee,
> For, Lord, that could not be,
> This heart would still refuse Thee;
> But Thou hast chosen me . . .
> My heart owns none above Thee;
> For Thy rich grace I thirst;
> This knowing, if I love Thee,
> Thou must have loved me first.[155]

At their first meeting, on 20 October 1846, the London Association of Strict Baptist Ministers and Churches authorized the sending of a circular letter from which we learn that 'The true catholic of general church of Christ is composed of the numberless millions of the chosen, beloved, and redeemed people of God . . .'[156] P. T. Forsyth may sum matters up:

> The Church is not made by men. It is no creature of humane sympathy or of voluntary association, even though these give

152. Ibid., 57.

153. Watson, *A Divine Cordial*, 77, 78. For Watson (d. 1686) see ODNB, SI.

154. C. Thomas, *Hinckley*, 38.

155. For Conder (1789–1855) see ODNB. I do not find this hymn in any current mainline Nonconformist hymnal, and I have never seen it projected on a screen during worship. Of course, it did not occur to Conder to incorporate an endlessly repeatable chorus . . .

156. Anon., *Circular Letter*, 253.

it local and practical form. It is not put together by consents, contract, or affinities. It is a new creation of God in the Holy Spirit, a spiritual organism in which we find our soul. Men unite themselves with the Church because already united with Christ, and because they are, in that very act of union with Him, already in spirit and principle organised into the great Church He created, and whose life He is.[157]

The *Westminster Confession* and its derivatives proceed to say of the saints that God enlightens their minds 'spiritually and savingly to understand the things of God, taking away their heart of stone, and giving unto them a heart of flesh, renewing their wills . . . effectually drawing them to Christ.' It is by the intervention of the Spirit that minds are enlightened and renewed; the saint, once blinds, now sees; and were it not for this work of the Spirit we should be like the man of whom R. T. Brooks engagingly wrote: 'he has lost his specs and cannot see to find them until he has found them!'[158] For their part, the saints, 'being quickened and renewed by the Holy Spirit [are] enabled to answer this call, and to embrace the grace offered and conveyed in it.'[159] In a word, the church comprises regenerate saints. To use the term so sadly hijacked by a particular brand of Christianity, the saints are 'born again.' The substantial confession of the General Baptist exiles to whom John Smyth ministered in the Netherlands affirms that 'the visible church is a mystical figure outwardly, of the true, spiritual invisible church; which consisteth of the spirits of just and perfect men only, that is, of the regenerate.'[160] In the nineteenth century John Brown remarked that 'As the existence of spiritual life in those who come together, a new birth from above, is the one indispensable foundation of a Congregational church, it is interesting to notice that it was the revival of spiritual life which first led to the revival of the Congregational system among the early English Separatists. The ecclesiastical idea did not come first, but the spiritual.'[161] As Morgan Llwyd put it, 'When the true shepherd speaks, and a man hears him, the heart burns within, and the flesh quakes, and the mind lights up like a candle, and the

157. Forsyth, *The Church and the Sacraments*, 34.

158. Brooks, *Renewal*, 4–5.

159. *Westminster Confession*, X.i, ii.

160. Lumpkin, *Baptist Confessions of Faith*, 136. For Smyth (d. 1612) see ODNB.

161. Brown, "Congregationalism," 124. For Brown (1830–1922) of Bunyan Meeting, Bedford, see *The Times*, 17 January 1922, 12.

conscience ferments like wine in a vessel, and the will bends to the truth: and that thin, heavenly, mighty voice raises the dead to life, from the grave to himself, to wear the crown, and wondrously renews the whole life to live like a lamb of God.'[162] In less poetic style the *Statement of the Christian Faith* (1956) of the Presbyterian Church of England declares that 'It is by the Holy Spirit that men are moved to acknowledge their sinfulness and commit themselves in penitence and faith solely to the love and mercy of God in Christ . . . [I]n his new life the believer is united in Christ with the outgoing love of God.'[163] Speaking of Congregationalism, R. W. Dale drew the ecclesial consequence: 'We believe that the Church of Christ is not an artificial society, consisting of persons who hold a common belief, and who have agreed to order their lives by a common rule, but a Divine creation. Those who belong to it have received a supernatural life, which reveals itself in supernatural acts and a supernatural character.'[164] P. T. Forsyth concurred: 'A Church is not made by Christian sympathies or affinities. Rather these are made by a Church. A Church is made by the Christian Gospel, its creative word of the Cross, its Holy Spirit.'[165] Lovell Cocks sums up as follows: 'To be regenerated is to have the "mind of Christ" . . . We do not become Christs, nor are we absorbed into the divine substance, but we are remade after the pattern of Him who is the image of God.'[166]

Owen Evans further points out that the participial form, *hoi hêgiasmenoi* or *hoi hagiozomenoi*, 'those who are sanctified,' occurs eight times in the New Testament.[167] The *Westminster Confession* characterizes the sanctified as follows: the saints are sanctified 'through the virtue of Christ's death and resurrection, by his word and Spirit dwelling in them; . . . they [are] more and quickened and strengthened in all saving graces, to the practice of true holiness, without which no man shall see the Lord.'[168] According to John Robinson, who had been pastor to the Pilgrims in the Netherlands, the church is 'A company of

---

162. Llwyd, *Gweithiau*, II, 236. Quoted by Nuttall, *The Holy Spirit*, 140. For Llwyd (1619–59) see DWB, ODNB, SI.

163. In D. M. Thompson, *Stating the Gospel*, 191.

164. Dale, *Essays and Addresses*, 73–74.

165. Forsyth, *The Church and the Sacraments*, 25.

166. Cocks, *By Faith Alone*, 154, 155.

167. Evans, *Saints*, 29.

168. *Westminster Confession*, XIII.i.

faithful and holy people (with their seed) called by the Word of God into publick covenant with Christ and amongst themselves.'[169]

Another way of speaking of the Holy Spirit in relation to the saints is to say that, on the ground of Christ's righteousness, they are justified, accounted righteous before God. This is not of their own doing, it is all of God's free grace. Moreover the faith that the saints place in God's saving act in Christ is itself a gift of God, so that none may boast (Ephesians 2:8–9). In the words of the General Baptist *Orthodox Creed* of 1679, 'Justifying faith is a grace, or habit, wrought in the soul by the holy ghost, through preaching the word of God, whereby we are enabled to believe, not only that the Messias is offered to us, but also to take and receive him, as a Lord and Saviour, and wholly and only to rest upon Christ, for grace and salvation.'[170] As the Presbyterian, Philip Henry, further observed, 'Though justification be an act absolved in one instant, yet the manifestation and assurance of it increaseth according as we increase in faith. Rom, 13: 11.'[171]

The remaining term in the constellation of terms characterizing the aspects of the Spirit's work in calling out the saints is 'adoption.' The underlying idea is that whereas Jesus Christ is the Son of God by right, the saints are God's sons and daughters by the adoption of grace, 'by which they are taken into the number, and enjoy the liberties and privileges of the children of God; . . . are enable to cry, Abba, Father.'[172] 'The encouragement contained in this tender appellation is inexpressible,'[173] writes Andrew Fuller. He further explains that 'Regeneration gives us a new nature; and adoption adds to it a *new name*, even that of sons and daughters of the Lord Almighty. Nor is it a mere name; for the richest blessings both in this world and in that which is to come are attached to it.'[174] If John Owen treated adoption

---

169. Robinson, *A Briefe Catechisme*, 1.

170. Lumpkin, *Baptist Confessions*, 314. Interestingly, the Particular Baptist, John Gill (1697–1771), for whom see ODNB, thought in terms of the believer's justification from eternity, and laid no emphasis upon faith in relation to justification. See Oliver, *English Calvinistic* Baptists, 4–12. This was one of a number of instances of inner-Baptist tension during the eighteenth century, which manifested themselves in various parts of the country. See on justification, for example, Douglas, *North of England*, 169–74.

171. Henry, *Life of Philip Henry*, 369. For Henry (1631–96) see ODNB, SI.

172. *Westminster Confession*, XII.

173. Fuller, *Works*, 491. For Fuller (1754–1815) see ODNB.

174. Ibid., 606.

more exhaustively, and in a manner which merits pruning of length and distillation of content,[175] Thomas Watson drove concisely to the heart of the matter: 'We have enough in us to move God to correct us, but nothing to move him to adopt us, therefore exalt free grace.'[176] Many examples might be given to show that the doctrine of adoption permeated the grassroots of orthodox Dissent, but one must suffice. The *Confession of Faith and Covenant* which the Baptists of Alcester agreed at their Church Meeting of 17 August 1712 includes the following affirmation: 'We believe that God's People . . . receive the Adoption of Sons by Jesus Christ & are put among the Children being made of the family and household of God & are joint heirs with Christ, are called by His Name, & having the Spirit of Adoption have boldness of access with confidence through faith in Him.'[177]

Sufficient has been said to show that the saints are the product of the gracious, prevenient, work of God the Holy Spirit. It is this work that underpins the ecclesiology of historic orthodox Dissent, epitomized by the Separatists, the ejected and their heirs. Far from this being an exclusive claim, I shall argue that Spirit's work is church-creating no matter by which confessional body it is processed. For the present, however, I remain with the Dissenters. With reference to one of the aspects of the Spirit's one work, Forsyth declared that 'It is the adoption of sons that gives us the fellowship of brothers'[178] (to which we might properly add 'and daughters' and 'and sisters'—as Andrew Fuller, here ahead of his time, interestingly did). The point is that the church is a visibly gathered company.[179] Except in extreme circumstances one cannot be a Christian in isolation, and even in such circumstances there is a spiritual affinity with all who belong to Christ. John Robinson said it long ago: 'One man cannot be a Church, which as Christ teacheth, . . . must be a company, however small soever, gathered together in his name.'[180] Albert Peel said it more recently: '*only one thing makes a* church—not officers, not creeds, not sacraments, but believing men and women, those who have been saved by Christ

---

175. See Owen's *Works*, II, ch. 10.

176. Watson, *A Body of Divinity*, 240.

177. The full text is reproduced by Roger Hayden, *Continuity and Change*, 212–28.

178. Forsyth, *Congregationalism and Reunion*, 47.

179. See further on what follows in this section, Sell, *Saints*.

180. J. Robinson, *A Briefe Catechisme*, 11.

and gathered together into a fellowship of the Divine life.'[181] To be a Christian is to be a member of the body, a branch of the Vine, and hence to be in inevitable relationship with all the saints—a term that, as Evans reminds us, is almost invariably used in the plural in the New Testament.[182] This was nowhere more clearly understood than by the Separatist, Robert Browne, who famously wrote, 'The Church planted or gathered, is a company or number of Christians or believers, which by a willing covenant made with their God, are under the government of God and Christ, and keep his laws in one holy communion . . .'[183] This line of testimony can be traced from the Separatists to the *Scheme of Union* of the United Reformed Church. Thus in the seventeenth century John Owen cautions, 'Let none . . . pretend that they love the brethren in general, and love the people of God, and love the saints, while their love is not fervently exercised towards those who are in the same church Society with them.'[184] Bernard Lord Manning nicely updated the advice for twentieth-century young people:

> You say you love Christ's Church. Well, here it is: Tom, Dick, Harry, and the rest . . . They are not very good. They are not very nice. But they have, in their own odd ways, heard Christ's call . . . They have made a covenant with God, and so joined themselves in the saved society with Him. It is little use your feeling mystical sympathy with St. Francis who is dead, with St. Somebody Else who never existed, with men of good will all over the world whom you are quite safe from meeting. If you do not love your brothers whom you have seen . . . you cannot, in fact, love those brothers (whom you call the Church) whom you call the Church whom you have seen.

The echo of I John 4:20 is loud and clear. Here is the realistic ecclesiology of the visible saints. It is what explains the denial by the Dissenters of the notion that the church is an optional extra to the gospel; on the contrary, it is integral to it. There is nothing casual about this ecclesiology. To be gathered with the saints is to embrace a God-given responsibility for the saints. To be numbered among God's covenanted people is

181. Peel, *Inevitable Congregationalism*, 70. His italics. For Peel (1887–1949) see ODNB, SI, WTW.

182. Evans, *Saints*, 84; cf. 124.

183. R. Browne, *A Booke which sheweth*, 253.

184. Owen, Sermon XXI on "Gospel Charity (Col. 3: 14)" in *Works*, IX, 262.

to enter into covenant with believers among whom one is placed—with all the joys, challenges, and responsibilities that that entails

Above all, to be visibly gathered is to be, as it were, gathered to and around the church's sole Head, Jesus Christ. Conversely, as John Owen insisted 'if Christ be not present with [the saints], they are no church, nor can all the powers under heaven make them so to be. And when any church loseth the especial presence of Christ, it ceaseth so to be.'[185] The idea flows down to the twentieth century in the words of Robert Mackintosh: 'Where Christian people are, there is Christianity, and there is the Church. Above all,—invisibly but most really present—Christ Himself is there.'[186] Bernard Manning was characteristically to the point (he speaks of Congregationalists, but Baptists also are congregationalists, and there is nothing in what he says that has not entered into the thought of the United Reformed Church):

> On the one hand Congregationalists have outdone all other Christians in the emphasis they have laid on the visible church and on the supreme importance of continuous personal exercise in it by every individual. On the other hand Congregationalists have clearly understood, frankly confessed, and effectually lived by the truth that this all-important visible church is a divine spiritual society, not an earthly historic society, and that it depends wholly on grace, not at all on law.[187]

Manning ought perhaps to have prefaced his remarks with the phrase, 'When they have behaved themselves . . . ,' for it should not be supposed that Congregationalists have impeccably lived up to their ideal. R. W. Dale, for example, accused his ilk of having 'exaggerated and misinterpreted the great Protestant principle that religion is an affair that lies altogether between a man and his Maker . . . The relations between the individual Christian and the Church have been ignored. The necessity for the Church has been implicitly denied.'[188] For the saints the Church is an inescapable reality because, as Forsyth wrote, *'the same act which sets us in Christ sets us also in the society of Christ.*

---

185. Owen, *On Spiritual Gifts*, in *Works*, IV, 499.

186. Mackintosh, "The Genius of Congregationalism," 115. For Mackintosh (1858–1933) see ODNB, SI; Sell, *Robert Mackintosh*.

187. Manning, *Essays in Orthodox Dissent*, 164.

188. Dale, *Essays and Addresses*, 92.

It does so *ipso facto*, and not by a mere consequence or sequel, more or less optional. To be in Christ is in the same act to be in the Church.'[189]

It must be confessed that the saints have not always understood that what they are visibly gathered into is the church catholic in one of its numerous local expressions. Lovell Cocks was crystal clear on the matter: 'Where the believers are, there is not *a*, but *the* Church—the holy catholic Church, with Christ as its Head and the Holy Spirit as its Guide.'[190] Dale illustrated the point in this way: 'The Church at Corinth is not a mere member of that "one Body" into which all Christians are "baptized" by "the one Spirit"; it is itself the "Body of Christ." The whole is present in every part.'[191] According to its statement of 1948 the Baptist Union Council concurs: 'Gathered companies of believers are the local manifestation of the one Church of God on earth and in heaven.'[192] When this has been forgotten 'granular independency' has resulted. No doubt it is better to have an ideal which one fails to attain than to have no ideal at all. Indeed the consciousness of failing may even prompt penitence and fresh resolve.

Be all that as it may, the idea of the saints as visibly gathered by the Spirit in the presence of Christ, the only Lord of the Church, is the positive principle that prompts the anti-establishment negative. Once again, the protest flows down from the Separatists. To John Smyth, Jesus Christ is 'the only King, Priest, & Prophet of his

---

189. Forsyth, *The Church and the Sacraments*, 61–62. I cannot here pursue in detail the pressing matter of those today who wish to claim the name of Christian, who regularly attend a particular place of worship, but who do not wish to profess their faith and become enrolled as visible saints. I do, however, find it hard to understand why a person called, regenerated, justified, adopted, sanctified, and engrafted into Christ by the Spirit would not by that fact be drawn towards, and wish to experience the closest possible fellowship with, the saints, and this with a view of sharing responsibility for the worship, mission and service of the church. I briefly offer three considerations: (a) to affirm that the church comprises Christians is not adversely to judge the condition or status—still less to predict the eternal destination—of any outside the churchly fellowship; (b) great harm had been done when theologians and others have drawn unwarranted negative implications from certain of their positive claims; (c) Jesus reminds us that the 'religious' will have some surprises when they discover who is in heaven—and who is not (see, for example, Luke 16:19–30). See further, Frykholm, "Loose Connections."

190. Cocks, *The Faith of a Protestant Christian*, 43–44.

191. Dale, *Essays and Addresses*, 158.

192. See *The Baptist Doctrine of the Church*, in Payne, *The Fellowship of Believers*, 152–53. Cf. The Baptist response to the Lambeth Appeal of 1920, ibid., 143–47.

Church,[193] and among the one hundred *Propositions and Conclusions* of his Amsterdam church is number 84, in which it is affirmed: 'That the magistrate is not by virtue of his office to meddle with religion, or matters of conscience, to force or compel men to this or that form of religion, or doctrine, but to leave religion free, to every man's conscience, and to handle only civil transgressions . . .'[194] Most famously of all, the General Baptist, Thomas Helwys,[195] declared that:

> our lord the King is but an earthly King, and he hath no authority as a King but in earthly causes, and if the Kings people be obedient and true subjects, obeying all humane laws made by the King, our lord the King can require no more: for mens religion to God is betwixt God and themselves; the King shall not answer for it, neither may the King be jugd betwene God and man. Let them be heretikes, Turcks, Jewes or whatsoever, it apperteynes not to the earthly power to punish them in the least measure. This is made evident to our lord the King by the Scriptures.[196]

We should note that these are not necessarily republican sentiments—indeed, the vast bulk of Dissent has never been republican. Rather, positively, the Separatists would have endorsed the line of the hymn had they known it: 'The Church's *one* foundation is Jesus Christ her Lord,' from which sentiment they drew the negative inference that there is no biblical justification for supposing that the church can properly have a monarch as its temporal head. This is the conviction to which the ejected ministers came when the spiritual freedom of the church was at stake. Those who could not give their 'unfeigned assent and consent' to the *Book of Common Prayer,* and who could not in conscience promise to use it, and only it, in services of worship, took this stand for two main reasons. First, many of them—and some more than others—had objections to the portions of the *Book.* This was nothing new. The members of Richard Fitz's clandestine 'Ancient Church,' meeting in 1567, bluntly declared that they had repudiated the 'relics of Antichrist,' that they had joined 'with those that have not

193. Smyth, *Works*, II, 471.

194. Lumpkin, *Baptist Confessions*, 140.

195. For Helwys (c.1575–c.1614) see ODNB.

196. Helwys, *A Short Declaration*, 69. See further on Helwys and his *Declaration*, Haymes, "On Religious Liberty"; Sell, "Separatists and Dissenters amidst the Arguments For and Against Toleration: Some Soundings 1550–1689."

yielded to this idolatrous trash,' or gone 'back again to the preach-
ings. &c. of them that have received these marks of the Romish beast.'
They had a particular aversion to 'Popish garments.'[197] More strongly
doctrinal objections were levelled against the *Book of Common Prayer*,
notably that it taught the unbiblical and hence untenable doctrine of
baptismal regeneration. Many deeply regretted the implication that
since formal written prayers only were to be used the practice of free
prayer was illegitimate. Further, the requirement of the episcopal ordination of ministers was abominated as sectarian. Above all, however, the determination to impose liturgical requirements by law was
to the ejected ministers a denial of the sole Lordship of Christ in his
church. They strongly held that it was not the prerogative of monarch
or parliament to prescribe the worship and ordering of the church.
While upholding the role of the civil magistrate in maintaining good
order, they insisted that in matters spiritual Christ alone must rule in
his church. From time to time the issue reared its head as the centuries
wore on. We have already heard the call of mid-nineteenth-century
Dissenters for a Free Church in a Free State. But one of the more en-
tertaining outbursts occurred at the beginning of that century. John
Gisburne's pilgrimage had been from Wesleyanism *via* the Baptists to
Unitarianism, and he was now pastor at Soham in Cambridgeshire.
He had been Andrew Fuller's assistant there, and was now the sole
pastor. Fuller had drawn up a doctrinal statement that every church
member was required to sign, but Gisburne refused. He compounded
his disobedience by preaching a somewhat inflammatory sermon
against the established Church. His sermon more or less reduces to
the following Aristotelian syllogism: All creatures having two heads
are monsters; The Church of England has two head—King Jesus and
King George; therefore the Church of England is a monster. This
caused more than a gentle fluttering in the dovecotes, and Fuller and
the London Unitarian, Robert Aspland,[198] a local boy, were called
upon to pour oil on troubled waters. Fuller did what he could, but
Aspland contented himself with saying that while he did not favour
uncouth language in the pulpit, Gisburne had simply stated the basic
principle of Nonconformity.[199] This basic principle, more temperately

197. Burrage, *The Early English Dissenters*, 13–14. For Fitz see SI.

198. For Aspland (1782–1845) see ODNB.

199. See Fuller, *A Narrative of Facts*; Aspland, *Bigotry and Intolerance Defeated*.

expressed, flows down into 'A Statement concerning the Nature, Faith and Order of the United Reformed Church' of the United Reformed Church: 'The United Reformed Church declares that the Lord Jesus Christ, the only king and head of the Church, has therein appointed a government distinct from civil government and in things spiritual not subordinate thereto, and that civil authorities, being always subject to the rule of God, ought to respect the rights of conscience and of religious belief and to serve God's will of justice and peace for all men.'[200]

The idea of the saints as visibly gathered by the Spirit around their only Lord is the key to the proper understanding of that crucially important feature of Baptist, Congregational, and United Reformed church life, namely, the Church Meeting (where the emphasis should be upon the first of the two words). Of the propriety of the saints' seeking Christ's will together, and of their competence to do so, the Separatist martyr, Henry Barrow, was in no doubt:

> It is manifest, that all the members of the church have a like interest in Christ, in his word, in the faith; that they altogether make one bodie unto him; that all the affairs of the church belong to that bodie together . . . The people of Christ, they are all inlightened with that bright morning star, that sonne of righteousness . . . They are an humble, meek, obedient people, they will heare and follow the true shepheard . . . [T]o them and everie one of them he hath given his holy sanctifying spirit, to open unto them and to lead them into al truth.[201]

As Dale further explained, 'The ground on which these great responsibilities are imposed on the commonality of the church is the union between Christ and all Christians. All who are loyal to Christ abide in Christ, and Christ abides in them.'[202] He might have added that all the members *together* have access to the mind of Christ by the Holy Spirit, thereby signifying that 'the priesthood of all believers' is a corporate term that is not to be construed atomistically, as if each member were an isolated and insulated 'priest.' The same idea was earlier conveyed by John Robinson who, having referred to the 'oil of gladness' with which God has anointed Jesus, and with which every member is anointed, continues,

---

200. D. M. Thompson, *Stating the Gospel*, 263.

201. Barrow, *A Brief Discoverie of the False Church*, 319, 522.

202. Dale, "The Early Independents," 42.

in this holy fellowship by virtue of this plenteous anointment, every one is made a king, priest, prophet, not only to himself but to every other, yea to the whole. A prophet to teach . . . himself and the rest; a priest, to offer up spiritual sacrifices of prayer . . . for himself and the rest; . . . a king to guide and govern in ways of godliness, himself and the rest . . . [T]here is not the meanest member of the body but hath received his drop or dram of this anointing.'[203]

He underlines the point that no member may say that he or she has no need of the other members by referring to 1 Corinthians 12:21.

In the opinion of T. T. James, 'The Church Meeting should be regarded by every member as of supreme importance . . . Whatever control the members of the Church exercise, and whatever decisions are made, these rest on the fact that membership is spiritual, and that the will of Christ finds expression through the members of the Church . . . It must always be remembered that [Church Meeting] is an Assembly of believing men and women seeking the mind and will of Christ.'[204] It is an extension of worship; it is where the saints, who have sat under the preaching of the Word and met at the table of the Lord gather, under the leadership of the one called to lead them to the throne of grace[205] to seek the mind of Christ regarding their mission and service.

203. J. Robinson, *Works*, II, 140–41. According to my teacher, the Presbyterian T. W. Manson, 'the priesthood of all believers lies in the fact that each believer offers himself as a sacrifice according to the pattern laid down by Christ; and—what is equally essential—that all these individual offerings are taken up into the one perpetual offering made by the one eternal high-priest of the New Covenant.' *Ministry and Priesthood*, 64. For Manson (1893–1958) see ODNB, WTW; Sell, "A Valued Inheritance of New Testament Scholarship"; Evans, "On Serving Two Masters."

204. James, *The Work and Administration of a Congregational Church*, 15, 16. For Thomas Theophilus James (1876–1954) see SI. A distinguished alumnus of Lancashire Independent College, he served as Moderator of the Lancashire Province of the Congregational Union from 1925 to 1945. There is some evidence to suggest that attendance at Church Meeting has declined in many churches; pressure of work, the mobility of the population, and boredom with the proceedings are among the explanatory factors proposed. There is no excuse whatever for the last. As to the others, such matters as day and time are amendable. In the opinion of Lovell Cocks, with which I heartily concur, 'the decay of the Church meeting means more than the decline of Congregationalism. It bears tragic witness to the decline of our faith in the Gospel. It means that we are refusing our responsibility, and with it our Christian maturity.' See *A Church Reborn*, 27.

205. And not under a business man who is 'good at meetings'! For the Church Meeting in relation to worship see Cocks, *A Church Reborn*, 26.

There is no higher authority.[206] As Guinness Rogers put it, 'The power [the church] possesses no prince or prelate can convey, and none can take away. It is a power which does not accrue from some natural right belonging to its members separately, or in their corporate capacity, but comes directly from the presence of Christ Himself in accordance with His own promise.'[207] Hence Forsyth's remark: 'Congregationalism . . . is High Church or it is nothing'[208]—a point which Henry Cook re-iterated on behalf of the Baptists.[209] Nathaniel Micklem amplified the principle thus: 'A local church meeting is the gathering of the Church catholic in that place; its spiritual authority is derived from the fact that it is the Church catholic and therefore the heir of the promises of Christ to lead and guide his Church.'[210]

In particular, the Church Meeting is not a democratic assembly holding to the principle of one person, one vote:[211] '*the democracy will recognise no authority but what it creates, the Church none but what creates it.*'[212] Indeed, 'no society which gives Christ the regal place the Church does can be a democracy. It is an absolute monarchy.'[213] Church Meeting is thus the occasion where the will of the Lord is sought, and the objective is not majority rule, but unanimity in Christ.[214] Sadly

206. See Selbie, *Evangelical Christianity*, 93.

207. Rogers, "Clericalism and Congregationalism," II, 235.

208. Forsyth, *Faith, Freedom and the Future*, 215. Cf. Forsyth, *The Church and the Sacraments*, 12–13; Berry, "The Churches of Christ," 195.

209. Cook, *What Baptists Stand For*, 32.

210. Micklem, *Congregationalism and the Church Catholic*, 72. For Micklem (1888–1976) see ODNB, SI, WTW.

211. Cf. Nuttall, *The Holy Spirit*, 120: 'the democratic form of the church-meeting [is] not an end in itself but a means of discovering "the government of the Spirit"; and . . . it was the church meeting which gave birth, in England, to political democracy, not *vice versa*.' In a note he observes that 'The earliest instance of *democratical* (1589) in the *Oxford English Dictionary*, and the second instance of *democracy* (1574; the first refers to Athens) are both from religious, not political, controversy.'

212. Forsyth, *Faith, Freedom and the Future*, 192. His italics. See further, Jenkins, *The Church Meeting and Democracy*; Sell, *Commemorations*, 349–61; Sell, *Testimony and Tradition*, 70–78.

213. Forsyth, *The Church and the Sacraments*, 12–13.

214. This is nowhere more important than where the call of a minister is con-cerned. With a view to unanimity in Christ (and not simply because ministers com-peting over a vacancy is unseemly) it is desirable that one minister only at a time be under consideration. My favourite atrocity story in this connection concerns Principal A. J. Grieve of Lancashire Independent College, who was famous for his wit,

not all the saints have appreciated this—or did my ears deceive me when a church member, walking to Church Meeting said to a recently admitted member, 'This is the meeting where we can all stick our oar in'? Even the erudite R. F. Horton of the well-heeled Lyndhurst Road Congregational Church, Hampstead, referred to his church members and lamented that 'They do not know what a Church Meeting is. In fifty years I have failed to teach them.'[215] Happily, there are other testimonies too, notably that of R. W. Dale:

> To be at a church meeting—apart from any prayer that is offered, any hymn that is sung, any words that are spoken—is for me one of the chief means of grace. To know that I am surrounded by men and women who dwell in God, who have received the Holy Ghost, with whom I am to share the eternal righteousness and eternal rapture of the great life to come, this is blessedness. I breathe a Divine air. I am in the new Jerusalem, which has come down out of heaven from God, and the nations of the saved are walking its streets of gold. I rejoice in the joy of Christ over those whom He has delivered from eternal death and lifted into the light and glory of God.[216]

Although such lyricism eludes me, my testimony is the same: I have known many Church Meetings of that sort, and they can still be known. I have, however, to concede that such godly concord is not universally experienced; why, otherwise, would the Yorkshire and

---

and for pungent and concise replies to correspondents on postcards. He received a letter from the secretary of a church who explained that the pastorate was vacant, and that he was approaching four theological college principals with a view to arranging that their three best students might be invited to preach with a view to becoming the church's next minister. When all twelve had been heard the Church Meeting would make its selection. Grieve's postcard read, 'The ministry is a calling not a race meeting. No students will be coming from this college.' students will be coming from this College.' See Frank Hewis's letter, "Twelve Runners," to *Reform*, April 1984.

215. Peel and Marriott, *Horton*, 186. Horton appears in some logic text books as illustrating ambiguous utterance. In connection with clerical dress he famously said, 'I will wear nothing to distinguish me from my fellow Christians.' For Horton (1855–1934) see ODNB, SI, WTW. C. J. Cadoux (1883–1947), for whom see ODNB, SI, WTW, puzzles me when he writes, 'voting in a particular church-meeting is an office not of universal or Catholic, but of purely local, concern.' See "Congregationalism the true Catholicism," 73. But (assuming that voting is an appropriate method of decision-making—which I doubt), (a) many decisions taken locally have wider-than-local reference and/or implications; (b) in any case, such voting is the concern of, and is undertaken by, catholic Christians.

216. Dale, "The Evangelising Power of a Spiritual Fellowship," 136.

Lancashire Particular Baptist Assembly of 1764 have felt it necessary to advise its members 'to avoid such subjects "as may tend to jangling" . . . [and] to speak calmly because "when persons are full of anger, they are incapable of expressing their own ideas, and wrath begets wrath."'[217] It remains to add that there exists ample recent Baptist testimony as to the nature and importance of Church Meeting, and of those authors to be noted, it is Paul Fiddes who most clearly sets the Church Meeting within the covenant idea of the Church.[218] What Robert Mackintosh wrote of Congregationalism applies equally to the Baptists: '"Democratic" control of policy, within the Church, may be the shell of Congregationalism, but never its kernel. The body of Congregationalism might continue to exist for a season, though it had ceased to be an expression of evangelical faith and life; but the soul which had animated it would be gone. And a body without its soul is a corpse.'[219]

The saints are not only visibly gathered in the presence of their Lord, they are willingly gathered: 'the Lord's people is of the willing sort,' declared Robert Browne.[220] This is not the voluntarism of those who are free to join, or not join, a society or club. It is not the voluntaryism of those who under the influence of individualism could later define the church as 'a voluntary association of believers in Christ for mutual edification and the advancement of the Kingdom of God.'[221] Undoubtedly the saints do gather, but in the first place, they *are gathered* by the Spirit, to whose call they are enabled by grace to respond, and with whom, together with the saints around them, they are in communion. 'Wherein standeth this communion of the Spirit?' asks John Robinson's *Catechisme*. The answer is, 'In the indwelling and operation of the gifts and graces thereof conveyed from *Christ* as the head, unto the Church as his body, and members one of another: Whence ariseth that most streit and divine conjunction, by which, as by the civill bond of marriage, the man and the wife are one flesh: so they who are thus joyned to *Christ* are one spirit.'[222] As the

217. Brown, *The English Baptists of the Eighteenth Century*, 89.

218. See, for example, Dakin, *The Baptist View*, 22–23; Payne, *Fellowship of Believers*, 156; Reynolds, *First Among Equals*, 82–83; Fiddes, *Tracks and Traces*, 54–56, 86, 171, 211.

219. Mackintosh, "The Genius of Congregationalism," 125.

220. R. Browne, *A Treatise of Reformation*, 162.

221. As lamented by Mackennal, *Evolution*, 186.

222. J. Robinson, *Catechisme*, 4.

ejected minister William Bartlet put it, 'This visible church-state is a free society of visible Saints, embodied or knit together, by a voluntary consent, in holy fellowship . . .'[223]

In making this claim the Separatists and their heirs were setting their face against the parochial idea of the church, with its implication that to be a Christian was to be born in England and to belong to that country's Church.[224] At a time when Roman Catholic Spain was the great enemy, this was treasonable talk, and the martyrdoms of Barrow, Greenwood and Penry[225] in 1593, and of others in surrounding years, was by no means unrelated to the desire of the authorities to have uniformity of religion as 'cement' holding the nation together against its foreign foes. There was political as well as theological motivation in Richard Hooker's assertion of the view that 'there is not any man of the Church of England but the same man is also a member of the commonwealth; nor any man a member of the commonwealth, which is not also of the Church of England.'[226] Not surprisingly, those who were disinclined to believe that a person becomes regenerate by baptism were not inclined to think that regeneration is a consequence of domicile. On the contrary, in Robert Browne's view, 'the Kingdom of God Was not to be begun by whole parishes, but rather of the worthiest, Were they never so few.'[227] When John Greenwood appeared before the Lord Chief Justice on 24 March 1588/9 he was asked, 'Do you not hold a parish the church,' to which he replied, 'If all the people are faithful, having God's law and ordinances practised amongst them, I do.' 'Then you hold that the parish do not make it a church?' Greenwood replied, 'No, but the profession which the people make.'[228] Among the lawyer Barrow's clinching arguments was a *reductio ad absurdum*. Having recited a list of prevalent sins in the land he continues, 'Neither hath all kind of sinne and wickedness more universally raigned in any

223. Bartlet, *A Model*, 30. For Bartlet (d. 1680) see SI, ODNB.

224. John Locke later went further: 'Nobody is born a member of *any* church; otherwise the religion of parents would descend unto children, by the same right of inheritance as their temporal estates, and every one would hold his faith by the same tenure he does his lands; than which nothing can be imagined more absurd.' See *A Letter Concerning Toleration*, 20, my italics.

225. For Penry (1559–93) see ODNB, SI.

226. Hooker, *Works*, III, 330.

227. R. Browne, *A True and Short Declaration*, 404.

228. Greenwood, *Writings*, 143.

nation at any time, than here at this present in this land; where all are received into the church, all made members of Christ . . . All this people, with all these manners, were in one daye [8 May 1559, when Elizabeth gave her assent to the Act of Uniformity of that year], with the blast of Queen Elizabeth's trumpet, of ignorant papists and grosse idolaters, made faithfull Christians, and true professors . . .'[229] Even those members of the present-day Church of England who might wish that all of their parishes comprised professed communicants, and who might wish they could repudiate the Separatists' suggestion that they never were, must nowadays surely recognize that many parishes are populated largely by subscribers to Asian faiths. And did not that gracious Methodist scholar, John Wilkinson, deliver a tap from an elephant's paw when he declared in a footnote, 'The establishment of the Parochial Roll is so far a recognition that the Church is not the nation, nor yet the baptized citizens'?[230]

Whether we focus upon the church as called and gathered, or as comprising saints who have responded willingly to God's grace, or who seek to order their worship and their churchly life in such a way that the only Lord of the church is honoured—or whether we hold all of these considerations in mind, we cannot escape the fact that there is throughout the conviction that there is a distinction of eternal significance between those who are in Christ and those who are not. Understanding that the church is called to be holy, the Separatists and Dissenters sought to live as those who are in the world (geographical), but not of the world (naughty).[231] Time and again they adverted to Paul's injunction, 'Come ye out from among them, and be ye separate, saith the Lord, and touch not the unclean thing, and I will receive you' (2 Corinthians 6:17). Indeed, as the quotation just given from Barrow makes crystal clear, their main complaint against the Church

229. Barrow, *A Brief Discoverie*, 283. I do not understand why Erik Routley wrote that 'if Congregationalists reject the parish-system to-day, it is for reasons very different from those for which Barrow rejected it.' There may be additional reasons for rejecting it (such, for example, as that not a few Anglican churches today seem to house gathered congregations of diverse doctrinal and liturgical stripes, and that a number of parishes are largely populated by persons of non-Christian faiths). But surely Routley did not think that Barrow erred in saying that being born in a parish did not make one a Christian?

230. Wilkinson, *1662 and After*, 198, n. 108.

231. Jesus' prayer (John 17:15) that his followers be not taken out of the world (geographical) would have been well known to the Separatists.

of England was that it was undisciplined. When, at his fourth examination, on 18 March 1588/9, Barrow was asked by the Lord Treasurer why he would not attend the parish church, he replied, 'Because all the profane and wicked of the lande are received into the body of your church.'[232] The Church of England had allowed itself to be invaded by 'the world'; it was quite undisciplined. Hence the Separatist hurling at it of such epithets as 'promiscuous rabble' and 'Antichrist.' It is important to underline the fact that Separatists were not in the first place Separatists from the Church of England, but from the ungodly world which, in their view, had invaded the Church of England. In *The True Church and the False Church* (1588), a work which may have been jointly written by Barrow and Greenwood, the principle of separation is more gently affirmed: 'The true planted and rightly established church of Christ is a company of faithful people; separated from the unbelievers and heathen of the land; gathered in the name of Christ, whom they truly worship, and readily obey as their only king, priest, and prophet.'[233] To the Baptist John Smyth, 'the Church off Christ is a compainy off faithful people I Cor. 1:2. Eph. 1:1., seperated frö the world by the word & Spirit off God. 2 Cor. 6, 17.'[234] The saints understood themselves as being separated unto the Lord—an understanding as old as the Old Testament,[235] and integral to the connotation of holiness.

As with the other themes we have pursued the idea of separation flows down the centuries. Some eighty years after the covenant of Richard Fitz's church was adopted, a covenant was signed on 16 August 1646 by five men and three women of Bury St. Edmunds, which includes the following affirmation:

> And wee being convinced in Conscience of the evill of the Church of England, and of all other states wch are contrary to Christ's institution. And being (according to Christes institutions and commandments) fully separated, not only from them, but also from those who communicate with them either publickly or privately. Wee resolve by the grace of God, not to returne unto their vaine inventions, their human devices, the abominable Idolatries or superstitious high places, which were

232. *The Writings of Barrow*, 179.
233. Barrow/Greenwood. *The True Church and the False Church*, 98.
234. Lumpkin, *Baptist Confessions*, 119.
235. See Evans, *Saints*, ch. 2, and 134.

built and dedicate to Idolatry. And wee seeing not only the necessity of this separation, but also the great need of continuing
in Christian fellowship, and societie, and that to be of the visible particular Church of Christ is most needful for the Saints
edification in this life . . . Wee do therefore, together with our
posteritie, Covenant, to become a peculiar Temple for the Holy
Ghoste to dwell in . . .[236]

Twelve years later the Congregationalists who appended 'The
Institution of Churches and the Order Appointed in them by Jesus
Christ' to their *Savoy Declaration of Faith and Order* declared that:

By the appointment of the Father all power for the calling,
institution, order, or government of the Church, is invested in
a supreme and sovereign manner in the Lord Jesus Christ as
King and Head thereof . . . [T]he Lord Jesus calleth out of the
world unto communion with himself, those that are given unto
him by his Father . . . Those thus called (through the ministry
of the Word by his Spirit) he commandeth to walk together
in particular societies or churches . . . The members of these
churches are saints by calling.[237]

Here we have the recapitulation of the points already discussed: the
call by the Spirit through the Word, the inescapable gathering of the
saints in church fellowship under the Lordship of Christ and, to resume the matter currently under consideration, their calling out of
the world. As the seventeenth century drew to a close the Baptists of
Great Ellingham resumed the theme in their covenant of 1699: 'We
. . . Covenant & agree together to separate ourselves wholly from the
worship of the world, and the Religion of the Times we are fallen into,
that we may (thro' the strength of Christ) keep our Garments unspot-
ted from the world.'[238]

The idea of separated saints was by no means exclusive to Baptists
and Congregationalists. Richard Baxter, the moderate episcopalian,
was among others who argued that 'The Church's separation from the
unbelieving world is a necessary duty: for what is the Church, but a
society dedicated or sanctified to God, by separation from the rest

236. J. Browne, *Norfolk and Suffolk*, 394; Grieve and Jones, *These Three Hundred Years*, 19–21.

237. D. M. Thompson, *Stating the Gospel*, 112, 113.

238. DeWeese, *Baptist Church Covenants*, 122.

of the world? 2 Cor. 6: 17, 18.'[239] In the nineteenth century the Strict Baptists of London underlined the challenge that separation, properly understood, entailed: 'The church of Christ, chosen, redeemed, and called out of the world, is to exhibit, in its separation from the world, in the exercise of all the graces of the Holy Spirit, in love to God, in benevolence to mankind, in harmony and affection amongst its several members, and in its consecration to the glory of God, the holiness, richness, and triumphs of that grace which bringeth salvation, Titus 2: 11 and 12.' At the beginning of the twentieth century P. T. Forsyth drew renewed attention to 'the act of Free Grace, which at once, and alone, separates the Church from the world, and gives it in the Holy Spirit of our redemption (and not merely our inspiration) a principle which is regulative for the Church in every age because it is what constitutes the Church above the ages.'[240] Here in one sentence is the pneumatological-ecclesiological unity that I am advocating throughout but, note, it entails the church-world separation. Manning put it bluntly to an Easter youth conference: 'To us Congregationalists there is the great distinction between the Saved Society, the Church, on one side and the world on the other.'[241] But nobody put the point so crisply as Dale: 'A Christian Church should consist of Christians.'[242] As Nathaniel Micklem later wrote, 'this seems to us so obvious that it is hard to believe that, before it could become the common property and accepted tradition of all the Free Churches, our Fathers had to rot in prisons and die for it.'[243]

I am tempted to wonder whether the truth is so obvious to some of those who stand in the tradition of Dissent today. It would take us too far afield to speculate in detail upon why this might be. It may arise because of the gulf that has arisen between Thomas Watson's advice that 'It is better to go to heaven with a few, than to hell in the crowd,'[244] and the view of those who, from the heyday of early twentieth-century theological liberalism onwards, have thought in terms of

---

239. Baxter, *A Christian Directory*, III, 53.

240. Forsyth, "The Evangelical Basis of Free Churchism," 685.

241. Manning, *Why Not Abandon the Church?* 35.

242. Dale, *Essays and Addresses*, 189.

243. Micklem, *God's Freemen*, 133.

244. Watson, *A Divine Cordial*, 89.

'a hell frozen over or turned into innocuous ashes'[245]; it may originate in the more recent anti-imperialistic desire not to be triumphalist;[246] it may be connected with that current spirituality which constantly tells myself and others that we are all on 'a journey', though whether it is a journey towards faith or a journey of faith is not normally specified, yet the two are distinct; it may result from forgetfulness of the fact that 'Detached from the Word, the supernatural action of the Holy Spirit becomes gradually the natural evolution of the human spirit.'[247] For whatever reason, the church, we are told, must be inclusive, and any hint of exclusivity must be denounced, notwithstanding that the saints comprise '*an eschatological community to which belongs the inheritance of the Kingdom of God,*'[248] and that we cannot serve both God and Mammon.[249] Undoubtedly churches must be welcoming to all sorts and conditions of people; moreover, they must go out to them with the gospel of God's grace proclaimed through speech and through self-sacrificing service. But there is an angularity to the gospel—it *matters* whether we are for Christ or against him; and thus there remains a profoundly important distinction between church and world, saints and seekers, and church and congregation. Guinness Rogers made the point long ago. He had Congregationalism in mind, but what he says has wider application: Congregationalism's 'ideal Church is a body of spiritual men converted by the grace of God, and living by faith in the Lord Jesus Christ. This is something radically different from a society of truth-seekers, resolved to live up to their light and to wait in the hope that more light will come.'[250] The distinction is derived from the gospel of God's sovereign, electing, grace, and it is the ground of the church's catholicity because all thus called and gathered comprise the one, holy, catholic, and apostolic church of God, no matter

---

245. Quoted by Horsch, *Modern Religious Liberalism*, 127–28.

246. I was astonished to read, in the first months of 2011, a letter from a biblical scholar to *The Christian Century*, in which he regretted what he judged to be the triumphalist note of 1 Peter 2:9, 'But you are a chosen race, a royal priesthood, a dedicated nation, a people claimed by God for his own . . .' I can only say that when I read that, knowing something of the churches and of myself, I feel more humbled by the privilege than puffed up with false pride.

247. Forsyth, *Faith, Freedom and the Future*, 95.

248. Evans, *Saints*, 130. His italics.

249. I have discussed inclusivity and exclusivity in relation to doctrine, ecclesiology, ethics and language, in Sell, *Enlightenment, Ecumenism, Evangel*, 325–76.

250. Rogers, *Church Systems*, 644.

under which denominational label they travel. Against any possible misunderstanding, let it be clearly understood that to be 'separated unto the Lord' is an unmerited privilege, not a ground for boasting; it challenges the saint to lead a life of divinely enabled holiness; but it is not an excuse for, still less a justification of, a quietism that shuns the very world (geographical) in which the gospel is to be proclaimed and unstinting service to be rendered.[251]

It remains to be added that the Separatist and Dissenting saints were well aware that they were still sinners. Had the Bible not reminded them of this—large parts of Paul's letters would not have been written had the saints been behaving themselves—the behaviour of their members would have made the fact obvious. Tares were not to be found only in the parish churches. On the contrary, they knew that 'No form of polity, indeed, no severity of discipline, can enable us to draw the line with unerring accuracy between "the saints and faithful brethren" and "those who obey not the Gospel of our Lord Jesus Christ"; but the attempt must be made.'[252] John Robinson granted that, although it should not be so, hypocrites 'doe creepe in through their owne hypocrisie,'[253] and the *Westminster Confession*, the *Savoy Declaration*, and the *Second London Confession* all allowed that despite the saint's sanctification, 'there abideth still some remnants of corruption in every part.'[254] However, 'all who are in the Church must be recognized as being also in Christ. They have to discharge duties which imply that they know the will of God, and desire to do it.'[255] The Dissenters thus sought to be a holy people disciplined under the gospel. This meant catechising the flock, carefully preparing candidates for church membership, exercising sacramental discipline,[256] as well as disciplining the wayward. Local

251. It is, of course, recognized that at certain times in the course of Christian history it has been necessary for the church to withdraw from the world (geographical), and to go underground, as the only means, humanly speaking, of preserving its life.

252. Dale, *Essays and Addresses*, 30.

253. J. Robinson, *A Briefe Catechisme*, 2.

254. *Westminster Confession*, XIII.ii; *Savoy Declaration*, XIII.ii; *Second London Confession*, XIII.ii.

255. Ibid., 131.

256. By this is especially meant upholding the view that the Lord's Supper is a sacrament of the church, not of the congregation (where the latter is not coextensive with the church). For this reason, within living memory, the Supper was regarded as an 'after service' which followed the 'preaching service.' The influence of the twentieth-century liturgical revival has taught many Dissenters that Word

Church Books are replete with instances of the last-mentioned activity. They concern such offences as falling asleep during the sermon, consorting with someone other than one's spouse, being drunk, and even, as at Chesham Baptist Church, 'passing "by the place of his own meeting to go and hear the organs and see the finery" at the local parish church.'[257] In Baptist and Congregational circles normal practice was for the minister first to have a confidential word with offenders; if that failed, the minister would raise the matter with the deacons; and as a last resort the case would be brought before the Church Meeting. It must freely be admitted that on occasion church discipline could badly backfire, and could even be enjoyed too much by those administering it. F. J. Powicke had some reason for characterizing eighteenth-century church discipline thus:

> [it] was vexatious and pragmatic. Members scrutinised each other's behaviour, scanned each other's doctrinal soundness, harassed their children with premature anxieties, grew formal in spirit and habit. The result was a type of piety which too long remained a characteristic of the Independent Church and drew forth a not undeserved ridicule. But it was no natural fruit of Independency. It was an excrescence—due largely to those social and political considerations by which Dissent was straitened, repressed, and cut off from sources of generous culture and aspiration.[258]

But however petty, and even on rare occasions, vindictive, such disciplinary procedures may have been, and no matter how frequently they veered in the direction of the legalistic 'policing of the saints,' the saints at their best understood that the objectives of church discipline were the honour of God, the peace of the church, the good example

---

and sacrament belong together since both testify to the gospel, the one by speech, the other by action; and hence the two have been brought together in the liturgy. But there was a theological logic to the older way, and the distinction between the liturgy of the catechumens and that of the faithful is venerable indeed. Of the ejected minister, Peter Ince (matric. 1731, d. 1683), an unfriendly witness wrote that 'He was a rigid disciplinarian of the Independent way [though his house at Thornhill, Dorset, was licensed for Presbyterian worship on 1 May 1672], so that he had a select number, who were termed the church, to the exclusion of the rest, who being hearers only, were left without the sacrament, or had to seek it elsewhere.' See Gunn, *A Memorial of the Nonconforming Clergy*, 14.

257. R. Brown, *English Baptists of the Eighteenth Century*, 35, quoting Champion, ed., *The General Baptist Church of Berkhamsted*, 32.

258. Powicke, "Historic Congregationalism in Britain," 265.

to weaker brothers and sisters, and, wherever possible, the restoration of offenders to fellowship: 'The *nature and end* of this judgment or sentence,' said John Owen, is '*corrective*, not *vindictive*,—for healing, not destruction.'[259] Eighty years ago Robert Mackintosh thought it conceivable that 'we have gravely lost by permitting such discipline to become a dead letter. Can a modern church, as a fellowship, do nothing to rescue those who are drifting upon the rocks? Does it discharge its full duty when it erases from its roll of members the names of those who have definitely lapsed? Is our life to-day too artificial to admit the simplicities of a more Christian practice?'[260] Sinners though the saints undoubtedly continue to be, the fact remains that 'The visible organised local church is for us the earthen vessel which carries the real presence of the Saviour.'[261] How can this be? Only by the grace of God.

THE CURRENT ECUMENICAL SITUATION AND THE AGE-OLD SECTARIAN THREAT

To recapitulate: the saints are those who are called by the Holy Spirit through the word of the gospel of God's prevenient grace. Their being called entails their regeneration, justification, adoption, and sanctification. To this divine summons they make their enabled, grateful, response of faith—itself a gift from God. One in Christ, they are visibly gathered in fellowship around the one Lord of the church, and they seek to honour him in their worship and churchly life and witness. They are a holy people, willingly separated unto the Lord; but they remain sinners who need the discipline of the church to encourage their faith and service and to pursue them with love when they are wayward. My contention is twofold. First, these are the positive points, rooted in pneumatology, which required the Separatists and later the ejected ministers to utter their 'No' to the impositions placed upon them. Secondly, these positive points were not comprehensively articulated during the several commemorations of the Ejectment, the books, tracts, and speeches of which were, understandably enough, directed to the religious and political circumstances of the times. Incidentally, the pneumatological points are almost entirely absent

259. Owen, *Works*, XVI, 171; cf. XV, 513; *Westminster Confession*, XXX.iii.

260. Mackintosh, "The Genius of Congregationalism," 110. See further on discipline, Sell, *Enlightenment, Ecumenism, Evangel*, 238–42, 339–55.

261. Manning, *Essays in Orthodox Dissent*, 117.

from a number of the manuals of church membership issued by the Dissenting traditions over the years. They have not given a clear answer to the question, 'Who are the saints, and whence do they come?' Instead they have concerned institutional matters, the ordering of the church, the sacraments and ministry of the church, the responsibilities of church members, and the like. Thus, for example, H. J. S. Guntrip raises one's hopes when he begins to answer his question, *What is Congregationalism?* by affirming that 'Congregationalism is first a foremost a thing of the spirit.' At first we may think that by an editorial slip the last word does not begin with capital letter; but a few lines on we learn that 'at its best the spirit of which Congregationalism is born is a rugged, sturdy strength of heart and mind . . .'[262] That able minister, Leslie J. Tizard, whose bibliography never ceases to amuse,[263] notes that the Dissenting forebears believed that the church comprises Christians. But what is a Christian? he asks. 'To be a Christian,' he replies, 'does not mean the acceptance of a creed,' it 'does not mean having a blameless past,' or that 'a high level of character has already been attained.' It means 'that you believe in . . . the God who was in Christ . . . That you will commit yourself to Christ and His way of life . . . [and] [t]hat you sincerely desire to live in fellowship with other Christians.'[264] The prevenient work of God the Holy Spirit is here conspicuous by its absence. It is not that material of this kind is unhelpful, but without the pneumatological roots it is unanchored. The emphasis becomes anthropocentric in that the texts turn upon what intending members need to know and what they are expected to do, rather than upon what God the Holy Spirit has already done.[265] Yet, as the Baptist Wheeler Robinson rightly said, 'The Free Churches stand or fall by the doctrine of the Holy Spirit, as every kind of Free

---

262. Guntrip, *What is Congregationalism?* 3. For Guntrip (1901–75) see ODNB, SI, WTW.

263. Because he followed up his book, *A Guide to Marriage*, with another entitled, *A More Excellent Way*.

264. Tizard, *Church Membership*, 6–11. For Tizard (1902–57) see SI, WTW.

265. Among happier Congregationalist examples of the genre are the following: Cooke, *Upon This Rock*, and Marsh, *For the Church Member*; and Dakin offers one of the more robustly theological popular accounts of *The Baptist View of the Church and Ministry*. See especially, 13–14. For Dakin (1884–1969) see *The Baptist Handbook*, 1970, 376.

Church must do.'[266] How, at the Bicentenary of the Ejectment could Alexander Maclaren content himself with the following unfortunate disjunctions: 'It is on the ground of their fidelity to conscience alone that these Nonconformists of 1662 deserve the homage which we pay them. It is not their theology, but their honesty; no[t] their creed, but their consciences; not their objections to the formulas of the Church, but their renunciation of advantages and endurance of persecutions because they would not mask their objections under a false uniformity—that we admire.'[267] In fact, the pioneers of Old Dissent assumed the truth of the pneumatological doctrines when they thought of the nature of the church. Most of them, after all, were Calvinists; and to any who may suppose that I am steering too close to the Calvinistic wind I have a twofold reply. First, the pneumatological roots of which I am speaking are nothing if not biblical. Secondly, Geoffrey Nuttall, himself no scholastic Calvinist, wrote this: 'Calvinistic sentiments would hardly be described as an accepted ideal in the Free Churches to-day. Yet there is much to be said for them on grounds of fidelity to Scripture and of an intellingent reaction to history and experience; and without them to undergird our gathered, communal and responsible churchmanship much of its *raison d'être* is taken away.'[268] When ecclesiology is sundered from these roots it all too easily degenerates into a matter of choice between one way of organizing the Church and another. Our Dissenting forebears did not suffer and die for the sake of having deacons rather than elders, believer baptism rather than paedobaptism, or even Calvinism rather than Arminianism. They suffered and died in the interest of God's right to call whom he will into the church by the Spirit, and for the sole Lordship of Christ within it.

It will not have escaped any who have followed the course of ecumenical dialogue over the past half-century that frequently, owing to the neuralgic issues of baptism, eucharist, and ministry, one has the impression of moving ecclesiological counters around the board. We have had more than a century of this sort of sharing. Whereas, as I myself can readily recall, the Tercentenary of the Great Ejectment was celebrated in a mood of ecumenical hopefulness, we are now, as I said

---

266. H. W. Robinson, *The Life and Faith of the Baptists*, 22. For Robinson (1872–1945) see ODNB.

267. Maclaren, "Fidelity to Conscience," 14.

268. Nuttall, "Calvinism in Free Church History," 427.

earlier, assured by some that we are living in an ecumenical winter. In this circumstance, when I ask how we are to commemorate the 350th anniversary of the Great Ejectment, I conclude, to resume my earlier suggestion, that the time is ripe for some lateral thinking. Let us break out of the mould of being content with asking, What can we learn of each other? What have we to share? These are not unimportant questions, but let us also drive deeper. Let us be radical in the sense of the Latin *radix*; let us go to the root and ask, What has God done? The answer is that in his love and mercy, by his Spirit through the Word, he has called out one holy, catholic, and apostolic church, and there is no other. Let our distillation of the insights of the ejected and their forebears focus once again on the pneumatological underpinnings of their ecclesiological stances. For this will both refresh our understanding of catholicity and encourage us to adjust matters ecclesiastical and much else besides in the light of God's saving act. It will also challenge us to repudiate the sectarianisms to which every Christian tradition is prone. I conclude by elaborating briefly on these points.

I have already expounded the Dissenting view of catholicity, but now I apply the idea to the ecumenical situation in which we find ourselves. The first thing we need to remember is that the church of the Lord Jesus Christ is *already one*; we do not have to create the unity—as if we could! Rather we have to manifest it and order our churchy life as if we believed in it. Far from this understanding of catholicity's being an insight exclusive to Dissenters, it is easily possible to mingle their affirmations with those of other traditions. As one of the fountainheads of that Reformed tradition to which the Separatists, Dissenters, and their united heirs belong stands Calvin. He could not have been more blunt: 'The church is called "catholic" or "universal," because there could not be two or three churches unless Christ be torn asunder—which cannot happen!'[269] Forsyth concurs: 'What the Gospel created was not a crowd of Churches but one Church in various places.'[270] To the Anglican, F. J. A. Hort, the unity of the church 'is a truth of theology and of religion, not a fact of what we call ecclesiastical politics.'[271] The Presbyterian, T. W. Manson said that 'We talk glibly about "our

---

269. Calvin, *Institutes*, IV.1.2.
270. Forsyth, *The Church and the Sacraments*, 68. Cf. Owen, *Works*, XV, 78.
271. Hort, *The Christian Ecclesia*, 168.

unhappy divisions"; but, in truth, so long as we are under one supreme Head, our divisions must remain essentially unreal.[272]

Essentially unreal they may be, but our divisions are pernicious in their actual effects. As Paul almost said—indeed, as he might well have said to the Corinthians, Now there are varieties of sectarianism but the same divisive spirit. Hear the seventeenth-century's Reformed pastor-ecumenist *par excellence*, Richard Baxter:

> I apprehended it a matter of great necessity to imprint true Catholicism on the minds of Christians, it being a most lamentable thing in the world to observe how few Christians in the world there be that fall not into one sect or another . . . and how lamentably love is thereby destroyed . . . And if they can but get to be of a sect which they think the *holiest* (as the Anabaptists and Separatists), or which is the *largest* (as the Greeks and Papists), they think then that they are sufficiently warranted to deny others to be God's Church, or at least to deny them Christian love and communion.[273]

Such attitudes dismember what God has made one in Christ by the Holy Spirit, and they still persist. At the heart of the problem is the Galatian heresy: the imposition of 'new circumcisions' which are permitted to take precedence over the gospel of God's grace, and to deny what he has already done. 'Without all controversy,' declared John Howe long ago, 'the main inlet of all the distractions, confusions, and divisions of the Christian world, hath been by adding other conditions of Church communion than Christ hath done.'[274]

No tradition is entirely free of the Galatian heresy. In whatever form it comes, it boils down to the insistence that unless and until you believe as we believe, order your church as we order ours, or subscribe to our ethical code, we will not have full fellowship with you. Now it must be granted that many such convictions are held in sincerity, but they are permitted to become church-dividing; that is the tragedy. They all have the effect of conditioning or constraining the sphere of grace. That is why we need the lateral thinking concerning the Spirit's work that will relativize them all and put them in perspective. It is manifestly the case that Christians will not agree on all doctrinal,

272. Manson, *The Church's Ministry*, 89.

273. Baxter, *Autobiography*, 95–96. Cf. Owen, *Works*, XVI, 186.

274. Howe, *Works*, V, 226.

ecclesiological, or ethical matters—we do not even do so within the denominational fortresses in which we shelter. But it is the height of arrogance to suppose that our agreements or disagreements ought to be more precious to us than the grace that has made us one already (whether we like it or not). Wherever the ecclesiological-sectarian spirit rears its head we need to take the pneumatological drill to it and dig it up.[275] My prescription, to repeat, is that by an exercise of lateral thinking we need to start not from where we have arrived, but from what God has done, and then adjust our churchly ways and relationships accordingly. In particular I shall suggest that from the Separatist-Ejected heritage we may distil the truth that by the Holy Spirit people may be both regenerated and visibly gathered in the fellowship of the one church. To put the point negatively, the Holy Spirit does not regenerate and then leave the saints in freewheeling isolation. Positively, the call to unity with Christ is the call to unity with all who are his. But in the church temporal 'his' are the visible saints. They are a community embodied in the world yet separated unto the Lord—a holy people. It ought therefore to be possible to know who they are and where they are. How, otherwise, could we conceive of the church as apostolic? In whatsoever locality those gather who call Jesus Lord—which they can do only by the Holy Spirit (1 Corinthians 12:3)—they are members of the church catholic; and they are so as visible, covenanted, anchored saints.

In view of the examples I propose to adduce I ought to say at the outset that I am neither concerned nor inclined to throw stones at those of other traditions. On the contrary, with mingled truthfulness and sorrow, I affirm that the history of the Reformed family, to which I belong, has probably witnessed more inner-sectarianism than any other. Our particular propensity has been so to elevate the mint and dill and cumin of doctrine that we have lost the Spirit. Thus, for example, it is not too much to say that the shape of English and Welsh Nonconformity owes as much to differences over the person of Christ as to any other Christian doctrine. By the end of the long eighteenth century the vast majority of Presbyterians of Old Dissent had become either Congregational or Unitarian, and numerous secessions

---

275. For some wider-than-ecclesiological examples of sectarianism see Sell, *Commemorations*, ch. 2.

had occurred in the process.[276] Of those who wished to elevate their doctrinal articles to the position of conditions of membership the eighteenth century the Arian Presbyterian, Ebenezer Latham, took a very dim view: 'Hereticks and schismaticks,' he declared, 'in the modern use of the words is but a sort of theological scare-crow, a kind of Billingsgate language in the Church'; and with reference to those who required a canon of doctrine in order to make for a united church he continued, 'That remedy for division is worse than the disease; 'tis adding human explications, the words of men, to the words of God . . . All their frightful anathemas are but ecclesiastical puffs . . . [T]hey usurp the throne of Christ.'[277] Latham's contemporary, the Arian Presbyterian Samuel Bourn, concurred: 'to *Substitute* any *Human Composures*, whether Articles, Creeds, Catechisms, Confessions, instead of the Gospel, as a Rule of Tryal . . . is to return back into the Tenets of Popery . . . If we pay that Regard to any Body of Men, tho' the most learned Assembly in the World, which is due to *Christ* only, we make a *Christ* of these Men; they are our *Rabbi*.'[278] Here are strikingly expressed reminders of the Dissenting conviction that while it is perfectly proper to set down the things commonly believed in statements and declarations of faith, it is in principle a sectarian act to require formal doctrinal assent as distinct from basic Christian testimony, as a condition of fellowship, and it may discourage openness to the Holy Spirit's subsequent guidance.

Further afield in the Reformed family, it has been said that if one wishes to understand some of the Reformed divisions, one needs to have been born within twenty-five miles of Grand Rapids. Again, when you consider that at the last count there were more than one hundred Presbyterian denominations in South Korea (most of them not related to the World Communion of Reformed Churches) you will surely agree that the eighteenth-century Scots were amateurs in the matter of inner-Reformed secession. In most divisions of this sort

276. See Sell, *Christ and Controversy: The Person of Christ in Nonconformist Thought and Ecclesial Experience*. In the middle decades of the nineteenth century the Strict and Particular Baptists divided over the same doctrine; see ibid.

277. Quoted by H. McLachlan, *Essays and Addresses*, 158. For Latham (1688–1754) see SI. Cf. Baxter, *Autobiography*, 138: 'I knew how ticklish a business the enumeration of fundamentals was.'

278. Bourn, *The True Christian Way*, 21. For Bourn (1689–1754) see ODNB, SI; Sell, *Dissenting Thought*, ch. 7.

politics and personal power struggles have not been entirely absent. In the last one hundred and fifty years some Reformed 'Galatians' have marched under the banner of biblical inerrancy with disturbing results. Happily, only the fringes of mainstream English and Welsh Dissent have been nibbled by this doctrine, but here and there it has fuelled the sectarian spirit. I call it a doctrine, but really it is a complex of doctrines. Thus whereas absolute inerrantists hold that the Bible is inerrant in every proposition asserted therein—its presumed history no less than its presumed science, relative inerrantists maintain that it is inerrant only in its principle doctrinal claims—a position that leads to further disagreement over what those might be. Inerrantists of all stripes are inclined to say 'We cannot have any dealings with mainstream ecumenism because unity must be in the truth and (*sotto voce*—or not) we have it,' and hence particular, and sometimes quaint or decidedly odd interpretations of the truth are elevated above the gospel of God's grace that has made us one, and this with sectarian consequences.[279] It was a conservative evangelical scholar, E. J. Carnell, who once ruefully remarked, 'When there are no modernists from which to withdraw, fundamentalists compensate by withdrawing from one another.'[280] I grant, with C. J. Cadoux, that 'A teacher or a book may be in fact inerrant: what neither he nor it can ever be is infallible, *i.e. unconditionally* inerrant, inerrant before and apart from proof.'[281] As he viewed his own Congregational tradition Forsyth lamented that 'we have become, first, individualists, and then denominationalists, at the cost of the great corporate Church mind which so ruled our Puritans and fed their Puritanism.'[282]

It is not a record of which to be proud, and it is not erased by the fact that the Reformed have in more recent time joined in more transconfessional unions of churches than most others. In what follows I do not wish to be understood as saying or implying that how the church orders itself, and what it believes is of no consequence. I am simply arguing that none of our doctrinal, ecclesiological, or ethical convictions and preferences should be elevated to such a degree that we grieve the Holy Spirit by denying his prevenient work and erecting barriers

---

279. See further, Sell, *Enlightenment, Ecumenism, Evangel*, 286–87.

280. Carnell, *The Case for Orthodox Theology*, 117.

281. Cadoux, "Congregationalism and the True Catholicism," 65.

282. Forsyth, *The Church and the Sacraments*, 43.

which would exclude from full fellowship those who are already his. If a person can say, however falteringly, that 'Jesus Christ is my Lord and Saviour' he or she can say it only by the Holy Spirit and I dare not withhold fellowship from such a person. Even if a person can only say, 'Jesus is my Master and I try to follow him,' I do not say 'You sound like an old-fashioned liberal theologian: come back when you've got a half decent Christology!' Undeniably these are credal affirmations, however brief; but they are also personal confessions which suffice to admit the confessors to the privileges and responsibilities of church membership.[283] Of course, the content of such brief confessions is not all that Christians need to know or believe, but I am convinced—and it is a biblical thought—that we should not erect creeds and confessions into tests of membership, still less force-feed babes in Christ on the alleged five points of Calvinism or, on the other hand, leave them all at sea on the Sea of Faith. I much prefer to stand with John Locke, who testified, 'A Christian I am sure I am, because I believe *Jesus* to be the *Messiah*, the King and Saviour promised, and sent by God.'[284] This, he thought, sufficed to indicate that a person is a Christian. He also thought that a fuller grasp of the faith was much to be desired, and elsewhere sought to elaborate upon it.[285] To make church membership conditional upon formal assent to detailed creeds, still more upon facility in detailed creedal exposition would be Pelagian indeed, and, incidentally, I fear, a remarkably effective way of depleting the ranks of most of our ministries. The Congregationalists who framed the *Savoy Declaration of Faith* had no qualms whatsoever about setting down the things commonly believed among them; but in their important Preface averred that 'Whatever is of force or constraint in matters of this nature causeth them to degenerate from the name and nature of confessions, and turns them from being confession of faith into exactions and impositions of faith.'[286] The fundamental objection to such a practice was articulated concisely by Bernard Manning: 'The grace of God . . . needs no legal machinery to protect it.'[287] If God the Holy Spirit has called, regenerated, justified, adopted, and sanctified

283. Cf. Micklem, *Congregationalism To-day*, 18–20.

284. Locke, *A Second Vindication*, 344–45.

285. See further, Sell, *John Locke*, ch. 6.

286. Thompson, *Stating the Gospel*, 63. Cf. Jenkins, *Congregationalism: A Restatement*, 41.

287. B. L. Manning, *Essays*, 114.

a person, and if Christ has accepted him or her, how can I dare do otherwise? Lovell Cocks was not wide of the mark when he declared that 'so far from not having a creed, a Congregational church is a creed made visible. It has no standing, no existence even, except as a fellowship of men and women who acknowledge Jesus as Lord.'[288] As I reflect upon the sectarianism that has divided the saints of Dissent and of the wider Reformed family I am increasingly inclined to the tolerant attitude of the eighteenth-century Arian Presbyterian, Samuel Chandler:

> if any man so believes the gospel, as to be influenced by it, to live as a Christian, whatever character he may be distinguished by, Calvinist, Arminian, Baxterian, Athanasian, Arian, Sabellian, Socinian, all are the distinguishing names of a party. I doubt not but there have been good men, and acceptable Christians amongst them all; and tho' they differ many of them from me in opinion, as I shall take the liberty to support and defend my own sentiments, I hope I shall ever do it, with the spirit which the gospel recommends.[289]

Where the worldwide church is concerned, no doctrine has been more susceptible to sectarian exploitation than ecclesiology. Accordingly, I turn briefly to the hoary themes that have traditionally perplexed and divided those who are one in Christ.

The World Council of Churches' much-studied convergence document, *Baptism, Eucharist and Ministry*, advises that 'If the divided churches are to achieve the visible unity they seek, one of the essential prerequisites is that they should be in basic agreement on baptism, eucharist and ministry.'[290] One may raise the question of the analysis of 'basic' in this proposition, and no doubt the term is preferable to 'absolute' in this context. But it is the emphasis upon the need for basic agreement on any x, y, and z that seems to me to put anthropological considerations before pneumatological ones; for the participants would not be in discussion at all if they did not already recognize their oneness in Christ by the Holy Spirit. Moreover, practically, the emphasis upon human agreement as an essential prerequisite can place one at the top of a slippery slope at the bottom of which lies the Galatian

288. Cocks, *A Church Reborn*, 20.

289. Chandler, *A Second Letter to . . . Guyse*, 97. For Chandler (1693–1766) see ODNB, SI; Sell, *Hinterland Theology*, ch. 4 and *passim*.

290. Anon., *Baptism, Eucharist and Ministry*, viii. Preface by William H. Lazareth and Nikos Nissiotis.

heresy. 'I could not possibly receive the sacrament from you, nor could I offer it to you,' said an Anglican friend of mine, 'because we don't believe the same things about it.' My friend would not regard himself as a biblical inerrantist but, psychologically, what is there to choose between them, for both say 'Only when you accept the truth in my way will I have full fellowship with you,' and ecclesiologically the sectarian result is the same. Nor does this attitude emanate only from those who claim the name of Catholic. The bold affirmation of J. H. Rushbrooke that 'Baptists . . . unchurch no others'[291] would seem to require qualification owing to the fact that there are Baptists of varying types who admit to church membership, and welcome at the Lord's table, only those who have been baptized by immersion as believers, and it is difficult not to construe this as a sectarian stance.[292] That was certainly how the Arian Presbyterian, Micaijah Towgood, saw it: 'The Table they . . . erect is not the Lord's Table, but a Table of their own; and as far as they thus eat in criminal separation from, and uncharitable seclusion of other acknowledged Christians, they eat not the Lord's Supper.'[293]

We later learn from *Baptism, Eucharist and Ministry* that 'participation in Christ's death and resurrection is inseparably linked with the receiving of the Spirit. Baptism in its full meaning signifies and effects both.'[294] It signifies it, but does it really effect it? I think not. 'Throughout the New Testament,' wrote the Congregationalist E. J. Price, 'baptism is the sign or symbol of an inner change wrought by Christ, and does not of itself produce that change in us or alter our relation of God.'[295] If we forget this we veer in the direction of *opus operatum* exposition, and that peril is close in the Anglican-Reformed

291. Rushbrooke, "The Baptist Communion in Britain," 41. For Rushbrooke (1870–1947) see ODNB.

292. Cook observes that 'there are some Baptist churches where Baptism is made entirely optional; the only condition of membership is personal faith in Christ.' *What Baptists Stand For*, 112. There are also Baptists who do not associate the baptism of believers with membership of the church. Wheeler Robinson explains that 'Entrance into the Church is regarded as distinct from baptism, though in practice it is usually combined with it.' *Life and Faith*, 84, n. 2. Cf. Marshall, "The Baptist Churches," 162–63; Sell, *Testimony and Tradition*, 72–74.

293. Towgood, *Catholic Christianity*, appended to J. Manning, *A Sketch*, 190. Cf. Towgood, *The Grounds of Faith in Jesus Christ*, 82–83, 87. For Towgood (1700–92) see ODNB, SI; Sell, *Dissenting Thought*, ch. 7.

294. Anon., *Baptism, Eucharist and Ministry*, 6.

295. Price, *A Handbook of Congregationalism*, 47. Cf. Forsyth, *The Church and the Sacraments*, 219–20. For Price (1882–1952) see SI.

international dialogue report, *God's Reign and Our Unity*. 'Baptism,' we there read, is 'in the strictest sense, constitutive of the Church.'[296] Similarly, 'we must say that the Eucharist is constitutive of the Church because in it Christ unites the disciples with himself.'[297] I became the Theological Secretary of the World Alliance of Reformed Churches at the point at which the final draft of this report was tabled for discussion. I failed utterly to remove the 'constitutive' language, but I gently pointed out that I did not endorse it. I concur with Charles Duthie, who wrote, 'I am not entirely happy about the present habit of finding the major point of Christian unity in baptism.'[298] Just as there are no saving doctrines in the sense that doctrines as such do the saving, so the sacraments as such do not constitute the church, or effect salvation. They witness to the gospel of God's prevenient grace, and they testify to what God has already done or, in the case of baptized children of the covenant,[299] can do, by the Spirit in the lives of those who are gathered and covenanted in his name; the presence of Christ is known in the sacraments, as it is in the preaching of the Word. 'The sacraments,' declared the incisive Robert Mackintosh, 'are a witness to God's grace—a channel for God's grace—everything the high churchman can call them, except a substitute for God's grace, or a shackle upon God's free Spirit.'[300] In my opinion it is only on the slenderest of biblical grounds that the doctrine of baptismal regeneration can be affirmed, and I can see no other way of justifying the view that regeneration is always contemporary with baptism. Others have been more successful in this challenge than I, sometimes with sectarian results. Thus, when a distinguished Nonconformist divine asked Archbishop Benson whether he would be interested in a joint Church of England-Nonconformist

---

296. Anon., *God's Reign and Our Unity*, 33. The document roots Christian baptism in the baptism of Jesus by John the Baptist—a move that many scholars would query for a variety of reasons.

297. Ibid., 41.

298. Duthie, "Responding to the Gospel," 246. For Duthie (1911–81) see W. D. McNaughton, *The Scottish Congregational Ministry*; Sell, *Hinterland Theology*, ch. 11 and *passim*.

299. Dale affirmed the 'larger truth' that children other than children of the covenant might be baptized. See *Essays and Addresses*, 182; *Manual*, 128–31.

300. R. Mackintosh, *Essays Towards a New Theology*, 434. In a typical utterance Mackintosh averred that 'Infant baptism stands as the one bulwark against the destruction of the Church in favour of the evangelistic committee.' See *The Insufficiency of Revivqlism as a Religious System*, 28.

evangelistic campaign the Archbishop replied, 'No; for you proceed upon the supposition that the non-church-going people require to be regenerated . . . but we proceed upon the belief that they are regenerated in baptism already.'[301] Once again we have a clear division as to who comprise the saints; once again we have an oblique defence of a parish system. No one put the opposing view more bluntly than Forsyth: 'All the baptized are not regenerated. Some regenerates have not been baptized.'[302] Yet if we take seriously the prevenient work of God the Holy Spirit, differences of opinion regarding the sacraments should not be permitted to divide those who are one in Christ, and no one who has confessed that Jesus Christ is Lord and Saviour should be excluded from them, except in rare disciplinary instances, and then in the hope of restoration to fellowship. That the sacraments, which witness to the catholicity of God's saving grace, should be permitted to become badges of sectarianism is tragic indeed.

The peril is never closer than where the Lord's Supper is concerned, and in this connection the hoary questions of apostolic succession and episcopal ordination come to the fore, and with them further opportunities for sectarianism. There should be no need in these latter days to argue the case that pipe-line theories of grace unwarrantably 'mechanize' grace, the personal, unmerited, favour of the personal God; nor to show that a continuous succession of ministers from Peter onwards is impossible to demonstrate from history. It should not even be necessary any longer to oppose the views of Kenneth Kirk,[303] Gregory Dix,[304] and Gabriel Hebert[305] among others who, notwithstanding the canons of the Church of England, make episcopacy the *esse*, not simply the *bene esse* of the church; for scholars such as T. W. Manson have conclusively shown that there was no handing on of authority from Christ to the first apostles of the institutional kind that such a theory requires;[306] and further, that Kirk's view that Jesus gave

---

301. Quoted by Edward White, "Broad Church doctrine," 169. For White (1819–98) see SI.

302. Forsyth, *The Church and the Sacraments*, 210.

303. Kirk, "The Apostolic Ministry," 8. For a searching review of this work see Nuttall, "The Apostolic Ministry." Kirk went so far as to claim that if the episcopally ordained ministry failed, the church would fall with it. Ibid., 40.

304. Dix, "Ministry in the Early Church," 303.

305. Hebert, *The Form of the Church*, 111, 113.

306. Cf. Bartlet, "Congregationalism, Essential and Relative," 42: 'Even had

the church the gifts of Word and sacraments and the ministry of grace, is not high enough, for 'Our Lord did better than that: He gave the Church Himself. His real and abiding presence in the Church is the supreme "means of grace" and the supreme "ministry of grace."'[307] To move to the other pole of Anglicanism, we do not have to agree with Hastings Rashdall that the idea of a special power conferred in ordination was 'invented in or about the year 1833,'[308] for it can be shown that *potestas* has been with us since the Middle Ages, when it emerged at least partly in response to the question, What is to be done in the case of those who sin after baptism? Answer: empower the priests to absolve the guilty. There thus developed a view of ordination that is, frankly, divisive.

We recall that the ejected ministers opposed the clause in the Act of Uniformity requiring episcopal ordination; and, consistently with this, they repudiated idea that ministers who had been ordained non-episcopally during the interregnum, required to be re-ordained. The classic instance is supplied by the ejected John Howe. Following the Restoration of the monarchy in 1660 the Bishop of Exeter, Seth Ward, asked him '"What hurt is there in being twice Ordained?" "Hurt, my Lord, says Mr Howe to him; the Thought is shocking; it hurts my Understanding; it is an absurdity: For nothing can have two Beginnings. I am sure, said he, I am a Minister of Christ . . . and I can't begin again to be a Minister."'[309] This is the principle that is echoed by Dissenters to this day, and it was trenchantly stated by Forsyth. He argued that 'The Episcopate replaced the Apostolate rather than prolonged it, taking some of its functions but not entitled to its prerogative,' and that the protest 'against polity as a condition of church unity'[310] stands. Elsewhere he underlined the point thus: 'Unity is in the Gospel, it is not in orders or sacraments, valuable as these are. The one is constitu-

---

Christ given the Apostles—as Dr. Hort expressly denies—a commission for *administrative or liturgical government* of His *Ecclesia*, pending the *Parousia*, it would have been under conditions excluding the very idea of a succession of them.' For Bartlet (1863–1940) see ODNB.

307. Manson, *The Church's Ministry*, 21.

308. Rashdall, *Principles and Precepts*, 153.

309. Calamy, *Memoirs*, 39.

310. Forsyth, *The Church and the Sacraments*, 46. Cf. Forsyth's student, Cocks, *The Faith of a Protestant Christian*, 46.

tive, the others but convenient.'[311] Not surprisingly, for all his love of the Church of England, Bernard Manning ruefully concluded that it had turned itself into an 'episcopalian sect.'[312] For this reason, he wrote, 'we decline still, as we have always declined, to have Episcopalian ordination of ministers and Episcopalian confirmation of Church members made into as sort of new circumcision within the limits of which alone is there the full and valid and regular operation of God's grace.'[313] Consistently with this W. F. Adeney had earlier declared his willingness to unite with his friends in the Church of England, 'if only they would let me be myself, would recognise me not only as a Christian brother, but also as already a member of the Christian Church, and as a Christian minister requiring no fresh ordination. But union by submission I respectfully decline.'[314] Associating his Arminian Methodist family with that of historic Dissent, Gordon Rupp opined that 'Doubt cast upon the integrity of our ministry is doubt cast on grace itself. And when these things are denied we must simply wait until our separated brethren shall come to a better mind.'[315]

We need not simply wait, of course; we can graciously draw their attention to the non-sectarian, pneumatological, underpinnings of ecclesiology; we can commend to them an ecclesiology which 'presupposes no priestly hierarchy, but the believing congregation of those who have been called out of darkness into a marvellous light, and who live on the promises of God in the Word of His grace';[316] and we can remain alert to any attempt to have discussions concerning the reconciliation of ministries fudged by loose language which supposes that what Dissenters have to offer Anglicans by way of completing their ministries is equivalent to what at least some Anglicans think is required to complete the ministries of the Dissenters.[317] The stumbling

---

311. Forsyth, *Congregationalism and Reunion*, 21–2.

312. Manning, *Essays in Orthodox Dissent*, 136.

313. Ibid., 133.

314. Adeney, "The More Excellent Way," 47.

315. Rupp, "Clerical Integrity," 147.

316. Whale, "Commemoration Sermon," 112. For Whale (1896–1997) see ODNB, SI, WTW.

317. Cf. John Huxtable's verdict on the Anglican-Methodist draft Service of Reconciliation in his book, *Christian Unity: Some of the Issues*, 67. For an account of Nonconformist ecumenical thought in the twentieth century see Sell, *Nonconformist Theology*, ch. 3. For Huxtable (1912–90) see ODNB, SI, WTW.

block here is what led that dedicated ecumenist, John Huxtable, to lament that the Church of England 'is to be the bridge Church over which no traffic ever flows.'[318]

From what the ejected regarded as untoward episcopalian demands there flows the sectarian doubt that has often been cast upon the sacraments as observed by Dissenters and later Nonconformists. Are they irregular, invalid, or not sacraments at all? With respect to the Lord's Supper Bernard Manning denounced all such ideas in no uncertain terms: 'The Supper of the Lord is either celebrated or not celebrated. The Body and the Blood of Christ are spiritually received or they are not received. We simply do not know what an irregular or an invalid celebration it. We do not deal in percentages with the grace of God . . . We are in the presence of God. When we can botanise about the Burning Bush, either it has ceased to burn or it has been consumed.'[319]

The gospel, and with it the Spirit's gathering work, comes first, and if we really wish to claim that the sacraments are sacraments of the church,[320] then we need to know who the saints are, and 'The condition of entrance into the Church is that first of all men should be "in Christ"'[321]—an insight distilled from the writings and experience of Separatist and ejected alike, and affirmed by Richard Baxter: 'it is a dishonourable doctrine against God and Christianity to say that

318. Huxtable, *As it Seemed to Me*, 71.

319. Manning, *Essays*, 116–17.

320. This is precisely why, just as with preaching the Word, lay persons (to use a common but awkward term—for ministers should not forget that they belong to the *laos* of God)—may be authorised by the church to conduct baptisms and the Lord's Supper. See John Whale's remarks in "The Views of the Congregational Church," 214. I find it odd that many who agree with liturgiologists that Word and sacrament belong together then proceed to sunder them by allowing any heretic to preach, whilst taking a much more stringent attitude towards the conduct of the Lord's Supper. Again, a wedge is driven between the dominical sacraments when many Christian traditions will accept baptisms performed with water in the name of the Trinity, but reserve the Supper to a priestly caste. I also find it puzzling when those who have most to say concerning the mystery at the heart of the Christian faith seem to know so clearly what happens at the Lord's Supper that they can be quite sure when Dissenters and their heirs gather at the Lord's table they are missing something of vital importance. When the saints gather at the table and pray for the presence of the Holy Spirit he does not send his apologies.

321. J. D. Jones, *Things Most Surely Believed*, 152. For Jones (1865–1942) see ODNB, SI, WTW.

God layeth his love and mans salvation so much on a Ceremony, as to damn or deny an upright and holy soul for want of it . . . The thing signified is necessary to salvation.'[322] Positively, what may be distilled from the witness of the ejected in relation to doctrinal and ecclesiological sectarianism is the following testimony of a distinguished follower in their line:

> What was fundamental was . . . the baptism of the Spirit and the feeding upon spiritual bread; was not episcopacy or ministerial ordination or ecclesiastical polity of any kind, for, [as Cromwell declared in his speech at the opening of the Little Parliament on 4 July 1643] 'the true succession' was 'through the Spirit,'[323] and the Spirit blew where it listed; was not in creeds or catechisms or liturgies or any forms which might quench the Spirit and darken what fresh light might be given. What was fundamental was the personal reception, both individually and communally, of the Spirit; was in the possession of the Spirit's gifts and graces; was in not grieving the Spirit.[324]

It must, however, be admitted that the Dissenters and their heirs have not been short of sectarian opportunities where the reception or admission of members is concerned. There is an older (but continuing) and a more recent way in which they have imposed ethical and religious terms of fellowship alien to the Bible; they have behaved like the Galatians and have fallen into sectarianism. Not, indeed, that warnings against such constrictions of grace were not given. The Arian Presbyterian, Samuel Bourn, who had a great interest in the education of the youth of the church, prefaced his *Three Catechisms* with these words addressed to parents: 'Let your Children know, that Religion is a *nobler Thing*, than Sectarian Bigotry, dry Opinions, and a fruitless Faith; that it lieth in the Image of God on the Soul, a Likeness to God and Jesus Christ in Justice, Kindness and Charity; that it consisteth in Heavenly Dispositions, devout Affections, in Rectitude of Spirit, Purity of Soul, and universal Goodness.'[325] Despite such exhortations some Dissenters found no difficulty in embracing legalisms of one kind or another, thereby justifying Robert Mackintosh's claim that

322. Quoted by Nuttall, *Richard Baxter*, 66.

323. Cromwell, *Letters and Speeches*, Speech 1, II, 331.

324. Nuttall, *The Holy Spirit*, 177.

325. Bourn, *Lectures*, xxi.

'Doctrinally and emotionally [the saint] was to live by grace; but his conduct was to be exactly the same *as if he expected to be justified by law.*'[326] It is not difficult to see how this could come about. It is the shadow side of a polity which expected the saints to provide evidence of a godly walk as a sign of their regeneration, and which enjoined separation from the wicked world. John Robinson declared that 'it is required to the constitution of a holy church of God, that the people be holy, or saints, and sanctified in Christ Jesus.'[327] But when the saints set about prescribing the forms of moral behaviour that were the evidential criteria of sanctification law could easily trump grace. Thus, for example, from the covenant which they signed on 28 December 1786 it seems clear that the Congregational saints of the village of Bluntisham were determined to make the narrow way even narrower by elevating specific moral duties into terms of fellowship: 'As a church of Christ we desire through grace not to countenance the works of darkness such as Adultery, Fornication, Uncleanness, Murder, Drunkenness and such like. And not to frequent public places of amusement such as Horse-racing, Playhouses, Dancing, Cardplaying, Gaming, nor to frequent Ale-houses, unless lawfully engaged . . .'[328] Sometimes pious legalism could leave the saints hoist with their own petard—as at Ramsgate. In 1767 the saints of that seaside town called to the pastorate David Bradberry, who had been converted under the ministry of George Whitefield. Bradberry agreed to accept the call provided that the church formally adopted nine articles as terms of communion. Of these the first eight were staunchly Calvinistic, the ninth read thus: 'That you will discourage the infamous practice of smuggling, as contrary to the law of civil society, and as expressly contrary to God's word.' This final clause was debated at length, but at last all nine articles were adopted, and Bradberry became the minister there. In 1786, two years following Bradberry's departure, the Church Meeting gathered in solemn session and rescinded the clause concerning smuggling because it had occasioned so much deception and hypocrisy.[329] The unsanctified thought occurs that those who elevate particular aspects of moral behaviour into terms of communion may be sorely tempted

326. Mackintosh, *The Insufficiency of Revivalism*, 8.

327. J. Robinson, *Works*, III, 66.

328. See Dixon, *A Century of Village Nonconformity*, 157.

329. Hurd, *These Three Hundred Years*, 4. For Bradberry (1735–1803) see SI.

hypocritically to list only those alleged sins that they themselves are not particularly inclined to commit: 'Don't go to the dance hall because it's a sink of iniquity; but if you're a tiny bit racist in your heart, the neighbours will never know.'

The more modern type of legalism is that which expects candidates for church membership to have undergone a specific type of experience—even a timed and dated one, and to be able to testify to it. From the earliest Separatist and Dissenting days the guidance was that 'Ther may none be admitted into the church of Christ but such as enter by publicke professions of the true faith.'[330] Furthermore, as John Robinson declared, such professions of faith were to be made 'not by men of lewd conversation, or apparently unsanctified,' but by those who were 'so far as men in charity could judge, justified, sanctified, and entitled to the promises of salvation, and life eternal.'[331] It would be a mistake to suppose that Dissenters were universally approving of the practice of 'giving in an experience.' While the Baptists and Congregationalists favoured such testimonies, the Presbyterians for the most part had reservations, and were content with an affirmation of faith. Baxter, the moderate episcopalian thought that the relating of spiritual experience tended towards fanaticism and irrationalism, and that from the standpoint of parish life, which he favoured, 'It tendeth to extirpate Godliness out of the Land, by taking a very few that can talk more than the rest, and making them the Church, and shutting out more that are worthy . . .'[332] Even some of those whose practice it was became, with the passage of time, somewhat disenchanted with the volubility of testimonies. Thus in 1764 the Yorkshire and Lancashire Baptist Association cautioned that 'constant repetition of the same thing, and a treading in the same steps, with scarce any deviation, tends to cloy the appetite and benumb the soul.'[333] Yet with hindsight Geoffrey Nuttall judged that the requirement of personal testimony 'contributed to the preservation of the Congregational churches from the tendencies to rationalism which developed within the Presbyterian churches.'[334]

330. Barrow, *A Brief Discoverie*, 280.

331. J. Robinson, *Works*, II, 333.

332. Baxter, *Rel.Bax.*, III, 67.

333. Quoted by R. Brown, *The English Baptists of the Eighteenth Century*, 88.

334. Nuttall, *Visible Saints*, 112. For other relevant factors see Sell, *Dissenting Thought*, ch. 5.

As the Evangelical Revival took hold of significant portions of Old Dissent, personal testimonies assumed an ever larger place in the lives of many churches. In some cases the emphasis upon conversion was so great as to reduce baptism to a detail—even to an optional extra, and the concept of the church as a covenanted body of saints was in some places replaced by that of a society of rescued sinners.[335] R. W. Dale made much of what he regarded as a declension, and in a typical remark he declared that 'The "Revival" was eager to save individual men. It knew little or nothing about the dignity, the power, the sacredness of the Church.'[336] It must be said that this was not universally true. John Briggs, for example, has rightly drawn attention to the prominent Baptist, John Fawcett, who was no less deeply committed to the church as a company of visibly gathered saints, as he was to evangelism.[337] Undeniably, however, stereotypical testimonies were frequently required for admission to church membership, and while the stereotypical is not necessarily the insincere, the requirement to employ the accepted 'language of Canaan' could become a badge of sectarianism at least to the extent that people felt excluded by it. Thus the youthful Joseph Parker, who felt that as a teenager his sins were not sufficiently dire, and hence that his testimony would be less than acceptably substantial and dramatic. 'So I stood outside the gate,' he tells us, 'crying bitter tears, because I had not sinned according to the quality and magnitude of another man's confession.'[338]

Robert Vaughan's cautionary words may stand: 'While resolved not to open the doors of the Church to the worldly, we should be careful that we do not close them against Christians.'[339] We have seen that the door could be closed by adding 'new circumcisions,' whether doctrinal, ethical or religious to the basic and only proper condition of

335. The number of local Congregational covenants declined noticeably after about 1820, with many churches establishing mission stations—a novelty as far as Congregational polity was concerned.

336. Dale, *Essays and Addresses*, 232; cf. ibid., 209; Dale, *History of English Congregationalism*, 590; Dale, *The Old Evangelicalism and the New*. Cf. Manning, "Some Characteristics of the Older Dissent," 289.

337. See Briggs, *English Baptists of the Nineteenth Century*, 14–15. For Fawcett (1740–1817) see ODNB.

338. Quoted by Dawson, *Joseph Parker*, 22. For Parker (1830–1902) see ODNB, SI. For more on the reception of members see Sell, *Enlightenment, Ecumenism, Evangel*, 343–47.

339. Vaughan, *Congregationalism*, 200.

membership, confession of faith in Jesus Christ as Saviour and Lord. Dale may sum up for us:

> *A Christian society which imposes any other condition of membership than faith in Christ is a sect, and not, in the highest sense of the term, a Christian church.* It is a private Christian club. It receives persons into membership, not because they are the brethren of Christ, but because they are the brethren of Christ professing certain religious opinions or observing certain religious practices . . . It is a society not for all Christians, but for a particular description of Christians. It is a sect—not a Church.[340]

I can well understand that to members of some Christian traditions—especially those concerned to 'guard the ark', and those, if such there be, who may be inclined to elevate institution above gospel—this will seem a most inadequate stance, perhaps because they give insufficient weight to the relationship of the Holy Spirit to ecclesiology which it has been my purpose to demonstrate. Having quoted so many of the Dissenting tradition, I conclude this section by quoting William Gordon Robinson, who as Robert Vaughan was the first, was the last Principal of my *alma mater*, Lancashire Independent College. He, I am persuaded, had the pearl of price: 'a genuine trust in the operation of the Holy Spirit, held humbly, prayerfully and expectantly by ministers and people in their private devotion and in their gathering at worship and in the Church Meeting is not only our ultimate safeguard in matters of faith. Even to call it a safeguard is to speak on too mean a level. It is of the essence of our existence.'[341]

CONCLUSION

Our preliminary investigation revealed that at different times and under different circumstances the Great Ejectment was either not publicly or widely commemorated at all, or was differently remembered as those concerned distilled what they deemed important from the events predating, surrounding, and following 1662. In our present situation that some have described as an ecumenical winter, and now that almost all the anti-Dissenter disabilities have been removed, we

340. Dale, *A Manual*, 50. His italics.

341. W. G. Robinson, "Congregationalism and the Historic Faith," 213.

have an unparalleled opportunity of inaugurating climate change of a most positive kind. This will involve us in an exercise of lateral thinking. Instead of focusing only upon such traditionally neuralgic issues as baptism, eucharist, and ministry with a view to enquiring what we have to learn and to share on these matters, we shall dig deeper. We shall ask not, What do we think? How do we order ourselves?, but What has God done? This will lead us to address the further, too frequently neglected, question, Who are the saints, and whence do they come? The approach to an answer will require us to bring together ecclesiology and pneumatology. The stance and experience of the Separatists and the ejected exemplify a protest *against* untoward ecclesiological impositions, which is at the same time a protest *in favour* of the prevenient work of God the Holy Spirit which itself has ecclesiological implications. Their witness reminds us that by God's prevenient grace the saints are called out, regenerated, justified, adopted, and sanctified by the Holy Spirit and gathered together as branches of Christ the Vine, the one Lord of the one church; and it should caution us against elevating doctrinal tests, churchly orders and practices, and ethical preferences above the gospel in sectarian, 'Galatian,' fashion, thereby excluding from full fellowship those with whom we are already one in Christ.

It has become clear that the tradition of English and Welsh religious Dissent, one of the focal points of which is the Great Ejectment, raises in a profound way the question of the permissible degrees of tolerance in the church. More particularly, it reminds us that our doctrinal, ecclesiological, and ethical stances are interpretative afterthoughts to the gospel of God's grace, savingly active at the cross and brought home to us by the Holy Spirit who has made us one in Christ.

I am well aware that what I have just written may be construed as an hostage to fortune; for it may be argued that my giving precedence to the work of the Holy Spirit in ecclesiology is itself an interpretative afterthought which should carry no more weight than other possible ecclesiological starting-points. To make this case, however, it would be necessary to show that the church originates elsewhere than in the work of God the Holy Spirit, who, on the ground of Christ's saving work, calls out, regenerates, and gathers the saints into union with the one Lord of the church and, visibly, with one another. I do not know how this could be done without implying that the church comes into being independently of God's gracious saving initiative to which an enabled response is made; and this would seem to me to scupper the gospel, and to be inconsistent with both the biblical witness and Christian experience. No doubt our interpretations will forever differ—that is the reality; but our saintly status is given—that is also the reality. If our churchly life were to accord with that fact our interpretations might more readily converge, and they would no longer be wielded as terms of fellowship or worn as badges of sectarian exclusion. We would put first what God the Holy Spirit has done, and all traditions might come to see the point of covenanted, anchored, enrolled sainthood—of knowing who the saints are. This would imply the repudiation of both an exclusively spiritual union of Christ's people which has the luxury of not being embodied in the world,[342] and of the idea that ecclesiastical institutions can be so boundary-less as to be to a greater or lesser extent effectively anonymous; and all such covenanted fellowships would be seen as expressive of the church's catholicity—of its oneness visibly expressed in many places and in many ways. T. H. Huxley tells us that when he first mastered the central idea of Charles Darwin's *The Origin of Species*, namely, that the trigger of evolution was the idea of the survival of the fittest, his reaction was, 'How extremely stupid not to have thought of that!'[343] Would that the whole church might have a 'Huxley moment,' and revisit its pneumatological origins in such a way that nothing would be permitted to shatter the one church that God by the Holy Spirit has made one in Christ. Until it does, and since I set out from him, I shall give Thomas Binney the penultimate word: 'I am a dissenter because I am a catholic; I am a separatist because I cannot be schismatical; I stand apart from some, because I love all; I oppose establishments because I am not sectarian; I care not about subordinate differences with my brother, for "*Christ* has received him, and so will I."'[344]

I come now to my final word. We have seen that while the ejected ministers were united in their stand for conscience, their motivations were not identical in all respects. Some, for example, were much more distressed by the requirement to abjure the Solemn League

---

342. John Whale declared that 'it would be an Irish result if the only discernible mark of the Church were its invisibility.' See *Christian Doctrine*, 134.

343. Huxley, "On the Reception of 'The Origin of Species,'" 2, 197.

344. Binney, *Dissent Not Schism*, 65.

and Covenant oath than others. We have also seen that during the years that have passed between 1662 and the present day, a number of themes have been distilled from the Great Ejectment by those who have given thought to it. It has been construed as a tale of conscientious struggle against great odds; as a repudiation of state interference in churchly affairs; as an impassioned plea for liberty of belief and worship. No doubt, with suitable qualifications, these themes have their place;[345] but my distillation of the significance of the Ejectment, which is informed by modern biblical criticism and the current ecumenical situation, is that taken individually these themes are partial, and even when taken altogether they do not strike deeply enough. They are all, as it were, on the side of protesting *against* (which was required in the circumstances of 1662), and thus they run the risk of overlooking the fact that the consciences of many of the ejected ministers were doctrinally informed in a positive way to a significant degree. Many of them were protesting *for* pneumatological convictions of great importance. They espoused and articulated the following fundamental, positive, principle as clearly as any before or since, namely, that on the ground of Christ's saving work, God the Holy Spirit, the original hunter-gatherer, both pursues sinners with grace, transforms them into willing saints, and gathers them into one catholic ecclesial fellowship which is both eternal and visibly embodied in the world, and over which Christ is the sole Lord. The continuing ecumenical significance of this doctrine is that we can say, 'Jesus Christ is Lord' only by the Holy Spirit's enabling; those who are the Lord's are to love one another (1 John 4:7–10); to exclude any of God's saints from full fellowship—above all from the table of the Lord—is to give precedence to gospel-denying new circumcisions, whether doctrinal, ecclesiological, or ethical; it is not a loving thing to do, and it rends asunder what God by the Spirit has done. It grieves the Holy Spirit. If I may, uncharacteristically, have recourse to 'marketing speak,' I would

345. John Huxtable, for example, qualified the plea for liberty thus: 'the liberty of which our fathers spoke was of a special kind . . . what never occurred to them was the notion that a man might choose this doctrine and reject that because one was congenial and the other repellent, that he might make temperament the arbiter of his way of worship or let whim determine the course of his behaviour. It is not the glorious liberty of the sons of God to be unfettered; to have freedom of conscience is to be the slave of Christ, and of Christ alone.' See *The Tradition of Our Fathers*, 9, 10. Huxtable here echoes Forsyth who speaks, using capital letters, of a 'FOUNDED FREEDOM' in *Faith, Freedom and the Future*, 336, 347.

say that the convictions in which these sectarianisms are rooted need to be 'rebranded' so that instead of operating as principles of exclusion they are regarded as differing expressions of views in a family united in Christ within which—as the Ejectment and our own experience also show—absolute uniformity of belief and practice cannot properly be imposed by either ecclesial or secular powers, and, if the attempt be made, it is doomed to fail. We shall still be able to disagree over many things for, as A. M. Fairbairn wisely remarked, 'toleration of difference is not indifference to truth.'[346] So, for example, standing as I do on theological grounds in the line of John Howe on this matter, I cannot imagine that I should ever be able to agree that the term 're-ordination,' like the terms 're-baptism,' 'unicorn' and 'the tooth fairy,' is anything other than a non-instantiated concept.[347] My point is that such disagreements should be put into perspective by the prior fact that the God of all grace has, by the Holy Spirit, already made us one in Christ, and engrafted us into the one church as branches of the one Vine. On this ground, and in Christ's name, my tradition calls all who are his to the table of the Lord; sadly, not all thus called come—or reciprocate. I am not arguing for the instrumentalist use/abuse of the Lord's Supper as a tool for advancing or effecting church unity, but for recognition of the fact that since the saints on earth comprise one holy, catholic, and apostolic church, they should gather together at the Lord's table in response to Christ's invitation no matter what their denominational 'home.' I repeat that none of us should elevate our understandings and articulations of the truth above the Holy Spirit's gracious call, which we have all heard, to which we have, by grace, responded, and by which we have been made one in Christ. Our differences of opinion and practice should be understood as occurring within the one family of visible saints, and not as between quarrelsome sects who hold one another at arm's length and refuse full pulpit and table fellowship. May we learn from the positive principles for which the ejected ministers stood to put God's prevenient grace first, and adjust our churchly ways accordingly; for where salvation is concerned God the Holy Spirit is the great leveller, and where ecclesiology and pneumatology are concerned he, as the one who calls the

346. Fairbairn, *Studies in Religion and Theology*, 150.

347. I tactfully omit the term 'Father Christmas' from this sentence for fear of distressing the saints.

one church into being, takes precedence over, relativizes, and where appropriate rebukes, all ensuing doctrinal interpretations and ecclesiastical arrangements.[348]

BIBLIOGRAPHY

Adeney, Walter F. "The More Excellent Way." In *The Congregational Year Book* (1913) 35–47.

Angus, Joseph. *Bicentenary Prize Essay. Christian Churches: The Noblest Form of Social Life; the Representatives of Christ on Earth; the Dwelling-place of the Holy Spirit.* London: Ward, 1862.

Anon. "1662 and 1912." In *The Christian World*, 22 August 1912, 10.

———. *Baptism, Eucharist and Ministry.* Geneva: World Council of Churches, 1982.

———. *The Baptist Doctrine of the Church.* London: Baptist Union of Great Britain and Ireland, 1948.

———. "The Bicentenary of the Bartholomew Ejectment." In *The Gospel Herald or Poor Christian's Magazine*, 31 = N.S. 8 (1862) 120–24.

———. "The Bi-centenary Scales Fairly Adjusted." In *The Earthen Vessel* 18 (1862) 101–2.

———. "Bicentenary Texts." In *The Gospel Herald*, 31 = N.S. 8 (1862) 222–24.

———. *Bulletin One*, 1960, and *Bulletin Two*, 1961 of the Joint Commemoration Committee, London: Independent.

———. "Churches' Disunity 'Rebuking Fact.'" *The Times*, 24 October 1962, 12.

———. *Circular Letter, on the Scriptural Constitution of the Churches of Jesus Christ, adopted by the Messengers of the London Association of Strict Baptist Minister and Churches.* London: Stephenson, 1846. Collected in Breed, *Calvinism and Communion*. Springfield, MO: Particular Baptist, 2008.

———. *Documents Relating to the Act of Uniformity of 1662.* London: Central United Bartholomew Committee and W. Kent, 1862.

———. "The Ejected Ministers. Mr. Francis Holcroft and Mr. J. Oddy." In *The Gospel Herald*, 31 = N.S. 8 (1862) 181–82.

———. *God's Reign and Our Unity: The Report of the Anglican-Reformed International Commission 1981–1984.* London: SPCK, 1984.

———. "The Great Ejectment Dispute." *The Guardian*, 6 January 1962, 4.

———. News items in *The Times* (1912), September 19, 4; October 1, 4; 3, 5; 5, 7; 18, 10.

———. Obituary of John Brown. In *The Times*, (1922), January 17, 12.

348. I append two personal observations in conclusion. (a) It is not too much to say that I have been working on the ideas enshrined in this chapter since I was fourteen years of age. (b) The opportunity of introducing Dissenting catholicity to colleagues in a wide variety of international bilateral dialogues was not the least of reasons why in the nineteen-eighties I accepted the Geneva-based post of Theological Secretary of the World Alliance of Reformed Churches.

———. Review of Charles Girdlestone, *'Black Bartholomew's Day.' How shall we best Commemorate, on August 24, 1862, the Bi-centenary of the Act of Uniformity? A Plea for Truth, and Peace, and Love. First published in "Evangelical Christendom" for January, 1862.* In *The British Quarterly Review* 35 (1862) 302–23.

———. Reviews. *The Baptist Magazine* 54 (1862) 372–77, 577–79.

———. *The Savoy Declaration of Faith and Order*, edited by A. G. Matthews. London: Independent, 1959.

———. *A Statement of the Christian Faith.* London: Presbyterian Church of England, 1956. In *Stating the Gospel: Formulations and Declarations of Faith from the Heritage of The United Reformed Church*, edited by D. M. Thompson, 184–97. Edinburgh: T. & T. Clark, 1990.

———. Tracts published in 1862 by the Central United Bartholomew Committee (*The First Protest*; *The Book of Sports*; *The Star Chamber and High Commission*; *The Ejection of the Episcopalians*; *The Savoy Conference*; *The Act of Uniformity*; *The Farewell Sunday*; *The Effects of the Ejectment*; *On the Prayer Book*; *On Clerical Subscription*; and *The Act of Toleration*).

———. "Vanity Fair of our Affluent Society." *The Times*, 25 August 1962, 8.

———. *The Westminster Confession of Faith.* In *Stating the Gospel*, edited by D. M. Thompson, 10–60. Edinburgh: T. & T. Clark, 1990.

Aspland, Robert. *Bigotry and Intolerance Defeated: or, an Account of the late Persecution of Mr. John Gisburne, Unitarian Minister of Soham, Cambridgeshire: with an Exposure and Correction of the Defects and Mistakes of Mr. Andrew Fuller's Narrative of that Affair: in Letters to John Christie, Esq. Treasurer of the Unitarian Fund.* Harlow, UK: Flower, 1811.

Barrow, Henry. *A Brief Discoverie of the False Church.* (1590). In *The Writings of Henry Barrow 1587–1590*, edited by Leland H. Carlson, 259–673. London: Allen & Unwin, 1962.

———, and John Greenwood. *The True Church and the False Church.* In *The Writings of John Greenwood, etc.*, edited by Leland H. Carlson, 95–102. London: Allen & Unwin, 1962.

Bartlet, J. Vernon. "Congregationalism, Essential and Relative." In *Essays Congregational and Catholic*, edited by A. Peel, 32–52. London: Congregational Union of England and Wales, [1931].

Bartlet, William. Ἰχνογραφία *or a Model of The Primitive Congregational Way.* London: Overton, 1647.

Baxter, Richard. *The Autobiography of Richard Baxter, being The Reliquiae Baxterianae Abridged from the folio (1696).* London: Dent, 1931.

———. *A Christian Directory: or a Summ of Practical Theologie.* 4 parts, London: White, 1673.

———. *Reliquiae Baxterianae.* Edited by Matthew Sylvester. London: Parkhurst et al., 1696.

Berry, Charles Albert. "The Churches of Christ and the Kingdom of God." In *Constructive Congregational Ideals*, edited by D. Macfadyen. London: Allenson, 1902.

Binney, Thomas. *Dissent Not Schism: A Discourse delivered in the Poultry Chapel, December 11, 1834, at the Monthly Meeting of the Associated Ministers and Churches, of the London Congregational Union.* 3rd ed. London: Robinson, 1835.

Bogue, David, and James Bennett. *History of Dissenters from the Revolution in 1688 to the year 1808.* 4 vols. London: printed for the authors, 1808–12.

Bourn, Samuel. *Lectures to Children and Young People in a Catechetical Method, Consisting of Three Catechisms.* London: Ford, 1838.

———. *The True Christian Way of Striving for the Faith of the Gospel. A Sermon Preach'd to a Congregation of Protestant-Dissenters, Ministers, and Private Christians: At their Yearly Meeting in Dudley in Worcestershire. One my 23, 1738, being Whitson-Tuesday*. London: Ford, 1738.

Breed, Geoffrey R. *Calvinism and Communion in Victorian Englan: Studies in Nineteenth-Century Strict Baptist Ecclesiology*. Springfield, MO: Particular Baptist, 2008.

Brooks, R. T. *Renewal*. London: Independent, [1949].

Brown, John. "Congregationalism: Old and New." In *Early Independents*, 177–202. London: Congregational Union of England and Wales, 1893.

———, ed.. *Volume of Proceedings of the Third International Congregational Council*. London: Congregational Union of England and Wales, 1908.

Brown, Raymond. *The English Baptists of the Eighteenth Century*. London: The Baptist Historical Society, 1986.

Browne, John. *History of Congregationalism and Memorials of the Churches in Norfolk and Suffolk*. London: Jarrold, 1877.

Browne, Robert. *A Booke which sheweth the Life and Manners of all True Christians*. (1582); *A Treatise of Reformation without tarrying for anie*. (1582); *A True and Short Declaration*. (c. 1583). In *The Writings of Robert Harrison and Robert Brown*, edited by Albert Peel and Leland H. Carlson, London: Allen & Unwin, 1953.

Burrage, Champlin. *The Early English Dissenters*. 2 vols. Cambridge: Cambridge University Press, 1912.

Cadoux, C. J. "Congregationalism and the True Catholicism." In *Essays Congregational and Catholic*, edited by Albert Peel, 53–77. London: Congregational Union of England and Wales, [1931].

Calamy, Edmund. *Memoirs of the Life of the Late Rev. Mr. John Howe, M.A.* London: Chandler, 1724.

———. *The Nonconformist's Memorial: Being an Account of the Ministers, Who Were Ejected or Silenced after the Restoration, Particularly by the Act of Uniformity, etc.*, abridged and corrected by Samuel Palmer, London: Harris, 1775.

Calvin, John. *Institutes of the Christian Religion*. Translated by Ford Lewis Battles, edited by J. T.McNeil, 2 vols. Philadelphia: Westminster, 1961.

Carlson, Leland, *The Writings of Henry Barrow 1587–1590*. London: Allen & Unwin, 1962.

———. *The Writings of John Greenwood, together with the Joint Writings of Henry Barrow and John Greenwood*. London: Allen & Unwin, 1962.

Carnell, E. J. *The Case for Orthodox Theology*. London: Marshall, Morgan & Scott, 1961.

Carter, A. C. *A Popular Sketch Historical and Biographical of the Midland Baptist College*. London: Kingsgate, 1925.

Champion, L. G., *The General Baptist Church of Berkhamsted, Chesham and Tring 1712–1781*. London: The Baptist Historical Society, 1985.

Clark, H. W. "The Ejection of 1662 in relation to Nonconformity." In *The Contemporary Review* 102 (1912) 228–38.

———. *History of English Nonconformity*. 2 vols. London: Chapman and Hall, 1913.

Cocks, H. F. Lovell. *By Faith Alone*. London: Clarke, 1943.

———. *A Church Reborn*. London: Independent, [1950].

———. *The Faith of a Protestant Christian*. London: Independent, 1931.

———. "We Must Sacrifice our Prejudices." *The British Weekly*, 30 August 1962, 1, 5.

Cook, Henry. *What Baptists Stand For*. London: Kingsgate, 1947.

Cooke, Leslie E. *'Upon This Rock.' Congregationalism, Its Heritage and Task*. London: Independent, 1939.

Cramp, John Mockett. *The Great Ejectment of 1662: A Lecture with an Appendix.* Halifax, NS: *Christian Messenger* Office, 1862.

Cromwell, Oliver. *Letters and Speeches.* Edited by T. Carlyle. 3 vols. London: Dent, 1908.

Dakin, A. *The Baptist View of the Church and Ministry.* London: The Baptist Union, 1944.

Dale, R. W. "The Early Independents." In *Jubilee Lectures . . . Delivered on the Occasion of the Jubilee of The Congregatioanl Union of England and Wales*, 2 volumes in one, 1:1–56. London: Hodder and Stoughton, 1882.

————. *Essays and Addresses.* London: Hodder and Stoughton, 1899.

————. "The Evangelising Power of a Spiritual Fellowship." In *Constructive Congregational Ideals*, edited by D. Macfadyen, 129–44. London: Allenson, 1902.

————. *History of English Congregationalism.* London: Hodder and Stoughton, 1907.

————. *A Manual of Congregational Principles.* London: Hodder and Stoughton, 1884.

————. *The Old Evangelicalism and the New.* London: Hodder and Stoughton, 1889.

Darwin, Francis, ed. *The Life and Letters of Charles Darwin.* 2 vols. London: Murray 1887.

Dawson, Albert. *Joseph Parker, D.D. His Life and Ministry.* London: Partridge, 1901.

DeWeese, Charles W. *Baptist Church Covenants.* Nashville, TN: Broadman, 1990

Dix, Gregory. "The Ministry in the Early Church." In *The Apostolic Ministry*, edited by Kenneth Kirk, 183–303. London: Hodder and Stoughton, 1946.

Dixon, R. W. *A Century of Village Nonconformity at Bluntisham, Hunts. 1787 to 1887.* London: Harris, 1887.

Doddridge, Philip. *Free Thoughts on the Most Probable Means of Reviving the Dissenting Interest.* London: Hett, 1930.

Douglas, David. *History of the Baptist Churches in the North of England from 1648 to 1845.* London: Houston and Stoneman, 1846.

Duce, Robert. *'Fire in the City': An Historical Play on the Great Ejection of 1662.* London: Independent, 1961.

Dunkerley, R., ed. *The Ministry and the Sacraments.* London: SCM, 1937.

Duthie, Charles S. "Responding to the Gospel." In *Vocation and Victory*, edited by J. W. Winterhager and A. Brown, 243–49. Basel: Brunner, 1974.

E., S.S. "The late Rev. Julius Charles Hare on the Acts of Uniformity." *The Evangelical Magazine* (1862) 25–28.

Elliot, Ernest. *A History of Congregationalism in Shropshire.* Oswestry, UK: Woodhall, Minshall, [1898].

Evans, Owen E. "On Serving Two Masters." In *The Bible in Church, Academy and Culture*, edited by Alan P. F. Sell, 124–41. Eugene, OR: Pickwick, 2011.

————. *Saints in Christ Jesus. A Study of the Christian Life in the New Testament.* Swansea: Penry, 1975.

Fairbairn, A. M. *Studies in Religion and Theology.* New York: Macmillan, 1910.

Fiddes, Paul S. *Tracks and Traces: Baptist Identity in Church and Theology.* Milton Keynes, UK: Paternoster, 2003.

Fletcher, Joseph. *The History of the Revival and Progress of Independency in England, since the Period of the Reformation.* (1847–49), 4 vols. London: Snow, 1862.

Forsyth, P. T. *The Church and the Sacraments.* London: Independent, 1953.

————. *Congregationalism and Reunion.* London: Independent, 1952.

————. "The Evangelical Basis of Free Churchism." *The Contemporary Review* 81 (1902) 680–95.

————. *Faith, Freedom and the Future.* London: Independent, 1955.

Frykholm, Amy. "Loose Connections: What's Happening to Church Membership?" *The Christian Century*, 31 May 2011, 20–23.

Fuller, Andrew. *A Narrative of Facts relative to a late occurrence in the County of Cambridge, in Answer to a Statement contained in a Unitarian publication, called the 'Monthly Repository.'* London: 1810.

———. *The Works of Andrew Fuller.* Edited by Andrew Gunton Fuller. Edinburgh: Banner of Truth, 2007.

Goadby, Bertha and Lilian. *Not Saints But Men, or the Story of the Goadby Ministers.* London: Kingsgate, [1908].

Goadby, Thomas. "The Black Bartholomew Commemoration." In *The General Baptist Magazine* (1862) 201–10, 241–47, 298–303.

Gough, Strickland. *An Enquiry into the Causes of the Decay of the Dissenting Interest.* London: Roberts, 1730.

Gould, George. "Sixteen Hundred and Sixty-two and Eighteen Hundred and Sixty-two." *The Baptist Magazine* 54 (1862) 69–80.

Greenhough, J. R. "The Day of St. Bartholomew." *The Baptist Times and Freeman*, 23 August 1912, 620–21.

Greenwood, John. *The Writings of John Greenwood, together with the Joint Writings of Henry Barrow and John Greenwood.* Edited by Leland H. Carlson. London: Allen & Unwin, 1962.

Grieve, A. J. and W. Marshall Jones. *These Three Hundred Years: Being the Story of Congregational Work and Witness in Bury St. Edmunds, 1646–1946. With an Introductory Chapter by Albert Peel, M.A., Litt.D, LL.D.* London: Independent, 1946.

Gunn, H. Mayo. *A Memorial of the Nonconforming Clergy of Wilts and East Somerset, in 1662.* London: Jackson, Walford and Hodder, 1862.

Guntrip, H. J. S. *What is Congregationalism?* London: Independent, 1942.

Hare, Julius Charles. *The Mission of the Comforter and Other Sermons. With Notes.* 2 vols. London: Parker, 1846.

Hayden, Roger. *Continuity and Change: Evangelical Calvinism among Eighteenth-Century Baptist Ministers trained at Bristol Academy, 1690–1791.* Milton under Wychwood, UK: Lynn, 2006.

Haymes, Brian. "On Religious Liberty: a Re-reading of *The Mystery of Iniquity* in London in 2005." *The Baptist Quarterly* 42 (2007) 197–217.

Healey, F. G. *Rooted in Faith. Three Centuries of Nonconformity 1662–1962.* London: Independent, 1961.

Hebert, A. G. *The Form of the Church.* London: Faber & Faber, 1944.

Helwys, Thomas. *A Short Declaration of the Mistery of Iniquity,* Amsterdam [?]: 1612.

Henry, Matthew. *The Life of the Rev. Philip Henry, A.M. With Funeral Sermons for Mr. and Mrs. Henry,* (1698) corrected and enlarged by J. B. Williams. Edinburgh: Banner of Truth, 1974.

Henson, H. Hensley. *Puritanism in England.* London: Hodder and Stoughton, 1912.

Hester, Giles. *Attercliffe as a Seat of Learning and Ministerial Education.* London: Stock, 1893.

Hewis, Frank. "Twelve Runners." Letter in *Reform*, April 1984.

Hooker, Richard. *The Works of that Learned and Judicious Divine, Mr. Richard Hooker.* 3rd ed. 3 vols. Oxford: Oxford University Press, 1845.

Hora, Mary. "English Nonconformity and the Invention of Tradition." *The Journal of the United Reformed Church History Society* 6 (2000) 409–28.

Horne, C. Silvester. "The Ejected Ministers." *The British Weekly*, 29 August 1912, 524.

Horsch, John. *Modern Religious Liberalism*. Chicago: The Bible Institute Colportage Association, 1920.

Hort, F. J. A. *The Christian Ecclesia*. London: Macmillan, 1897.

Howe, John. *The Works of John Howe*. Edited by Henry Rogers. 6 vols. London: 1862–63.

Hurd, Alan G. *These Three Hundred Years: The Story of Ramsgate Congregational Church 1662–1962*. Ramsgate, UK: Published by the church, [1962].

Huxley, T. H. "On the Reception of 'The Origin of Species.'" In *The Life and Letters of Charles Darwin*, vol. 2, edited by Francis Darwin, 179–204. London: Murray, 1887.

Huxtable, W. John F. *As it Seemed to Me*. London: The United Reformed Church, 1990.

———. *Christian Unity: Some of the Issues*. London: Independent, 1967.

———. *The Tradition of Our Fathers*. London: Independent, 1962.

———. "The Obedience of the Dissenter." *The British Weekly*, 22 February 1962.

Jackson, W. David. *Our Heritage and Opportunity*. London: The Baptist Union of Great Britain and Ireland, 1962.

James, T. T. *The Work and Administration of a Congregational Church*. London: Congregational Union of England and Wales, 1925.

Jenkins, Daniel T. *The Church Meeting and Democracy*. London: Independent, 1944.

———. *Congregationalism: A Restatement*. London: Faber and Faber, 1954.

Jones, J. D. *Things Most Surely Believed*. London: Clarke, 1908.

Jones, R. Tudur. *Congregationalism in England 1662–1962*. London: Independent, 1962.

Jordan, E. K. H. *Free Church Unity. History of the Free Church Council Movement 1896–1941*. London: Lutterworth, 1956.

Kirk, Kenneth E. "The Apostolic Ministry." In *The Apostolic Ministry*, edited by Kenneth Kirk, 1–52. London: Hodder and Stoughton, 1946.

Larsen, Timothy. "Victorian Nonconformity and the Memory of the Ejected Ministers: The Impact of the Bicentennial Commemorations of 1862." In *The Church Retrospective*, edited by R. N. Swanson, 459–73. Woodbridge UK: Boydell, 1997.

Lewis, H. Elvet, "Introduction" to *The Ejectment of 1662 and the Free Churches*, 1–7. London: National Council of Evangelical Free Churches, [1912].

Llwyd, Morgan. *Gweithiau*. Edited by T. E. Ellis and J. H. Davies. 2 vols. Bangor, UK: Jarvis and Foster, 1899, 1908.

Locke, John. *A Letter Concerning Toleration* (1689). In *John Locke, A Letter Concerning Toleration in Focus*, edited by John Horton and Susan Mendus. London: Routledge, 1991.

———. *A Second Vindication of the Reasonableness of Christianity*. London: Churchill, 1697.

Lumpkin, W. L. *Baptist Confessions of Faith*. Philadelphia: Judson, 1959.

Macalpine, George W. "A.D. 1662—Uniformity or Unity?" *Transactions of the Baptist Historical Society* 3 (1912–1913) 111–16.

Macfadyen, D., *Constructive Congregational Ideals*. London: Allenson, 1902.

Mackennal, Alexander. *Sketches in the Evolution of English Congregationalism*. London: Nisbet, 1901.

Mackintosh, Robert. *Essays Towards a New Theology*. Glasgow: Maclehose, 1889.

———. "The Genius of Congregationalism." In *Essays Congregational and Catholic*, edited by Albert Peel, 103–25. London: Congregational Union of England and Wales, [1931].

———. *The Insufficiency of Revivalism as a Religious System*, bound with his *Essays Towards a New Theology*. Glasgow: Maclehose, 1889.

McLachlan, H. *Essays and Addresses*. Manchester: Manchester University Press, 1950.

Maclaren, Alexander. "Fidelity to Conscience." In *The Ejectment of 1662 and the Free Churches*, 9–35. London: National Council of Evangelical Free Churches, [1912].

McNaughton, William D. *The Scottish Congregational Ministry 1794–1993*. Glasgow: The Congregational Union of Scotland, 1993.

Manning, Bernard Lord. *Essays in Orthodox Dissent*. (1939). London: Independent, 1953.

———. *The Making of Modern English Religion*. (1929). London: Independent, 1967.

———. "Some Characteristics of the Older Dissent." *The Congregational Quarterly* 5 (1927) 286–330.

———. *Why Not Abandon the Church?* (1939). London: Independent, 1958.

Manning, James. *A Sketch of the Life and Writings of the Rev. Micaijah Towgood*. Exeter, UK: 1792.

Manson, T. W. *The Church's Ministry*. London: Hodder and Stoughton, 1948.

———. *Ministry and Priesthood: Christ's and Ours*. London: Epworth, 1958.

Marsh, John. *For the Church Member*. London: Independent, 1946.

Marshall, Newton H. "The Baptist Churches." In *Evangelical Christianity*, edited by W. B. Selbie, 131–67. London: Hodder and Stoughton, [1911].

Matthews, A. G. *Calamy Revised. Being a Revision of Edmund Calamy's Account of the Ministers and Others Ejected and Silences, 1660–2*. Oxford: Clarendon, 1988.

Micklem, Nathaniel. *God's Freemen. A Tract for the Times*. London: Clarke, [1922].

Mourby, Adrian. "Why do the English Hate Opera?" *Opera Now* (March-April 2011) 126.

Neal, Daniel. *The History of the Puritans, or Protestant Nonconformists from the Reformation in 1517 to the Revolution in 1688*. (1732–38). 3 vols. London: Tegg, 1837.

Nightingale, Benjamin. *The Story of the Lancashire Congregational Union 1806–1906: Centenary Memorial Volume*. Manchester: Heywood, [1906].

Nuttall, Geoffrey F. "The Apostolic Ministry." *The Congregational Quarterly* 25 (1947) 109–16.

———. "Calvinism in Free Church History." *The Baptist Quarterly* 22 (1968) 418–28.

———. "The Emergence of Nonconformity." In *The Beginnings of Nonconformity*, 9–32. London: Clarke, 1964.

———. "The First Nonconformists." In *From Uniformity to Unity 1662–1962*, edited by Geoffrey F. Nuttall and Owen Chadwick, 149–87. London: SPCK, 1962.

———. *The Holy Spirit in Puritan Faith and Experience*. Oxford: Blackwell, 1946.

———. "Reconstruct to Hear the Word!" *The Congregational Quarterly* 21 (July 1943) 253–56.

———. *Visible Saints. The Congregational Way 1640–1660*. Oxford: Blackwell, 1957.

———, and Owen Chadwick. *From Uniformity to Unity 1662–1962*. London: SPCK, 1962.

Oliver, Robert. *History of the English Calvinistic Baptists 1771–1892*. Edinburgh: Banner of Truth, 2006.

Owen, John. *The Works of John Owen*. Edited by W. H. Goold. (1850–1853). 16 vols. London: Banner of Truth, 1968.

Parker, Constance M. *The Congregational Road. A History of Congregationalism. A Nine-Week Lesson Course for the 'Over-Elevens'.* London: Congregational Union of England and Wales, 1962.

Payne, Ernest A., "Baptist-Congregational Relationships." In *Free Churchmen, Unrepentant and Repentant*, 93–104. London: Kingsgate, 1965.

———. *The Baptist Union: A Short History*. London: Kingsgate, 1958.

————. *The Fellowship of Believers: Baptist Thought and Practice Yesterday and Today.* Enlarged edition. London: Kingsgate, 1952.

Peel, Albert. *The Congregational Two Hundred 1530–1948.* London: Independent, 1948.

————. *Inevitable Congregationalism.* London: Independent, 1937.

————. *These Hundred Years: A History of the Congregational Union of England and Wales 1831–1931.* London: Congregational Union of England and Wales, [1931].

Peel, Albert, ed. *Essays Congregational and Catholic: Issued in Commemoration of the Centenary of the Congregational Union of England and Wales.* London: Congregational Union of England and Wales, [1931].

———— and Leland H. Carlson, eds. *The Writings of Robert Harrison and Robert Browne.* London: Allen & Unwin, 1953.

———— and J. A. R. Marriott. *Robert Forman Horton.* London: Allen & Unwin, 1937.

Phillips, George. "Freedom in Religious Thought." In *The Fourth Freedom: Essays on Congregationalism and its Enduring Witness*, 35–74. London: Independent, 1943.

Powicke, Fred. James. "English Congregationalism in its Greatness and Decline (1592–1770)." In *Essays Congregational and Catholic*, edited by Albert Peel, 279–309. London: Congregational Union of England and Wales, [1931].

————. "Historic Congregationalism in Britain." In *Volume of Proceedings of the Third International Congregational Council*, edited by John Brown, 260–69. London: Congregational Union of England and Wales, 1908.

————. *A History of the Cheshire County Union of Congregational Churches.* Manchester: Griffiths, 1907.

Rashdall, Hastings. *Principles and Precepts.* Oxford: Blackwell, 1927.

Reynolds, Geoffrey G. *First among Equals: A Study of the Basis of Association and Oversight among Baptist Churches.* Published by the author, 1993.

Roberts, H. P. "Nonconformist Academies in Wales (1662–1862)." In *Transactions of the Honourable Society of Cymmrodorion, Session 1928–29* (1928–29) 1–98.

Robinson, H. Wheeler. *The Life and Faith of the Baptists.* London: Kingsgate, 1946.

———— and J. H. Rushbrooke. *Baptists in Britain.* London: The Baptist Union, 1937.

Robinson, John. *A Briefe Catechisme concerning Church Government.* London: 1642.

————. *The Works of John Robinson, Pastor of the Pilgrim Fathers, with a Memoir and Annotations by Robert Ashton.* 3 vols. London: Snow, 1851.

Robinson, W. Gordon. "Congregationalism and the Historic Faith." *The Congregational Quarterly* 29 (1951) 202–13.

————. "A Fellowship of Convictions. The Real Meaning of 1662." *The Christian World*, 2 November, 1961, 2.

————. *A History of the Lancashire Congregational Union 1806–1956.* Manchester: Lancashire Congregational Union, 1955.

Rogers, James Guinness. *The Church Systems of England in the Nineteenth Century.* London: Hodder and Stoughton, 1881.

————. "Clericalism and Congregationalism." In *Jubilee Lectures . . . Delivered on the Occasion of the Jubilee of The Congregational Union of England and Wales.* 2 volumes in one, 2:35–39. London: Hodder and Stoughton, 1882.

Routley, Erik. *The Story of Congregationalism Briefly Told.* London: Independent, 1961.

Rupp, E. Gordon. "Clerical Integrity—1662." *The Expository Times* 74 (1962–63) 145–48.

Rushbrooke, J. H. "The Baptist Communion in Britain." In *Baptists in Britain*, edited by H. W. Robinson and J. H. Rushbrooke, 35–59. London: The Baptist Union, 1937.

Seed, John. "History and Narrative Identity: Religious Dissent and the Politics of Memory in Eighteenth-century England." *Journal of British Studies* 44 (2005) 46–63.

Selbie, W. B. *Evangelical Christianity: Its History and Witness*. London: Hodder and Stoughton, [1911].

————. "The Religious Principle of Congregationalism." In *Mansfield College Essays*, 21–41. London: Hodder and Stoughton, 1909.

Sell, Alan P. F. *Christ and Controversy: The Person of Christ in Nonconformist Thought and Ecclesial Experience*. Eugene, OR: Pickwick, 2012.

————. *Commemorations: Studies in Christian Thought and History*. 1993. Reprint. Eugene, OR: Wipf and Stock, 1998.

————. *Enlightenment, Ecumenism, Evangel: Theological Themes and Thinkers 1550–2000*. Milton Keynes, UK: Paternoster, 2005.

————. "Geoffrey Nuttall in Conversation." *The Journal of the United Reformed Church History Society* 8 (2009) 266–90.

————. *Hinterland Theology: A Stimulus to Theological Construction*. Milton Keynes, UK: Paternoster, 2008.

————. *John Locke and the Eighteenth-Century Divines*. 1997. Reprint. Eugene, OR: Wipf and Stock, 2006.

————. *Nonconformist Theology in the Twentieth Century*. Milton Keynes, UK: Paternoster, 2006.

————. "Rectifying Calvin's Ecclesiology: The Doctrinal and Ecumenical Importance of Separatist-Congregational Catholicity." In *John Calvin's Ecclesiology. Ecumenical Perspectives*, edited by Gerard Mannion and Eduardus Van der Borght, 143–68. London: T. & T. Clark, 2011.

————. *Robert Mackintosh, Theologian of Integrity*. Bern: Lang, 1977.

————. *Saints: Visible, Orderly and Catholic: The Congregational Idea of the Church*. Geneva: World Alliance of Reformed Churches and Allison Park, PA: Pickwick (now from Wipf and Stock), 1986.

————. "Separatists and Dissenters amidst the Arguments For and Against Toleration: Some Soundings 1550–1689." *Enlightenment and Dissent* (forthcoming).

————. *Testimony and Tradition: Studies in Reformed and Dissenting Thought*. Aldershot, UK: Ashgate, 2005.

————. "A Valued Inheritance of New Testament Scholarship." In *Studia Doctorum Theologiae Protestantis*, 1, 57–76. Koloszvár, Romania: Kolozsvári Protestáns Teológiae Intézet, 2011.

————. ed., *The Bible in Church, Academy and Culture: Essays in Honour of the Reverend Dr. John Tudno Williams*. Eugene, OR: Pickwick, 2011.

Shaftesbury (Anthony Ashley Cooper), third Earl of. *A Letter from a Person of Quality to His Friend in the Country*. London: 1675.

Shepherd, Peter. *The Making of a Northern Baptist College*. Manchester: Northern Baptist College, 2004.

Skeats, Herbert S., and Charles S. Miall. *History of the Free Churches of England 1688–1891*. London: Alexander and Shepheard, [1891].

Smyth, John, *The Works of John Smyth*. 2 vols. Edited by W. T. Whitley. Cambridge: Cambridge University Press, 1915.

Stillingfleet, Edward. *Irenicum: A Weapon-Salve for the Churches Wounds*. (1661). Reprinted in *The Philosophy of Edward Stillingfleet*, vol. 1. Bristol: Thoemmes, 2000.

Stoughton, John. *Church and State Two Hundred Years Ago: A History of Ecclesiastical Affairs in England from 1660 to 1663*. London: Jackson, Walford & Hodder, 1862.

Stovel, Charles. "The Chairman's Address." *The Baptist Handbook* (1863) 133–41.

Surman, Charles E. *Alexander James Grieve, M.A., D.D. 1874–1952*. Manchester: Lancashire Independent College, 1953.

Swanson, R. N., ed. *The Church Retrospective*. Woodbridge, UK: Boydell, 1997.

Taylor, John. "The Bicentenary of 1662." *Transactions of the Congregational Historical Society* 19 (1960) 18–25.

Taylor, John, and Clyde Binfield, eds. *Who They Were in the Reformed Churches of England and Wales 1901–2000*. Donington: Tyas, 2007.

Thomas, Clifford. *The History of the First Nonconformist Congregational Church in Hinckley*. Hinckley, UK: published by the church, 1962.

Thomas, T. Gwyn, and Joseph Jones. *Brecon and Radnor Congregationalism: 1662 Commemoration Volume*. Merthyr Tydfil, UK: Williams, 1912.

———. Thompson, David M. *Stating the Gospel: Formulations and Declarations of Faith from the Heritage of The United Reformed Church*. Edinburgh: T. & T. Clark, 1990.

Thompson, David M. *Stating the Gospel: Formulations and Declaration of Faith from the Heritage of The United Reformed Church*. Edinburgh: T. & T. Clark, 1990.

Thompson, Joseph P. "The Bicentenary of Nonconformity." *The Congregational Quarterly* (Boston) 4 (1862) 191–97.

———. et al. "A Fraternal Address." *The Congregational Quarterly* (Boston) 4 (1862) 369–72.

Tizard, Leslie J. *Church Membership*. London: Independent, 1943.

Towgood, Micaijah. *Catholic Christianity; or, the Communion of Saints, earnestly recommended to all professing Christians, particularly to the Brethren of the Anti-paedobaptist Persuasion*. Appended to James Manning, *A Sketch of the Life and Writings of the Rev. Micaijah Towgood*. Exeter, UK: 1792.

———. *The Grounds of Faith in Jesus briefly stated, and Shewn to be a solid Foundation for Peace and Joy unspeakable. With an earnest Recommendation of Catholic Christianity, and the Communion of Saints. Addresses to A candid Society of Christians at the Close of his Ministrations amongst them*. London: Buckland, 1784.

Urwick, William, ed. *Historical Sketches of Nonconformity in the County Palatine of Cheshire. By Various Ministers and Laymen in the County*. London: Kent, 1864.

Various. *The Apostolic Ministry*. London: Hodder and Stoughton, 1946.

———. *The Beginnings of Nonconformity*. London: Clarke, 1964.

———. *Bicentenary of the Bartholomew Ejectment in 1662. St. James's Hall Addresses*. London: Jackson, 1862.

———. *Congregationalism through the Centuries*. London: Independent, 1937.

———. *Early Independents. Six Tracts written to Commemorate the Tercentenary of the Martyrdoms of Greenwood, Barrowe, and Penry in 1593*. London: Congregational Union of England and Wales, 1893.

———. *The Ejectment of 1662 and the Free Churches*. London: National Council of Evangelical Free Churches, [1912].

———. *The Fourth Freedom: Essays on Congregationalism and its Enduring Witness*. London: Independent, 1943.

———. *Jubilee Lectures . . . Delivered on the occasion of the Jubilee of the Congregational Union of England and Wales*. 2 volumes in one. London: Hodder and Stoughton, 1882.

———. *Mansfield College Essays presented to The Reverend Andrew Martin Fairbairn, D.D. on the Occasion of his Seventieth Birthday November 4 1908*. London: Hodder and Stoughton, 1909.

Vaughan, Robert. *Congregationalism: or, the Polity of Independent Churches, Viewed in Relation to the State and Tendencies of Modern Society.* 2nd ed. London: 1842.

———. *English Nonconformity.* London: Jackson, Walford and Hodder, 1862.

———. *I'll Tell You. An Answer to 'How Did They Get There?' A Tractate Touching the Ejected of 1662.* London: 1862.

Venables, George. *How Did They Get There? Or the Non-conforming Ministers of 1662. A Question for those who would Celebrate the Bi-centenary of St. Bartholomew's Day, 1662.* 3rd ed. London: Wertheim, Macintosh and Hunt, 1862.

Waddington, John. *Bicentennial Prize Essay: Congregational Church History from the Reformation to 1662.* London: Jackson, Walford & Hodder, 1862.

———. *Congregational History 1850–1880.* London: Longmans, Green, 1880.

Walker, Williston. *The Creeds and Platforms of Congregationalism.* 1893. Reprint. Boston: Pilgrim, 1960.

Watson, Thomas. *A Body of Divinity.* 1692. Reprint. London: Banner of Truth, 1965.

———. *A Divine Cordial.* 1663. Reprint. Grand Rapids: Sovereign Grace, 1971.

Whale, John S. *Christian Doctrine.* London: Collins Fontana, 1957.

———. "Commemoration Sermon." In *Congregationalism through the Centuries,* 102–12. London: Independent, 1937.

———. "The Views of the Congregational Church." In *The Ministry and the Sacraments,* edited by R. Dunkerley, 211–18. London: SCM, 1937.

White, Edward. "Broad Church Doctrine and Independency." In *Jubilee Lectures . . . Delivered on the Occasion of the Jubilee of the Congregational Union of England and* Wales, 2 vols in one, edited by ?, 2: ?–?. London: Hodder and Stoughton, 1882.

Wilkinson, John T. *1662 and After: Three Centuries of English Nonconformity.* London: Epworth, 1962.

Williams, Frederick Smeeton. *Bicentenary Nonconformist Memorial: The Story of Black Bartholomew.* London: Yates and Alexander, [1862].

Winterhager, J. W., and Arnold Brown. *Vocation and Victory: An International Symposium presented in Honour of Erik Wickberg, LL.D.* Basel: Brunner, 1974.

Index of Persons

Index of Subjects